PRAISE FOR

Admission Matters: What Students and Parents Need to Know About Getting into College

3rd Edition by Sally P. Springer, Jon Reider, and Joyce Vining Morgan

All families will see themselves in this book and benefit from reading it. *Twice.* This commonsense book is the one I'll use when my son embarks on his college search adventure.

Monica Inzer, dean of admission and financial aid, Hamilton College

Crystal clear and concise, yet surprisingly comprehensive. The authors cover everything about the college admission process—which too often appears mysterious or secretive—in simple, understandable terms. I wish I had picked this book up before my daughter sent in her applications.

Kirk Brennan, director of undergraduate admission, University of Southern California

If you are serious about a college search, you should get the best book available and that is what you just found with *Admission Matters*. The years of expertise of the authors are mightily evident on every page.

Gary L. Ross, vice president and dean of admission, Colgate University

Admission Matters should be required reading for every high school student about to embark on a college search. It's remarkably thorough and insightful.

Jennifer Delahunty, dean of admissions and financial aid, Kenyon College

Since its debut, *Admission Matters* has been the single best resource available to help students and their families avoid the increasing barbarity of the "admission market-place." The new edition continues that noble tradition by providing essential information and tools to make the college admission process sane, humane, and perhaps even, for its fortunate readers, a great voyage of personal growth and discovery.

Michael Beseda, vice president of enrollment, Willamette University

I love this book—it is so easy to read, realistic, and spot on with its advice. Besides the great information, the quotes, charts, and examples are well placed and help make sense of the often confusing and overwhelming college admission process. It is a "must-read" resource for any student applying to college.

Bob Bardwell, school counselor and director of school counseling, Monson High School, MA

Thorough, careful, and clear—*Admission Matters* is a great guide for the experienced parent, the first-time parent, and students considering colleges of all types.

Maria Furtado, director of admission, Eckerd College, and past chair, Colleges That Change Lives

For students and parents desperate for timely, expert information and advice about college admissions, this new edition of *Admission Matters* is just what the doctor ordered. It is filled with wise, up-to-date facts and insider knowledge that only seasoned professionals such as Sally P. Springer, Jon Reider, and Joyce Vining Morgan know. Students and parents are going to love it.

Marjorie Hansen Shaevitz, author and founder, adMISSION POSSIBLE, www.admissionpossible.com, selected blogger *Huffington Post College Blog*

Although I've been in the admissions counseling field for almost twenty years, the book gave me new insights and perspectives that will help me in my daily work with students and their families. The book is a great resource covering the most current topics and trends in the ever-changing field of college admission.

Kathi Moody, school counselor, Lynnfield High School, MA

Admission Matters is a touchstone book on the topic written by deeply experienced, thoughtful, and respected professionals who realize that applying to college is both a practical and emotional experience for students and parents. Highly recommended.

Philip Ballinger, assistant vice president for enrollment and director of admissions, University of Washington

A clear, calm, and comprehensive guide. Whether you know a little or a lot about the college admission process, you will find this book filled with valuable advice from real experts. Loaded with good information, this will help both students and parents navigate an often daunting and confusing process.

Debra Shaver, dean of admission, Smith College

This important book and its respected and experienced authors provide an antidote to the anxiety felt by many families as they navigate the college admissions process. You can get in, you can afford it, and you can have a valuable experience.

Jeff Rickey, vice president and dean of admissions and financial aid, St. Lawrence University

This is probably the most thorough book of its kind. On top of that, it is full of accurate advice that should help all students and parents get a better perspective and relieve a great deal of the stress that revolves around today's college admission hype. It is a great resource, even for college counselors!

William S. Dingledine Jr., certified educational planner; past president, Southern Association for College Admission Counseling (SACAC)

Admissions Matters is a *must* read for anyone who is seeking to understand the admissions landscape of today—and make no mistake, it's different than it was just a few short years ago. This book offers wonderful guidance and wisdom for all.

Nanette H. Tarbouni, director of college counseling, John Burroughs School, MO

ADMISSION MATTERS

What Students and Parents
Need to Know About Getting
into College

THIRD EDITION

Sally P. Springer, Jon Reider,
Joyce Vining Morgan

JB JOSSEY-BASS™
A Wiley Brand

Cover design: Michael Cook
Cover image: Skip O'Donnell at iStockphoto

Published by Jossey-Bass
A Wiley Brand
One Montgomery Street, Suite 1200, San Francisco, CA 94104-4594—www.josseybass.com

Jossey-Bass books and products are available through most bookstores. To contact Jossey-Bass directly call our Customer Care Department within the U.S. at 800-956-7739, outside the U.S. at 317-572-3986, or fax 317-572-4002.

Wiley publishes in a variety of print and electronic formats and by print-on-demand. Some material included with standard print versions of this book may not be included in e-books or in print-on-demand. If this book refers to media such as a CD or DVD that is not included in the version you purchased, you may download this material at http://booksupport.wiley.com. For more information about Wiley products, visit www.wiley.com.

Library of Congress Cataloging-in-Publication Data
Springer, Sally P., date
  Admission matters: what students and parents need to know about getting into college/Sally P. Springer, Jon Reider, Joyce Vining Morgan—Third edition.
    pages cm
Includes bibliographical references and index.
ISBN 978-1-118-45027-7 (pbk.); ISBN 978-1-118-63465-3 (ebk.); ISBN 978-1-118-63454-7 (ebk.); ISBN 978-1-118-63443-1 (ebk.)
1. Universities and colleges—United States—Admission. 2. College choice—United States. I. Title.
LB2351.2.S67 2013
378.1'617—dc23   2013000296

Printed in the United States of America
THIRD EDITION
PB Printing   10 9 8 7 6 5 4 3

Contents

Acknowledgments

The third edition of *Admission Matters*, like the two before it, was born out of desire to help students and parents navigate the college admissions process in a thoughtful, hopeful, and calm manner. Many people have shared our goal and helped us, in ways both large and small, as we wrote this book. We are grateful to all of them: Karla Baldwin, Barry Beach, Jack Blattner, Lynne Debie, Jeffrey Durso-Finley, Reta Gasser, Ines Gomez-Ochoa, Kiyoe Hashimoto, David Hawkins, Mollie Hope, Marybeth Kravets, Stephen McGrath, Mary Morrison, Daniel Parrish, and Anne Richardson. Our understanding of admissions in Canada and the United Kingdom was greatly enhanced by Leanne Stillman of the University of Guelph and Kate Burns of Oxford University. A very special thank-you goes to Frances Fee, who lent her time and expertise for a second time to ensure that our chapter on financial aid contained the most up-to-date and authoritative information available anywhere. The third edition was built on the foundation of previous ones, and we want to acknowledge and thank once again those who contributed to the first two editions: Bill Caskey, Cindy Clark, Marilyn Geiger, Fred Hargadon, Arleen Jones, Bruce Madewell, Gail Martinez, Dorothy Missler, George Rooks, Mary Ryan, Courtenay Tessler, Jill Theg, Leon Washington, and Fred Wood. Although Marion Franck was not an active contributor to the third edition, her insights and wisdom remain an integral part of *Admission Matters*.

We are indebted as well to the Jossey-Bass editorial team for the third edition—Kate Bradford, senior editor; Nana Twumasi, editorial program coordinator; and Susan Geraghty, production editor—for so capably and cheerfully guiding us through the publication process. We are also grateful to Lesley Iura, now vice president and publisher at Jossey-Bass/Wiley, and Dimi Berkner, senior marketing manager, for their continued enthusiasm for *Admission Matters*.

Finally, we want to thank the thousands of high school and college students whose lives we have touched over the course of our careers, both in the classroom and as counselors. Their dreams and aspirations have encouraged us to try to ease the path for others yet to undertake the college admissions journey.

FROM SALLY . . .

Admission Matters began over ten years ago as an effort to write the book I wish I'd had when the first of my two children was applying to college. Erik's college journey inspired me to begin writing, and Mollie's subsequent journey inspired me to keep going until the book was finished. Little did they know at the time how their experiences would ultimately benefit tens of thousands of other students. Along the way I have had the privilege of working with very talented collaborators—Marion Franck for the first edition, Jon Reider for the second, and Joyce Vining Morgan and Jon for the third. I am grateful to each of them for signing on to a project that quickly became much more than any of us could have envisioned. I am in greatest debt, then and now, to my wonderful husband, Håkon Hope. Across three editions he has provided abundant and unwavering love and support that made it possible for me to devote the time and energy needed for a project of this scope. Truly, there would be no book without him.

FROM JON . . .

Who knew that collaborating among three authors could be so easy? Sally and Joyce have been ideal partners: smart, careful, and helpful. After close to 30 years in the admission profession, "on both sides of the desk," as we say, I find too many friends and colleagues who have provided kindness, mentoring, and insight to begin to cite them. My contributions to this book reflect the influence of all of them. I learned the most from the educational journeys of my two children, Rebecca and Abby, each of whom wisely took her own path in applying to college. I learned, as every parent must, the important lessons of when to engage (hire the rental car) and when to pull back (the essay is theirs!). Finally, I want to thank Sam for her constant support and wisdom. Her ideas and care are everywhere in this book, in its heart.

FROM JOYCE . . .

For years, when students or parents asked for the best book on college admissions, I'd say "*Admission Matters!*" Sally and Jon, thank you for inviting me to join your team; writing with you has been a joy. Like anyone with a few decades of experience, I have a lot of other people to thank, too. First, my own three children—David, Jamie, and Kira—who taught me to listen. My students were my next teachers and inspiration. When I moved to The Putney School and college counseling, I was mentored by Harry Bauld, Hugh Silbaugh, and Brian Cohen and supported by an extraordinary faculty; the mentoring and support expanded as I worked with high school and college colleagues in college admission counseling across New England and across the country. I am profoundly grateful to all of them, and hope that they see their wisdom reflected in the third edition of this book. And most of all, I thank my patient and ever-encouraging husband, Brian Morgan, himself a perceptive educator, whose enthusiasm for this project made my work possible.

April 2013

Sally P. Springer
Davis, California

Jon Reider
Redwood City, California

Joyce Vining Morgan
Putney, Vermont

To our children

Introduction

The past few years have been a time of rapid and extraordinary change in the world of college admissions. Families are focusing more than ever before on the cost of a college education as tuition continues to rise. At the same time, they are seeking assurance that a school and major will lead to a successful career after graduation. Pressure to do well on standardized tests keeps increasing, yet more schools are adopting test-optional policies, where test scores may not matter at all. While some colleges report record numbers of applications and admit rates now in the single digits, other schools have openings well into the summer before the start of the new school year.

In this thoroughly revised third edition of *Admission Matters*, we have worked hard to address these changes and many more so that you, our student and parent readers, will understand what they mean for your family as you begin the college admissions journey. We have also expanded the scope and depth of the book so that students with disabilities, international students, and transfer students will find much-needed guidance to address their special circumstances. In addition, athletes, artists, and homeschoolers will find additional help as they plan and apply. We want *Admission Matters* to continue to be the most up-to-date, clear, insightful, supportive, and practical book on college admissions to be found anywhere.

We feel we are especially well qualified to be your guides. Among us, we have almost 100 years of experience in secondary and higher education in the roles of high school teacher and college counselor, college admissions officer, college professor and administrator, and independent educational consultant. We are also proud parents of successful college graduates, some of them recent. Collectively we have worked with thousands of students across the United States and abroad. We are delighted that our readers in the general public have found *Admission Matters* enjoyable and easy to read, and we are honored that professional colleagues use it widely as a text in courses on college admissions for those studying to be counselors themselves.

Admission Matters explains

- How rankings motivated by profits contribute to the application frenzy
- How the admissions process really works, and what you can, and cannot, control
- How you can build a list of colleges that are a good fit for you and submit strong, competitive applications to gain admission to them
- How colleges use standardized tests and how you can best prepare for them
- What changes in standardized testing policies at many schools mean for you
- When an early application makes sense, when it can be a mistake, and how to tell the difference
- How financial aid works, what you can expect from it, and how you can increase your chances of receiving more
- What you—student and parent—can do to work together in appropriate and respectful ways throughout the admissions process to achieve a happy outcome

And much more.

It is easy to understand how college admissions has become an ordeal for many students and their families. Each year more students vie for a limited number of freshman spots at some of the best-known colleges. Application numbers in general continue to break records at many schools. Families find themselves caught up in a high-stakes competition in which they are uncertain about the rules and even more uncertain about the outcome. Parents feel uncomfortable trying to support their children in a process that they do not completely understand and are not sure they can afford. Even those who consider themselves knowledgeable may quickly find that much of what they know is out-of-date or based on unverifiable hearsay.

But college admissions does not have to be, and should not be, an ordeal. A clear understanding of the process can empower students and their families to make good choices for themselves and allow them to retain their balance and sanity at the same time. That has always been our goal.

We have written this book to demystify the college admissions process by explaining how it works and to level the playing field for those without access to extensive assistance from knowledgeable high school counselors, or sometimes any counselors at all. It will also help those who have access to good counseling but would still like some extra support. Our advice will help students applying to any four-year college, not just those seeking admission to a selective one.

While *Admission Matters* focuses on the admissions process for students who plan to enter a four-year college as a freshman, we recognize the critically important role of community colleges in higher education, both in awarding associate degrees and as an entry point, through transfer, to a four-year college. Many students choose community college for financial or personal reasons or because their high school record does not allow direct entry into the four-year college of their choice. In this new edition, we address the transfer process for community college students as well as others. Community college is an important educational option that can open many doors, and we note with interest the small but growing number of community colleges that offer four-year as well as two-year degrees.

Although *Admission Matters* is a comprehensive guide to college admissions, you may want more information on certain topics than space allows us to include. We provide a list of resources, many of them on the Web, that give detailed information on topics such as financial aid and athletic recruiting to supplement our own coverage. To keep *Admission Matters* as up-to-date as possible, we are maintaining a website with free updates keyed to the pages in this book throughout the lifetime of this edition. You can find it at www.admissionmat ters.com. We welcome your feedback.

This third edition of *Admission Matters* features a new team of writers. Sally Springer has over 30 years of experience as a psychology professor and senior university administrator on both the East and West Coasts. She has devoted her entire career to higher education and has essentially not left school since she entered college at age sixteen. Associate chancellor emerita at the University of California, Davis, she received her bachelor's degree from Brooklyn College of the City University of New York, where she was a commuter student before venturing cross-country to Stanford University for her doctoral and postdoctoral work in psychology. She has been a volunteer admissions reader for the Office of Undergraduate Admissions at UC Davis and is a member of the National Association for College Admission Counseling, the Independent Educational Consultants Association, and the Higher Education Consultants Association.

Jon Reider is director of college counseling at San Francisco University High School. He was formerly the senior associate director of admission at Stanford University and a lecturer in the humanities for many years. He is a winner of a Marshall Scholarship to the University of Sussex, where he received a master's degree in sociology, and he also holds a bachelor's degree and a PhD from Stanford in history. He was elected to Phi Beta Kappa, was a Danforth Graduate Fellow, and received the Walter J. Gores Teaching Award for Outstanding Undergraduate Teaching. He is a prolific writer and speaker in the national college admissions world.

Joyce Vining Morgan is a certified educational planner specializing in college admission with an online individualized practice. She has over 17 years of experience in college admissions, including service as director of college counseling at the Putney School in Vermont and as vice president of the New England Association for College Admission Counseling. Earlier in her career, she taught in several disciplines in a number of public and private schools and colleges. She holds a PhD in Slavic languages and literature from Yale University and a bachelor's degree in Russian from Manhattanville College. She is a member of the National Association for College Admission Counseling, the Independent Educational Consultants Association, and the Higher Education Consultants Association and an associate member of the Overseas Association for College Admission Counseling.

We hope *Admission Matters* will become a trusted road map to help you through the college admissions journey.

CHAPTER 1

Why Has College Admissions Become So Competitive?

Applying to college was a pretty simple process for members of the baby boom generation born between 1946 and 1964. Those bound for a four-year college usually planned to go to a school in their home state or one fairly close by; many considered a college even 300 miles from home to be far away. Few students felt the need to apply to more than two or three colleges, and many applied to just one. They chose their colleges most often based on location, program offerings, cost, and difficulty of admission, with a parental alma mater sometimes thrown in for good measure. For the most part, the whole process was fairly low key. If students did their homework carefully before deciding where to apply, the outcome was usually predictable. Of course, there were surprises—some pleasant and some disappointing—but nothing that would raise the issue of college as to the level of a national obsession.

IT USED TO BE SIMPLE ... BUT NOT ANYMORE

Fast-forward about 50 years to the second decade of the twenty-first century. Media headlines tell a story very different for students applying to college now: "College Admission Tougher Than Ever,"[1] "The Escalating Arms Race for Top Colleges,"[2] "High Anxiety for Students Awaiting College Admissions Letters,"[3]

"When Parents 'Too Invested' in College Admissions Make Their Children Anxious,"[4] "More Students in Limbo as College Wait Lists Grow,"[5] and "College Applications Increase Stress."[6]

Colleges themselves make equally jarring announcements. In spring 2003, Harvard announced that for the first time, it had accepted just under 10 percent of the students who applied for freshman admission for the class of 2007, or about 2,000 out of 21,000 applicants. This was a new low not only for Harvard, but for colleges nationwide. But there was more to come. By spring 2012, the admissions rate at Harvard had fallen to 5.9 percent out of an applicant pool of over 34,000 for the class of 2016, and at least seven other colleges, all but one on the East Coast, had joined Harvard in the "under 10 percent" club.

In the Midwest, the University of Chicago reported an admissions rate of slightly over 13 percent for the class of 2016, down from almost 35 percent just five years earlier. Some public universities reported record-low admit rates as well. On the West Coast at the University of California, Irvine, for example, about 36 percent of applicants were admitted in the spring of 2012; the campus had admitted over 55 percent five years before.

These are just a few of the many colleges reporting record-breaking numbers of applications and record-low rates of admission, continuing a trend that began a decade and a half earlier. What has happened to change the college admissions picture so dramatically in such a short time?

The Echo Boom

The simple explanation seems to be supply and demand: there are more high school graduates than ever competing for seats in the freshman class. After declining somewhat in the late 1980s and early 1990s, the number of students graduating from high school in the United States has risen steadily. In 1997 there were 2.6 million graduates; in 2003, there were 3 million; by 2011, the number of high school graduates had grown to 3.4 million. Although the numbers are now declining slightly, they are projected to stay above 3.2 million until at least 2028.[7]

Part of the increase is the result of immigration, especially from Asia and Latin America, but most of the growth is due to the children of the baby boom generation that

> I don't think anyone is complacent about getting a high-quality applicant pool.
>
> HARVARD UNIVERSITY
> ADMISSIONS OFFICER

created the great demand for higher education in the decades after World War II. Known as the echo boomers or the millennial generation, these children are part of the largest group of high school graduates in history.

Social Changes

But it turns out that the problem is not just numbers. Application numbers have risen much faster than the age cohort due to important social changes. Not only are more students graduating from high school each year, but a greater percentage of them are interested in going to college. A college education is increasingly seen as the key to economic success in our society just as a high school diploma was once the minimum requirement. Studies confirm the value of a college diploma in terms of lifetime earnings, and many desirable careers require education beyond the bachelor's degree. As a result, more students are seeking to attend four-year colleges, including students from underrepresented minority groups whose college participation rate was previously low.

At the same time, colleges themselves have increased their efforts to attract large, diverse pools of applicants. Many have mounted aggressive programs to spread the word about their offerings nationally and internationally. Through colorful view books mailed directly to students, e-mail blitzes, visits to high schools by admissions officers, college nights at local hotels, and information booths at college fairs, colleges are reaching out to prospective freshmen in both the United States and abroad with unprecedented energy and at great expense.

Started in earnest in the 1980s when the number of college-age students dropped temporarily, these marketing efforts have continued and expanded even as the number of students applying has soared. Sophisticated marketing techniques are used not only by colleges that may have problems filling their freshman class, but also by colleges with an overabundance of qualified applicants. Colleges want to attract the most academically qualified, talented, and diverse applicants from which to select their freshman class, and they increasingly go to great lengths to do so. And it works! As a result, more and more college-bound students have become aware of and are willing to seriously consider colleges far away from where they live.

The Role of the Internet

The Internet has also played a major role in how students approach college admissions. Although printed material and in-person presentations are still helpful ways for students to learn about different colleges, the web is now the primary source of information for students. Students can visit campuses through sophisticated online virtual tours and webcams and find answers to many of their questions from FAQs posted on their websites or by tracking college-sponsored blogs. Colleges have invested heavily in technology to help showcase themselves.

Finally, the Internet has made it easier than ever to apply to college. Students no longer have to send for applications, wait for them to arrive in the mail, and then fill them out by hand. Applications can be completed and submitted online, saving a lot of the time and effort that a traditional paper application once required. Simplifying things even more, over 500 colleges now accept the Common Application, a standardized application that can be filled out once (often along with a school-specific supplement) and submitted online to up to 20 participating colleges.

With admission harder to predict, students are now submitting more applications than ever before. Eight to 10 applications are now the norm at many private schools and high-performing public high schools; 12 to 15 or more applications are not uncommon. The Common Application, and technology in general, has made it easier for students to apply to an ever-larger number of colleges.

> As word spreads about the competition for college admission, students respond by applying to even more colleges to increase their chances of acceptance. In so doing, they end up unwittingly contributing to the very problem they are trying to solve for themselves.
>
> HIGH SCHOOL COUNSELOR CONCERNED ABOUT THE TREND

All of these factors taken together—growth in the population of eighteen year olds, greater interest in college, sophisticated marketing efforts, ease of access to information, and the ability to apply made possible by the Internet—help explain why it is harder to get into college now than ever before.

But that is not the whole answer.

Where the Real Crunch Lies

Most people are surprised to learn that with relatively few exceptions, four-year colleges in the United States still accept most of their applicants. In fact, each May the National Association for College Admission Counseling posts a list on its website of over 200 colleges still seeking applicants. Many of these have vacancies well into the summer for their freshman class that enrolls in the fall despite the social and demographic changes we have outlined. How can this fact be reconciled with the newspaper headlines (not to mention firsthand reports from students and parents) about a crisis in college admissions?

It turns out that the real crunch in admissions—the crunch that drives the newspaper headlines and the anxiety that afflicts many families at college application time—applies to only about 100 colleges that attract applicants from all over the country and the rest of the world and that are the most selective in admissions. What's wrong with all the rest? Nothing, of course, except that they aren't in that list of 100. Bill Mayher, a private college counselor, summarizes the problem succinctly: "It's hard for kids to get into colleges because they only want to get into colleges that are hard to get into."[8]

> It's hard for kids to get into colleges because they only want to get into colleges that are hard to get into.
>
> BILL MAYHER, PRIVATE COLLEGE CONSULTANT

WHAT IS SELECTIVITY ALL ABOUT?

The percentage of students offered admission to a college is a major factor in determining its selectivity. As the number of applications to a college increases, its admissions rate decreases. Another key factor affecting selectivity at a given college is the academic strength of the applicant pool since applicants tend to self-select when applying to certain colleges, especially some smaller ones, known for their academic rigor. Such schools may accept a higher percentage of those who apply because their applicant pools tend to be smaller and more uniformly strong. Both of these factors—admissions rate and strength of the applicant pool—help determine the selectivity of a particular school. Complicating matters even more is that some schools have different admissions processes for different programs, with some programs much more selective than others.

Our Definition of Selectivity

To simplify our discussion here, we define *selectivity* only in terms of admissions rate and define a selective college as one with an overall admissions rate of less than 50 percent. We further divide selective colleges into four categories: ultra-selective colleges (those admitting less than 10 percent of applicants), super-selective colleges (those admitting less than 20 percent of applicants), highly selective colleges (those admitting less than 35 percent of applicants), and very selective colleges (those admitting less than 50 percent of applicants).

These are artificial classifications, of course, and they don't consider the self-selection factor we noted above, but they give a sense of the relative difficulty of gaining admission. Although over 2,000 nonprofit four-year institutions of higher education in the United States admit 50 percent or more of their applicants (and most admit at least 75 percent), many students focus their attention on the 100 or so colleges that fall into the four groups we have just defined.

The students applying to selective colleges (and especially those we define as super-selective and ultra-selective) are the ones experiencing the "crisis" in college admissions. The crisis does not affect those applying to community colleges or seeking admission to the many colleges that accept most or all of their applicants. Nevertheless, it is very real to those who are applying to selective colleges now or expect to apply in the next few years. You (or your child) may be one of them. Our book will help you understand all aspects of the college admissions process, build a college list that is right for you, and submit strong applications.

If you'll be applying to less selective schools, this book will help you too. All students need to understand the admissions process, and all face the challenges of identifying colleges that will be a good fit and then submitting effective applications. We wrote *Admission Matters* to help all students take the college admissions journey successfully.

⚹ Colleges by Admissions Rate for the Class of 2016

Ultra-selective (less than 10 percent of applicants admitted)
- Brown University
- Columbia University
- Dartmouth College
- Harvard University
- MIT
- Princeton University
- Stanford University
- Yale University

Super-selective (less than 20 percent of applicants admitted)
- Amherst College
- Bowdoin College
- Cal Tech
- University of Chicago
- Claremont McKenna College
- Cornell University
- Duke University

- Georgetown University
- Harvey Mudd College
- Johns Hopkins University
- Middlebury College
- Northwestern University
- University of Pennsylvania
- Pitzer College
- Pomona College

Super-selective
(*continued*)
- Rice University
- University of Southern California
- Swarthmore College
- Vanderbilt University
- Washington University, St. Louis
- Washington and Lee College
- Wesleyan University
- Williams College

Highly Selective (less than 35 percent of applicants admitted)
- Bard College
- Barnard College
- University of California, Berkeley
- Boston College
- Bucknell College
- Carleton College
- Carnegie Mellon University
- Colby College
- Colgate University
- Colorado College
- Davidson College
- Emory University
- George Washington University
- Grinnell College
- Hamilton College
- Haverford College
- College of the Holy Cross
- Lafayette College
- Lehigh University
- UCLA
- Macalester College
- New York University

- University of North Carolina
- Northeastern University
- University of Notre Dame
- Oberlin College
- Pepperdine University
- Reed College
- Scripps College
- Trinity College (Connecticut)
- Tufts University
- Tulane University
- Vassar College
- University of Virginia
- Wake Forest University
- Washington and Jefferson College
- Wellesley College
- College of William and Mary

Very Selective Colleges (less than 50 percent of applicants admitted)
- American University
- Baylor University
- Binghamton University
- Boston University
- Brandeis University
- Bryn Mawr College
- University of Connecticut
- Connecticut College
- Cornell College
- University of California, Davis
- Denison University
- Dickinson College
- University of Florida
- Fordham University

- Franklin and Marshall College
- Gettysburg College
- University of California, Irvine
- Kenyon College
- University of Maryland
- University of Miami
- University of Michigan, Ann Arbor
- University of Minnesota, Twin Cities
- Mount Holyoke College
- Occidental College
- Rensselaer Polytechnic Institute
- University of Richmond
- University of Rochester
- University of San Diego
- University of California, San Diego
- University of California, Santa Barbara
- Sarah Lawrence College
- Skidmore College
- Smith College
- St. Lawrence University
- Spelman College
- Stony Brook University
- Texas Christian University
- University of Tulsa
- Union College
- Villanova University
- Wabash College
- Whitman College

Note: This list is not all-inclusive.

WHY IS THERE SO MUCH INTEREST IN A SMALL GROUP OF COLLEGES?

What is behind the intense interest in the small group of colleges and universities that is driving the headlines about a crisis in college admissions, and in particular, why is there a mystique surrounding the colleges in the Ivy League, as well as a few others accorded similar status? Just what benefits do these elite colleges bestow (or do people believe they bestow) on their graduates?

Prestige, of course, is one obvious answer. By definition, the more selective a college, the more difficult it is to get into and the greater the prestige associated with being admitted. The student enjoys the prestige directly (after all, the student is the one who was admitted!), and parents enjoy prestige by association. Parents are often the primary driver of the push toward prestige, but students also report similar pressures from peers in high school. Over the last generation, going to a highly ranked college has become a status symbol of greater value than almost any other consumer good, in part because it cannot simply be purchased if you have enough money.

> Lots of times it's kids, I think, trying to define themselves by their school choice, not so much choosing the school that's right for them, but trying to look good through it. I'm not sure if they get it from parents or from other kids or from teachers. But they get it from somewhere.
>
> VOLUNTEER IN COUNSELING OFFICE AT PRIVATE HIGH SCHOOL

Although some people openly acknowledge considering prestige in college choice, many more cite the assumed quality of the educational experience as the basis for their interest in an elite college. But this rationale often depends on the unstated and untested assumption that a good indicator of the quality of something is how much others seek it. This means that selective colleges are presumed to offer a better education: the more selective, the higher the quality. But is this really true?

Take the eight colleges in the Ivy League, for example: Harvard University, Yale University, Princeton University, Brown University, Dartmouth College, University of Pennsylvania, Cornell University, and Columbia University. One counselor we know refers to them as the "climbing vine" schools to take away some of the unconscious allure of the common brand. The Ivy League originally referred only to a football league. (Only seven colleges belonged at first. Brown University eventually joined as the eighth member, although several other colleges were considered possibilities at the time.)

Over time, though, the term *Ivy League* became synonymous with prestige and a very strong academic reputation rather than an athletic league. The admissions rate of each Ivy places it in the ultra-selective or super-selective category. Certainly each has fine students and faculty renowned for their research. Everyone agrees that they are excellent schools, but do the Ivies automatically offer undergraduates a better educational experience than many other institutions? The answer, commonplace to those in academic circles but surprising to much of the public, is assuredly no.

THE RANKINGS GAME

A major contributor to the mystique of selective colleges has been the annual rankings of colleges published by *U.S. News and World Report*. The first rankings, published in 1983, were based solely on surveys of college administrators. Over time, the rankings became so popular that they outgrew the magazine itself

> Harvard is perhaps the most overrated institution of higher learning in America. This is not to imply that Harvard isn't a good school—on the contrary, Harvard is an excellent school. But its reputation creates an unattainable standard; no school could ever be as good as most people think Harvard is.
>
> COMMENT BY A HARVARD STUDENT

and became a separate annual guidebook simply called *Best Colleges*. A dozen or so other ranking guides have emerged as competitors, and in some cases, like the contrarian *Washington Monthly*, a foil to *U.S. News*.

Although *U.S. News* no longer exists as a print magazine, the rankings continue through the guidebook and an accompanying website published every year in August that feature extensive information and advice about applying to college, as well as rankings based on both reputational and complex statistical formulas. The yearly rankings, though, drive the sales of *Best Colleges* and generate a lot of media attention and controversy among those, including us, who believe the ranking process is fundamentally flawed. One vocal critic, Lloyd Thacker, founder of the Education Conservancy and a prominent voice for reform of the college admissions process, refers to the ranking business as the "ranksters."

While president of Stanford University, Gerhard Casper expressed his concern about the rankings to the editor of *U.S. News* as follows: "As the president of a university that is among the top-ranked universities, I hope I have the standing to persuade you that much about these rankings—particularly their specious formulas and spurious precision—is utterly misleading."[9]

What Goes into the *U.S. News* Rankings

A little less than one quarter—22.5 percent to be exact—of a college's ranking is based on reputational ratings it receives in the poll that *U.S. News* conducts annually of college presidents, provosts, admissions deans, and a small group of high school counselors. The administrators are asked to rate the academic quality of undergraduate programs at schools with the same mission as their own (for example, liberal arts colleges or research universities) on a scale of 1 to 5 from "marginal" to "distinguished," with an option to respond "don't know"; the counselors are asked to rate schools in both categories. Many of those who receive the questionnaire acknowledge that they lack the kind of detailed knowledge of other colleges that they would need to respond meaningfully. The response rate is usually fairly low: less than 50 percent for college administrators and less than 15 percent for the high school counselors.

The remaining 77.5 percent of a college's ranking is based on data collected in five categories, each weighted in the final calculation as follows: retention and graduation rate (20 percent), faculty resources (20 percent), student selectivity (15 percent), financial resources (10 percent), alumni giving (5 percent), and graduation rate performance (7.5 percent).[10]

Each of these five categories in turn contains several submeasures. For example, *U.S. News* has derived student selectivity from several kinds of data for the freshman class: admissions rate, the 25th and 75th percentiles of SAT or ACT scores, and the percentage of students in the top 10 percent of their high school class. This last item is frequently not reported to colleges by high schools, so it is based on information from just a portion of the freshman class. It is assumed, but never but proven, that these data can measure a good education.

The *U.S. News* Formula

All of the measures we have just described are collected annually for each college and put into a formula that weights the different kinds of data and then computes an overall "ranking." To avoid comparing apples with oranges, *U.S. News* ranks campuses of the same type, so that research universities and liberal arts colleges, for example, are ranked separately. (We'll discuss the differences between these two kinds of institutions, as well as others, in chapter 4 when we look at factors to consider in choosing colleges.) Only the first 100 colleges in each group are ranked individually; after that, the schools are grouped alphabetically by tiers. Every few years, *U.S. News* slightly modifies its formula, mostly recently to reduce the reputation factor from 25 percent to 22.5 percent, ostensibly to demonstrate its precision and respond to criticism.

Overall, the rankings don't change much from year to year, although a school's position may bounce up or down a few notches due to a change in the formula or some aberration in a statistic reported for a given year. Does its quality relative to its peers really change significantly in one or two years? We think not. Critics of the rankings like Lloyd Thacker argue that meaningful changes in college quality cannot be measured in the short term and that *U.S. News* changes the formula primarily to appear fresh and up-to-date—and to sell more guidebooks.

> Now more than ever, people believe that the ranking—or the presumed hierarchy of "quality" or "prestige"—of the college or university one attends matters, and matters enormously. More than ever before, education is being viewed as a commodity . . . The large and fundamental problem is that we are at risk of it all seeming and becoming increasingly a game. What matters is less the education and more the brand.[12]
>
> LEE BOLLINGER, PRESIDENT OF COLUMBIA UNIVERSITY

Admissions Rate and Yield

Although it plays only a small role in the *U.S. News* formula, a college's admissions rate or selectivity is the one figure that captures the public's attention and the most headlines. A decline in the admit rate from the previous year is often interpreted as a reflection of a college's increased quality, not just the result of successful marketing. Sample headline: "College X Admits Record Low Percentage of Applicants." This is news.

Factors That Affect Admissions Rate

Aggressive outreach to students to encourage them to apply, although they know that only a fraction of those applying will be admitted, is the easiest way for a college to become more selective. While most colleges engage in outreach with more noble goals, the result is the same. Rachel Toor, a former Duke University admissions officer, vividly describes her own experience: "I travel around the country whipping kids (and their parents) into a frenzy so that they will apply. I tell them how great a school Duke is academically and how much fun they will have socially. Then, come April, we reject most of them."[13]

Colleges can also lower their admissions percentage by limiting admission offers to those students who are most likely to enroll. A college's yield—the percentage of admitted students who actually decide to enroll—can affect its admissions rate. Yields vary greatly from college to college, from more than 80 percent at Harvard to less than 20 percent at some others.

Ways Colleges Can Increase Their Yield

If a college has a high yield, it can admit fewer students and still fill its classes. If it has a low yield, it has to admit more to meet enrollment targets. A college can raise its yield by admitting a larger percentage of the incoming class by early decision, often referred to as ED. Through an ED application, students submit a completed application by November 1 or November 15 rather than the traditional January 1 deadline, in exchange for an admission decision by mid-December rather than in the spring. The catch is that an ED application is binding on the student, meaning that the student is obligated to attend if admitted, subject to the availability of adequate financial aid. So a student admitted by ED is a sure thing for a college. We'll talk much more about ED and its cousin, early action, in chapter 7, but we mention it now because it indirectly increases a college's yield and thereby reduces its overall admit rate. Some colleges currently admit from a third to a half of their incoming freshman class under ED, leaving many fewer seats available for the much larger number of students applying in the regular admissions round.

A college may also increase its yield and lower its admit rate by rejecting or, more likely, wait-listing, students they consider "overqualified" because the college believes the student won't accept the college's offer of admission and will go elsewhere. The dean of admissions at one such college realistically defended the practice at his institution as follows: "We know our place in the food chain of higher education. We're not a community college. And we're not Harvard."[14] This practice is not common, but it is not rare either. We'll have more to say about it in chapter 5.

Finally, a college may increase its yield by preferentially admitting students who have shown that they are strongly interested in that school in some way beyond simply submitting an application. We'll talk more about "demonstrated interest" and its role in admissions in chapter 5.

Some More Concerns About Rankings

Critics have pointed out that while the *U.S. News* variables can contribute indirectly to educational quality (perhaps higher salaries lead to better faculty, and smaller classes mean more personal attention), educators do not agree on how those variables can be used to measure the quality of a college. To make things worse, colleges can manipulate some of the factors in the *U.S. News* formula to raise their standing. As much as college leaders disparage rankings, they are too high profile and too influential among the general public for colleges to ignore them.

> I overheard a conversation at a reception for the parents of newly admitted students at Elite U. A mom was chatting with a young admissions officer who was mingling with parents on the lawn of the president's house. "I have a question I'd like to ask you," she said. "Since Elite U takes less than 15 percent of those who apply, why does the university work so hard to encourage more applications?" The admissions officer was silent for a moment. "I'm afraid you'll have to ask the dean of admissions that question," she said.
>
> PARENT OF PROSPECTIVE FRESHMAN

Alumni, boards of trustees, and even bond-rating agencies on Wall Street pay close attention to the rankings and expect to see "improvement." Under pressure, some colleges have actively worked to look better in ways that have little to do with educational quality but will boost the school's ranking. One common but harmless approach is the production of elegant, full-color booklets that typically highlight a college's new programs and facilities, as well as its ambitious plans for the future. In addition to distributing them for fundraising and recruitment purposes, some college presidents send them to their colleagues at other campuses in the hope that the booklets will raise awareness of their college and possibly lead to a higher reputation rating when the *U.S. News* questionnaire arrives the following year. No one knows if this actually works, but some colleges expend considerable effort in the hope that it does.

Another tactic is selective reporting of data. Colleges have always had some leeway in how they report their statistics, and they naturally want to present themselves in the most favorable light for the ratings. In the past, for example, some colleges excluded the scores of recruited athletes in their reported SAT scores. Athletes often have lower SAT scores than other freshmen and would lower the average score, and hence the college's ranking, if they were included. *U.S. News* says they have stopped this practice, but it is hard to know for sure. Even more troubling are recent disclosures by several well-known colleges that admissions staff misrepresented data used in the rankings in an apparent effort to enhance their school's position.

WHY ARE RANKINGS SO POPULAR?

It is not surprising that students and parents turn to rankings like those published by *U.S. News* when they think about colleges. Deciding where to apply isn't easy, and having supposed experts do the evaluating is an attractive alternative to figuring things out on your own, especially if you have no experience. As a society, we are obsessed with rating consumer goods in the quest for the best. We accept ratings that assess washing machines, restaurants, football teams, hospitals, and movies, so why not colleges too?

The Limitations of Rankings

College rankings, though, are very different. The rankings simply don't measure what people think they measure: the educational experience for an individual student. Doing that requires a personalized look at a college through the eyes of a potential student. Although you no doubt have much in common with your friends and classmates, you also differ in important ways, so no standardized ranking can hope to evaluate how you as an individual might fare at a certain college.

There is no easy substitute for investing the time and effort to determine which colleges will be a good fit for you. Merely knowing which ones are the most selective or enjoy the highest reputations among college administrators (which, in large measure, is what the *U.S. News* rankings are telling

> Students may have a better sense of their potential ability than college admissions committees. To cite one prominent example, Steven Spielberg was rejected by the University of Southern California and UCLA film schools.[15]
>
> STACEY DALE AND ALAN KRUEGER, RESEARCHERS WHO STUDIED THE LONG-TERM EFFECTS OF ATTENDING DIFFERENT TYPES OF COLLEGES

you) doesn't get you very far toward finding a place where you will thrive and learn. Readers interested in more information about *U.S. News* and other college rankings can access that information through the Students and Parents link on the National Association for College Admission Counseling website at www.nacacnet.org.

Another Option: The National Survey of Student Engagement

For the past decade, the National Survey of Student Engagement, abbreviated NSSE and pronounced "Nessie," based at Indiana University, has attempted to measure quality and satisfaction by asking students direct questions about their educational experiences and how they spend their time. Unfortunately, many highly regarded colleges do not participate in NSSE, including most of the ones we call selective. And some colleges that do participate do not make the results public.

Representative Questions from the National Survey on Student Engagement 2013

1. During the current school year, about how often have you done the following? Response options: Very often, Often, Sometimes, Never
   a. Talked about career plans with a faculty member
   b. Worked with a faculty member on activities other than coursework (committees, student groups, etc.)
   c. Discussed course topics, ideas, or concepts with a faculty member outside of class
   d. Discussed your academic performance with a faculty member

2. During the current school year, to what extent have your courses challenged you to do your best work? Response options: 1 = Not at all to 7 = Very much

3. How would you evaluate your entire educational experience at this institution? Response options: Excellent, Good, Fair, Poor

4. If you could start over again, would you go to the same institution you are now attending? Response options: Definitely yes, Probably yes, Probably no, Definitely no

Used with permission of the Trustees of Indiana University.

Although NSSE is not used or reported as broadly as it might be, we think you should know about it, since it suggests some important dimensions in assessing educational quality. (You can learn more about NSSE and see which colleges participate in it at www.nsse.iub.edu.) We applaud NSSE's questions and recommend that you ask similar ones on your own when you research and possibly visit colleges. We talk more about college visits in chapter 5, where we provide a link to a series of questions that NSSE suggests you ask when you tour schools.

"I'll MAKE MORE MONEY IF I GRADUATE FROM AN ELITE COLLEGE": ANOTHER MYTH

Let's return now to the basic question of why there is so much interest in the group of the most selective one hundred colleges. Okay, you say, you now see that name recognition and rankings do not necessarily indicate educational quality. But maybe that is irrelevant. Isn't the real value of an elite college education the contacts you make while there? Everyone knows that the rich, the famous, and the well-connected attended these colleges. Wouldn't attending one of them increase your chances of getting to know the right people, getting into a prestigious graduate school, or getting an important career-enhancing break— all eventually leading to fortune if not fame?

The Association Between Income and College Selectivity

Several studies have been interpreted as supporting this conclusion. Years after graduation, graduates of elite institutions on average earn more than graduates of less well-known colleges, just as the income of college graduates is higher those with a high school education. The simple interpretation is that attending a selective college is responsible for the income difference. But economists Stacy Dale and Alan Krueger investigated another possibility in two studies conducted a decade apart.[16] Perhaps, they hypothesized, the students who apply to elite colleges have personal qualities to begin with that lead in some way to later income differences. Their research suggests that the kind of college that students attend is less important than their inherent ability, motivation, and ambition.

> We didn't find any evidence that suggested that the selectivity of a student's undergraduate college was related to the quality of the graduate school they attended.[17]
>
> STACY DALE, COAUTHOR OF DALE AND KRUEGER STUDIES

The Characteristics of the Student, and Not the College, Are Key

In their first study, Dale and Krueger compared income figures for individuals who were accepted by elite colleges and attended those colleges with the income of people who were accepted by elite colleges but chose to attend a less selective college. They found no difference in income between the two groups. The only exception was that students from low-income backgrounds who attended an elite college had higher incomes later in life. The data even suggested that simply having applied to an elite college (that is, having high aspirations), regardless of whether a student was accepted, was the critical factor in predicting later income.

A second study, conducted 10 years later with a much larger number of participants, confirmed and extended the earlier findings. When Dale and Krueger controlled for a student's grade point average and test scores on entering college, there was no difference years later in the income of students who attended elite colleges versus those who had applied, were denied, and subsequently attended less selective schools. In both studies, students of similar academic ability who had the self-confidence and motivation to envision themselves attending a selective college showed the economic benefit normally ascribed to those

> My advice to students: Don't believe that the only school worth attending is one that would not admit you. That you go to college is more important than where you go. Find a school whose academic strengths match your interests and that devotes resources to instruction in those fields. Recognize that your own motivation, ambition, and talents will determine your success more than the college name on your diploma.[18]
>
> ALAN KRUEGER, COAUTHOR OF DALE AND KRUEGER STUDIES

who actually attended such a college. As before, though, there were differences for some subgroups of students. Black and Hispanic students, as well as those from less-educated or low-income families, did show significantly increased future earnings associated with attending a selective college.

GETTING INTO GRADUATE SCHOOL

What about admission to graduate school? Does attending a selective college affect your chances of getting into a highly regarded law, business, medical, or other graduate program? A disproportionate number of graduates of selective colleges attend prestigious graduate and professional schools. But here too, perhaps students admitted to selective colleges bring personal qualities with them that make their subsequent success in gaining admission to these schools after graduation more likely. Those same students may have done just as well if they had gone to a less selective college.

Dale and Krueger did not have the data in either of their studies to rigorously test this hypothesis; they could draw firm conclusions only about income. In their first study, however, they found that people who went to a selective college were no more likely to obtain an advanced degree than those who were admitted to a selective college but chose to attend a less selective school. In addition, the data suggested that it was the qualities of the students themselves, and not anything associated with the college they attended, that predicted where they went for graduate study. Students admitted to a selective college but chose to attend a less selective one seemed to fare just as well when it came to graduate or professional school admissions as those who actually attended a more selective college.

THE IMPORTANCE OF FIT

We believe that the college selection process should be about finding colleges that are a good fit for you. A number of factors contribute to fit—academic, extra-curricular, social, and geographical, among others—and the determination of fit will be different for different people. Assessing fit takes time and effort and is much harder to do than simply looking at a list of rankings. It is not a shoe that you slip on once and decide if it fits well.

This book does not try to dissuade you from selecting a college on the basis of prestige—you have lots of company. However, in chapter 4, we discuss many other important dimensions to consider in selecting colleges and encourage you to think carefully about them. Finding a good fit does not mean that there is just one perfect school for a student. Rather, it means exploring many factors that can lead to your academic and personal success.

You may find that in the end, you are making the same choices as you would have before, but your choices will be more informed. You may even find yourself seriously considering other options that you had previously overlooked. Either outcome is fine. We simply want to help you understand as much as possible about yourself, the college admissions process, and colleges themselves so that you can make the best choices for you.

Stephen Lewis, former president of Carleton College, stated it well: "The question should not be, what are the best colleges? The real question should be, best for whom?"[20]

CHAPTER 2

What Do Colleges Look for in an Applicant?

One often hears that college admissions decisions are just not predictable. Everyone knows that it is harder to get into some colleges than ever before, but the criteria for admission seem to be getting murkier and murkier. For example, a student may be admitted to a super-selective college yet find herself placed on the wait list at a less selective one. Or a student is admitted to three colleges but denied by three others, all about the same in terms of selectivity. Why aren't decisions more consistent?

Even more puzzling are cases involving students from the same high school who apply to the same college. One student may have a significantly stronger academic record than his classmate, yet be denied by a college while the classmate receives an acceptance to the same one. Why wasn't the student with the stronger record accepted also? And although many colleges claim they use exactly the same admissions criteria for early decision applications as they use for regular decision applications, anecdotal as well as documented evidence strongly argues that early applicants often have an edge in the admissions process. Why should when you apply make so much difference?

This chapter will help you understand the many factors colleges take into account in their review of applications. Knowing what colleges look for as they sort through thousands of applications can help you make sense out of the admissions process and provide you with what you need to approach it with confidence.

We have no magic bullet or formula that will guarantee you acceptance to a college that does not admit everyone who applies or that does not admit students by their numbers alone. But the more you know about how colleges go about selecting their freshman class, the wiser you will be in approaching the tasks before you—from choosing colleges, to preparing your applications, to dealing with the successes and, yes, even the disappointments that may occur at the end.

HOW COLLEGE ADMISSIONS HAS CHANGED

Before we begin, we'll share a little history that dramatically illustrates how college admissions have changed over the years. About 80 years ago, colleges that are now considered among the most selective filled their classes in ways that reflected the times. Yale University, for example, filled its class of 1936 from a total of 1,330 applicants. Of that group, 959, or 72 percent, were accepted, and 884 of them subsequently enrolled.

Yale Then

Almost 30 percent were the sons of Yale University alumni, known as legacies. Many of those admitted were students from feeder schools—elite prep schools with headmasters whose close relationships with college admissions officers virtually assured the admission of their graduates to the school of their choice. Less than 20 percent of the freshman class graduated from a public high school.[1] Women were not eligible then to apply to Yale; they had separate elite colleges, known as the Seven Sisters, which had similar admissions practices. Also excluded were young men who, no matter how bright and accomplished, did not fit the mold of privilege and wealth, to say nothing of race, religion, and ethnicity. But few of the latter even considered applying; everyone understood the criteria for admission.

Another example, this one from about 60 years ago, makes a similar point. The following description comes from a book on the history of college admissions:

> Until the 1950s admissions staffs typically consisted of one professional and possibly a secretary to take care of clerical work. Often, a dean would split responsibilities between admissions and some other aspect of administration or teaching. Colleges could function effectively with such a simple admissions structure because students tended to apply only to their first choice college, and

they were usually accepted. A close collaboration between admissions officers and guidance counselors also facilitated such modest staffing. Admissions officers visited selected high schools, interviewed candidates for admission, and then usually offered admission to students on the spot. Philip Smith, [former] dean of admissions at Williams College, recounted a visit as an admissions officer in the late 1950s. After he interviewed students, Smith sat down with eight teachers; he was given a pat on the back and a Scotch, and was expected to offer admission to all the candidates right then.[2]

Yale Now

Today, of course, institutions like Yale University and Williams College pride themselves on the diversity of their student body and actively recruit high-achieving men and women from all backgrounds. The 1,975 men and women invited to join the Yale University class of 2016 were selected from an applicant pool of almost 29,000; of the 1,320 enrolling, just 13 percent were legacies. Fifty-five percent of the class came from public high schools. This example is typical of the current admissions picture at similar colleges as well. Those who in a prior era would have easily been assured of admission by virtue of birth or circumstance no longer are. The rules have changed.

CHANGING TIMES AT YALE UNIVERSITY

	Class of 1936	Class of 2016
Number of applicants	1,330	28,975
Accepted (%)	72%	6.8%
Size of freshman class	884	1,356
From public high schools (%)	Less than 20%	57%
Legacies (%)	30%	13%

WHAT MATTERS NOW

The web pages of most colleges provide general information about the characteristics they are seeking in their prospective freshmen. This information may even include details about how the college weights grades, test scores, or extracurricular activities in the final admissions decision. This material is surprisingly consistent from school to school. It's as if they had all attended the same admissions training program. But information on the web page is the public version of the admissions story. It is vague on purpose, though not intended to mislead. This is just all they can legitimately disclose in a general way. The private version is what actually goes on behind closed doors as admissions officers read through many thousands of applications to select a freshman class that may have just a few hundred places. We don't mean to suggest an atmosphere of smoke-filled rooms and sneaky deals being made. It is just that the process can be enormously complex and subtle, and it may vary somewhat for each applicant. In this chapter, we will discuss the criteria that colleges generally take into account in their evaluation. In chapter 3, we will turn our attention to the review process itself.

Students and parents are often surprised when they learn about the full range of criteria that admissions officers at many colleges consider. Although some criteria are well known and predictable (for example, grades and test scores), others are not, and not all schools use all criteria. The level of competition for admission to the most selective colleges can also come as a big surprise to those who have not had recent firsthand experience with college admissions.

THE ACADEMIC RECORD

The heart of a college application is the student's academic record: the courses taken and the grades they achieved in those courses over the course of a high school career. Colleges almost uniformly state that they are looking for students who show convincing evidence of being able to do well in a demanding academic program and that they place the greatest weight in admissions decisions on that record.

How Challenging Is Your Academic Program?

Many colleges provide students with guidelines about the kinds of preparation they expect successful applicants to have in high school—the number of years of English, mathematics, foreign language, and so forth.

> Students and parents sometimes ask if it is better to get an A in a regular course or a B in an AP course. My answer is that it is best to get an A in the AP course.
>
> COMMENT BY A HARVARD ADMISSIONS OFFICER AT A GROUP INFORMATION SESSION, FOLLOWED BY NERVOUS LAUGHTER FROM THE AUDIENCE

⚔ What Do Admissions Committees Look At?

Academic Record

- Grades
- Class rank
- Rigor of curriculum

Standardized Test Scores

- SAT
- ACT
- SAT Subject Tests

Engagement Outside the Classroom

- Extracurricular activities
- Community service
- Work experience

Personal Qualities

- Letters of recommendation
- Essays
- Interview report

Hooks and Institutional Priorities

- Legacy connection
- Donation potential
- Underrepresented race or ethnicity
- Recruited athlete status
- Socioeconomic and geographical background
- Exceptional talent

What Kinds of Courses Should You Take?

Williams College, for example, a super-selective liberal arts college in Massachusetts, provides the following guidelines to prospective students:

> By far the most important aspect of your application is your high school transcript. We want to see that you have done well while tackling a challenging (and well-balanced) course load. To be competitive, applicants should pursue the strongest program of study offered by their high schools, taking whatever honors or advanced level courses are available. A program of study should ideally include a full four-year sequence in English and mathematics; study of one foreign language for three or, preferably, four years; and three years of study each in the social sciences and laboratory sciences. These are not absolute requirements for admission, but they are recommendations for developing a compelling high school record.[3]

The guidelines at Williams are similar to those at some of the most selective colleges. Guidelines at less selective schools may be less stringent, for example, fewer years of foreign language or mathematics, but they still emphasize the importance of the academic preparation needed to gain admission.

Why Colleges Like a Challenging Curriculum

Colleges expect students to take advantage of opportunities their school may offer to challenge themselves academically through honors or Advanced Placement (AP) courses or by participating in the International Baccalaureate (IB) program that is offered at some high schools. This is especially important at selective colleges. Admissions officers like to see these courses since they are college level and culminate in rigorous subject matter tests scored by independent graders using calibrated standards. Strong performance in these courses (and on the tests themselves) indicates that a student can do college-level work. It has also become fairly common in some communities for high school juniors and seniors to take classes at a local community college, a nearby four-year college, or online in subjects where the students have exhausted their high school's offerings. College admissions officers also favorably note these classes. If opportunities for challenging classes are open to you, a selective college will expect you to have taken advantage of them.

Be Reasonable and Stay Sane

But what exactly is expected? When students return from college visits over spring break or the summer, they frequently report that they heard that colleges expect students to take the "most demanding" program available. But what is the "most demanding" program? Is it five APs a year, or would six be better if you can squeeze another one in? What if your school doesn't offer as many APs as the other high school across town? Are you at a disadvantage? (No, you aren't, because colleges learn about this from information that your school sends along with your transcript.)

Many students ask, and we admit it is hard to answer: "Should I take every AP course I can?" Our answer is a highly qualified, "It all depends." Are these all courses you are likely to do well in? Are they well taught? What are you doing in the rest of your life: activities, family responsibilities, just living a daily life? In other words, there is a different answer for each student. It is unfortunate that these admission officers can't add a few simple words to their advice: "Be reasonable; stay sane; take what you can manage and do well in." This would go a long way toward relieving some of the pressure some students at some high schools feel to take every honors or AP course in sight.

Course Load and Grades Are Both Important

The bottom line, however, is that a straight A record will not make up for a weak course load at many selective colleges if your school offers the option of more advanced course work. High grades are important, but the rigor of your course load is just as important. Many high schools reward a student who has taken a challenging course with a weighted grade at the end of the semester. If an A in a regular course is worth four points, for example, an A in an AP class may be worth five points. Grade weighting sometimes extends to the pluses and minuses that a student may receive as well, so that an A+ in an AP course might be assigned 5.25 points, while an A– in such a course might be worth 4.75 points. The weighting of honors, IB, and AP classes can result in some astronomical grade point averages (for example, a GPA of 4.6) for students who take heavy loads of such courses and do exceptionally well in them. Such students represent a very small fraction of high school students overall, but they are disproportionately represented in the applicant pools of the most selective colleges.

Colleges May Recalculate Your GPA

It may be disheartening for students to learn that some colleges recompute each applicant's GPA in unweighted form, including only the years (usually tenth, eleventh, and twelfth) and classes (usually academic "solids" such as English, foreign language, math, science, and social studies) they consider most academic. Admissions officers do this to have a relatively common standard for discussion. But rest assured that despite any recalculation, they will look carefully at the quality of the courses you are taking, within the context of the opportunities you have had. A high GPA in a less challenging curriculum will definitely be less well received by a selective college than a more mixed record in a challenging one.

An Upward Trend Is a Good Thing

In addition, colleges consider improvement and decline over time: two students may have identical GPAs in comparable courses, but one has improved over time while the other's grades have declined. The evaluation of these two students' academic records will be very different; admissions staff will view the improving student much more favorably. This is another example of how the evaluation process considers an applicant's record in context.

Putting the GPA in Context

While colleges place great emphasis on grades and courses, they recognize that grades can be hard to evaluate in isolation. Everyone, including college admissions officers, knows that some high schools (and some teachers) are generous with top marks, while others have more rigorous standards. Grade inflation has become a serious problem at many high schools, both public and private. According to the College Board, 44 percent of students in the high school graduating class of 2011 who took the SAT reported GPAs of at least A–. Less than 20 years earlier, the figure was just 32 percent.

How Colleges Deal with Grade Inflation

Grade inflation is a major reason that colleges like to see students do well on AP tests in addition to excelling in the courses themselves. The AP tests taken at the end of the academic year are scored by the College Board according to national norms (or international norms, in the case of the IB), so a student who gets a 4 or 5 on an AP exam (scored 1 to 5, with 5 as the highest possible) has demonstrated excellent mastery of the material, independent of his or her local teacher's grading standards. Colleges typically invite, but do not require, students to self-report AP test scores, and you are under no obligation to report disappointing scores. But admissions officers like to see AP test results from the AP courses you have taken through your junior year as a way to gauge the rigor of the courses themselves.

The Role of Class Rank

Some high schools, mostly public, assign a class rank to students on the basis of GPA. Class rank provides information about a student's grades relative to his or her classmates, and colleges have found it makes the task of evaluating grades easier. But fewer and fewer high schools are now computing class rank. Private schools in particular have been reluctant to rank their students, since they believe it promotes a more competitive environment in their school and magnifies small differences in achievement so that students below the very top are disadvantaged. Class rank also does not take into account the strength of the student body overall. A student ranked in the lower half of the class at one school might have ranked in the top 20 percent at an easier school. Increasingly, public high schools are recognizing these same drawbacks and have stopped ranking their students as well.

The absence of explicit class rank makes the job of admissions officers more challenging, but colleges adapt to it and use the information that is available to get a sense of where students stand in their class, more or less. Even if they don't have class rank from a high school, they can compare the GPAs of the different students applying from the same high school, or to previous years, since these standards change only slightly from year to year.

The School Profile

High schools generally include a school profile with each transcript sent as part of a college application. The profile summarizes the school's curriculum and grading policies so that a college can get a general idea of how a student has performed relative to his or her peers. A profile may show the grade range for each decile or quintile of the senior class and list the AP, IB, and honors courses offered, as well as the percentage of students who go on to four-year colleges directly from that high school. It may also include statistics about the student body such as the SAT and ACT distributions, the number of students taking and passing AP tests, and so forth. Colleges use this information to supplement data on class rank or to provide much-needed context when class rank is not provided.

Colleges also require students to have a school official, usually a counselor, complete a recommendation form, called the secondary school report (SR on the Common Application) that includes an evaluation of the rigor of a student's academic program relative to the offerings at the high school. This is another way for colleges to calibrate a student's grades while trying to ensure that students from schools that do not offer many advanced classes are not penalized for not having taken a program chock full of them.

Part of the college mania we noted in the Introduction to this book is the frequently quoted tidbit that Harvard denies over 75 percent of the high school valedictorians who apply each year. Several other ultra-selective and super-selective colleges also deny a majority of their valedictorian applicants. But if you reflect on this for a minute, it is not really surprising. There are over 27,000 high schools, both public and private, in the United States, with more being founded every year as charter schools expand. Each of them has a student (or often several students) who achieved the highest grades. Clearly grades can't be the whole story in college admissions; there are just too many students with very high grades and too much variation in what those grades really mean for grades alone to determine who is admitted to a selective college. So the common parental complaint, "My child had perfect grades but still didn't get into College Q" is no surprise to the admissions officer at the other end of the phone the day after students receive their decisions.

STANDARDIZED TESTS

Most colleges require standardized tests such as the SAT or the ACT. The question students ask most often is how much the tests count in admissions decisions. David Erdmann, dean of admissions at Rollins College, has given the most candid answer of all: "At most institutions, standardized test scores count less than students think and more than colleges are willing to admit."[4] Chapter 6 is devoted to a discussion of these tests in detail.

Standardized tests seem to be more "objective" to both colleges and students because they are independent of the varying grading standards of high schools. They also help separate students from each other since grades alone no longer do that well due to widespread grade inflation.

But the tests are not without their critics, and most colleges are wary of relying too heavily on them because of doubts about what they really measure and lingering concerns that they may be biased in some way. Of special concern is the growth of the test prep industry that often "guarantees" significant score improvements for students who take special courses that can cost a thousand dollars or more. Clearly the only ones who can benefit from this assistance are those who can afford to pay for it.

In response to these concerns, some colleges have made standardized tests optional—the decision whether to submit scores is left to the student. We talk about test-optional schools and how to find them in chapter 6. More schools are going test optional all the time.

Despite calls to eliminate standardized tests entirely from the college admissions process, most colleges, including public universities for which it is a crucial piece of information, will probably continue to use them for the foreseeable future. With grades difficult to interpret, most colleges are unwilling to give up the additional information, however imperfect, that these tests provide.

ENGAGEMENT BEYOND THE CLASSROOM: THE EXTRACURRICULAR RECORD

Many colleges not only expect students to be strong academically but also to be interesting, contributing members of both the school community and the community at large. Admissions officers used to talk about the importance of being well rounded and showing evidence of leadership in extracurricular activities. Now they more often speak about having a "well-rounded class" composed of students who each have exceptional talent or commitment in one or two areas. This summons up the ubiquitous buzzword: *passion*, that elusive quality that all teenagers are supposed to have discovered in themselves by the time they apply to college.

The shift in language reflects the realization that there are just so many hours in the day for any adolescent and that achieving excellence in a given area can take up most of those hours. As David Gould, former dean of admissions at Brandeis, has said, "The embodiment at age seventeen of a Renaissance person is difficult to find. We realized we could accomplish the same thing [for our freshman class] with lots of different people."[5] So colleges examine whether a student has made a sustained commitment to an activity over a number of years in high school; thus, involvement in one activity over time can be more helpful than involvement in several more briefly.

We think *commitment* is a better term than *passion*, and it is the one we choose to use.

Extracurricular Activities

But just what does *exceptional talent* or *commitment* mean? In general, the more selective the college, the higher the bar in evaluating extracurricular activities and leadership. Involvement in debate, for example, can range from participating on a team to winning occasional local tournaments, to having a winning record at the regional, state, or national level. At more selective colleges, higher levels of achievement are needed to impress admissions officers. Being a dedicated member of the school orchestra is good, but being first violinist and concertmaster is better. Better still is winning regional, state, national, or even international competitions as a soloist. We'll address the special case of athletic talent later in this chapter under the topic of hooks.

Colleges like to see evidence of leadership in an applicant as well. Serving as president of an active high school club, or as a student body officer, or editing the high school newspaper or yearbook are all examples of common high school leadership activities colleges see. Again, the more selective the college, the greater the expectation that applicants will hold leadership positions and that they will be at the highest levels, possibly extending beyond the high school to local, regional, and state organizations, where applicable.

Colleges differ, however, in the emphasis they place on leadership. Fred Hargadon, a long-time dean of admissions at Stanford and Princeton, was well known for preferring to see evidence of perseverance in applicants rather than leadership per se. It can also be difficult to assess leadership meaningfully, since the same position can vary greatly in importance and responsibility from high school to high school.

Community Service

Colleges like to see that a student has been willing to contribute time and effort to help others through community service, though it is not formally required any more than sports, the arts, or student government are. There are many ways to do this, and in fact some high schools require community service for graduation that may include activities like tutoring other students; volunteering at a soup kitchen, hospital, or homeless shelter; or fundraising for a worthy cause. Just as in extracurricular activities, sustained involvement over time is the key, and a major time commitment will have more impact on an application than one that is less extensive. Generally a leadership role in a community service activity, in addition to a major time commitment to it, will have the most impact of all since it reflects the student's altruism, energy level, and ability to work effectively with others.

Work Experience

Most college applications give students an opportunity to list their work experience. Depending on its nature, paid work can nicely complement a student's special interests (for example, designing web pages or working with developmentally disabled children). Work can also demonstrate personal responsibility and leadership ability if the student has a job in which he or she supervises others. Finally, an extensive work commitment can reflect a student's modest socioeconomic background and indicate that her income is important to her and her family. Admissions officers know that work responsibilities of this type can limit the amount of time a student can devote to other activities, so work can compensate for an otherwise limited extracurricular record.

Follow Your Interests

In chapter 9, we will discuss how you can share information about your extracurricular, community service, and work experiences as part of your application. Students sometimes try to join activities they think will look good to college admissions officers, like community service. In reality, admissions officers want to see students who have sustained their involvement in one or more activities and grown from them. It doesn't much matter what those activities are. A long list filled with activities that require little time or devotion is not helpful. This is one of those cases where less is more.

Second-guessing what activities colleges are seeking is usually futile—and not much fun. Do what you love. It makes much more sense to get involved in what really interests you than to try to fit your interests to some preconceived (and likely inaccurate) idea about what colleges want to see.

> Students who do activities out of their own interests and passions and who create activities for themselves stand out—even if the activities were done down the street and not in an exotic locale. Students who do activities because their parents pay for them and they need résumé dressing are a dime a dozen and blend into the overall pool.
>
> PARENT WITH EXPERIENCE IN THE ADMISSIONS PROCESS

PERSONAL QUALITIES: THE PERSON BEHIND THE PAPER

You know that your written record—test scores, GPA, and even a list of extra-curricular activities—doesn't tell the whole story of what kind of person you are right now and what kind of person you might become. For that reason, many colleges request qualitative information as well: letters from people who know you, essays, and in some cases an interview.

Letters

As you'll see in chapter 9, many schools, including almost all selective private colleges, require or recommend a letter of recommendation from a student's high school counselor and one or two letters from teachers. (The University of California system and some other public colleges are notable exceptions.) Admissions officers look at letters for evidence that a student has, for want of a better word, "sparkle." They are looking for someone who is smart, intellectually curious, good-hearted, talented, and energetic, but most of all, they are looking for insight into how you learn.

Some Letters Are More Useful Than Others

Letters of recommendation can vary widely in their usefulness. Sheila McMillen taught English at the University of Virginia and served one year as a reader in the undergraduate admissions office. This is how she described her experience reading letters:

> I had to take into account that the harried guidance counselors at a large urban school, writing hundreds of recommendations, often did not know the applicant well—this letter would be short and vague. The applicants attending private schools, where the rate of college acceptances is an important recruiting tool, received four-page tomes from their counselors . . . Fairness demanded that I factor in the inequity, but invariably I was told more—though in hyperbolic terms—about the private school student than I ever learned about the public school one.[6]

Although four-page letters are very rare from any counselor, private or public, the lesson here is clear: regardless of where you go to high school, try to get to know your counselor, even if your opportunities are limited. Some students go to schools with low student-to-counselor ratios and can get to know a counselor easily. Others have to work harder at it. It's not always easy, and it isn't fair, but it is worth the effort to try.

Get to Know Your Teachers

It helps to get to know several teachers well since you may have to ask one or two of them to write on your behalf. Being memorable (in a positive way) and actively participating in your classes are the best ways to ensure that your teachers will have something helpful to say. Hold on to your best papers and projects from your classes. At letter-writing time, you may want to remind a teacher about the work you did in his or her class. A few colleges (for example, Reed College, Sarah Lawrence College, Bard College, and Mount Holyoke College) even ask applicants to submit a graded academic paper, so you may have additional uses for work that you have saved. In reading such a paper, the college is trying to evaluate both your analytical and writing skills (beyond the minimal sample on the SAT or ACT), as well as your high school's academic standards.

The Essay

Perhaps no other part of the application process besides standardized tests is as dreaded as the essay. The essay asks students to expose themselves to a stranger who will be judging their person, not just their grades and scores. It is also something students have not done much of before; they know colleges want high grades and scores, but what exactly does a college want in an essay? Just what does it mean to "be yourself" in an essay?

How Do Colleges Use the Essays?

The essay is an opportunity for a student to show how she writes and, more important, how she thinks and how she has been able to learn from her experiences. The essay is also the only part of the application over which you exercise complete control, and if you have something valuable to say, it can make an impact.

College admissions officers see the essay as one more way to gain insight into who the student is. With so many applicants with similar grades, GPAs, and activities, the essay allows the student to convey his or her own individuality. So look at the essay as an opportunity to be thoughtful about yourself, not as something to be dreaded. An effective essay leaves the reader feeling that he has gotten to know the student and likes what he sees.

How Much Do Essays Count?

How much do essays count in admissions decisions? A survey attempting to answer this question found that students and parents rated the essay as more important than admissions officers said it was. This is not surprising, considering the time and energy students put into writing it, while admissions officers must of necessity read them quickly. Nevertheless, the results confirmed that the essay can still make a difference in the admissions decision.[8]

A good essay can strengthen an application to a selective school, particularly if your grades and test scores are already strong. Not surprisingly, a boring, poorly written, arrogant, or silly essay can hurt your chances, especially if your qualifications are borderline. But even if your record is very strong, a weak essay can spoil your chances at a college with many strong candidates to choose from. An essay that falls in the middle—neither strong nor weak but simply flat—doesn't give the reader a reason to accept you beyond what is in the rest of your file. A wise student tries to have as many factors in the plus column as possible—including the essay, which can be a positive experience if you start early. We'll talk more about writing your essays in chapter 8.

Interviews

Interviews are perhaps the most misunderstood part of the college admissions process. In some cases, they can be helpful in the overall evaluation of candidates, and at the same time students can learn more about a college through an interview. Its importance varies from school to school: many offer no interviews at all.

In a small percentage of cases, an interview can produce new information—either exceptionally positive or exceptionally negative. Students who act boorishly or immaturely in an interview could damage their chances, but

> Save for the few instances in which candidates write essays so completely lacking in taste as to make us marvel at the fact that they even bothered to apply, in my experience no one is ever admitted solely on the basis of a great essay and no one was ever denied admission solely on the basis of a poor essay.[7]
>
> FRED HARGADON, FORMER DEAN OF ADMISSION AT PRINCETON UNIVERSITY

> Most applicants compete not with the whole applicant pool but within specific categories, where the applicant-to-available space ratio may be more, or less, favorable than in the pool at large . . . Students in the selected categories, which vary from institution to institution, have a "hook" because they help meet institutional needs.[9]
>
> PAUL MARTHERS, FORMER DEAN OF ADMISSIONS AT REED COLLEGE, REFLECTING ON ADMISSIONS PRACTICES AT SELECTIVE INSTITUTIONS

short of such exceptionally negative (and rare) behavior, an interview is unlikely to affect the outcome of an admissions decision negatively. Most of the time, an interview roughly confirms what is already available in the application.

If nothing else, participating in an interview indicates your interest in a college. As we will see in chapter 5, demonstrating interest may be part of the decision-making process at some colleges, especially in close cases. We'll talk more in chapter 9 about the different kinds of interviews, what you can expect, and how you can make a good impression.

HOOKS AND HOW THEY HELP

In admissions parlance, a *hook* is a special characteristic a college deems desirable over and above the qualities it is seeking in its students in general. They are institutional priorities that can be powerful factors, tipping the outcome in favor of the applicant at a college that receives many more applications from qualified students than it can accept. Hooks can be controversial, and they can vary greatly in detail from college to college and from year to year at a given college. In our discussion of hooks, we simply want you to understand the different factors that may go into crafting a freshman class. If you have a hook, it can help. If you don't have a hook, that's okay. There is lots of room for unhooked students.

Legacy Status

A legacy is a child of an alumnus or alumna who received an undergraduate degree (and the alum doesn't even have to be famous). Some colleges, like MIT and the University of Pennsylvania, even count grandchildren of alumni as legacies, and a few, like Stanford, consider children to be legacies if a parent received an undergraduate or graduate degree there.

Why Do Colleges Give Legacies Preference?

Colleges are usually eager to enroll legacy children, since they believe that legacies are likely to have a strong commitment to the parent's college and will likely accept an offer of admission and become enthusiastic, contributing students. In short, they are good for school morale. Parents, in turn, like the idea of having a child follow in their footsteps. Another reason for the legacy practice is a college's desire to be seen as a humane, caring community, even a family of sorts. A legacy child is joining the college family.

But the bottom line plays a major role as well. Giving special admissions preference to legacies can be a wise financial decision for colleges since they all depend heavily on contributions. All colleges and universities regularly solicit alumni for donations. Tuition pays only part of the cost of educating a student at a private institution, and fundraising and other forms of external support are critical for colleges to operate successfully. Many public research universities also now receive much less than half of their funding from state sources and tuition. But the legacy hook is not based solely on the prospect of donations. Even if the parent has never given money to the college, the child is still a legacy, and that can help.

While legacy status may factor in admissions at a small percentage of public institutions, it plays an important role in admissions at most private ones. Some private colleges, in fact, have special information sessions for legacy applicants, special legacy-only interviews, and staff assigned to deal specifically with legacy concerns. Legacy preference is a double-edged sword for a college that becomes more selective and has to deny admission to many legacy applicants. A spurned legacy parent is likely to remember. The college has to walk a fine line between upholding its standards and looking after its "family."

> We take a look at the level of loyalty—contributions, alumni interviewing, etc. that graduates have maintained over the years. If alumni have been engaged in the community since they left, supporting them in return just makes sense.[10]
>
> CHARLES DEACON, DEAN OF ADMISSIONS AT GEORGETOWN UNIVERSITY

How Big Is the Legacy Advantage?

At many private colleges with low admissions rates, legacies tend to be admitted at up to two or three times the overall rate of admission. Part of the difference in admissions rate is no doubt explained by the fact that the legacy pool overall is usually somewhat stronger than the general applicant pool and that many legacies choose to apply early, which by itself can boost the chances of admission. But clearly a separate, distinct boost comes with legacy status at many institutions. Being a legacy by no means ensures admission, however, especially at colleges that have low admissions rates to begin with.

> If it weren't for the generosity of alumni, we would not be able to provide the education we do. So yes, we do give preference.[11]
>
> THOMAS PARKER, DEAN OF ADMISSION AND FINANCIAL AID AT AMHERST COLLEGE

The Legacy Admissions Controversy

The practice of legacy admissions has come under fire from time to time as inconsistent with the values of equal opportunity. Critics claim that because most alumni of selective colleges are well-off Caucasians, the use of legacy status as an admissions factor amounts to affirmative action for well-to-do white students. Colleges, however, claim that the legacy preference is small while the benefit to the institution is potentially great. For now, legacy status continues to be a hook, and an important one, at most private colleges.

Development Admits

Many selective colleges have a small number of so-called development admits each year—students who would be unlikely to be admitted were it not for their potential to bring significant donations to the college. The children of alumni who are major donors to a college get a double hook when they apply: as legacies and as development cases. In addition, even the nonlegacy children of wealthy donors or potential donors who have contributed significant sums of money to a college (or will do so) are also hooked.

How big a donation does it have to be? This varies from college to college, and, not surprisingly, colleges do not advertise what those amounts might be. Colleges justify development admits because of the institution's need for additional funding to support the school. The development office may or may not be actively involved in recruiting such students, but they are certainly gracious and welcoming to these families. Once they apply, development prospects are usually flagged for special admissions consideration. In these cases, admissions staff evaluate whether the student can "do the work," not an easy thing to define, that will allow him or her to graduate from the institution.

Development admits don't significantly affect the admission of other students because there are very few of them. Nevertheless, the practice is kept low profile to avoid publicity that would call attention to it. This changed, at least briefly, with the publication of *The Price of Admission* by Daniel Golden, a *Wall Street Journal* reporter who threw new light on these often controversial practices.[12] The colleges were generally not pleased with the publicity.

Recruited Athletes

Outstanding athletic ability is yet another important institutional priority or hook. Most colleges have active athletics programs that they see as integral to the college experience. The student body and alumni, even the faculty, want their teams to win. So does the development office, whose fundraising success may reflect teams' win-loss record. Most colleges allow coaches to identify a limited number of athletes whom they can strongly support for admission.

Who Is a Recruited Athlete?

We define a recruited athlete as one who earns a spot on the coach's final list for admissions purposes. The more important the sport at a college, the greater the weight of a coach's recommendations for admission. For basketball and football, the two highest-profile sports on most campuses because they can produce significant revenue for the school, the coach's recommendation counts for a lot. Although some recruited athletes have fine academic records that would earn them admission independent of their special talent, some do not.

> The kids who get in on sports, they're good enough students to go there and hang in there, but they're not always students who were good enough to have gotten there on academics alone.
>
> HIGH SCHOOL SENIOR WHO UNDERSTANDS THE ATHLETIC HOOK

What Is the Admissions Advantage for Athletes?

In *Reclaiming the Game*, William Bowen, former president of Princeton University, and his associate, Sarah Levin, present data illustrating what they call the "admissions advantage" for athletes at Ivy League colleges—the difference between the average admissions probability for a recruited athlete and the average admissions probability for any other applicant after controlling for differences in their academic records.[13] The percentage point difference for male and female athletes was 51 percent and 56 percent, respectively.

Since the average probability of admission in the Ivy League at that time was around 15 percent, they reasoned that a boost of 51 percentage points meant that a typical male athletic recruit had an admissions probability of 66 percent (the 15 percent base rate for everyone added to the 51 percent athletic advantage). The average male recruited athlete, then, had four times the chance of being admitted to an Ivy League college than a male student with a comparable academic record who was not a recruited athlete and had no other hooks.

Analyzed the same way, the admissions advantage for underrepresented minorities and legacies turned out to be much smaller. Using the same Ivy League data set, Bowen and Levin report that the admissions advantages for underrepresented men and women were 26 percent and 31 percent, respectively. For male and female legacies, the respective admissions advantages were 26 percent and 28 percent. Although the Bowen and Levin data are 15 years old, experienced counselors believe that their conclusions generally hold today as well. Exceptional athletic ability may be the strongest college admissions hook of all, aside, perhaps, from development, where the data are not public and the numbers are small. We'll talk at greater length about athletes and college admissions in chapter 10.

Underrepresented Students

Being a member of a traditionally underrepresented group (African American, Native American, or Hispanic) can also be a hook at colleges eager to diversify their student bodies. Asian Americans are occasionally included in this group, especially at colleges in parts of the country, such as the rural Midwest, South, and Northeast with low Asian American populations, but usually they are not. Most colleges believe that a diverse student body is an essential part of a high-quality educational experience for all students, and many applicants list diversity among the various attributes they are seeking in a college.

Efforts to Increase Diversity

Colleges are becoming increasingly proactive in seeking out and supporting underrepresented students in the admissions process, since they may have less access to information about college, especially financial aid, and may not even consider applying beyond their local university. Some colleges offer to fly in groups of minority and first-generation-to-go-to-college applicants in the fall of their senior year so the students can get a taste of their college. Students can apply for some of these programs directly, while other schools require a counselor nomination to be considered, often asking for transcripts, test scores, and a counselor's endorsement before issuing a formal invitation.

The diversity hook in college admissions is formally known as race-sensitive admissions or, more commonly, affirmative action. Race-sensitive admissions policies were challenged on the constitutional level in a case heard by the Supreme Court in 2003. The Court ruled against the University of Michigan's policy of awarding an additional 20 points, out of a possible 150, to students who fell into one of three racial categories (100 points were sufficient to earn admission to the university). The majority of the Court believed that a system that automatically awarded a substantial bonus to those belonging to particular groups placed too much emphasis on race. At the same time, the Court upheld racial and ethnic diversity as a "compelling state interest" and reaffirmed the importance of giving colleges and universities some leeway in this area of admissions. Although colleges can no longer use a simple point system to achieve diversity, the Court's ruling allows them to continue use race as part of the decision mix in more subtle ways.

Current Status of Affirmative Action

Most colleges that practice race-sensitive admissions were unaffected by the ruling, since they did not use a point system. They have continued to consider race in the admissions process as they have in the past to ensure a diverse student body. The ruling does not affect campuses that do not practice race-sensitive admissions like the University of California and University of Florida, since state laws there prohibit public universities from using race-sensitive admissions in any form. Ensuring diversity without directly considering race has been a major challenge for those campuses.

As of this writing, the Supreme Court is considering another challenge to the constitutionality of affirmative action, *Fisher* v. *University of Texas*. The outcome will determine whether affirmative action in higher education may continue to be practiced in its current form.

Socioeconomic and Geographical Diversity

Many colleges are eager to assemble a freshman class from a wide variety of backgrounds. Colleges are particularly interested in identifying students who are the first in their families to attend college, often called "first-gen" students, and have succeeded against the odds. High school students from disadvantaged backgrounds who do well in school despite the challenges of low income or poor schools, or both, are likely to be highly motivated, successful college students.

Geographical diversity is another variable that many colleges consider in selecting their freshman class, since geographical diversity is often correlated with diversity of life experience. Students who come from underrepresented parts of the country can benefit when it comes to admission to a selective college. But the definition of "underrepresented region" is relative; it depends in part on the college in question. Although few students from Nevada may apply to Colby College in Maine, Pitzer College in California is likely to have an ample supply from which to choose. Talented students from sparsely populated Wyoming or rural Mississippi are in short supply everywhere.

Major exceptions to the geographical diversity advantage are selective public institutions such as the University of Texas, the University of North Carolina at Chapel Hill, and the University of Virginia, which have higher academic standards for out-of-state students because they have many more highly qualified applicants than they can accept. Until recently, we would have included the various campuses of the University of California in this list, but a crisis in funding has led these campuses to actively recruit and even favor out-of-state and international students because they pay substantially higher out-of-state tuition. And while many private colleges seek geographical diversity in their student body, they may also give a small preference to students from their own local area in an effort to build goodwill with the community. Tufts University, Duke University, and Northeastern University are among those that acknowledge this kind of preference.

Special Talents

Still other hooks include exceptional talent—as a musician, dancer, actress, or ice skater; as a visual artist or published writer; or as a scientist, among others—that a college would like to have represented in its student body. An Olympic ice skater, an actress who has appeared in commercial films, the author of a published novel, and the winner of a major Intel science award—all of these applicants have hooks based on exceptional talent that will catch the attention of admissions committees. A diverse class with a wide range of exceptional talents is an interesting class. Some of these talents (e.g., the science award winner or the published author) may connect to the educational mission of the school. Others may just add some glamour. Although the majority of students admitted even to the most selective colleges do not have a special talent at this level, some do. If you are fortunate enough to have a talent, it will be a definite plus when it comes to an admissions decision. In chapters 9 and 10, we'll explore how students with special talents can bring these to the attention of admissions officers.

Are Hooks Fair?

Are hooks fair? This is a tough question. If you have one, you are likely to be glad of it; few students are willing to give up an advantage, real or imagined. If you don't have a hook, and most applicants don't, you may feel that the system is structured against you. Unfortunately, this contributes to the widely held idea that college admissions is a game and you have to exploit the fine points of the game to win. If you find yourself feeling this way, just remember that most students admitted to every college do not have a hook, and that most students are admitted on the basis of the normal mixture of criteria: grades, test scores, activities, essays, and recommendations.

FITTING IT ALL TOGETHER

We hope this chapter has given you a good sense of the many factors that play a role in selective college admissions. Another important consideration—the timing of a student's application—is covered in chapter 7, which deals with early acceptance programs. There is no single answer to how college admissions offices weight these factors and what process they use to make their decisions. Each college is free to shape its own admissions policies and practices based on college priorities, tradition, and, sometimes, the previous experience of a newly hired admissions dean. In the next chapter, we will consider how most colleges generally go about the actual process of reviewing applications to reach their decisions about whom they will admit.

CHAPTER 3

How Do Colleges Make Their Decisions?

For most students and their parents, the college admissions process is shrouded in mystery. Hundreds of thousands of students apply every year to colleges across the spectrum of selectivity. Each application presents the academic and personal accomplishments of a teenager hoping for admission. After a period ranging from a few weeks to several months, the college's verdict arrives: the student is accepted, denied, wait-listed, or, in the case of some early applicants, deferred until a later round of decision making.

This chapter will focus on what goes on behind the scenes between the time a student submits an application and the time the mail carrier (or, much more often these days, the Internet) delivers the college's response. We end the chapter with a brief discussion of the roles that high school counselors, college access programs, and parents can play in helping ensure a happy outcome. We also include a short section on independent educational consultants since increasing numbers of families are seeking their services.

WHO WORKS IN ADMISSIONS?

College admissions officers have varied backgrounds. Some make college admissions their careers and have many years of experience, or they can be younger people, spending a few years in admissions before embarking on other careers.

Often the latter are recent graduates of the college where they work who display the energy, maturity, and dedication to do a good job in a very demanding position.

Admissions staff tend to be ethnically diverse with varied personal interests and backgrounds. It is rare today for a college not to have one or several Asian, Hispanic, and African American staff members. In addition to being sensitive to diversity, colleges consciously want different sets of life perspectives to be heard at the table at decision time. The regular admissions officers who represent the school have the most important role in the actual decision-making process. The larger schools with many thousands of applications also hire seasonal readers to help read applicant files, although they do not usually participate in making the final decisions.

Helping Build the Applicant Pool

Evaluating applications is only part of an admissions officer's job, however. Admissions officers typically do much more than read applications and make decisions. They work with the dean of admissions, who develops the strategy for marketing the college. This includes planning all the brochures, letters, e-mails, and other outreach that come from the admissions office, as well as the website that has become the major way students and parents get easy access to information about a college. The staff decides who will get which mailings and when they will get them. Applications and view books are sent to all students who request them, though both are rapidly being phased out in favor of electronic materials, especially the application itself. Special unsolicited mailings from some colleges target selected students as early as the sophomore year. We'll talk more about these unsolicited communications in chapter 5.

Ambassadors and Gatekeepers

Because outreach to prospective students involves much more than e-mail and letters, admissions officers also serve as ambassadors, personally spreading the word about their college. Each fall, they spend up to six to eight weeks on the road visiting high schools to meet with students and counselors. Typically they visit four high schools a day.

Colleges usually assign their staff to specific regions of the country (and increasingly to other countries), and these visits help officers learn more about the high schools in those areas, and for whom they will later read the applications. Officers also participate in college nights at hotels or other venues (schools, libraries, private homes of alumni) in their assigned region. These events, sometimes hosted by a single college but often by several together, help familiarize parents and students with a college and help the college reach more students than just those at the high schools they can arrange to visit. Some schools hold events in the spring to reach juniors before the following year's application cycle begins. We will discuss these at greater length in chapter 5.

Admissions officers also conduct group information sessions on their home campus for visitors to the college. Spring, summer, and fall bring a steady stream of high school students and their parents to visit colleges. These one-hour information sessions, along with a student-led campus tour, attempt to communicate to visitors what makes the college special. Admissions staff also respond to an enormous volume of e-mail and phone calls, answering questions on every conceivable topic and forwarding questions to other college staff and faculty. It is an intense, busy job.

Once the fruits of the admissions officers' outreach efforts arrive—the large pool of applications from eager, well-prepared high school seniors—the primary focus of their work shifts. Formerly ambassadors, admissions officers now take on the role of gatekeepers, determining who is admitted and who is denied. From gregarious greeters and public speakers, they become more solitary, reading applications in their offices and homes for much of the winter, emerging once the decisions have been made to greet the spring and the hordes of accepted students.

WHAT HAPPENS TO YOUR APPLICATION?

Once almost exclusively a paper-based process, college applications are now submitted and reviewed primarily online. Most students submit their applications electronically (the Common Application is now exclusively online), and more and more high schools are submitting counselor and teacher recommendations and transcripts electronically as well. SAT and ACT scores are also transmitted electronically once a student has designated the schools that should receive them. Any material that arrives at the admissions office by regular mail is usually scanned so that it can become part of a student's electronic file. Once a file is complete, with all parts accounted for, it is ready for review.

Who Will Be Reading Your File?

A typical college may read an application twice, and sometimes more than that, depending on the file itself. (Not all colleges fit this pattern, however, with some using a less intensive process.) Of the two people who review a file, one is frequently the admissions officer assigned to the region where an applicant attends school. Sometimes this same officer may have visited the student's high school earlier in the fall and may also have conducted a formal regional presentation at a hotel in a nearby city. The other evaluator is often randomly selected from among the remaining group of admissions officers or readers. The admissions office wants one reader with specific expertise and one with a broader view of the entire pool. Sometimes both evaluators are randomly selected. Many colleges assign an admissions officer the task of recruiting applicants from a specific minority group. This officer may read the file of students of color as a third reader. At a few colleges (Caltech and Georgetown University are examples), faculty members may also read files, but many more use faculty as occasional evaluators of special talents—mathematical, musical, and so forth—when a professional assessment is needed.

What Are the First Steps?

Each of the two readers assigned to a file reads it thoroughly. The first person to read a file is usually responsible for extracting key information and entering it into an electronic snapshot. Grades, class rank, SAT scores, notations about the strength of the student's curriculum, codes for extracurricular activities—all get entered for an at-a-glance view of the application in objective terms. Other factors are noted as well—any special interest in the applicant by coaches or the development office, minority background, exceptional talent, and so forth.

Both readers then prepare written summary comments highlighting what is most significant in the candidate's essay, letters of recommendation, and personal qualities that convey a sense of who the student is beyond a list of grades and activities. The first reader, whether an admissions officer or seasonal reader, usually makes more detailed notes than the second reader. Those notes are then generally read out aloud if the file finds its way to committee discussion. A straightforward application might take only 10 to 15 minutes to read and work up. A complex file could take 30 minutes to digest fully.

Admissions staff typically have to read 30 files a day during peak reading season, which normally runs from early January through mid-March. Long days and weeks are the norm once reading begins. On many campuses, an admissions officer may read a thousand files or more over the application cycle.

How Is an Application Evaluated?

Usually each evaluator assigns a numerical rating along at least two dimensions—academic qualifications and personal qualities—as well as an overall judgment or recommendation that combines the two in some way. The scale used by colleges can vary—from 1 to 5 at one, from 1 to 9 at another. Some have a separate rating for athletics, others for intellectual curiosity. But the idea is the same: to rate applicants in a standardized way along those dimensions.

Evaluators may have a list of specific qualities to rate as a key to guide them in assigning ratings on the broader dimensions. At Wesleyan University, for example, the academic rating is a rough average of the ratings, from 1 to 9, with 9 the highest possible, in three academic categories: academic achievement, intellectual curiosity, and commitment.[1] SAT or ACT scores get factored into this overall academic rating as well. Where applicant pools are strong and many students have top grades and strong academic programs, test scores can play an important role in separating students out on a linear scale. They can be the one factor that allows readers to tell applicants apart.

At Wesleyan, a rating of 4 in academic achievement is used for those with "fair to good recommendations" with "some weaknesses apparent in application." A rating of 5 is reserved for students with a "solid academic" load, and a rating of 6 or 7 is used for "an excellent academic record in a demanding curriculum." The top ratings of 8 or 9 go to those with a "flawless academic record in the most demanding curriculum." A rating of 5 in intellectual curiosity would go to a student described as "conscientious," while "strong interest and activity" in "research, independent projects, competitions, etc." would receive a rating of 6 or 7. A student with a "sophisticated grasp of world events and technical information" and "passionate interest in numerous disciplines" would receive 8 or 9 on the intellectual curiosity dimension. Other colleges use similar rating systems but don't try to average the ratings; instead, they simply total the ratings to get an overall score. Personal qualities, or extracurricular strengths, are rated similarly, with each reader assigning an overall "personal" rating or scores based on different aspects of the record, such as evidence of unusual commitment to community service, leadership, or engagement in activities. Wesleyan has two nonacademic categories, personal and extracurricular, each on a 1–9 scale.

Rating systems such as the one at Wesleyan are based on your overall record through high school. Although you will never know the ratings assigned to you by a college, we describe it to show you how your high school years can be sifted, analyzed, and reduced to numbers so that applicants can be roughly compared to each other. There may still be a lot to be discussed after an application is rated, but it is not surprising that the higher the ratings, the more likely the student is to be admitted.

TENTATIVE DECISIONS

Once a reader or an admissions officer completes the ratings and notes for a given applicant, it is the moment of decision—his or her call on the applicant's status: admit, deny, wait-list, or perhaps something less definitive such as admit-minus or deny-plus, which will lead to further discussion. This call can be a very difficult, even subjective one, though the reader is expected always to use professional judgment. In reality, most applicants to most colleges can succeed if success means simply doing well enough to be able to graduate within four years. Who, then, should be given that opportunity?

College Priorities

At this point, the full range of a college's priorities plays out, along with the personal preferences and inclinations of the readers. Colleges are complex academic communities that seek to create a rich, stimulating environment academically, culturally, athletically, and socially. As we discussed in the previous chapter, this means crafting a class that includes not only academic superstars, but winning athletes, talented performers and musicians, students from all parts of the country and a diverse array of ethnic and socioeconomic backgrounds, the children of alums, as well as some whose parents are willing and able to make exceptionally generous donations.

These categories are not necessarily mutually exclusive, but realistically few, if any, students can excel in everything. Thus decisions are made about individual students so that the class as a whole embodies the priorities of the campus. Here the hooks we described in chapter 2 come into play. When there are lots of applicants to choose from with similar grades and test scores, the admissions staff has considerable leeway in exactly who the accepted students will be. Institutional priorities can play a big role in the outcome.

Clear-Cut Admit or Deny?

Sometimes the decision is clear-cut. Some applicants are so outstanding in ways important to the college that the decision is obvious to both reviewers of a file: admit. In some cases, a file may be sent right to the dean with a recommendation to admit after only one reading by an experienced admissions officer. Colleges that compute a rating total may automatically admit students who score at or above a very high threshold without further review.

Similarly, at the other end of the continuum, files are prescreened to identify applicants who fall far short of a college's standards. Identifying these before they are thoroughly read helps readers save their time for the stronger files that require careful consideration. These decisions can be made on the basis of grades, test scores, or some other easily detected major weakness, relative to the rest of the pool, that cannot be offset by other factors. It may sound harsh to learn that some files get a decision after only five minutes of evaluation, but that can be the case. The number of applications is usually too large for every file to receive the same level of analysis.

Sometimes a file is forwarded for review, and after careful consideration, both readers independently recommend denial. At highly competitive colleges with many more applicants than spots in the freshman class, this is often the fate of applicants who do not distinguish themselves in some way, even if their grades and scores are competitive. You don't have to have done anything wrong or have a serious flaw. You just are not distinguished enough from the rest of the pool. You DSO (don't stand out) and you are LMO (like many others). Here, too, this can be the end of the decision process or, depending on the college, the dean or another senior staff member may review the file briefly to confirm the decision others have made. Colleges using ratings totals may also establish a threshold at the low end: students who score below the threshold will be denied without further review.

The Gray Zone

The most difficult decisions have to be made for those in the middle of the pack—the deny-plus or admit-minus applicants whose ratings total falls between the obvious deny and admit thresholds or the ones referred to committee for additional review. A good number of applicants fall into this gray zone. These applicants have a lot that makes them attractive to the two reviewers, but so do many other applicants. Here the decisions get tougher—more personal and more human—and, as a consequence, more unpredictable and, to some extent, mysterious, at least as seen from the outside.

> Years ago, Dartmouth College let me sit in on its process. I was struck by some of the vagaries. For example, the time—if your application came up at nine-thirty in the morning when everybody was full of energy, that made a difference, as opposed to coming up at five o-clock in the afternoon when people are thinking, "I'd rather be somewhere else."[2]
>
> JOHN MERROW, THE MERROW REPORT

HOW THE FINAL DECISION IS MADE

The final round is often review by committee.

Committee Discussion

Consisting of all or a subset of the senior admissions officers (or subcommittee chairs), the committee typically hears an oral overview of each applicant who is referred to it. That overview is usually provided by the admissions officer from the applicant's geographical region who serves as the student's advocate in the discussion. One young admissions officer, when asked what he had learned in his first year that he could apply in his second, replied, "I learned who it was worth bringing to committee. You can't bring them all." Questions go back and forth, thoughts are exchanged and debated, and then a final, usually decisive, vote is taken: admit, deny, or wait-list (or defer, in the case of early action or early decision). At some colleges, the committee may review and act on all decisions, even the easiest ones; other colleges do not use committees at all.

Difficult Choices

Regardless of how the process unfolds, clearly many of the final decisions are difficult ones that might have turned out differently on another day and with another set of reviewers. The qualitative nature of admissions reviews, along with all the dimensions that a college may consider in crafting its class, creates a lot of uncertainty. Two equally wonderful students apply to a college, and one is admitted, but the other is not. Why?

Unfortunately, there may or may not be a clear answer, or the answer may be one that makes you uncomfortable. As Shawn Abbott, now assistant vice president for admissions at New York University, has stated, "Most of the highly selective institutions in the country could easily fill their

---

I applied early to Yale and was rejected. I had great grades, high SATs, lots of extracurriculars, blah, blah, blah. Everyone thought I was a shoo-in—my parents, my teachers, my relatives, my friends. Then I was rejected. Just plain rejected. I was bummed out for a few days but got over it. But my mom couldn't understand how this could happen. She sent a nice e-mail to the admissions office asking for reasons. This is what they wrote back:

> Realize the personalities on Yale's committee are distinctive to Yale, as are the personalities on admission committees at other schools. And even within a given school, there are sometimes multiple committees that have different constellations of personalities presiding and voting as they see fit. Also within a single committee, three people may like an essay, recommendation, extracurricular activity, etc., but four or even three others on the committee may feel very differently. Such a divided sensibility would result in an unfavorable outcome. Frequently committee members do not agree, which leads to some tough arguments and split votes. This does not mean that the applicant is not extraordinary; it just means that not enough people voted favorably.

I'm not sure this made her feel any better.

HIGH SCHOOL SENIOR

---

classes twice over with candidates possessing similar academic credentials."[3] The decisions cannot always be easily explained or defended, and colleges almost never explain their decisions to applicants, and only rarely even to school counselors beyond a few generalities. It is easier for them to talk about the "tremendous quality and size of the applicant pool" and "what a tough year it was."

THE SPECIAL CASE OF THE MOST SELECTIVE COLLEGES

Parents and students need to realize how complex and fundamentally messy college admissions decisions at selective colleges can be. The purpose of sharing this information is not to discourage you, but to help you approach college admissions with a flexible mind-set and encourage you to develop a list of good-fit colleges that includes some where your admission is pretty much assured.

The Outcome Can Be Unpredictable

Almost no one's record will guarantee him or her admission to the most selective colleges in the country. There are too many variables, including institutional priorities that are not under your control in the admissions equation, to predict the outcome with absolute certainty. Knowing this may initially be disillusioning, but it can also be liberating. It can help you understand, in both your head and heart, that the admit or deny decision made in the admissions office of a selective college is not an evaluation of your worth as a student and as a person. And equally true, the decision does not measure the success of a parent's child-rearing efforts.

Appreciating what goes on behind the scenes in the college admissions process can help explain some of the puzzling situations with which we began this chapter. A student with a terrific record may receive serious consideration at several highly selective schools. But because of the judgments involved, the differing needs of each college, and the qualitative nature of the review process, some schools may admit her, while others may end up wait-listing or even denying her instead: same application, similar schools, different outcomes.

> It looks to the family that this is a perfect student, but most of the students look like that. We're making hairline decisions.[4]
>
> ANN WRIGHT, FORMER VICE PRESIDENT FOR ENROLLMENT, RICE UNIVERSITY

But It Is Not Random

Although the result of an admissions review may be unpredictable, it is not random. A super-selective college may have a 15 percent admissions rate, but that does not mean that all applicants to that college have the same 15 percent chance of admission. The overall admissions rate for a college is just that—an overall rate that does not take into account the factors that make an individual applicant more or less likely to be accepted.

If a college collected and shared more information about its admissions process, in principle you could know the probability of acceptance for a male legacy with a midrange (for that school) ACT score and 3.9 unweighted grade point average in a demanding curriculum. Maybe the chances of acceptance for a student with that profile are 70 percent, not the 15 percent figure for the overall applicant pool.

> I have seen some kids get into selective schools with unlikely stats, and some with very high stats get turned down. As a rule, though, the better the kid's stats, the better the chances. Every applicant does not have the same odds.
>
> EXPERIENCED PRIVATE COUNSELOR

But even then, a fair amount of uncertainty about the outcome would remain. A 70 percent chance of admission means that on average, seven out of ten applicants with that profile will be admitted, but three will not. What may seem like a fair outcome to one of the chosen seven may still seem capricious to the unlucky three. Although the same chance of admission applies to all ten, the outcome for a given individual can be very different.

THE ROLE OF YOUR HIGH SCHOOL COUNSELOR

Ideally your counselor will know you well and have the knowledge and time to help you identify a list of good-fit colleges, as well as provide you with information about and assistance with the application process itself. The more background work you do on your own, researching colleges and learning about the college admissions process, however, the more productive your time with your counselor will be. As we will discuss in chapter 9, your counselor will also prepare the secondary school report that many colleges require. The report often serves both to recommend you and evaluate your academic record relative to that of your classmates.

We realize that at many schools, heavy workloads with hundreds of counselees make it impossible for many counselors, even the most dedicated and hard working, to do all they would like to do. There is no ignoring that the college admissions process is easier for students who have extensive, high-quality assistance from their high school counseling office. If help from your school is limited, the best approach is to take advantage of what is available and be prepared to fill in the gaps yourself. Rest assured that you are far from the only student to do so. If you are willing to make the effort and continue reading this book carefully, you will do just fine.

HOW COLLEGE ACCESS PROGRAMS CAN HELP

If you are the first in your family to attend college or come from a high school without a strong college-bound culture, you may find that you need more help than your teachers, counselors, and parents are able to provide by themselves. Fortunately, many nonprofit community-based as well as federally funded college access programs are there to support you and students like you across the country.

College access programs vary in exactly what they do and how they do it, but most offer one-on-one counseling for college, tutoring, assistance with understanding and seeking financial aid, opportunities to visit colleges, and more. They usually don't have large budgets for advertising, but work through schools and other organizations in the community to let students know about their work and how to get involved. Check with your high school counselor about programs that may operate in your area.

Another valuable resource is TRIO, a set of federally funded college opportunity programs designed to help students from disadvantaged backgrounds pursue a college degree. Upward Bound and Educational Talent Search are the best known of the TRIO precollege programs, serving almost 400,000 students each year through participating colleges around the country. A directory of all TRIO programs by state and region can be found at the Council for Opportunity in Education website at www .coenet.us.

Online resources can also help. Websites designed primarily for first-generation students include KnowHow2Go at www.know-how2GO.org, sponsored by the American Council on Education, the Lumina Foundation

> Students who don't have a family history of higher education need support and encouragement from home, school, and their community. But the important message is that the opportunity for college is there for any student who wants it.[5]
>
> MATT RUBINOFF, EXECUTIVE DIRECTOR, CENTER FOR STUDENT OPPORTUNITY

for Education, and the Ad Council; and I'm First at www.imfirst.org, an online community founded by the nonprofit Center for Student Opportunity. Both offer support, advice, and encouragement on the road to college. Signing up, for free, gives you access to a wide range of resources on either site (and both in English and Spanish on KnowHow2Go). I'm First features college search tools that will help you research and connect with colleges that are especially welcoming to first-generation students, and the Center for Student Opportunity publishes the *College Access & Opportunity Guide*, a first-of-its-kind comprehensive college guidebook designed to help first-generation, low-income, and minority students as they plan for college.

SHOULD YOU CONSIDER HIRING AN INDEPENDENT COLLEGE COUNSELOR?

In many areas of the country, independent, fee-based counselors have become much more popular than they were just a few years ago. Independent counseling services can range from a few hours of help with college selection and applications to multiyear "platinum packages" that provide extensive guidance, costing $40,000 or more, geared to preparing students as young as the eighth grade for admission to selective colleges. The platinum package approach is quite rare, however, and the vast majority of independent counselors charge much more modest fees for their services, sometimes reducing their fees for less-affluent families and offering pro-bono services through local college access organizations.

Although we believe that the services of an independent counselor are never a necessity, under certain conditions they can be quite helpful. When parents and students have limited access to good counseling at school, an independent counselor can help a student do an honest self-analysis and develop a list of colleges to consider. An independent counselor can also act as a gentle buffer between parent and child when it comes to deadlines—the counselor, not the parent, becomes the taskmaster. When school counselors lack the time, independent counselors may help a student play to her strengths in an application by suggesting specific activities or interests to highlight in application essays as well as provide guidance about interviews. Finally, independent counselors can often help with the financial aid side of the application, answering questions and helping families understand a process they may find daunting.

All of this is light-years away from the "platinum package" approach to college counseling that involves retaining an expensive, multiyear personal trainer who essentially makes admission to an elite college the center of every life decision her teenage client makes. We think that is an unwise and an unnecessary investment of the few remaining years of childhood, and it puts too much emphasis on living only for the sake of getting into the "right" college. Nor is it good training for college and adulthood when a young person will have to make his or her own way in the world.

> Ironically, you want to look unpackaged and raw—someone like me can be behind the scenes and make someone look raw without over-packaging them.[6]
>
> "PLATINUM PACKAGE" INDEPENDENT COUNSELOR WHO SEES ONLY HALF OF THE IRONY

If you do hire an independent counselor, always remember that you need your high school counselor to know you as well as possible so he or she can write an effective recommendation for you. You cannot substitute an independent counselor for your high school counselor. Professional independent counselors should be willing to discuss the advice they give you with your school counselor if they are asked to do so. Information about working with an independent counselor can be found on the websites of the Independent Educational Consultants Association (IECA), www.iecaonline.org, and the Higher Education Consultants Association (HECA), www.hecaonline.org. Both IECA and HECA have a searchable directory of member consultants on their sites.

THE PARENTS' ROLE

Parents of course play an important role in their child's college admissions process long before an application is even filed. A loving home where education is valued is the most lasting gift a parent can give a child. When it comes time to seriously begin thinking about college, however, you can take some specific steps to help your child deal with an unfamiliar and sometimes daunting process.

Teens differ in the kind and amount of help they will need and are willing to accept, however, so you will have to see what works for both of you. We provide specific suggestions in the following chapters for ways to support your child. For now, we offer a word of caution about overinvolvement. Marilee Jones, former dean of admissions at MIT, has vividly described what can happen at the extremes when parents lose perspective:

> More and more, today's parents are getting too involved in their child's college admissions process, and in many cases, their actions and attitudes are getting out of hand. At MIT we've been asked to return an application already in process so that the parent can double-check his/her child's spelling. We've been sent daily faxes by parents with updates on their child's life. We've been asked by parents whether they should use their official letterhead when writing a letter of recommendation for their own child. Parents write their kids' essays and even attempt to attend their interviews. They make excuses for their child's bad grades and threaten to sue high school personnel who reveal any information perceived to be potentially harmful to their child's chances of admission.[7]

Fortunately, antics like these are exceptional, but many behaviors that might seem less extreme are still worth avoiding. One counselor gives this advice: "It seems very important at the moment, to get everything just right. The temptation to micromanage is strong. You have experience, and you are probably correct. They are young and have no experience. But they will be your children for the rest of your lives. Don't do anything between now and May 1 of the senior year (or even after that) that might hurt your long-term relationship with your child. Whatever the short-term benefit, it isn't worth it." This same counselor steamed open his daughter's SAT scores when they arrived in the mail so that he could see them while she was away at camp. Sometimes it is hard to take your own advice. Overinvolvement sends a clear signal to both the child and the college that he can't make it on his own. Neither message is a good one.

CHAPTER 4

How Colleges (and Students) Differ

Finding What Fits

Everyone knows some students who have been thinking about where they want to go to college since sixth grade and who know exactly where they want to go. It may be mom's alma mater somewhere on the other side of the country, or the well-regarded state university the student has heard about all his life, or a school whose football team has often been on TV on New Year's Day. But scratch beneath the surface, and ask those same students why that particular college is their first choice and you might not get much of an answer. When you ask them what other colleges they are considering if, heaven forbid, they are not accepted at their top choice, you may find them unwilling to even consider such an unthinkable outcome.

At the other extreme are students, and we know lots of them, who have a hard time even beginning to think about a list of potential colleges. Not only do they not have a first choice, they don't have any well-defined choices at all—nor even a clear idea of where to begin.

Most students, of course, fall somewhere in between. They have some ideas about college choices but no good way to determine whether those choices are really the best ones for them. Regardless of where you are at this point in your thinking, reading this chapter and the next will help you build your college list with confidence.

SO MANY CHOICES: HOW DO YOU BEGIN?

For all students—even those who think they know what they want—the first step in developing a good college list is an honest self-assessment. A bit later in this chapter, we'll discuss what should go into that assessment. We'll then spend much of this chapter showing the important ways that colleges differ. In chapter 5, we'll show you how to take all of this information and use it to identify schools for your own personal college list.

> My original criteria for choosing a college were (1) it had to have cute squirrels (2) it had to be bigger than my high school and (3) PE should not be required. But my school does have PE; you have to take a whole year. Their squirrels are vicious. And it's about the same size as my high school. So I violated all three of my criteria. I'm sure I could have found my own niche somewhere else, too, but I absolutely love it here.
>
> COLLEGE SOPHOMORE HAPPY WITH HER CHOICE

There Are No Perfect Colleges

At the outset, we want to emphasize that as much as the websites and campus tour guides would have you believe otherwise, there is no such thing as a perfect college. The college application process is all about fit—finding colleges that are a good match for you based on your interests, abilities, values, aspirations, and preferences, both social and academic. The more you know about yourself and the more you know about colleges, the better that fit can be. Although no perfect college exists, you can find many where you will be perfectly happy. That is a key point to accept. Even if you eventually apply early decision to a college because you are convinced that it is *the* college for you, you could actually have chosen many where you would be happy.

You Are in Control

In deciding where to apply, you have full control. Based on your research, you create your list of colleges. The colleges do not decide for you, even though they are marketing themselves to you like crazy. Make the most of the opportunity and select carefully. Later in the college admissions process, control will shift from you to the admissions offices, where the colleges decide whom to accept. At that point, you simply wait patiently for the review process to play out. Finally, at the end of the process, control shifts back to you as you decide which offer of admission to accept, ideally from among two or more fine choices that you are happy with.

Doing Your Homework

But we don't want to get ahead of ourselves. We are still back at the beginning, laying the foundation for building a list of good-fit colleges. Thoughtfully considering your own preferences as well as how colleges differ, and then narrowing the list carefully to the right choices for you, are critical parts of the admissions process. College rankings certainly can't do this for you. They only tell you what someone else thinks. Doing your homework to identify a group of good-fit colleges is easily half the battle.

SOME QUESTIONS TO ASK YOURSELF

Be honest with yourself as you try to answer the questions that follow. Most students find some of these questions easy to answer and others much more difficult. You may have strong preferences or weak ones. Perhaps you have never thought about your preferences before, and maybe you just plain don't know. That's okay. You have lots of company regardless of which description fits you.

- **What are your academic interests?** Do you have a strong interest in a particular field, such as nursing or engineering, and plan to work in that field after college or pursue graduate study in that area? How specialized is your field of interest? Or are you undecided about a major and want to explore different options before making a commitment? Are you somewhere in between?

- **What kind of student are you?** Are you strongly self-motivated to achieve, or are you somewhat less ambitious academically (although you may have done very well)? Do you thrive on intellectual engagement with bright and talented peers, or is that less of a priority? Do you need to be at or near the top of your class to feel good about yourself, or is lower down okay if the competition is stiff? Are you willing to actively seek out help or resources if you need them, or do you want them easily available with little effort on your part? Do you want to be independent or looked after to some degree?

- **How do you learn best?** Does the format of your classes matter to you? Do you prefer large classes with no pressure to participate actively, or small classes where you can contribute to the discussion and you always have to be prepared? Do you want a mix of both?

- **What activities outside class matter most to you?** Do you enjoy being involved in a number of different activities at once, or do you prefer to focus on one or two? Do you want to participate in athletics in college, either competitively or just for fun? How specialized is your sport, and how good are you? Is your sport relatively unusual like squash or fencing, and therefore available on only some campuses? Do you want to be active in community service? Do you strive to be a leader in whatever you are involved in, or is being a contributor okay?

- **How important is prestige to you?** Do you want people to be visibly impressed when they hear where you are going to college? Would you be disappointed if they have never heard of your school or don't know much about it? Even if this is true, why is this important to you when balanced against other factors? We caution you to balance this factor against others because the most prestigious schools are also the most selective.

- **Do you want a diverse college?** Do you want a campus that is highly diverse in gender, race, ethnicity, and/or sexual and religious preferences? Or would you prefer a more homogeneous campus, or does it not matter to you? How important to you are campus programs that openly welcome and celebrate diversity?

- **What kind of social and cultural environment would you like best?** Would you like to join a fraternity or sorority? How do you feel about a campus with, or without, a strong Greek presence? Do you want a campus known for its sense of community, or would you prefer to "do your own thing"? Do you like the feeling of knowing almost everyone, or are you comfortable with a large campus where you will never know most of the students? Do you prefer an artsy environment, a politically active one (liberal or conservative), or something else? Preppy or not? Do you want lots of options on how to spend a Friday night, or will a smaller list of possibilities work for you?

- **Where do you want to live for the next four years?** Do you want or need to stay close to home, or are you interested in experiencing a new part of the country? Do you like big cities, or do you prefer a small town or suburban setting? Are you open to all options? Do you want guaranteed on-campus housing for four years, or are you happy or at least willing to live off campus, maybe as soon as sophomore year? Do you want to be near skiing, surfing, lots of bookstores, museums, a shopping mall? What kind of weather do you like, and what kind can you tolerate?

Try to keep these questions in mind as you research colleges. As your list develops, you may be surprised by changes in your preferences and by just how flexible you really are (or aren't). The self-assessment process is designed to help you identify your preferences so you can begin to consider colleges systematically. At the end of this chapter, you'll find a questionnaire to help you record all of your preferences for later use in evaluating specific colleges. It is also available at www.admissionmatters.com.

You also need to know how colleges vary. Institutional mission—the goals a college sets for itself—is key to understanding how one type of college differs from another.

LIBERAL ARTS COLLEGES

Undergraduate education is the primary, and often the only, mission of a liberal arts college. Union College, Beloit College, Davidson College, Knox College, and Claremont McKenna College are examples of liberal arts colleges. They award most of their degrees to undergraduates in the liberal arts and sciences disciplines, which include the social sciences like sociology and anthropology, sciences like physics and biology as well as mathematics, and humanities and arts fields like English, music, and classics.

The focus that liberal arts colleges place on these academic fields distinguishes them from colleges with more practical programs, such as engineering, education, or business—although some liberal arts colleges do both. Smith College and Union College, for example, are liberal arts colleges that offer a major in engineering; Skidmore College has education and business majors, while Harvey Mudd College and Bucknell University, both well known for strong engineering programs, are classified as liberal arts colleges because they award a high percentage of degrees in fields other than engineering.

> There is something special about a liberal arts college. You see your friends all over campus; the president actually knows your name. Professors have their class to dinner. You feel like you belong.
>
> PARENT OF STUDENT AT A LIBERAL ARTS COLLEGE

Most liberal arts colleges enroll only undergraduates, but some have very small graduate programs as well. Again, the key to classifying a school as a liberal arts college is how much it focuses on educating undergraduates in liberal arts and sciences disciplines. Liberal arts colleges are typically highly residential: most students live on campus or in campus-owned housing. Most of the liberal arts colleges in the United States are private and charge higher tuition fees than public universities.

The Academic Program

As we noted above, a liberal arts college provides students with a sound foundation in core areas such as English, philosophy, history, psychology, music, physics, and mathematics. They also often offer interdisciplinary programs that draw from several different fields, like women's studies, philosophy of science, and international relations. Liberal arts programs are not directly career focused, although many have internship programs to connect students to careers loosely related to their subject of study. There are also ample opportunities for students to participate in faculty research as well as independent research projects. The faculty at liberal arts colleges believe that a broad, nonvocationally oriented education that emphasizes critical thinking and analysis is excellent preparation for any later career choice, as well as for graduate and professional school. In fact, graduates of liberal arts colleges succeed in all walks of life.

Campus and Class Size

Enrollment at liberal arts colleges typically ranges from about 1,000 to 2,500 undergraduates, although a small number, like Bucknell University and Wesleyan University, have over 3,000 students. Since they enroll few, if any, graduate students, total enrollment is about the same as the size of the undergraduate student body in comparison to research universities that may be half and half. Regardless of campus size, classes at liberal arts colleges are usually taught exclusively by faculty members, without the help of graduate student teaching assistants (TAs). Small classes generally mean many opportunities to write, contribute to class discussion, and receive individualized feedback on your academic progress.

Since many liberal arts colleges are located in small towns and in suburbs, student life tends to center around the college and its extracurricular activities.

Some, however, are in big cities; for example, Barnard College is in New York City, Goucher College is in Baltimore, Trinity College is in Hartford, and Rhodes College is in Memphis. Obviously a smaller school cannot offer as many courses in a subject as are offered at larger institutions, but undergraduates take only a dozen or so courses in their major anyway, so there are always enough courses to satisfy the most eager learners. At some colleges, cross-registration with nearby colleges makes it possible to expand the options. Consortiums like the Claremont Colleges (Pomona College, Claremont McKenna College, Scripps College, Pitzer College, and Harvey Mudd College) and the Tri-College group (Swarthmore College, Haverford College, and Bryn Mawr College) are good examples. In addition, at liberal arts colleges students get to know their teachers and classmates well and form close bonds. These relationships contribute to a strong sense of community that is the identifying mark of a liberal arts college.

Athletics and Activities

Many liberal arts colleges have athletic programs at the National Collegiate Athletic Association (NCAA) Division III level. As we will discuss in chapter 10, the NCAA divides its member teams into three categories, Division I, Division II, and Division III, in descending order of athletic competitiveness. With fewer students and a less intense level of competition than that found at Division I schools, liberal arts colleges usually have a higher percentage of their students playing varsity sports than other types of schools.

This same general principle applies to other extracurricular activities. With fewer students vying for a newspaper job or a seat in the violin section of the orchestra, a greater percentage of students can get involved. But the scale of the activity may be smaller. The campus newspaper at a liberal arts college may come out just once a week, while a larger school is likely to have a daily (and bigger) paper. There may be fewer organized activities to choose from at a liberal arts college compared to a larger school, but regardless of the absolute number, students always find many options for involvement. Students can start new activities if they want to. You'll keep bumping into your friends, acquaintances, and professors even in diverse activities, because the community is small. At Hendrix College in Arkansas, the servers in the campus dining hall know all the students by name.

RESEARCH UNIVERSITIES

In contrast to liberal arts colleges, research universities have three interconnected missions: research, public service (especially public universities), and teaching undergraduate and graduate students. Research generates new knowledge, and through public service, the knowledge generated is shared with society at large. Yale University, Duke University, the University of Michigan, and the University of Nebraska are examples of research universities. An institution is classified as a research university based on the number of doctoral degrees it awards each year across a number of fields. About two-thirds of research universities are public and one-third private.

> My mother kept talking about the small class size at the great liberal arts college we visited, but I didn't care about that. I liked the idea of having just about every possible option open to me.
>
> FRESHMAN HAPPY AT A LARGE RESEARCH UNIVERSITY

The Role of Research

More so than at liberal arts colleges, faculty members at research universities are evaluated, promoted, and given raises on the quality and quantity of their research as well as the quality of their teaching. At the strongest and best-known research universities, faculty members do research at the frontiers of their fields using well-equipped research laboratories and libraries.

This does not mean, however, that these schools ignore undergraduates. You are still important, but you are not the center of the enterprise as you are in high school or at a liberal arts college. In fact, learning from professors who are very active in research is a valuable opportunity for undergraduates, particularly those majoring in the sciences or social sciences, where new research can rapidly change a field. It is exciting to learn from teachers whose research will appear in tomorrow's headlines and next year's textbooks and who can convey firsthand what discovery and scholarship are all about.

Research universities offer many opportunities for undergraduates, not just graduate students, to become involved in faculty research projects, but you have to be energetic in seeking them out. Liberal arts colleges also offer many research opportunities, and there may be less competition for them but their variety may be smaller, like the curriculum in general.

Campus and Class Size

Research universities come in all sizes. They range from quite small (Caltech, for example, has fewer than 1,000 undergraduate students and about 1,200 graduate students) to medium (Harvard University has about 6,700 undergraduates and 14,500 graduate students) to very large (University of Texas, Austin, has about 38,400 undergraduates and 12,700 graduate students). Most research universities enroll about 20,000 to 25,000 students, graduate and undergraduate combined.

Classes at research universities, particularly at the introductory level, may be quite large, with several hundred students in each one. The large lecture classes are usually accompanied by small discussion or lab sections, often taught by graduate students serving as TAs. Research university faculty generally teach fewer classes per term because of their other responsibilities, and thus they may be less accessible to undergraduate students than faculty at liberal arts colleges.

How you feel about all of this will depend on how much contact you want with professors and how much you care about the relative anonymity of large classes. Research universities also vary greatly in the extent to which they use TAs for undergraduate instruction. While often enthusiastic and committed teachers, TAs have less teaching experience than faculty, and they may be hard to find when you need letters of recommendation for a job or graduate school.

Athletics and Activities

Research universities and their Division I teams dominate the media for big-time college athletics for players and for those in the stands cheering wildly for the home team. Homecoming on many research university campuses is often scheduled around a home football game, and returning alums join current students in rooting for their alma mater. Intercollegiate athletics can be an important part of the liberal arts experience as well, but it is generally at a more subdued level, and football may not even be part of the picture.

Research universities generally host a wide range of activities and clubs and often have major performing arts halls on campus. Liberal arts colleges also host a wide range of activities, but the scale tends to be somewhat smaller, reflecting the smaller size of the student bodies on those campuses.

Honors Programs

Research universities, especially public ones, often have honors programs or other special opportunities for their most academically motivated and able students. These programs may offer small discussion-based seminars, honors housing, and special advising and mentoring opportunities, among other features. To a degree, honors programs replicate some of the most attractive features of a small college at a much lower cost. Good examples can be found at the University of Michigan, University of Texas, Austin, Pennsylvania State University, Arizona State University, UCLA, and a number of others. These programs can be wonderful opportunities for highly qualified students to learn in smaller classes and receive the personal attention of a liberal arts college in a setting that also provides the advantages of a large research university. At some schools, applicants have to apply separately for the honors program when they apply for admission, while other schools do not require an application but invite students to participate based on their strong academic credentials.

WHAT'S IN A NAME?

Don't let the name of an institution mislead you. Bucknell University, Colgate University, and the University of Richmond, for example, are liberal arts colleges, while Dartmouth College and the College of William and Mary are medium-sized research universities. You'll need to look deeper than the word *college* or *university* in its name to determine a school's actual mission and the kind of educational experience it provides. In this book, we use the terms pretty much interchangeably, although we probably use the term *college* more often for simplicity. Much more important than the name is what the actual undergraduate education is like.

It also pays to watch out for similar names that can be easily confused. As examples, Trinity College and Wesleyan University are both in Connecticut, but Trinity University and Wesleyan College are in Texas and Ohio, respectively. The University of Miami is located in Florida, but Miami University of Ohio is located—you guessed it—in Miami, Ohio. We could offer more examples, but you get the idea.

Despite all the attention they get, you may be surprised to learn that research universities and liberal arts colleges make up a little less than 25 percent of all four-year colleges and universities in the United States. The remaining schools generally fall into one of three additional categories: master's universities, general baccalaureate colleges with diverse programs, and specialized colleges.

MASTER'S UNIVERSITIES AND BACCALAUREATE COLLEGES

Master's Universities

Master's universities, both public and private, typically offer undergraduate degrees in the liberal arts and in some applied fields such as business, engineering, education, or nursing, but they award more than half of their degrees to students enrolled in graduate programs leading to the master's degree. Although there are major exceptions, most master's universities draw a large majority of their undergraduate and graduate students from their own area of the country.

As a rule—but again with major exceptions in the private sector like Villanova University, Elon University, and Loyola Marymount University—at these campuses a significant percentage of students commute from home or live off campus. Master's universities are about evenly divided between public and private control. San Francisco State University, Morehead State University (Kentucky), and Jacksonville State University (Alabama) are examples of public master's universities. The size of master's universities varies widely. Average class size varies too, although in general, classes tend to be somewhere in between those of a liberal arts college and a research university.

Most master's universities have Division II athletic programs. Campuses with a high percentage of undergraduate students living on campus generally have a rich array of extracurricular activities available. Less residential campuses may have many activities available as well, but a lower percentage of students tend to be involved in them.

Because master's universities vary so widely along so many different dimensions, you will need to pay particularly close attention to the college attributes you are looking for when you consider them. Some have the feel of a liberal arts college, while others are more like smaller-scale research universities.

Baccalaureate Colleges with Diverse Programs

Baccalaureate is simply another word for *undergraduate*. Baccalaureate colleges with diverse programs primarily emphasize undergraduate education just like liberal arts colleges, but they award more than half of their degrees in applied fields like business, nursing, and education. Some of these campuses enroll significant numbers of older students returning to college and part-time students, as well as traditional-age full-time undergraduates. About 85 percent of schools in this category are private. Examples are Elizabethtown College (Pennsylvania), Asbury College (Kentucky), Carroll College (Montana), and High Point University (North Carolina). The majority enroll under 2,000 students, although some are larger. Baccalaureate colleges tend to be regionally focused like master's universities, but they are generally much more residential than the average master's university.

Baccalaureate colleges with diverse programs with a high percentage of students living on campus for freshman year and beyond generally offer a full array of on-campus activities, including intercollegiate and intramural athletics. Athletics at these schools tend to be Division III, with some campuses belonging instead to the National Association of Intercollegiate Athletics, another collegiate athletics governing organization.

Considering All the Options

Master's universities and general baccalaureate colleges vary widely in selectivity, but only a small percentage would be considered selective using our definition of a school that accepts fewer than half its applicants. They can be affordable and accessible alternatives to liberal arts colleges or research universities and can be a wonderful choice for many students. General baccalaureate colleges can be especially attractive to students who would like the benefits of a smaller residential school while pursuing an undergraduate degree in an applied field like nursing, sports management, or criminal justice.

The approach to finding a good fit that we will describe later works just as well for colleges in these categories as it does for research universities and liberal arts colleges. The most important thing is to understand the mission of each school you are considering and what the undergraduate experience will be like. Once you understand that, how a school is classified really shouldn't be important to you at all.

SPECIALIZED PROGRAMS

Yet another kind of college is the highly specialized school such as a music conservatory (for example, Juilliard School or the New England Conservatory of

Music), art institute (for example, California Institute of the Arts or the Rhode Island School of Design), or undergraduate business (for example, Babson College or Bentley College, both in the Boston area) or engineering school (for example, Cooper Union in New York, Rose-Hulman Institute of Technology in Indiana, and Colorado School of Mines). The service academies like West Point and the Air Force Academy, with their focus on military training and a career in the military, fall into this category as well. Some specialized programs, such as Juilliard and the service academies, are highly selective in admissions.

Should You Consider a Specialized College?

Specialized schools are appropriate for students with highly focused, well-developed interests and clear career goals. A student who wants to be a professional musician and is committed to a career as a performer, for example, may decide that a conservatory is the best fit. A student planning to study civil engineering may opt for a school that prepares only engineers. And so forth.

Other students who want to study these same subjects may find that attending a liberal arts college or a master's university, for example, will allow them greater educational breadth in addition to courses in their special area of interest. It is much easier for a student to explore other fields if the courses are readily available. If your interests later change, even though you don't expect them to, it is almost always simpler to switch majors within a given college than it is to switch colleges.

Learning More About the Options

Which way to go depends a lot on your level of commitment to your field of interest: you need to be very sure about what you want to study and do after college when you apply to specialized schools. The Resources section at the back of *Admission Matters* provides links if you want to explore the option of more focused study. The section also includes links to information about service academies as well.

Specialized programs usually have specific requirements for admission that require demonstrating your particular talent or skill at a high level, and students often have to start assembling the different pieces during their junior year. So find out early what is needed. We'll talk more about specialized options for artists and performers in chapter 10.

COLLEGES WITH SPECIAL AFFILIATIONS

Some colleges have historical affiliations with an appealing distinctive environment.

Religious Affiliations

Many fine institutions in the United States have a religious affiliation that goes back to their founding. Some, like Duke University and Wesleyan University, no longer have such an affiliation, although they had one years ago. Others have religious affiliations that vary widely in terms of how active they are. Perhaps best known among schools with religious affiliations are the Jesuit colleges, such as Georgetown University, Notre Dame University, and Boston College. Davidson College was founded by Presbyterians; Swarthmore College and Haverford College are still officially considered Quaker colleges; Brigham Young University remains a formal part of the Mormon Church; St. Olaf College is Lutheran; and Brandeis University has its early roots in Judaism. There are hundreds more. Most colleges with religious origins welcome students of all backgrounds, but sometimes a majority of the students at those colleges are affiliated with the founding religion. Students who profess a faith other than the founding religion will find a welcoming college environment where the practice of faith is valued.

The extent to which founding religion is a visible part of everyday campus life varies greatly from school to school. At some, it is readily accessible to those who seek involvement, but pretty much in the background for everyone else. At other schools, it is very much a part of the everyday campus experience, with mandatory chapel attendance and other religion-based requirements. Some web-based research will help you sort this out fairly easily.

Historically Black Colleges

Known as historically black colleges and universities, or HBCUs for short, about 100 colleges in the South and a few in the North have traditionally enrolled almost exclusively African American students. Established when many American universities were closed to African Americans, these colleges continue to provide an important educational option for African American students (about 35 percent of all African American college students) who would like a college experience in a nurturing African American community. Most, like Howard University, are coeducational, but a few, like Spelman College and Morehouse College, enroll only women or men, respectively. These colleges provide a supportive environment and successfully launch their students on careers of distinction. More information about HBCUs can be found in the Resources section at the back of this book.

Women's Colleges

For most of the twentieth century, some of the best-known colleges in the United States were single sex. By the mid-1970s, almost all formerly all-male colleges opened their doors to women, and colleges that had once been women-only became coed. Yale University, Williams College, and Claremont McKenna College (once known as Claremont Men's College) are formerly male-only institutions that are now about 50 percent women. Connecticut College, Goucher College, and Sarah Lawrence College, former women's colleges, now enroll both men and women.

A number of high-profile women's colleges have elected to remain open to women only, however, and as a group they are an academically strong and attractive option for students who would welcome the kind of empowering environment that an all-female student body provides. Women-only colleges include Stephens College, Wellesley College, Mount Holyoke College, Agnes Scott College, Smith College, and many others.

A few women's colleges are part of a formal consortium whose member colleges share resources and facilities. Scripps College, for example, is a member of the Claremont Colleges in Southern California. Scripps students can take courses, use the libraries, and eat in the dining halls at the other four campuses that are members of the consortium, and vice versa. They also share sports teams with Claremont McKenna College and Harvey Mudd College. Other colleges have arrangements with individual colleges; Barnard College, for example, has a cooperative arrangement with Columbia University. Bryn Mawr College has a similar working relationship with Haverford College and Swarthmore College. These arrangements provide students with coeducational experiences while still retaining the ambience of a women's college. Research has documented that alumnae of women's colleges are more positive about their experiences than alumnae of coed schools. Some major figures in contemporary American life like Hillary Clinton and Diane Sawyer are graduates of women's colleges.

More information about women's colleges can be found at www .womenscolleges.org.

EARNING YOUR DEGREE ABROAD, IN ENGLISH

American students have still more options. The combination of quality education and immersion in a different culture can entice some to earn their degree, in English, at a wide range of programs abroad, like those at the American Universities of Paris, Rome, Cairo, and Beirut or like the bachelor's programs at Utrecht University in the Netherlands or Sophia University in Japan. An increasing number of US universities also have campuses abroad. But to date, most American students who decide to study abroad full time look to universities in the English-speaking world, particularly in Canada and the United Kingdom.

> While there are many similarities between living in the States and Canada, the multitude of cultures I have found up here is amazing. You see so many people from so many different nations live, work, and study together. It really opens your eyes to the world.
>
> STUDENT ATTENDING COLLEGE IN CANADA

Canada

Canadian universities offer the advantage of being nearby, almost all of them being located within a hundred miles of the US border. While Canada has many fewer universities than the United States, you can find world-class specialized programs and liberal arts degrees, with campus environments similar to those in the United States. Because one of every six Canadians was born outside Canada, Canadian campuses are extraordinarily multicultural. They are also unique in having broadly available co-op programs that offer paid work experience as part of their educational programs and tuitions half to two-thirds that of comparable US colleges.

All but a couple of Canadian universities are public, and their quality of teaching and research is continually assessed, sometimes by provincial or regional authorities as well as by university overseers. Most undergraduate degrees are four years, but some provinces offer a three-year bachelor's degree with an optional fourth year "honours" degree for those who wish to go on to a graduate program. Since Canada has two official languages, you can also study in French or in a bilingual university program, especially in the eastern provinces.

As in most American universities, you do not have to have a specific major in mind when you apply, but you usually apply to a broad school, such as Natural Sciences, Social Sciences, Arts (including the humanities), and Business. The general model is similar to most US public universities. Most Canadian schools are medium-sized to large, like American state schools; small liberal arts colleges are less common.

The United Kingdom and Ireland

Farther away and culturally diverse in a different way, the universities of the England, Wales, and Northern Ireland have special appeal if you are ready to concentrate on one academic subject or, in the case of Scotland and the Irish Republic, an initial three or four subjects within a given field of study such as science or business. The whole approach is very different from the American emphasis on liberal arts, with students in all majors either required or encouraged to take courses across the full spectrum of the curriculum.

As in Canada, tuition is much lower than at comparable universities in the United States but can vary according to the subject studied, with sciences being more expensive than the humanities. Degrees typically take three years, occasionally four years (mostly in Scotland), depending on the program and university, with degrees in the professions taking up to seven years. Through the Erasmus Programme, you may be able to study or work abroad for a semester or a year to teach or train in any of 33 European countries as part of your degree.

Campus life is rich and lively, but not quite like North American universities. For example, though sports are just as competitive, varied, and spirited as sports in North America, they are clubs sponsored by student unions (student governments) rather than by the university itself. Many universities have traditions, both solemn and silly, that have endured, sometimes for centuries. Continental Europe and the Near East are accessible and close, making vacations unsurpassed opportunities to travel affordably. The best all-around online resource for research about schools is UCAS at www.ucas.ac.uk for the United Kingdom and the Irish Universities Association at www.iua.ie for the Irish Republic.

Language is worth mentioning here: both island nations use familiar words in a very unfamiliar way. A catalog is called a prospectus, "faculty" is what we call "department," residence halls are called "accommodations," and teachers may be called "staff," "lecturers," or "tutors." North American English speakers might want a glossary to translate their native tongue into British English.

WHICH KIND OF COLLEGE IS BEST FOR YOU?

What kind of college is best for you? Well, as with most things in life generally and in college admissions, it depends. It depends on your personality, your learning style, and your academic interests. If, after doing some research and introspection, do your preferences seem to align better with one type of college than another? If so, you have made a major step forward. You may also find, though, that you do not have a clear preference. Many students feel comfortable in different kinds of settings, and their final choice depends on where they are admitted as well as the other factors that they discovered as part of their self-assessment. In this section, we'll look at some characteristics of colleges to consider as you reflect.

Location, Location, Location

When you close your eyes and try to imagine yourself in your ideal college environment, what do you see? Do you envision a bustling city, with the excitement, anonymity, and diversity that accompany it? Or do you envision a more bucolic setting, perhaps near a small town, with expansive lawns and a slower pace? Or something in between? Despite the trend for students to think more nationally rather than locally when considering colleges, the majority of students still go to college in their home part of the country—those in the South go to southern schools; westerners tend to stay west of the Rockies; those in the Northeast usually choose a school in that area; and so on. Some students, however, see college as an opportunity to explore a different part of the country and factor this into their college search plans accordingly.

> I was really surprised by my son's reaction to certain colleges. The original Birkenstock-wearing California kid, he fell in love with a small liberal arts college in rural Massachusetts (enrollment 2,000) as well as a large research university in New York City (enrollment 23,000). Go figure.
>
> OBSERVATION BY SURPRISED PARENT

Weather and Culture

Each area of the country has its own weather and, more important, elements of its own culture. Try to keep your mind and options open, and don't automatically rule out a part of the country without carefully considering why. Be aware, though, that a campus in rural Maine or the Upper Midwest that is gorgeous when you visit in the fall could be less appealing in winter if you don't care for snow. Cultural differences can also pose a challenge for some. We know a young woman from the East who was determined to go to the most prestigious college that accepted her, no matter what. She chose to attend an ultra-selective college on the West Coast for that reason and ended up miserable because she thought it rained too much and that everyone was too laid back. Few people would describe Stanford University that way, but she did. The fit, for her, was a poor one.

Be Sure to Do Your Homework

If you find yourself drawn to colleges in other parts of the country, be sure to do your homework to determine what life would actually be like if you were to spend four years there. Be aware of possible differences in food, politics, weather, and life in general. In addition, it can sometimes be a little harder to get home for the holidays from more remote colleges. We know parents who want a "one-plane-ride" school for their child. On the other hand, living in a different part of the country can be wonderful if you are open to change.

> My son grew up in a town with a big university, and that's what he's used to. When we toured small schools, he would say, "This is their union? This is their athletic facility?"
>
> MOTHER OF COLLEGE FRESHMAN HAPPY AT A LARGE UNIVERSITY

Size

Colleges vary greatly in size. Some have fewer than a thousand undergraduate students, and a handful have as many as 45,000 or more, with the rest somewhere in between. As we saw earlier, private liberal arts colleges tend to be among the smallest, while the largest campuses are research universities, usually public.

How Size Affects the Feel of a Campus

Size can play a major role in how a campus feels. Michael Tamada, former director of institutional research at Occidental College and now at Reed College, has reflected on the differences: "A small college is like a small town; simply walking through the quad, you will pass by familiar faces of people whom you know. A large university is more like a city; as you walk through the quad or hallways, you'll mainly see faces of strangers, with an occasional encounter with someone who you know. These

> At UC Santa Cruz, I thought, "This is so neat," but my son said, "This is the boonies." At UCLA, I thought, "He'll get lost in a place like this," but he came back beaming.
>
> CALIFORNIA PARENT

experiences can be comforting, stifling, liberating, or alienating depending on your personality."[1]

Size and the Educational Experience

Size affects not only the ambience of a campus, but often the educational experience as well. For one thing, a larger campus usually has a broader choice of programs and courses. You will find majors in symbolic systems, botany, public policy, and many foreign languages. But the downside is that the larger the campus, the larger the classes, at least at the introductory level and possibly beyond. Exceptions to this, as we mentioned earlier, are the honors programs within a college or university. If you care about class size, you'll want to find out about the size of specific classes in your likely major. They will probably be smaller in philosophy or history than in economics or biology, which are among the most popular majors on many campuses. The low student-faculty ratios that colleges often cite may mislead you about the size of actual classes, since all faculty are counted, even those who do little or no undergraduate teaching.

There is no right or wrong when it comes to size. Preferences vary from person to person. Some students find it helpful to visit different-sized colleges near home, even if they are not interested in attending them, just to see what schools of different sizes are like.

The Intangibles

Size, location, and curriculum: all of these are readily observable and easily described and compared. More difficult to assess and compare are the many factors that contribute to the feel of a campus—the ambience—both academically and socially. There is no right or wrong ambience—each person will have his or her own set of preferences and needs. What is important is finding a set of colleges that feels right for you.

Where Do Students Live?

Most colleges with residence halls require or strongly recommend that freshmen live on campus but are more flexible when it comes to sophomore, junior, and senior years. So you should ask, "Where do most students live after freshman year? On or off campus? How far away do students live if they are off-campus? Do they seem generally satisfied with their housing options?" Campuses where most students live on or near campus tend to feel more like a community than those with many commuters.

Campus safety can be an issue for some. Is the campus well lit at night? Is an escort service available for a student who is working late at night in a library or lab and would prefer not to walk back to the residence hall alone? (These services are now very common.) Is access to residence halls secure? Unfortunately, no campus is immune from crime, but a campus can take steps to reduce it.

Federal law requires every college to publish an annual Clery Report providing statistics about crime on campus. Entering "Clery Report" on a college's home page will take you to that institution's report. A visit to the campus security office can also provide helpful information if safety is an issue of particular concern to you or your family.

What Is the Campus Social Life Like?

Do fraternities and sororities play a big role on campus? What percentage of students affiliates with a Greek organization, and how many live in a fraternity or sorority house? Do the answers fit with what you are looking for? Campuses also differ in terms of their ethnic, racial, and geographical diversity. Some are very diverse, others less so, and some are quite homogeneous. Colleges readily provide information about the gender and racial mix of their student body, as well as their geographical diversity. These numbers can help give you a sense of their diversity. But if you are interested, you can go further than this: Are there special housing arrangements for minority students who want them? How do the different groups get along? Do they integrate or self-segregate? You need to ask.

Other factors contribute to the social atmosphere as well. How big a role does athletics play on campus? Is there a lot of school spirit, and does social life tend to revolve around home football Saturdays or other big events? Does this appeal to you? Finally, some campuses are known for their liberal, eclectic student bodies, while others have a reputation for attracting more conservative students. These labels develop and stick because people like to put colleges into categories. The labels may not be real, or they may be out of date as the campus has changed. Each school probably has more variety inside it than is usually ascribed to it from the outside. Think about what you want to experience, but be cautious about the labels just as you are about the rankings. They may serve the marketing purposes of the college more than your own.

What Is the Intellectual Atmosphere of the Campus?

Campuses differ in their reputations for academic intensity. Although some students work harder than others at any college, some colleges seem to have greater expectations for intellectual engagement among their students. And at some campuses, students seem to place greater demands on themselves. Campuses known for intellectual rigor and the work ethos of the student body can be exciting places in which to live and study. They can be perfect matches for some students—and a poor one for others. Swarthmore College, Reed College, and the University of Chicago fit this description quite well, but there are many others too.

Ultimately, however, academic intensity is subjective. Different people assess it from their own perspective. We encourage you to do some thoughtful research both about colleges and yourself. High school students who are overtly intellectual are often hesitant to admit this because it rarely makes them the most popular kid in their class. But every college is looking for students with intellectual vitality. Your own assessment of a campus is, after all, the only one that really counts in the end.

How Do Students Spend Their Time Outside Class?

A typical full-time student takes three or four courses each term, and classes rarely meet every day as they usually do in high school. That leaves lots of time outside class, not all of which is needed for studying. How do students spend their free time? Do they belong to a wide choice of student groups? More important, are there activities in your areas of interest, including new interests that your high school didn't have? Are the recreational facilities attractive and accessible? What do students do on Saturday night? If you visit a campus, ask your tour guide how she and her friends spent last weekend.

Campuses also vary somewhat in their tolerance for alcohol use by underage students. Excessive and abusive use of alcohol among college students is a serious national problem and at all types of colleges except the most religiously observant. Although no college encourages underage students to drink alcohol, they differ in how strictly they enforce their own rules and state law and hence in how much drinking occurs on campus. So you should find out: Do students feel pressured to drink by their classmates, or can you be comfortable in abstaining? Are alcohol- and substance-free residence halls available for those who want them?

MAJORS, CAREERS, AND CURRICULUM

What is a college major, or concentration, as it is called at some schools? A student majoring in a particular field must take a certain number of credits in that field and in related fields to help build knowledge and skills in that subject. The major will require some specific courses for everyone, say, statistics for psychology or organic chemistry for chemistry majors, while other courses are electives, so you can choose which courses to take from a large array. At some schools, you can also declare a minor in another field that still gives you in-depth knowledge of a second area but requires fewer credits. Double majors and occasionally triple majors, for the very energetic, are sometimes available, and some schools allow students to design their own custom majors with the help of an academic advisor. Some programs in the health fields or engineering, for example, have requirements that begin in freshman year.

> They're so right about freshmen changing their majors. I've changed from electrical engineering to computer science to pre-dental to political science—and I've only been here a semester.
>
> UNDECIDED FRESHMAN AT A RESEARCH UNIVERSITY

Selecting a Major

Students often feel under pressure to pick a major while applying to college. Some schools, especially some public ones, admit students at different rates, depending on the major they declare on their application. The most popular majors may have additional requirements for admission and be more selective than less popular majors. If you are admitted to the school but not to the specific major you hoped for, it may be difficult, and maybe even impossible, to switch later. Find this out before you specify a major on your application.

Most schools, though, simply ask students about potential interests, but don't hold them to it. In fact, "undecided" is one of the options offered on the Common Application and is the most popular initial "major." While some students enter college with a clearly defined plan of study that they pursue until graduation, others are completely undecided or change their minds at least once before they receive their degree.

As educators, we like the model that lets students explore their interests for the first two years of college before they have to commit to a major. That gives you time to take courses in different areas to see what really excites you and captures your interest. How are you supposed to know you would like to study psychology or philosophy until you take a course in college? While this is ideal from our viewpoint, we know that some schools require students to commit to a major earlier.

The Relationship Between Major and Career

Excellent information about college majors and the careers they can lead to can be found on the BigFuture website of the College Board at www.bigfuture.org. Colorful and easy to use, the career planning tools on the website describe a large number of college majors as well as the careers for which these majors are good preparation. Projections about job prospects for each career are also provided. The site's search engine helps you identify colleges offering a particular major.

Especially interesting are the wide range of career opportunities open to students who major in humanities subjects like English or history or French. People in these majors work in all walks of life. A banker we know majored in history and says he likes to hire English majors because much of the work in banking involves writing and speaking. A resource like the BigFuture website can be very reassuring to students who love a subject and want to study it but aren't sure how it might translate into a job after graduation. BigFuture is available to anyone for free. Another resource, My Road to College (http://myroad .collegeboard.com), contains more extensive career and major planning information, including an interest inventory, and is available free to students who take the PSAT. You can also purchase access for a nominal fee through the College Board website if you have not taken the PSAT. An additional helpful, and free, resource is College Majors 101, available at www.collegemajors101.com.

College websites and admissions material will help you sort out specifics of the major or majors you are interested in at a given school as well as school policy toward selection and changing majors. If you still have questions about flexibility in choosing majors and when they must be declared after reading those materials, ask for help from the colleges you are considering. A quick e-mail to the admissions office should get you answers to any remaining questions you have.

Majors and Choosing a College

As we noted earlier, some students enter college with a clearly defined plan of study, while others are completely undecided. How should this play into your thinking about colleges? If you are interested in special programs (for example, engineering, dance, business, sports management), whether a school has such a program can be important.

There's More Flexibility Than You Think

But notice that we said "can be important" rather than "is important." It turns out that things may be more flexible than you think, at least in some fields. Say, for example, that you want to study engineering. While you will certainly want to look at schools that offer engineering degrees, you may be interested to learn that many schools without engineering programs partner with engineering schools to offer what is known as a 3/2 program. The student spends three years at the first school, usually majoring in physics or mathematics and receiving specialized advising for 3/2 students, and then transfers to a school with an engineering program for an additional two years. At the end of five years, the student receives two degrees: a bachelor's degree in math or physics from the first college and a bachelor's degree in engineering from the second one. As a bonus, the student has had a broad-based liberal arts education that may set her apart from other engineering graduates on the job market. We have never met a graduate of a 3/2 program who regretted having a liberal arts background in addition to her engineering degree.

Different Paths to the Same Destination

As another example, consider a student who wants to become a marine biologist. Most jobs for marine biologists require a graduate degree, and it turns out that the best preparation for graduate study in marine biology is a solid foundation in biology and chemistry, something that any college's major in biology or biochemistry would readily provide. So there is no reason to limit yourself to the relatively few schools that offer an actual major in marine biology when considering undergraduate colleges. Similarly, few colleges have a formal journalism or architecture major, but all of them offer an English and an art major.

The same general principle applies to students who are interested in business as a career. The natural tendency for such a student is to look for a school with a business major, and there are many options. But a recent survey of employers showed that overall, many actually prefer to recruit students who majored in something other than business—perhaps economics or international relations—because they value students with a broader background than a business major typically provides.

Yet another example is the student who wants to be a doctor. Many students think you have to major in "pre-med" when in fact many schools have no such major. A student who is pre-med must simply take certain courses that are required for entry into medical school, but beyond that, they can (and should) major in any field that interests them. "Pre-med" at most schools is simply a term used for an advising program that helps students select the courses needed for medical school and assists them with the admissions process; it is not a major by itself. Successful medical school applicants come from all sorts of majors, from classics to history to psychology to Russian as well as biology, so study something you really enjoy and will do well in. Students who major in something not usually associated with medicine may even have an edge in the admissions process, all other things equal, since they may stand out from the pack in a positive way.

Each of these examples, and there are many others, illustrates that what may seem to be the obvious path to a given career may not be the only one, and it may not even be the best one in some cases. If you have a career in mind when you are applying to college, be sure to do some research into the various paths and majors that will lead to that career. You may find some surprising options.

Remember also that the average student switches major at least once before graduation. Ideally, look for colleges that offer the kinds of programs that fit your interests, as well as the flexibility to switch fields if your interests change.

Dual-Degree Programs

Some schools offer special dual-degree programs that allow students to obtain a bachelor's degree and a graduate degree, often in less time than it would take if the two were pursued separately. These programs can be attractive to students with focused career objectives. In some dual BS-MD programs, for example, a student receives both degrees at the end of seven years, dual BA-JD programs can be completed in six years, and dual BA-MBA programs take just five years. These programs generally save a year of time and thus a year of tuition. Similar programs exist for BA-MA programs in some fields at some schools, as well as in other professional fields. Smaller schools offering these programs usually have cooperative arrangements with a university that offers graduate degrees, and large universities may offer both parts themselves. In either case, being accepted to a dual program means that if you do well, you won't have to go through a second admissions process to achieve your educational goals. Many of these programs, especially the dual BS-MD programs, are highly selective.

General Education Requirements

Another important aspect of the curriculum is how a college organizes its general education (GE) requirements. Students tend to focus on majors when looking at colleges, overlooking another important part of the curriculum.

What Is General Education?

General education refers to an effort to ensure that every student, regardless of major, will emerge from college with the background considered necessary to be an educated person. This means exposing the student majoring in the humanities to the social sciences and sciences and the engineering student to the humanities and social sciences. College is often the last chance students have to encounter such a broad range of fields, and the benefits of that encounter can be lifelong. Most colleges believe that this is an important part of a student's education, and so they build GE into the requirements for graduation.

Forms GE Can Take

General education means different things at different schools. Some schools have what is known as distribution requirements—a Chinese-menu-style approach in which a student must select a number of courses in the sciences, humanities, and social sciences from a long list. Another approach is the core curriculum—a small set of specially designed courses that all students must take. Sometimes a set of core courses is combined with a distribution requirement. Some colleges no longer require courses identified with different disciplines and instead focus on exposing students to different skills, such as quantitative reasoning, moral reasoning, and global citizenship, through an array of courses.

Some schools have limited GE or no formal requirements at all. Brown University, Amherst College, Hamilton College, and Wesleyan University have no GE requirement. These schools hope that their students will not specialize too much and that they will still take a broad range of courses, but of their own free will. Naturally these schools are very popular with students who want a lot of freedom. Wesleyan University goes a step further and grants university honors at graduation only to students who fulfill broad liberal arts "general education expectations," which include introductory courses in mathematics and the natural sciences, social and behavioral sciences, humanities, and the arts.

Be sure to find out how GE is handled by the colleges you are exploring, so you won't be surprised or disappointed once you enroll. In the end, you are not likely to have to take more than one or two courses more because of GE than you would have anyway, so the requirements can be quite enjoyable once you see how much choice you actually have.

HOW EASILY CAN YOU GET ADVICE AND HELP?

Almost all students need advice at various points in their college career, whether it involves help in selecting courses, deciding on a major, securing an internship, or applying for jobs or graduate school. A recent study showed that students at public colleges ranked access to good academic advising as the most important aspect of their educational experience; students at private colleges ranked it second, after instructional effectiveness.[2] Both groups ranked financial aid, campus climate, and campus life much lower in importance.

Academic Advising and Help

Given the importance of advising, families pay surprisingly little attention to it when exploring colleges. Colleges vary widely in the quality and accessibility of their advising services, so it is well worth trying to find out what you can about them. College websites are a good place to start. Check to see what a school says about its advising program. Is there a good description of how advising at the school works for both freshmen and more advanced students? Is information provided about how the college assists students in identifying and securing internships? What kinds of pre-professional advising are available, and how extensive is it? What kinds of academic support services are available to help a student in academic difficulty?

Descriptions, though, are just a beginning. Try to find out how effective advising is by talking with current and former students. Schools are usually happy to provide the names of students willing to answer questions by e-mail, and if you visit a campus, you'll be able to talk directly with students you meet. You want to hear that advisors are available when needed, informed and able to provide useful information about requirements and courses, able to direct students to sources of help when they have academic difficulty, and able to provide guidance about special opportunities, career interests, and postgraduation plans. You also want to learn about the kinds of support services that are available from centers that can assist students with writing papers to tutoring centers that help with study skills as well as specific subject matter.

Pre-Professional Advising

For students interested in professional degrees like law, medicine, or other health professions, good advising about course work, extracurricular activities, and the application process itself, including interviews, can be crucial. Colleges often have offices or specific faculty who do such advising. Find out what kind of help is provided and the record of students gaining admission to the kind of professional program you are interested in.

Internship opportunities—a chance to tackle a real job, whether paid or not, while still a student—can be very helpful not only in exploring careers but in obtaining a first job. Northeastern University and Drexel University offer co-ops, alternating semesters of academic study with semesters of full-time employment. Many other colleges have offices specifically devoted to matching students with internship opportunities. What kind of internship and career center do the schools you are interested in have? How helpful are they in finding internships for students? Is résumé and interviewing help provided? Can the services be used even after a student graduates? How many and what kind of recruiters come to campus each year? All of these are legitimate questions to ask as you explore how colleges differ.

Help for the Unexpected

Students occasionally get sick or injured and need to go to the campus health center. Some experience psychological difficulties and need counseling or psychiatric care, and some just get lonely or homesick. What kinds of services assist students facing these challenges? Are support services available in residence halls to help students make a smooth adjustment and provide help when they hit a bump in the road? Is the campus health center well staffed, or do students use other nearby resources?

Advance Planning

Overall, you want to know how well the campus takes care of its students. It is well worth asking these questions, probing more deeply into the areas of special interest to you. In particular, we strongly encourage parents of students with prior mental health problems or learning disabilities to contact the appropriate campus offices to discuss the available support services. We'll talk more about this in chapter 11. You want to be sure that appropriate help will be there when it is needed.

WHAT MAKES FOR A QUALITY UNDERGRADUATE EXPERIENCE?

Up to this point, we have been discussing your preferences and interests and how you should identify colleges that match those preferences and interests. But what about quality? How can you assess the quality of the undergraduate education you would receive at a college?

The late Ernest Boyer, president of the Carnegie Foundation for the Advancement of Teaching, identified a number of key characteristics associated with a quality educational experience.[3] We've selected a few that we think are especially important. These criteria have nothing to do with the selectivity of a college, and they can be found anywhere—at a liberal arts college or a research university, a master's university or baccalaureate college, a small or large campus, in an urban setting or a rural one:

- **Does the college do a good job of helping students make the transition to college life?** Is there a program to orient new students to campus life? (These are now universal, but it's good to know what it entails.) Is there a good advising system to help students throughout their college careers? (Complaints about advising are also almost universal. It's hard for colleges to get this right.)
- **Does the college give priority to developing written and oral communication skills, not only in basic introductory classes for freshman but also in all fields?** This is sometimes called Writing Across the Curriculum. Do students

do lots of writing throughout their college careers? Are there ample opportunities for students to give oral presentations? The best way to learn to write and speak effectively and to think critically is to practice those skills; there are no shortcuts.

- **Does the college encourage quality undergraduate teaching through teaching evaluations, programs for faculty to improve teaching, and rewards for good teaching?** Are teaching evaluations obtained at the end of every course and used to provide feedback to the faculty? Do students feel challenged intellectually by their teachers?

- **Does the college encourage students to be active rather than passive learners?** Is independent, self-directed study encouraged? Do students have opportunities to participate in faculty research projects, small breakout sections of large classes, and internships?

- **Does the campus offer a wide range of activities—lectures, concerts, athletic events—that encourage community, support college tradition, and foster social and intellectual exchange?** Do students from varied backgrounds have enough extracurricular activities to choose from? Does everyone feel like a welcomed member of the campus community?

Although we acknowledge that no college is perfect, we think that Boyer's criteria are helpful as you ask questions about colleges. The more a college meets these quality criteria along with your own personal criteria, the greater your chance is of having a good experience.

DETERMINING YOUR PRIORITIES

This chapter was designed to help you learn more about colleges and more about yourself. This may seem like a lot. To know all this about a college would take a while, and you are still in high school, after all, with plenty to do. So this is an ideal plan. Some parts will be more important to some readers of this book. But while everything is still fresh in your mind, we encourage you to fill out the "Determining Your Priorities" questionnaire. Your answers will help you identify the best colleges for you. Chapter 5 will show you how to get information about specific colleges that match your priorities.

☒ Determining Your Priorities

This questionnaire will help you identify what is most important to you as you think about choosing colleges. Questions are divided into three categories: Physical Environment, Academic Environment, and Extracurricular and Social Environment. Answer each question as accurately as you can. For each one, note whether your preference is very important (V), somewhat important (S), or not important (N) to you.

Physical Environment	Your Preference	Importance		
		V	S	N
1. How far from home would you like to live? Close by? Easy or longer drive? Accessible by plane?				
2. Do you prefer a large city, small city or town, suburb, or country environment?				
3. Does weather matter to you? Is there an area of the country where you do not want to live?				
4. What size college do you prefer: small (fewer than 2,500), medium (fewer than 10,000), large (fewer than 20,000), or very large (more than 20,000)?				
5. Do you want to live on or off campus after freshman year?				
Other:				
Other:				

Academic Environment	Your Preference	Importance		
		V	S	N
1. Do you have a preference between a liberal arts college and research university?				
2. Are there specific majors or courses that you want a college to offer?				
3. Do you prefer small classes, large classes, or a mix?				
4. Are you interested in a specific major?				
5. Are there any special curricular features that you want (core curriculum, honors program, and so forth)?				
6. What kind of intellectual environment do you prefer? Exceptionally rigorous, midrange, less intense?				
7. Do you want a "name brand" or prestigious college?				
8. Do you need special support services (e.g., learning disabilities, health issues)?				
Other:				
Other:				

Extracurricular and Social Environment	Your Preference	Importance		
		V	S	N
1. Are there particular extracurricular activities or special facilities that you would like to have available?				
2. Do you want to participate in certain sports at the varsity level? At the club sport or intramural level?				
3. How big a role should athletics play on campus?				
4. Do you want fraternities and sororities to be available and an important part of campus life?				
5. How diverse a campus do you want? What kinds of diversity are you seeking?				
6. Do you want a campus with a special focus such as religious affiliation or women only? Are you open to considering them even if you are not actively seeking such a focus?				
7. Do you seek a particular kind of atmosphere? Artsy, politically active, cohesive community, other?				
Other:				
Other:				

Miscellaneous	Their Preference	Importance		
		V	S	N
1. Do your parents have any requirements?				
Other:				
Other:				

List the preferences you have identified as very important or somewhat important in the spaces provided below. Then rank them in order of importance to you within each group. This list will guide you in identifying colleges before you apply and will help you in making a final decision once your acceptances are in.

Priorities Summary

The following preferences are very important to me:

_____

_____

_____

_____

The following preferences are somewhat important to me:

_____

_____

_____

_____

CHAPTER 5

Where Should You Apply?

In chapter 4, you began to build your college list by considering how colleges differ and identifying your personal preferences. This was an important first step because you need to have at least a rough idea of what you are looking for in order to find it. Your ideas about what you want may change along the way, but with over 2,200 nonprofit four-year colleges in the United States alone, you can't start by looking at them one by one.

By doing your self-assessment, you now have some specific criteria in mind to guide your search. But how do you go about identifying the colleges that fit your criteria and that may, in turn, be a good fit for you? In this chapter, we will take you through those next steps. There is no one right way to build a college list, but we are going to suggest some ways that you'll find very helpful.

START AT YOUR COUNSELING OFFICE

Your high school counseling office can be a good place to begin your college search. Some well-funded public schools and most private schools have counselors whose sole job is to work with students on all aspects of the college admissions process. Other schools fold college counseling duties into the job description of school counselors, who may have other duties besides college advising. Still others have an arrangement that is in between these two: a college specialist provides general college guidance for students, but a student's regular school counselor provides support as well.

We know that schools vary greatly in what college planning help they offer students and that massive student-to-counselor ratios can make it very hard to get help even if it is in principle provided. Whatever the arrangement at your school, take full advantage of the available resources. You can make up for what is missing, or augment what is provided, by carefully reading and using the information in this book. *Admission Matters* was written so that all students can have access to the help they need.

Use Naviance If You Have It

More and more schools are providing web-based tools to assist their students with the college admissions process. One of the most popular is Naviance, a program that lets you search for colleges that meet criteria you specify. Doing a college search using the SuperMatch college search engine on Naviance and then posting the schools that look promising to you on your Naviance account will help you keep track of schools as well as share them with your counselor, who will be able to see what you post. Similar search engines are readily available, so if your school doesn't have Naviance, you can still achieve the same good results, as we will discuss shortly.

Input from Your Counselor

Your counselor may be able to combine his or her knowledge about colleges with your academic record and personal preferences to help you expand and revise the list you generate using a college search tool or other resources. The more specific your criteria are, the more your counselor can help you. Counselors may know more about some colleges than others, but a preliminary list of schools generated with help from your counselor can get you going. If you can't get one, don't worry; you'll be able to develop a fine list using the tools we will be sharing with you.

Regardless of whether or not your counselor helps you develop an initial list, if you haven't already built a relationship with your counselor, this is a good time to start. Remember that he or she will be preparing your secondary school report, including writing a letter on your behalf if colleges on your list require one, as many do, so helping your counselor know you will serve you well. Wait until after winter break of your junior year, when your counselor is finished advising the seniors, and make an appointment to introduce yourself if you haven't already been invited to do so. You want to give a face to your name even before you start to seek your counselor's advice about college. Continue this contact as needed throughout the admissions process. In a big public school, you will have to be more proactive in getting to know your counselor.

In chapter 9, we will talk about how you can be sure your counselor has the information about you that she will need even if you don't meet her for the first time until senior year. This can sometimes happen despite your best planning when there are staffing changes at the start of a new school year or where counselor caseloads are very large.

Your List Is Just Beginning

The initial list you may get from talking with your counselor is just that, a beginning. You'll also want to talk with your parents, other family members, friends, classmates, and others who know you well and may have suggestions. Don't worry if your list is long at this point. You'll have plenty of opportunities to narrow it down later. Your list will eventually look like an inverted pyramid: very broad at the top (beginning) and narrow down at the bottom (end).

USE A COLLEGE SEARCH TOOL

Online search engines are powerful tools that can help zero in on schools that may be an excellent match for you. Fortunately, good college search engines (including SuperMatch, the same search tool found on Naviance) are available to anyone with access to a computer and Internet connection. We encourage you to try several of them because they might turn up different results. They can be used to augment a list that you have already started or even to build one from scratch.

BigFuture

The BigFuture website at www.bigfuture.org that we discussed briefly in chapter 4 can help you identify colleges using criteria that are important to you, like size, location, majors, sports, activities, average net price, and the academic record of a recent incoming class. The search engine also lets you rate how important each criterion is to you: don't care, nice to have, or must have. This "fuzzy logic" approach is very powerful.

The search engine then presents a set of schools that meet your criteria, starting with those that satisfy them 100 percent. The top of the list shows the number of schools returned in the search. Clicking on any college on the list takes you to a quick summary of information as well as in-depth information about the college. You can save the schools you are interested in and easily compare them to one another using the comparison tool. The search engine is colorful and easy and fun to use, and you can instantly see how changing one or more of your criteria can expand or contract your list.

SuperMatch

The same search engine that students use through Naviance, SuperMatch, is available for free to anyone at www.collegeconfidential.com/college_search. SuperMatch uses the same fuzzy approach as BigFuture, so your list will consist of schools that both match your criteria perfectly as well as those that match them only to some extent. Some of the specific criteria used in SuperMatch align with those used in BigFuture, but others, like graduation rate, ethnicity, and great college towns, are different. As a result, you are unlikely to get exactly the same results with the two search engines, but that's a good thing. You will likely be able to expand your list by using more than one. That is just what you want to do at this point.

College Navigator

The U.S. Department of Education has a search tool, College Navigator, which serves a similar function as the BigFuture search feature. You can find it at http://nces.ed.gov/collegenavigator/. College Navigator isn't as colorful as BigFuture or SuperMatch, and it doesn't let you indicate the importance of different criteria, but it has an extensive list of majors to choose from and lets you specify the SAT or ACT ranges that you would like to include in your search results. The College Navigator site also contains links to the online *Occupational Outlook Handbook* that lets you explore job prospects in different occupations, as well as a link that will take you immediately to the net price calculator at any college. (We will go into more detail about net price calculators, a tool that can help you estimate your actual out-of-pocket cost at different colleges, in chapter 12 when we discuss financial aid and the cost of college.)

More About Search Engines

Online searches are easy and fun to use. Pay special attention to colleges that appear on different lists because they may be particularly good matches. With all search engines, if you get hundreds of results, you will need to narrow down your search criteria, and if you get very few hits, you will have to broaden them. Each of the search engines makes it easy to add or drop criteria used in a search, so you can work with each one to see how your criteria affect the results.

MEETING COLLEGE REPRESENTATIVES

Up to this point, you have been adding schools to your list. We are not yet done suggesting ways you can find additional schools, but we would like to shift our attention to ways to both add to your list and possibly narrow it down at the same time.

The College Fair

Usually held in the fall or spring in cities all over the United States and internationally, a college fair is an opportunity for you to meet with admissions representatives from many colleges all assembled in one place. At college fairs, many college representatives, either admissions officers or alumni volunteers, stand at individual tables arranged alphabetically. A college fair can be a very efficient way to gather information and get some questions answered. You can learn about unfamiliar colleges, as well as gather information about colleges already on your list. We encourage you to attend a college fair in your junior year if one is offered near you and use it to learn more.

How to Approach a College Fair

Sometimes, though, a fair can be a free-for-all, with students and parents crowding the tables of the most popular colleges. In this case, the best you can usually hope to do is to pick up some marketing literature and add your name to the mailing lists for colleges that interest you. Less well-known colleges will be much more accessible at the fairs. Go right up, introduce yourself to the rep, and ask anything you want. Be active! They are there to serve you. It can help if you already know something about the college and ask informed questions. "Can you tell me about your neuroscience program [or field hockey team]?" is better than, "Do you have a neuroscience major?"

In addition to having representatives from many colleges, college fairs often feature presentations on different aspects of the college admissions process with an opportunity for you to ask questions. They are free and open to everyone, including parents. Your high school counseling office will have information about dates and locations of fairs in your local area. The National Association for College Admission Counseling also posts an up-to-date list of its large, national college fairs on its website, www.nacacnet.org.

Try a Virtual College Fair

A virtual college fair is an easy way for you to get many of the benefits of an in-person fair without actually having to leave home. Each month, hundreds of colleges participate in College Week Live, a day-long event that gives students and parents an opportunity to engage in live chat, instant messaging, and interactive question-and-answer sessions with students and admissions officers at colleges that interest them. These virtual fairs also feature keynote talks on different aspects of the college admissions process, such as financial aid. Many of the events are recorded and accessible, so even if you miss all or part of the fair on a given day, you can view the question-and-answer panels and keynotes later. You can check the schedule for the next virtual fair and other special events, as well as view the archived presentations at www.collegeweeklive.com.

Meet with the College Representatives Who Visit Your High School

Between Labor Day and mid-November, admissions staff travel to selected high schools across the country to speak with interested students. There are far too many high schools, however, for reps to visit every one of them, and they tend to visit schools where they think they are likely to find potential applicants.

Watch for Announcements

If reps do visit your school, try to attend at least a few of the visits. Watch for announcements of visits by your counseling office, and attend those that most interest you if you can take the time from class. It is fine to come even if you are just curious and know nothing previously about the college; it can be a great way to learn about a new school. But, again, it makes a better impression and is a better use of your time and theirs if you already know at least the basics.

Usually lasting about 30 to 60 minutes, visits include a short presentation and question-and-answer period with the college admissions representative.

Representatives typically do several over the course of a day, so they cannot spend a lot of time at one school. If you attend, they will ask you to fill out a card, so you will get on a list of students who have shown interest in the college and you will receive paper and electronic mailings. With small groups, the admissions officer may jot down brief notes about the students he or she has met for later reference.

How Attending Can Help

Coming to a high school visit is an easy way to show interest in a school, something that may play a role in the college's eventual admissions decision, as we discuss later in this chapter. More important, the visit can provide information that will help you decide if you want to apply. Prepare some questions in advance based on your interests. The visiting rep may even be the first reader of your file if you decide to apply, so making a favorable impression, even just showing your face, can be helpful later.

Occasionally admissions representatives conduct individual student interviews as part of the school visit or perhaps on the nearest weekend. If you are already on the school's mailing list, the college will notify you of this in advance. But don't hesitate to contact the admissions office of a college to see if a representative will be coming to your area since interview slots can fill up quickly. We'll talk more about interviews and what to expect during them in chapter 9.

The Visiting Road Show

A number of colleges sponsor regional events intended for parents and students in addition to, or in lieu of, high school visits. This allows them to reach more students than they can by just visiting high schools. These events may include a presentation by an admissions officer and young alums, a slide show, and the opportunity to get printed materials and ask questions. Students who have previously expressed an interest in the college by requesting material may get a special invitation, but the events are always open to all students and parents, and colleges notify high schools in advance. The events are usually held in the evening or on a weekend afternoon in a large meeting room at a hotel or other public place.

Some colleges combine their efforts and offer a joint session. For example, Harvard University, Duke University, Georgetown University, Stanford University, and the University of Pennsylvania travel together across the country every year and hold a joint program called "Exploring College Options" in over 50 cities. In this way, they draw more people than any one college would by itself. Five smaller schools in the Pacific Northwest—Lewis and Clark College, Reed College, University of Puget Sound, Whitman College, and Willamette University—travel together as the Pacific Northwest College Consortium. Some women's colleges, including Wellesley College, Barnard College, Bryn Mawr, Mount Holyoke, and Smith College, have a similar arrangement, as do the Colleges that Change Lives, a group of less well-known colleges noted for their life-changing success with students. There are many others, whose groups may shift somewhat from year to year.

Families attending these joint events typically hear a short presentation on each institution followed by a question-and-answer session. Even if you don't ask questions yourself, you'll benefit from hearing the answers to questions others ask. Colleges put the schedule of their regional trips on the web. It is worth checking college websites to see if colleges that interest you will be sponsoring a program near where you live.

READ WHAT THEY SEND YOU (BUT DON'T LET IT GO TO YOUR HEAD)

If you've already taken the PLAN, PSAT, ACT, or SAT and checked the box saying you would like to receive information directly from colleges, you are probably finding your mailbox and e-mail inbox filling with glossy mailers and enthusiastic

---

My mom got really excited when the letter from Elite Liberal Arts College arrived. It was personally signed by the dean of admission himself and really encouraged me to apply. I did pretty well on the PSAT, so that's probably how they got my name. I had visited the college and liked it, and my mom said a personal letter meant they were very interested in me, too. I decided to apply. In May the thin envelope arrived—rejected. This time, the letter wasn't hand signed. A computer inserted the dean's signature. No big deal. I gave the letter to my mom, who files everything. When she was putting it away, she pulled out the original letter from the dean and noticed something strange. Both came from the same person, but the signatures were different. The light bulb went on. The dean hadn't personally signed the first letter either. Staff members in his office probably took turns signing his name on thousands of "personal" letters that went out. We read too much into it.

COLLEGE FRESHMAN

---

e-mails from colleges. Colleges buy the names and e-mail and postal addresses of students who meet certain criteria (for example, geography, scores above a certain point, interest in a specific major, or religious affiliation) from the testing agency. They use the information to develop a targeted mailing list of students who might be interested in their institution. We suggest that you read the literature you receive and then check out the colleges that seem interesting. Then file those in any way that enables you to retrieve them later should you need them.

Sometimes colleges send personalized letters rather than brochures to encourage students to seek more information and then apply. Be wary of reading too much into a personalized "search" letter from a college, particularly one from a highly selective college. These colleges send out tens of thousands of letters to students who score well on standardized tests or have other desirable demographic characteristics. This helps them build a strong pool of candidates, but they know they can accept only a small percentage of them. Colleges justify this on the grounds of greater diversity and spreading the word about their college more widely. The problem is that these warm and flattering letters can lead a student and his or her family to believe that the student has an inside edge on admission.

The following phrases come from actual search letters:

- "I hope that this is the beginning of a long-term relationship between you and Williams and that you will be interested enough to keep us in mind as you apply to schools in the fall."
- "We are writing to offer our congratulations on your academic achievements and to encourage you to consider the opportunities available at Harvard as you plan your academic future."
- "As you continue to explore a wide variety of colleges and universities, I am eager to share with you the enclosed snapshot of the University of Chicago."
- "We recently learned of your exceptional testing performance and think you may find NYU to be a great fit for you."

In the vast majority of cases, search letters simply mean you might be a viable candidate—no more and no less. They are certainly nice to receive, but remember that it is just sophisticated marketing from the colleges.

HOW TO NARROW THINGS DOWN

If you have followed our advice up to this point, by now you have a long list of colleges—colleges that may be a good fit but that you need to learn more about before deciding for sure. We are going to turn our attention now to some tools that will help you do that effectively.

Using BigFuture

One of the tools we think is especially helpful we have already mentioned: the BigFuture website at www.bigfuture.org. It is not only a search engine to help you identify colleges that meet certain criteria, but also a rich source of factual information about the academic programs, sports, extracurriculars, tuition, and admissions practices at each of them. It is a great way to get an overview of a school.

College Guidebooks

Another useful tool as you narrow your list is a "big book" that provides anecdotal and statistical information about a wide range of colleges. There are several of them, including the *Fiske Guide to Colleges* and the *Insider's Guide to the Colleges*.[1] Each one is published annually and contains basic factual information about colleges similar to what you would find on BigFuture as well as descriptive information about the academic and social life on campus based on student interviews. This information, including representative comments from students, can give you a feel for the campus beyond the numbers. The good news is that the comments in these books are free of direct college marketing efforts. The bad news is that much of the information is anecdotal and not fully reflective of the complexity of the colleges they describe. Overall, though, we have found the descriptions, at least of the colleges we are familiar with, to be quite accurate.

One major drawback of such books is that they contain information on fewer than 400 colleges and inevitably focus on those that are among the best known. Don't worry if some colleges on your list are not in one of these books—there are other good ways to get the kind of information you would find there anyway.

College Websites

College websites are perhaps the single most valuable source of information about a college. True, a college is not going to tell you that the dining hall food is tasteless or that faculty members are hard to reach outside of class (you'll have to discover this in other ways) but clicking on "admissions" or "prospective students" from a college home page will lead you to much useful information. You'll usually find recent campus news and sports results, statistics about the most recent freshman class, a description of the entrance requirements, and the academic programs and majors available. Links to academic departments give you detailed information about faculty and their specializations, as well as a list of courses offered.

Check Out Deadlines, Requirements, and Special Features

The website will also likely highlight any special features of the undergraduate experience at that college, including opportunities for study abroad, community service, and involvement in athletics at all levels, and even about the surrounding community. Colleges try to make their web pages attractive and easy to use, since they know that many students and families use the Internet extensively.

Information about application deadlines and testing requirements is prominently featured on most sites, along with the application and detailed instructions. You can also request by e-mail to be added to a college's mailing list. You'll generally receive a view book with lots of pictures of the college, an application form and instructions if the school still accepts paper applications, and information about financial aid. Some colleges may send follow-up mailings as well—sometimes lots of them. The admissions web page is also a good place to learn about visiting the college, including listings of nearby hotels and airport shuttle companies, and how to set up an interview if they are offered.

Ways to Get a Good Feel for a Campus

Increasingly common are admissions chat rooms that allow prospective students to talk to admissions officers and current students. Admissions websites post the details of these chat sessions, which anyone can join. Some colleges have admissions blogs, accessible through their websites, where admissions officers and others post useful information and comments. You can also read most student newspapers online. It is worth checking them out to get a feel for the hot issues on campus.

Reading a Catalog

Prospective students typically don't spend much time reading college catalogs, also known as college bulletins, but they should. Designed primarily as an official reference for current or newly admitted students, a catalog is usually a no-nonsense document fairly free of the influence of glitzy marketing efforts but overflowing with a wealth of information.

The catalog describes courses and requirements for all the majors and lists the faculty in each department and may even identify who teaches each course. You can tell how many courses they offer, how much variety there is, and whether a department has a special emphasis. It also explains graduation requirements such as general education courses and a senior thesis, information about dual-degree programs and honors programs, the academic calendar, housing policies, and the honor code. The catalog may also contain information about opportunities to study abroad, internship programs, and other features of the campus.

Because of the cost, colleges rarely provide free paper catalogs on request, but they post their catalog on their website, making it accessible to all. Some colleges have gone green and have stopped printing catalogs altogether. In either case, all of the information you would find in a printed catalog is available on the web.

A catalog can also help you figure out how to study a field in which the college does not offer a formal major. For example, you might find courses in criminology in sociology, psychology, and political science or courses in architecture offered through art, economics, and urban studies.

Additional Sources of Information on the Web

Several websites offer prospective students access to comments about a school provided by current or former students. These sites help you get a sense of the culture and atmosphere on a campus from those who have actually experienced it. They are far from scientifically conducted surveys of opinions, but they can provide useful information if you keep their limitations in mind.

College Prowler

College Prowler is an online and in-print guidebook that uses student comments to grade campuses (A-B-C-D) on their academics, athletics, campus housing, diversity, social life, local atmosphere, and other areas. In addition to student-authored summaries for each topic, the site includes comments from individual students, by topic, who have chosen to post their perspectives for everyone to see.

Students have told us that they found College Prowler especially helpful once they had narrowed their list of schools based on objective criteria like programs, size, selectivity, and other factors. College Prowler gave them insights into the feel of a campus that helped them narrow their list even more. Remember, though, that sites like College Prowler do not claim to have scientifically sampled the student body for their input. While any student can post a comment, those who take the time to do so are generally either very happy with their school or very unhappy. You generally don't hear from the middle of the pack.

Unigo

Unigo is a site that features student-submitted photos, videos, and comments about schools. Comments for each college are not sorted by topic as they are on College Prowler, but instead are displayed as a series of questions and answers for each individual reviewer. Unigo users can search for comments by reviewers similar to them in terms of major, gender, home state, and political leanings. Many reviewers sign up to be "service providers" for Unigo and make themselves available for 30-minute video chat sessions with prospective students willing to pay $30 for the opportunity to speak with a current student.

College counselors are also available for a video chat, but a 60-minute session will cost you $99.

> On paper every college looks more or less the same. But when you go there, you get a totally different feel if you know what to look for. You have to see whether you like the atmosphere. If you can imagine yourself there, then maybe it's for you.
>
> COLLEGE SOPHOMORE WHO WENT TO SCHOOL FAR FROM HOME

THE COLLEGE VISIT

Once you have learned as much as you can about a preliminary list of colleges from indirect sources, you may find campus visits to be extremely helpful in narrowing your list further. Some students take a college tour to look at several colleges, usually with parents or an organized group, during spring break in their junior year. A tour at that time allows you to see schools while classes are in session and the campuses are fully alive. A visit usually includes an hour-long group information session led by an admissions officer, sometimes with a student participant as well, and a group tour led by a student tour guide. Both help you get a quick overview of a college and answer some questions you may have.

Go Beyond the Formal Visit Programs

Don't limit your visit to the formal tour and information session, however. Try to spend some time on your own exploring the campus. The student union and the library are good places to check out. Have lunch in the union or school dining commons, and get a feel not only for the food but also for the pace of the campus. Sit down at a table with some students and ask them about what they like about the school and what they would like to see improved. Of course, you need to remember that they are a very small and random sample, but most students enjoy talking about their college, and you will get honest responses. Read the notices posted on the bulletin boards. What is being advertised? What are the upcoming events on campus? Pick up the school paper; better yet, go to the newspaper office and scan several back issues. Walk through the library and see how the students are studying. Are they studying at all, and if so, are they mostly working alone, or are they interacting in small groups? Is the library well lit with lots of comfortable places to sit?

> I had a bench test. At the end of every campus visit I found a bench and sat on it. I thought, "Is this the place for me?"
>
> HIGH SCHOOL SENIOR

Be Sure to Ask Questions

Most important, look around at the students and try to imagine yourself among them. Don't hesitate to ask questions. A tour guide's job is to answer them, but most students you will meet on your visit will be happy to offer their perspectives as well. Remember, they were visiting campuses too not so long ago. Keep your list of questions handy—the ones that are important to you and are not answered in written materials or on the website. Everyone has an opinion if you are willing to listen! Remember also to take notes about what you see. If you visit several colleges in a row, the details begin to run together, so you'll need notes to keep everything straight in your mind. Taking photos can also help. Cell phones make this an easy task.

Depending on your interests, you may also want to try to speak with a coach in your sport or a professor in your major field of interest as part of your visit. The admissions office can help you arrange such meetings, which you should set up well ahead of time. You can easily find e-mail addresses of faculty and the coaches on college websites.

⌧ Things to Do on a College Visit

Items marked with an asterisk must usually be arranged in advance.

- ☐ Take a campus tour led by a current student.
- ☐ Attend a group information session.
- ☐ Fill out a visitor card at the admissions office and pick up a catalog, view book, and application.
- ☐ Have lunch in the student union or dining hall. While there, scan the postings on the bulletin boards, and pick up a copy of the student newspaper. Browse in the bookstore, especially among the textbooks, not just the college gear.
- ☐ Walk through the library. Does it look like a comfortable place to study?
- ☐ Check out the recreational facilities that interest you.
- ☐ Sit in on a class.*
- ☐ Stay overnight in a dorm with a student.*
- ☐ Have a formal interview.*
- ☐ Meet with a coach or faculty member in your area of interest.*
- ☐ Ask students you meet what they like best about the campus and what they would change if they could.
- ☐ Explore the nearest town and transportation options.
- ☐ Sit on a bench, and watch students walk by. Can you imagine yourself happily among them?

Check Out the National Survey of Student Engagement Guide

We suggest you check out a wonderful brochure, "A Pocket Guide to Choosing a College: Are You Asking the Right Questions on a College Campus Visit?" Published by the National Survey of Student Engagement (NSSE) at Indiana University that we discussed in chapter 1, the NSSE guide provides a series of questions you might consider asking about the level of student engagement at a college: how much contact students have with professors, how good the advising system is, and how students can arrange to do research, for example. You can download it for free under the Students and Parents link at www.nsse@indiana.edu.

Timing Your Visit

We don't recommend seriously visiting colleges before the second half of the junior year. You may be an exception, but most students aren't ready to focus on specific colleges before that. They haven't had time to do the preliminary reflective thinking about themselves, and

> When you visit a college, it is a good idea to stand in the busiest part of the campus with a map in hand and try to look confused. Then wait to see how many people come to your aid. Although this is not a scientific sample, it will give you a sense of the campus environment in terms of friendliness and willingness to help.[2]
>
> JOSEPH GREENBERG, PROFESSOR EMERITUS AND FORMER REGIONAL DIRECTOR OF ADMISSIONS, GEORGE WASHINGTON UNIVERSITY

all they see are the buildings and how the students are dressed. In one case we know, a father told his daughter that her upcoming visits in the spring of her senior year to make a final choice would be especially useful because she had seen all the colleges the summer before her junior year. She said, "Oh, I don't remember anything from that trip, Dad. That was your trip."

Summer, Spring, or Fall?

The summer is a popular time to visit campuses, since it fits well with vacations. All colleges offer tours and information sessions in the summer even if classes are not in session. However, depending on the location, things may be pretty quiet without classes or many students around.

Visits in the fall of senior year can be a great way to see a campus after your thinking about colleges has progressed. You may also have the additional option of scheduling an overnight stay in a dorm with a student host through the admissions office. (This is not available at all colleges; usually the bigger or more popular the college, the harder this is to arrange. You can usually set this up on your own if you know someone there.) Staying overnight is a great way to get to know current students and to learn what students talk about at 10:00 p.m. in the dorm. Students who visit during the school year can also often sit in on a class in an area that interests them. This is usually a lecture class where a visitor is not intruding or even noticed. Although you don't want to draw general conclusions from just one class, notice whether the professor is well organized and clear in his or her presentation and if students are attentive and engaged—not texting their friends on their phone or surfing the Internet during the lecture.

The disadvantage of a fall visit is missing some school back home in the crucial first part of your senior year. If you can schedule fall visits with minimal disruption to your academic schedule, then consider them; otherwise, plan ahead and visit in the spring of your junior year and over the summer.

Look Beyond the Superficial

Remember, though, that many factors can affect your initial impression of a campus, including the personality of the tour guide and the weather that day. Colleges know that students relate best to other students, so they hire as tour guides energetic, enthusiastic students who enjoy their college and eagerly present it in the best light. Sometimes, though, a guide may be poorly trained, or just new at it, and less than an ideal ambassador for a campus. In this case, try to keep an eye on the bigger picture. The guide is not the entire school. Similarly, a campus seen in beautiful weather has a big leg up on one seen in the pouring rain. Try to keep this in mind as you compare your impressions of different colleges. No matter how long you spend on campus, you are seeing only a tiny slice of its life, good or bad.

My first-choice school invited me to a weekend program even before I was formally accepted. I had visited the campus once before, but now I was going to stay overnight. I didn't know what to expect, but I was excited about going. I was put in with this pretty crazy girl, and she and her friends were doing all this drinking and stuff. I was really scared because I wasn't expecting that. I had no experience with alcohol. I think the workshop leaders knew what was going on, but they just said things like, "Be careful at night." I came home and thought, "I don't really fit in at that campus." Later I learned I was in the part of the campus known for party dorms. I wonder if I had had a different roommate, if I would have had a different feeling. Anyway I chose another school, and I like it so much here that I didn't want to come home for Christmas.

COLLEGE FRESHMAN

How Can Parents Help?

Although some students visit colleges on their own or with organized tour groups, most visit with their parents. Whether the trip is part of a vacation or scheduled specifically for the purpose of looking at colleges, the parent perspective can be a valuable lens through which to view colleges. This can be quality time with your child, but remember that ultimately it is the student who must want to go to the college, regardless of the parents' views. As a parent, your extra set of eyes and ears on the visit serves as a sounding board for reactions. Virtually all campuses invite parents to join their children on the formal tours, but be sure to give your child plenty of freedom to look at what interests him and to ask the questions he wants to ask. If financial aid is a concern, this is a good time for parents to visit the financial aid office.

> We're just starting the search all over again. If I had known it would be this exhausting, I would have had my children further apart.
>
> MOM OF TWO

What If You Can't Visit?

What if scheduling or cost prevents you from seeing a campus firsthand? Fortunately, many resources can help fill that gap, such as view books, catalogs, and virtual online tours available on campus websites that we discussed earlier in this chapter. Some websites even feature collections of college tour videos that you can view for free. One such site is YouniversityTV at www.youniversitytv.com. Its over 500 six-minute videos can give you quick visual overviews of participating campuses. Another good source is CampusTours at www.campustours.com.

Consider e-mailing short questions about campus life (including, "What do you like best?" and, "What would you most like to change about your campus?") to several current students. Admissions officers can usually provide the names and e-mail addresses of current students (often called "student ambassadors") willing to respond to such queries. Use these opportunities to fill in the gaps in your knowledge. Your high school counselor may also have the names of graduates of your high school who attend different colleges. Once you have some names, you can often find contact information through college online directories. We have found that current students, especially from your home town, are always willing to share their experiences with you.

SHOWING THAT YOU ARE INTERESTED

Some colleges try to identify who is seriously interested in them by tracking how much contact a student has had with the college—such as requesting an interview, chatting with a representative at a college fair or a high school visit, e-mailing a question to an admissions officer, visiting campus—and using that information when making the final decision. They see a student who has initiated contact at least once with a college as more likely to enroll than a student who has not (for example, one whose first contact with the college is the electronic arrival of the application on the deadline, called "stealth applications"). This student is a better bet for admission. Given hard choices among candidates with similar credentials, demonstrated interest can make the difference between an offer of acceptance and placement on the wait list at some colleges.

Trinity University in Texas is one school that openly lets students know that this is important to them. Its admissions criteria state, "Visiting campus, emailing or calling an admissions counselor, attending a Trinity In Focus program, talking with a representative when they visit your high school, and stopping by our table at a college fair are some of the ways to show the Admissions Committee that you are genuinely interested in attending Trinity."[3]

> To think that when my older son applied we refrained from contacting colleges because we thought we were doing admissions offices a favor by not cluttering up their e-mail or phone lines. We won't pester them, but we won't have the same worry when our younger son applies.
>
> PARENT OF COLLEGE SOPHOMORE WITH ANOTHER CHILD IN THE ADMISSIONS PIPELINE

Not all colleges are this refreshingly candid, however, and not all consider demonstrated interest in the admissions process. In general, this counts less at the super-selective colleges that already have the highest yields. They have little to gain by showing preference to those who try to demonstrate interest. Trinity University is far from unique, however, and it is perfectly all right to ask an admissions officer if demonstrated interest plays a role in decisions on their campus.

SELECTIVITY AND YOUR COLLEGE LIST

We mentioned earlier in this chapter that the admissions profile of current students is one of the factors that you can put into the hopper when running college searches on the BigFuture website. Even if you don't make it a factor initially in your college search, as you finalize your list, the likelihood of being admitted to a given college should play an important role in deciding whether to apply.

Good Bets, Possibles, and Long Shots

A wise student distributes college choices among three categories based on the likelihood of admission. The first category, which we call "good-bet" colleges, includes those where you are almost certain to be admitted given your record and the recent admissions profile of the schools. The next category, "possible" colleges, involves chances that can range from "pretty likely" to "50–50" to "not too likely." It is the broadest of the categories and, in an ideal list, should have the most colleges. The final category, which we call "long-shot" colleges, includes those where the college's acceptance rate by itself (under 10 percent or 20 percent) or in conjunction with your own record makes admission very unlikely.

These three categories correspond to popular terminology with which you may be more familiar: "safety, target, and reach" colleges. We feel that our terms—good bet, possible, and long shot—more accurately capture the objective reality of college admissions rather than the scale of your hopes. Whatever the language used, the issue is selectivity, not quality. The problem is in confusing the two. Just because a school is a long shot doesn't mean it is desirable for you. It is just popular and therefore hard to get into.

The most common and ultimately most painful mistake is to think that if you apply to a large number of long-shot schools, your chance of being admitted to at least one of them increases. We call this the lottery principle: the more lottery tickets you buy, the better are your chances of winning, even if only slightly. This does not apply to selective college admissions. Even if schools do vary somewhat in their admission practices, by and large they are looking at the same information and looking for the same qualities in applicants. There is no more depressing scene than to get bad news from 10 famous colleges in one week. Ten long-shot schools, one possible, and one good bet do not comprise a good list.

> I wish I had applied to more "middle range" schools. I feel like I overshot on most of my schools and then didn't like the others.
>
> HIGH SCHOOL STUDENT IN SPRING OF SENIOR YEAR

Determining Your Chances

How can you tell what your chances of admission are at different colleges? The BigFuture website can be very helpful here. The admissions tab for each college will take you to data from one or two years ago showing the SAT and ACT range for the middle 50 percent of freshmen, as well as the percentage of freshmen ranking in the top 10, 25, and 50 percent of their high school classes for students whose high schools reported class rank. If your high school has Naviance, this is even more useful, since it standardizes the grade point averages (GPAs) for just your high school.

How to Identify Good Bets

The middle 50 percent of SAT and ACT scores helps you place your own scores in a better context of what the student body looks like than the average score. The data also include the percentage of applicants accepted. If you significantly exceed the midrange of standardized test scores of incoming freshmen and have a GPA that places you at the high end of the previous freshman class, the college can be considered a good bet for you if its overall acceptance rate is at least 50 percent. The higher the acceptance rate, the lower your test scores or GPA can be relative to the midrange of freshmen for the college to be considered a good bet.

What Makes a College a "Possible"

A "possible" college takes many forms. It can be one where your grades and test scores place you in the middle range of the freshman class and the admissions rate is 50 percent or higher. At another possible college, your scores might significantly exceed the midrange of freshmen, but the admissions rate is 35 percent or even somewhat less. The higher your scores are relative to the average freshman, the lower the admissions rate can be for a school to be a possible one for you. But the lower the admissions rate, the less that objective data like test scores and GPA matter in the end as long as both are in the ballpark for recently admitted students. When the admit rate is very low, lots of nonacademic factors like essays, recommendations, and special talents and other hooks end up making the difference between students who are admitted and those who are not.

The Long Shots

Finally, long-shot colleges are ones where, given your profile, you have less than a 35 percent chance of admission. For almost all students, even those with terrific stats, all colleges falling in the ultra- and super-selective categories (those with admissions rates under 20 percent) should be considered long shots. The many factors that affect the admissions decision make it a challenge to predict a successful outcome at such schools. It is much easier to predict when a student will not be admitted because of lower grades and scores.

Of course, highly selective or very selective colleges, as we have defined them (admit rates between 35 and 50 percent), are long shots for lots of good students as well, depending on their records relative to those of the freshman class. Highly selective colleges that admit less than 35 percent of applicants can be possible colleges for those with exceptional academic records that place them well into the top quarter of the college's freshman class. You can never get perfect precision about this. All you can hope for is an educated guess. That is why you need a balanced list, with several options in each category. You want to have choices in April.

> A few years ago I had a student—#3 in his class—who was bringing in his applications one by one. I saved them up for a while without looking at them, then took them home over the weekend to work on them. As I filled out one after another I thought to myself, "Oh, no, he hasn't applied to seven schools, he applied to the same school seven times."
>
> HIGH SCHOOL COUNSELOR REFERRING TO A STUDENT WHO DID NOT HAVE A RANGE OF COLLEGES ON HIS LIST

CHECK OUT THE DATA

With growing numbers of college applicants, the explosion of test preparation services, and a national trend of grade inflation, GPA and test scores at selective colleges have been increasing every year, along with the number of applications. The websites of the colleges themselves have the most up-to-date numbers. Most colleges put the statistics for their entering class on the web by the fall. The previous spring, most colleges issue press releases, also found on websites, that give data about the students who were just offered admission. These numbers are often more impressive than the numbers for enrolled students that will appear in the fall, since many colleges accept top applicants who choose to go somewhere else. Just be sure you know what data are being presented: Are they for admitted students (all of those who received offers of admission) or enrolled students (freshmen who actually accepted offers of admission the previous spring)?

The Common Data Set

Another good source of data about specific colleges is the Common Data Set. This is a collaborative project among colleges and a number of publishers in which the colleges agree to provide standardized statistical data each year, including detailed information about the composition of the freshman class, along with admission and wait list numbers and test score midranges. The participating publishers, including *U.S. News* and the College Board, present parts of the data through their websites. Some of the colleges choose to post the entire report itself. You can usually find the report, if available, by checking the college's institutional research office web page or by entering "Common Data Set" as a search term on the campus website. Reports usually appear around January for the class that entered the previous fall, making the data very current. The Common Data Set can provide a fascinating glimpse into admissions results if schools choose to share them publicly.

> My son seemed to narrow down his list very quickly. Columbia, NYU, UCLA. Five other top schools. Just one safety would have been a good idea. I wasn't as engaged as I should have been.
>
> FATHER OF SON DENIED EVERYWHERE WHO IS NOW "COMPLETELY HAPPY" AT A SCHOOL THAT WASN'T ON HIS LIST BUT SHOULD HAVE BEEN

Scattergrams Can Help

Although data from a big guidebook or college websites can help you in assessing your chances of admission to a given college, important additional information on your chances of admission from recent admissions results for students at your high school is even more precise.

What Is a Scattergram?

A scattergram is a graph of the GPA and SAT (or ACT) scores of students who were accepted, denied, or wait-listed at a college over a period of several years. It is an easy, visual way to determine where your own credentials fall in the context of other students at your school who have recent application experience at that college. You usually need at least five data points (meaning that at least five students have applied to this college) for the scattergram to be really useful, however, so if your school has not had many students apply to a particular college recently, the information will be of limited value. Some high schools prepare their own scattergrams, but thousands of high schools now use Naviance to generate scattergrams in a standard format using the high school's own data. You can save yourself a lot of heartache if you take the graphs seriously. If your statistics are way out of the range of students who have been accepted recently from your school, you are not likely to a lucky exception, barring some exceptional hook. By browsing, you can also find some good bets this way.

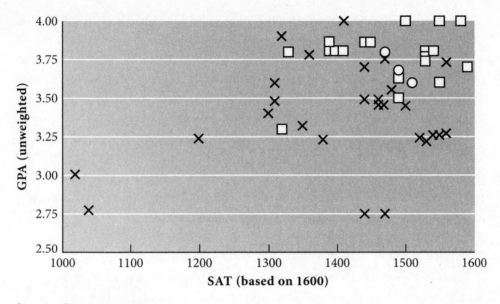

SAMPLE SCATTERGRAM

Limitations of Scattergrams

Keep in mind, though, that no matter how many points on a scattergram, it displays only two dimensions: standardized tests and GPA. These are just part of your application at many selective schools. The other factors—extracurricular activities, letters of recommendation, essays, and special talents, for example— may be critical to the outcome and help explain why, when two students have identical GPAs and test scores, one was admitted and the other was not. One counselor asks students what they make of this, and when they shake their head in bewilderment, she says, "The colleges read the files. Something else is in the file that makes a difference."

Remember that institutional priorities play an important role in admissions decisions. The sample scattergram vividly illustrates this point. It is based on real applications from students at a high-performing high school to a selective private university and shows that although admission offers tended to go to students with higher GPA and SAT scores, that was not always the case. Other factors, such as legacy status, athletics, or affirmative action, may have played an important role in determining the outcome in some cases. At best, scattergrams provide ballpark, not definitive, information.

Even if your school does not systematically collect the kind of information that goes into a scattergram, your counselor may be able to tell you about the recent admissions experience of students from your high school who applied to specific colleges. If few or no students have applied to a particular school, however, there obviously won't be much to share.

HOW LONG SHOULD YOUR COLLEGE LIST BE?

One of the first questions students have when they think about developing a college list is how many schools it should have. There is no one-size-fits-all answer to this question, but here are some guidelines to consider.

A Balance of Good Bets, Possibles, and Long Shots

In general, it is a good idea to develop a college list with one to three good-bet colleges that you would be happy to attend. This is important: these have to be schools that you like, not just ones you can get into. If you can't find such schools, it means you are not looking hard enough. It is critical to spend significant time and energy selecting these colleges. Too often students select them as an afterthought, which can be painful, if, at the end of the admissions process, you must choose one of them. A good list of good-bet colleges is a crucial cushion in what can otherwise be a very uncertain process. Two to four possible colleges and two to three long shots can round out the final list.

The Numbers Will Vary

These guidelines lead to college lists ranging in length from five to ten. But some students apply to fewer than five colleges (and they do just fine if they are well chosen and not all long shots) and others to 12, 15, or even more if they are especially eager for acceptance at possible or long-shot colleges or need substantial financial aid. Shorter lists are fine as long as they include at least one or two good bets that a student would be happy to attend. Longer lists add to the expense and time involved in applying, since many colleges now have their own supplemental essays even if they use the Common Application. So do your research, and whittle the list down to a reasonable number. Some high schools limit the number of applications a student can file by restricting the number of counselor recommendations and transcripts they are willing to submit for a single student. By limiting the number of colleges, a high school is telling students to research their choices carefully and to make each one count.

Early Applications and Your College List

In chapter 7, we discuss early decision and early action options that involve identifying one college as your top choice and submitting an application to that college by an early deadline in exchange for early review. Under the right circumstances and at the right schools, you can reap a significant advantage in submitting an early application, but it doesn't eliminate the need to develop your full college list carefully. If you are not admitted early to your first-choice college, you will have your carefully researched list of alternatives ready to go. Always have a plan B.

THE KEY TO A GOOD COLLEGE LIST

The key to developing an appropriate list is to be sure that you can actually see yourself happily attending any college on it. It is certainly reasonable to prefer some more than others, but because the outcome of the admissions process can be so unpredictable, you need a balanced list. We would like to propose a slightly different and more radical idea: consider all the colleges on your final list "first choices." In other words, aside from a possible early action or early decision school, don't rank your schools by preference too early. Enjoy the idea of any of them.

> We went to Harvard. I didn't want to apply. I thought, "Harvard's going to be stuck up and it's not going to be very nice." But Dad said, "No, you're going to apply just to apply."
>
> STUDENT WHO SAYS, "HARVARD HAD A REALLY NICE REJECTION LETTER."

It also makes good sense, and is common courtesy, to apply only to colleges you would seriously consider attending. Sometimes students get caught up in a prestige game and decide to apply to colleges in which they have no real interest just to see whether they will be admitted. This phenomenon is so common, in fact, that counselors have a name for it: trophy hunting. Parents sometimes directly or indirectly contribute to trophy hunting. Though seemingly harmless except for the waste of time and money, trophy hunting may hurt the chances of other students at your high school who really want to go there. As we discussed in chapter 2, colleges want to accept students who will actually attend. They also want a diverse student body, so the number of students a given college will accept from one high school may be informally limited, even though they have no quota or target number. If you apply to a college knowing you would not attend and you are accepted, you may inadvertently cause the denial of another student, even a good friend, at your school who is seriously interested in that college.

Developing a college list can be an exciting and demanding process for you and your family. We encourage you to begin with a careful self-assessment using the "Determining Your Priorities" questionnaire at the end of chapter 4. Make special note of characteristics that are very important or somewhat important to you. Then use the results of your assessment to develop a list of possibilities, narrowing that list as you learn more about the schools themselves and their degree of selectivity in relation to your own record. A good college list comes from thoughtful introspection, as well as thorough research about colleges. The College Research Worksheet in Appendix A will help you organize your ideas as you do your research. The worksheet can also be found and easily duplicated at www .admissionmatters.com.

A WORD ABOUT FINANCES

At this point, we would like to introduce another factor in the equation as you consider colleges: finances. Although some students can cover the cost of their education from family resources, many more need financial aid to cover all or part of the cost. A great deal of financial aid is available, with the largest amounts going to those with the lowest incomes and thus the greatest need. Middle-class and upper-middle-class families eligible for aid must often assume loans for part of their college expenses, although a few schools with large endowments have eliminated loans as part of their financial aid packages. A strong academic record or outstanding talent may result in merit aid—scholarships that don't depend on demonstrated need. How much is your family willing and able to contribute to your education, especially in a challenging economic climate? How much borrowing is comfortable for you and your family? Finances alone shouldn't dictate your college list, but they can't be ignored either.

Chapter 12 will give you some important information about financing a college education and direct you to online calculators that can give you a sense of what your out-of-pocket cost would be at different colleges. Colleges use complex formulas to determine financial aid in an effort to be fair and equitable. But a college may not be able to give you and your family as much as you feel you need because of an increase in requests for financial aid. In case financial aid does not work out as well as you had hoped, it is always a good idea to include on your list at least one college you know you can afford, probably a public university in your home state where you will be charged in-state tuition and where you are very likely to be admitted—in other words, a good bet that is also low cost. We call this a "financial good bet." You want your admissions experience to end happily regardless of the admission or financial aid decision you receive from any given college.

CHAPTER 6

The Big Tests

S tandardized tests—what they actually measure, how you can prepare for them, and the role they play in your getting accepted to college—are at the heart of probably the most anxiety-provoking part of the college admissions process. Each year millions of high school students get up early on a Saturday and spend the morning filling in little ovals on a test grid, concerned that their dreams for college hang in the balance.

This chapter will help you understand how standardized tests fit into the college admissions picture and how you can approach them with confidence. It will explain what the SAT, the best-known and most controversial of these tests, is all about. It also covers the ACT, another widely used standardized test, and we will look at the differences and similarities between the two. We'll discuss why and how colleges use standardized tests in the admissions process in the first place and how more schools are making these tests optional in their admissions process. We'll also help you decide which of the two tests to take and suggest how to best prepare for it.

> The SAT has become a symbol of all the anxieties, concerns, fears, and frustrations in the college admissions system.[1]
>
> LEE BOLLINGER, PRESIDENT OF COLUMBIA UNIVERSITY

WHAT IS THE SAT SUPPOSED TO TEST?

Your parents may remember when the SAT was called the Scholastic Aptitude Test. First developed in the mid-1920s as an adaptation of the Army Alpha test used to assign duties to recruits during World War I, the Scholastic Aptitude Test became widely used as an important tool in college admissions after World War II. Colleges facing unprecedented numbers of applications from returning veterans needed an efficient way to evaluate them. The idea of testing "aptitude" for college in a standardized way as part of the admissions process became popular as the number of applications soared.

The SAT Now

Almost 70 years later, a version of the Scholastic Aptitude Test is still widely used in the admissions process at many colleges, although with considerably more caution. The Scholastic Aptitude Test, originally designed to measure just what its name suggested, has morphed into the SAT Reasoning Test, or just SAT for short. According to the College Board, the organization that owns and administers the SAT, the SAT now tests "the reading, mathematics and writing skills and knowledge students acquire as part of a rigorous high school curriculum. The SAT also measures how well students can apply their knowledge, a factor that educators and researchers agree is critical to success in college."[2] The idea of testing something called aptitude, a term that suggests natural intelligence, has been put aside.

The SAT has long been challenged as culturally biased and unreliable in predicting success in college. Critics point to the substantial disparities in average scores of African Americans and Hispanics compared to white or Asian students, as well as strong correlations between socioeconomic status and performance on the SAT. Critics also cite data showing that high school grade point average (GPA) better predicts first-year college grades than the SAT does.

For those who appreciate history, it is more than a little ironic that the arguments against the SAT today are basically the same ones offered in support of the original Scholastic Aptitude Test by those who promoted its use after World War II. Educators at that time knew that economically disadvantaged students rarely had access to education of the caliber offered at prep schools. Thus, they argued, these students would be at a disadvantage on subject matter tests that had traditionally been staples of the college admissions process. However, tests of more abstract reasoning ability like the Scholastic Aptitude Test, the argument continued, would be less closely tied to high school quality, allowing good students to shine regardless of where they went to school. Additional support for the test

On the one hand, [standardized tests] are portrayed as an evil that should be purged from our society; on the other, they're viewed as a trustworthy measure of the academic standing of students, schools, and communities—perhaps even the quality of American education.[4]

REBECCA ZWICK, PROFESSOR OF EDUCATION AT THE UNIVERSITY OF CALIFORNIA, SANTA BARBARA, AND FORMER EDUCATIONAL TESTING SERVICE RESEARCHER

came from statistical studies at that time showing "that general verbal and mathematical ability tests predicted college grades better than did achievement tests in particular subjects."[3] New research now suggests just the opposite.

What Is in the SAT?

The SAT is a paper-and-pencil test with questions that fall into three categories: Critical Reading, Mathematics, and Writing. Students receive separate scores ranging from 200 to 800 in each of the three categories. The scores are then added together to get a total score, with a maximum possible score of 2400. Without breaks, the SAT takes 3 hours and 45 minutes.

A given test has ten sections, although the order of the sections varies from test to test:

- One 25-minute Essay section, which always comes first
- Two 25-minute Math sections (one with 20 multiple-choice and one 8 multiple choice and 10 grid-in)
- Two 25-minute Critical Reading sections (24 multiple choice each)
- One 25-minute multiple-choice Writing section (35 multiple choice)
- One 20-minute Math section (16 multiple choice)
- One 20-minute Critical Reading section (19 multiple choice)
- One 25-minute experimental section in Math, Critical Reading, or Writing (composition varies)
- One 10-minute multiple-choice Writing section (14 multiple choice), which always comes last

The Critical Reading category has fill-in-the blank vocabulary questions as well as reading passages with questions that test your understanding of what you read. Math questions cover material from Algebra I and Geometry, with a few questions that require knowledge of Algebra II. The Writing category includes three types of grammar questions as well as a short written essay in response to a prompt consisting of either a pair of quotations or a short paragraph from a real text. The essay assignment asks the student to write an argument in response to the prompt. You have 25 minutes to take a position one way or the other and support it with examples taken from your reading or personal experience. You can answer this either way; you are graded on the structure of the argument, not whether you get the "right" answer.

⌦ Writing Prompt from October 2012 SAT

Think carefully about the issue presented in the following excerpt and the assignment below:

> The idea of caring about only the people of one's own country seems outdated. Some people still defend this attitude, claiming that if we are going to expend resources to help people, we should help those of our own country first. But national boundaries are meaningless lines that shift over time. There is no reason why a citizen of one country should not feel just as responsible for the well-being of people in other countries as for the well-being of those in his or her own country.

Assignment: Should we care just as much about people in other countries as we do about people in our own country? Plan and write an essay in which you develop your point of view on this issue. Support your position with reasoning and examples taken from your reading, studies, experience, or observations.

The essays are handwritten in pencil but later scanned into a computer and scored on a scale from 1 to 6 by two independent readers. Essays that do not respond to the prompt receive a zero, no matter how well written. The scores from the two readers are then added together to obtain an essay score ranging from 2 to 12. If the two readers differ by more than one point, your essay will be read by a third, more senior reader. The essay score counts about a third of the overall Writing score, or about a ninth of the entire test, after it is combined with the score on the multiple-choice portion of the writing test to produce a final score between 200 and 800. Colleges can read your actual essay if they wish when you submit a score report. Your score report shows both your multiple choice score and your essay score, so you can see how well you did on each part.

Finally, every test includes an experimental section with questions that the College Board is testing out for use in future SAT exams. You are not graded on those questions and you don't know which section won't count to encourage you to try as hard as you can on all of them.

WHAT IS THE ACT SUPPOSED TO MEASURE?

The ACT is a second widely used standardized college admissions exam. It is also used by midwestern states like Illinois, Colorado, and Iowa to assess educational achievement of all high school students, college bound or not.

The ACT Has a Different Philosophy

Unlike the SAT, which began as the work of a Princeton psychologist in the mid-1920s, the American College Testing Program began in 1959 through the efforts of a University of Iowa statistician who had developed a statewide testing program for Iowa high school students. The ACT started with a very different philosophy from the SAT, one closely tied to specific instructional goals rather than assessment of abstract reasoning ability.

Today virtually all colleges in the United States that require a student to take a standardized test for admission accept either the SAT or the ACT, although historically the SAT has been the more widely used test on the East and West Coasts, with the ACT more common in the Midwest. Overall, the ACT has received less of the intense criticism than the SAT, although one group, the National Center for Fair and Open Testing (also known as FairTest), finds serious flaws in all types of standardized testing, including the ACT.

What Is in the ACT?

The ACT has four parts—English, Math, Reading, and Science—with an optional Writing part that consists of an essay. Most selective colleges require the essay if you choose to submit ACT scores instead of the SAT. You need to check with the colleges where you plan to apply. The basic test takes 2 hours and 55 minutes without breaks. Each section, with the exception of the essay, is scored from 1 to 36, with the ACT Composite score being the simple average, rounded to the nearest whole number, of the scores on the four parts. The optional essay adds 30 minutes to the test.

The test always follows the same fixed sequence:

- One 45-minute English section (75 multiple choice)
- One 60-minute Math section (60 multiple choice)
- One 35-minute Reading section (40 multiple choice)
- One 35-minute Science section (40 multiple choice)
- One 30-minute Essay (this is optional)

The English section tests your knowledge of grammar and usage by asking you to select options that correct punctuation and other errors in written material as well as options that improve clarity of expression. The Math section includes questions using Algebra I, Algebra II, Geometry, and some elementary trigonometry, although there are only a few trigonometry questions on the test. The Reading section tests reading comprehension using reading passages, each followed by 10 questions. The Science test, contrary to its name, is a test of scientific reasoning rather than a test of scientific knowledge. Everything you need to answer each question is presented in charts, graphs, and brief descriptions of experiments, and you answer questions based on this information.

The Writing section is very similar to the essay portion of the SAT: you must respond to a prompt with a persuasive essay in 30 minutes. As with the SAT essay, an ACT essay is read by two readers who will assign scores of 1 to 6, and the two will be totaled for a final score ranging from 2 to 12, with a third reader called in if scores differ by more than one point. The essay score is combined with the English score to yield a Combined English/Writing score from 1 to 36, but this score is not included in the Composite score.

The essay was added to the SAT in 2004, and the ACT followed suit shortly after. College administrators had complained for years that writing, the verbal skill most used in college, was not being tested. But the new essay test was criticized almost immediately by college writing teachers because the task of writing a 25- to 30-minute essay on a subject you had never seen until that moment contradicted most college writing experiences, where you write about the material you know from the course you are taking. Even more important, you have no opportunity to edit and revise your work. Many colleges are vague about how important the writing section is to them, and some make it clear that they do not consider it in the admissions process at all.

HOW MUCH DO STANDARDIZED TESTS COUNT?

"Okay," you say. "All of this is interesting, but what does it mean for me? Just how important are standardized tests, and how should I approach them?" In chapter 2, we quoted David Erdmann, admissions dean at Rollins College, as saying, "At most institutions, standardized test scores count less than students think and more than colleges are willing to admit." This is a fairly accurate statement about the importance of standardized tests.

At many selective colleges, standardized test scores count significantly in the evaluation of a student's academic strengths but less than GPA, class rank (if available, but increasingly rarely reported by high schools), and the rigor of the student's course work. At some other colleges, particularly public ones that have specific GPA requirements for admission, higher test scores can offset lower grades. Some schools, like those in the California State University system, even have published formulas showing how this trade-off works. So test scores can indeed be important, depending on the school's philosophy and your other credentials. At the same time, more colleges are becoming test optional, so a student can decide whether or not to submit scores. We will talk more about test-optional schools later in this chapter.

Scores Are Evaluated in Context

At most colleges that are not formula driven, admissions officers take into account many factors that might affect your scores and evaluate them relative to your opportunities and life circumstances. For example, parental education and income correlate strongly with scores (more education and higher income are associated with higher scores), so admissions officers expect to see higher scores from the prep school–educated son of two professional parents than from the inner city–educated son of working-class, immigrant parents. The same score can mean something different for two different applicants.

The Middle 50 Percent of Scores

Colleges usually report scores for the middle 50 percent of their class rather than averages. This is how they appear in the "big books" like the *Fiske Guide* and in the

U.S. News rankings. In general, the more selective a college, the higher the scores of students falling in the middle 50 percent of its freshman class. College A, for example, may report that the middle 50 percent had SAT math scores ranging from 480 to 600. This means that 25 percent of freshmen had a math SAT score below 480, 25 percent had a score of 610 or above, and the remaining 50 percent had scores in between. Knowing that the math midrange for the freshman class was 480 to 600, for example, tells you more than simply knowing that the average score was 540. It also reminds you that many admitted students were admitted with a score below 540, information that is lost when you have only the average.

College B may report that the middle 50 percent of its freshman class had SAT math scores of 600 to 710. Comparing the two sets of numbers, we can see that 75 percent of the freshmen at College B had a math score of 600 or above, while only 25 percent of the students at College A reached that level. A 480 would place you right at the 25th percentile for College A but at a much lower percentile at College B.

Percentile and Likelihood of Admission

Of course, many factors other than standardized test scores influence admission to a college that evaluates applications holistically. Scores are just one part of your complex profile. In general, if your test scores fall roughly in the middle 50 percent range of a selective college's freshman class SAT or ACT distribution, they won't hurt or help your chances for admission much, but the greater you diverge from the middle, up or down, they will help or hurt your chances accordingly.

In the example just discussed, a math score of 720 or greater would fall in the top 25 percent of the freshman class at College B and would probably help your case for admission. Just how much a higher score will help depends on the actual score, the weight the college places on it, the rest of your record, and the college's selectivity.

Scores falling in the lowest 25 percent of the freshman class for a selective college (590 or less in this example) would usually need to be offset by some compelling factors for you to be a viable candidate at that college, especially if the college is quite selective. Scores in the bottom 25 percent of a school's freshman class will not by themselves automatically disqualify you. By definition, 25 percent of the students in the class must have scores that fell at or below the 25th percentile. But realistically, scores in the lower end of a college's freshman class will reduce your chances of being admitted if the college does not accept a large percentage of its applicants. Some of the students admitted in the bottom quartile may have had a special admissions hook, such as athletics, first-generation background, or some other factor that proved compelling and offset their scores.

In reality, as an applicant to a college that requires or recommends the SAT or ACT, you have no sure way of knowing how important your scores will play in the admissions decision. Given all this uncertainty, the smart approach is to try to obtain the highest scores you can with reasonable preparation, with an emphasis on *reasonable*.

⊠ What Does the SAT Midrange Mean?

College A—Math Midrange of 480 to 600

25 PERCENT OF STUDENTS SCORED	50 PERCENT OF STUDENTS	25 PERCENT OF STUDENTS
less than 480	scored 480 to 600	scored 610 or more

College B—Math Midrange of 600 to 710

25 PERCENT OF STUDENTS SCORED	50 PERCENT OF STUDENTS	25 PERCENT OF STUDENTS
less than 600	scored 600 to 710	scored 720 or more

HOW SHOULD YOU PREPARE?

Test developers know that a person's score on a given test is based on three factors. First, how much do you know about the subject matter being tested? If a question requires a certain kind of calculation, you probably won't get it right if you don't know how to do it. The second factor involves test-taking skills: How comfortable are you taking such tests in general, and how familiar are you with the construction of this test? Finally, and most disconcerting, each test score has a random component—the luck of the draw—on the day of the test. No exam can exhaustively test your knowledge. It can sample it only at a certain moment. The specific questions on a given test may or may not reflect your broader knowledge.

You might not be feeling your best that day. There is no box to check if you have the flu, though you can cancel your scores within a few days of taking the test.

An SAT score report shows a score for each part, as well as a score range. A math score of 650, for example, has a score range from 620 to 680. By reporting a score range, the College Board is suggesting that if you took different editions of the test within a short period of time, your performance might vary a bit but would probably fall within this 60-point spread. This variation would occur independent of any attempts to improve your score through studying or familiarizing yourself with the format of the test. Colleges ignore the score range and count the actual score, just as students do.

Forms of Test Prep

Test preparation comes in many forms. You can successfully prepare with just a book (Kaplan and Princeton Review, the two largest companies offering class-room-based SAT and ACT preparation, both publish books they claim contain much of the same material covered in their courses) or a class that costs $1,000 and meets 12 times for three hours each, all the way to individual one-on-one tutors, who typically charge $100 an hour or more. Still other options are test prep software with similar content to what you would find in a book, as well as online courses for those who want the structure of a course but greater flexibility in timing. At elite private schools and high-performing public schools, most students do significant test preparation, often with private tutors. Some schools also arrange for a test prep company to offer a course at the school. The test prep companies are, of course, eager to offer their services.

Companies offering prep courses sometimes guarantee that a student's score will increase by a certain number of points, though they only rarely offer a refund. A student who does not improve by the guaranteed amount can simply take the course again for free—not exactly what anyone is really eager to do.

How Does Test Prep Work?

Good preparation for the SAT or ACT should focus on both subject matter and test-taking skills. You need to be motivated, you need enough time to absorb the lessons, and you need to study relatively close to the date of the test. It is not a good idea to study over Christmas, do nothing afterward, and then take the test in March. You need to keep your preparation going.

Mastering Content

The shorter the prep program, the greater its emphasis on test-taking skills, since subject matter preparation generally takes longer. Both approaches can be helpful, however. If you don't have a rich vocabulary, for example, questions that require knowing unfamiliar words will be difficult. Building a vocabulary is an important part of SAT preparation since some questions directly test vocabulary, although the English language has far too many words to learn them all. Preparation books and programs try to ensure that students master the words that most commonly appear on the tests. The Kaplan approach, for example, has always taught the Latin and Greek roots from which many obscure English words are derived. Reading a lot of Dickens will teach you these words too, and you get to read great literature at the same time, though that does take a lot longer.

Similarly, knowing simple mathematical formulas may be critical to solving some of the math problems. Test preparation focuses on the basic math concepts that test takers are assumed to have mastered. This can be especially helpful for students who have not had recent experience with them. Practice on writing and grammar is part of test prep as well. For the ACT, practice interpreting data from charts and graphs is included, since the Science section tests those skills.

Building Up Test-Taking Skills

But for many good students with strong verbal, math, and writing skills, the most valuable part of standardized test preparation deals with test-taking skills, including simply developing the stamina to stay focused through such a long test. Practicing tests under timed conditions can be important, as is learning how to approach various questions.

Questions tend to fall into predictable categories, and being very familiar with the types of questions that appear frequently can really help. In addition, the people who develop test questions know the kinds of answers that careless mistakes produce. These are called "distractors." You can be sure to find some easy wrong answers among the multiple-choice options. Identifying these repeated, careless errors can raise scores significantly just by itself.

What Type of Test Prep Works Best?

No one knows for sure what type of test prep works best. The kind of large-scale, carefully controlled research that would be needed to compare the effectiveness of different preparation approaches to each other and to no preparation at all hasn't been done to our knowledge. The conclusions that can be drawn from a few studies are very limited. Common sense suggests that as long as similar content is being taught, the particular method of preparation shouldn't matter as long as the student is willing to commit the time and effort needed to slog through the program and take the practice exams that appear to be critical in improving scores.

Both the College Board and the ACT publish their own test guides. The College Board publishes *The Official SAT Study Guide: Second Edition*, which contains ten practice tests and prep materials and costs about $22. Similarly, *The Real ACT Prep Guide* contains five practice tests and prep guidance at a list price of $31. Other commercial publishers and test preparation companies also publish self-help guides filled with strategies and tips on how to do well. If you have the self-discipline to coach yourself with a book or computer program (some are low cost or even free, such as the one at www.number2.com), or both, these can be highly effective forms of test prep.

Once again, you need to assess yourself honestly. If you are motivated to work from a book or software program consistently and diligently in a timely manner, you can save yourself and your parents literally hundreds or even thousands of dollars and get results similar to those you would have obtained from an

⊠

I was on this incredible emotional teeter-totter about the SAT. On one hand, I wanted to do well. On the other, I felt that my SAT score did not make or break who I am. It was a strenuous time because I tried to have a balance of a good social and academic life. Should I go watch a movie with my friends and have fun, or stay home and study for the SAT two more hours? Most of the time I chose the academic path. However, I do remember being at a school dance (I had to work at the dance since I was in student government) the night before the SAT. I was sitting in the coatroom with a fat SAT book, and my friends kept coming up to me saying, "You're studying at a dance? Oh, come on!" Needless to say, they convinced me to put the book down, and I never regretted it. It's simple: if you don't know the material already, you're not going to learn it in a few hours, so there's no use cramming. For this same reason, my band teacher never let us play the day of a concert. If you don't know it by now, you're not going to."

COLLEGE JUNIOR

⊠

in-person course or tutor. But the key is applying yourself. The course or tutor has the advantage of providing structure for you and, in the case of the tutor, personalized structure and instruction. But neither is necessary or sufficient to improve your score. How can you maximize your chances of doing well on the ACT or SAT, regardless of how many times you take it? The fact is that for most students, preparation and serious practice in any form will help. And for some, it may help a lot.

Remember also that the outcome will be hard to predict. Your scores may go up very little (or even decline a bit because of the random error that is inherent in any test), or they may go up a lot if they were on the low side to begin with. (They won't go up much if your scores were already very high, since there just isn't much room for them to go up.) We believe the best approach to test preparation is a reasonable one that doesn't disrupt your schoolwork and extracurricular activities. Preparation is unreasonable if it takes over your life. As with all other aspects of college admissions, stay balanced, and keep things in perspective.

WHICH TEST SHOULD YOU TAKE?

Why Has the ACT Become More Popular?

Some colleges requiring SAT Subject Tests (discussed below) will accept the ACT with Writing in lieu of both the SAT and the SAT Subject Tests because they regard the ACT as more curriculum based. This is a big advantage of the ACT if you are applying to schools like Bryn Mawr College, Duke University, Boston College, and Rice University that currently allow this option.

Unlike the SAT, the ACT doesn't penalize the student for wrong answers. Because of the penalty, you should only guess on the SAT when you can eliminate at least one of the answers to increase the odds that you will actually get the question right and avoid the deduction. On the ACT, you can randomly guess even if you can't eliminate any answers. This doesn't make the ACT test any easier because every student gets the same benefit from guessing and the scores are scaled relative to each other, not on an absolute scale. The contrasting side, which is rarely discussed, is that the ACT is more time intensive: you have more questions per time period. The SAT is time based as well, but there are fewer questions per time segment.

Some people think that the ACT is more student friendly, down to earth, or less "sneaky" than the SAT. It is said, for example, that SAT questions resemble

SAT–ACT Score Comparisons

SAT Critical Reasoning + Math (Score Range)	ACT Composite Score	SAT Critical Reasoning + Math (Single Score)
1600	36	1600
1540–1590	35	1560
1490–1530	34	1510
1440–1480	33	1460
1400–1430	32	1420
1360–1390	31	1380
1330–1350	30	1340
1290–1320	29	1300
1250–1280	28	1260
1210–1240	27	1220
1170–1200	26	1190
1130–1160	25	1150
1090–1120	24	1110
1050–1080	23	1070
1020–1040	22	1030
980–1010	21	990
940–970	20	950
900–930	19	910
860–890	18	870
820–850	17	830
770–810	16	790
720–760	15	740
670–710	14	690
620–660	13	640
560–610	12	590
510–550	11	530

deductive puzzles that reward the kind of test takers who like puzzles. The ACT is more straightforward: you either know the answer or you don't. These beliefs have contributed to the growing popularity of the ACT. But in fact most students do about the same on both tests when they take both, and that is why colleges accept either without stating a preference. There is no good research that shows that a certain kind of student (by gender, academic interests, or socioeconomic background) tends to do better on one, yet claims to this effect still regularly emerge. Some think there is a code that can be cracked. Of course, some actually do score better on one than the other, but you can't know in advance if you will be among them.

Consider Trying Both

Our advice is to take whichever test appeals to you more, see how you do, and if you don't do as well as you hoped, consider taking the other one to see if something in the style of the test is holding you back. Of course, you do not have to actually take the tests to compare them; practice tests can serve the same purpose. If you decide to take the ACT itself rather than a practice test, be sure to check if your schools require the ACT writing test as well. You need to register for that at the same time; it is not included automatically, as the essay is with the SAT. Just remember to keep all of this in perspective and don't emphasize the whole testing enterprise too much.

WHEN SHOULD YOU TAKE THE SAT OR ACT?

The SAT is offered seven times during the school year: October, November, December, January, March, May, and June; the ACT is offered six times in September, October, December, February (except in New York State), April, and June. Currently neither test offers a summer date.

Taking the Test for the First Time

A good time to take the test for the first time is the second half of the junior year, although some students choose to take the test in the fall. You can register for the SAT at www.collegeboard.org or the ACT at www.act.org by using a credit card. The fees are currently $50 for the SAT and $50.50 for the ACT with Writing. Fee waivers are available through high school counseling offices for low-income students who cannot afford the cost. The test is offered at many sites, mostly at

	SAT	ACT
Sections	Math Critical Reading Writing (includes essay)	Math Reading English Science Reasoning Optional Essay
Scoring	Each section 200–800 Maximum total 2400 Essay scored 2–12	Each section 1–36 Maximum composite 36 Optional essay scored 2–12
Test length	Approximately 3 hours 45 minutes including essays	Approximately 3 hours without essay; 3 hours 45 minutes including essay
Essay details	Required part of test Essay written at the start 25 minutes total	Optional part of test Essay written at the end of test 30 minutes total
Format	Multiple choice and completion (for some math questions only)	Multiple choice only
Question order	Questions presented in order of difficulty within each section	Questions randomly ordered within each section
Scoring basis	Random guessing penalized	No penalty for random guessing
Online information test registration	www.collegeboard.org	www.act.org

large high schools, but the sites vary on different dates. Details are available online on the websites and in printed materials in high school counseling offices. Because some test sites fill up quickly, it is good to plan ahead and register early to get the site of your choice so you don't have to drive a long distance to take the test. Students must submit a current photo with their online or paper registration request, and you must bring a picture ID to the test. This requirement was added in 2012 as a fraud prevention measure.

Obtaining More Than Your Scores

Scores on both tests are mailed a few weeks after the test date or are available online (or by phone for a fee) about two weeks after the test. The same website where you register for the test will release your scores through your password-protected account. For the January, May, and October SAT test dates, you can pay a small fee and get a copy of the actual test you took along with an answer key. The ACT offers a similar service for the December, April, and June tests. Getting the actual questions and answers can be a good idea for students who may take a test again. It can be a very helpful test preparation tool for the next round, although it will take several weeks after the test to receive your materials. You can sign up for the service when you register for a test or within five months of taking an eligible SAT test or within three months of taking an eligible ACT test.

How Often Should You Take the Test?

Once you get your first set of standardized test scores, you can decide whether you want to take the test again. A lot will depend on how competitive your scores are for the schools you are considering applying to and whether you are up for putting in more time preparing for the test. Students applying to more selective colleges tend to take the SAT or the ACT more than once. You can take the SAT or ACT as many times as you want, but actually only a small percentage of students take them even twice, and an even smaller percentage three times or more. Three times is a reasonable practical maximum. Taking it more than that is probably not the best use of your time and is unlikely to result in significant further improvement.

Choosing the Scores to Send

If you decide to retest, you can take the test later in the spring of your junior year or in the fall of your senior year. Both the College Board and the ACT keep track of all of your scores and allow you to decide which test scores you wish to submit to a college if you have taken a test more than once. All three parts of a given test administration are reported, but students can choose which test dates they want to report. The College Board will send all scores unless you specifically elect Score Choice when you request your scores to be sent. There is no extra charge for Score Choice, and you can choose which tests you want to send, as the name suggests. The ACT charges a separate fee for each test date it sends, so it won't send more than one unless you ask and pay the required fee for each college.

Superscoring Your Results

Students often ask if colleges will count their highest scores on the different parts of a standardized test regardless of when they obtained those scores (for example, the highest score on Critical Reading, Math, and Writing obtained across two or more test dates). So if you took the SAT twice and did better on Math the first time and Critical Reading the second time, you should send both. Using Score Choice to send just one would actually hurt you. Most schools do, in fact, "superscore" standardized test scores in this way, particularly for the SAT. A major exception to this are all campuses of the University of California, which counts the highest overall score on a single test date. Superscoring is done less frequently for the ACT, but it is becoming more common. Some schools that currently superscore the ACT are Middlebury College, Millsaps College, New York University, and the University of Georgia. The best way to check a school's policy is through its admissions website.

Some selective colleges, including Stanford University, Yale University, the University of Southern California, Johns Hopkins University, Pomona College, Rice University, and the University of Pennsylvania, still ask students to submit all their standardized scores (sometimes including all SAT Subject tests as well), although they too superscore the results. For schools that do not require you to submit all scores, you are free to choose the scores you wish to submit, remembering that in most cases, the schools will superscore from among the test results that you send. However, we have asked dozens of college admissions officers if it could ever hurt a student to submit all scores, even if not required, and they ALL said no. They know that students take test prep, have good test days and bad ones, and in general get different scores on different days.

The College Board developed Score Choice a few years ago (the ACT has had it for many years) to reduce student anxiety. Ironically, it has had the opposite effect for some students, who now worry about which scores to send to which colleges. Our best advice is to ignore Score Choice and send all your scores to every college. It makes things simpler and will not hurt you.

⊠

I definitely wanted to do well on the SAT, but my parents totally supported me and told me that they would be proud of whatever score I got, so I wasn't too scared. What I know now is—having gotten a good score but wishing I got a great score—I wish I had studied my behind off. I bet I could have gotten an amazingly outstanding score if I had pushed myself that much harder. I improved my math and verbal scores by taking it a second time; my overall score went up 90 points, so I wonder . . . if I had taken it a third time, especially with studying, how would I have done?

   On the other hand, taking the test was not a defining moment in my life. I'm at the college where I wanted to be, so the test didn't hurt me or change my plans for the worse or anything. It was a pretty unremarkable event.

COLLEGE SOPHOMORE

⊠

HOW DO THE PSAT AND PLAN FIT INTO THE PICTURE?

Both the SAT and ACT come in shorter, less expensive versions that you may be able to take at your school before you tackle the full-length test. The PSAT (or Preliminary SAT), the short version of the SAT, is traditionally offered in October to high school juniors, although at some schools, sophomores and sometimes even freshmen can take it. The PLAN, the short version of the ACT, is offered to sophomores from August to May at the discretion of the school. Neither test has an essay: the writing part of the PSAT consists only of multiple-choice grammar questions. Unlike the full-length versions of the tests, registration for the PSAT and PLAN is handled by the high school, not the testing agencies.

Getting Some Early Practice

The PSAT and PLAN give students experience taking a standardized college test and provide detailed reports along with the test results that give students valuable information about their strengths and weaknesses so that they can better prepare for the "real thing." The maximum score on the PSAT is 240 (rather than 2400 on SAT) and 32 on the PLAN (rather than 36 on the ACT). Both tests also include unscored sections on career interests that may provide useful guidance as well.

Some schools offer the PSAT only, some the PLAN only, and some offer both. Check with your school counselor to find out which tests are offered and when. If a test is not offered at your school, you may be able to make arrangements to take it through a nearby school that does offer it. Planning in advance is important. Neither test will appear on your high school transcript, and colleges do not receive reports of your scores. The test results are basically for your and your counselor's use, so we encourage you to take advantage of the opportunity to take one or both. There is one exception to all of this, however, and we turn to that now.

The National Merit Scholarship Competition

The PSAT (but not the PLAN) serves as the screening mechanism for the National Merit Scholarship Program, a large, nonprofit scholarship and recognition program. It is also used to identify students for the National Achievement Scholarship program (for African Americans) and the National Hispanic Recognition program.

Each spring, the National Merit Scholarship Corporation contacts the 50,000 high school juniors who score in the top 2 percent of those taking the PSAT nationwide the preceding October and invites them to identify two colleges they would like to have notified of their honor. The qualifying score for 2012–2013 was 200 out of 240 and is the same for all states. If you are included in this group, many colleges will like getting your name, and it will count as demonstrated interest at those places that normally consider demonstrated interest in the admissions process. But it doesn't show that much demonstrated interest, so don't think that's all you have to do in this regard. Colleges do not receive your actual PSAT scores; they only know that you scored at or above the cutoff threshold.

Being Named a Semifinalist

In September of their senior year, about 16,000 of the 50,000 students notified the previous spring learn that they have been selected as National Merit Scholarship semifinalists. Eligibility for semifinalist status is determined state by state, with the cutoff score based on the top 1 percent of scores in each state. For 2012–2013, the cutoff score ranged from a low of 200 in Wyoming, West Virginia, and North Dakota to a high of 221 in Massachusetts, the District of Columbia, and New Jersey. It was 220 in California, 216 in Texas, and 215 in New York. The state cutoffs may vary slightly from year to year and are not widely publicized. However, you can call the National Merit Scholarship Corporation's offices at (847) 866–5100 to get the most recent cutoff score for your state if you are curious. The remaining 34,000 students who are not named semifinalists are named "commended students" and receive a certificate.

Who Wins a Scholarship?

Semifinalists are invited to submit an essay, transcript, SAT scores, and a school recommendation to be considered for finalist status. About 90 percent of semi-finalists become finalists, and about half of those subsequently receive a monetary award directly from the National Merit Corporation itself, a participating company that one of their parents works for, or one of about 200 participating colleges eager to have National Merit finalists enroll at their college. A National Merit finalist who receives any scholarship is known as a National Merit Scholar.

While this is certainly an honor, and no one ever turns down the money, too many students are named finalists, and even more are commended, for National Merit recognition to carry much weight at the most selective colleges. Some of them, including the entire Ivy League, MIT, Stanford University, and others, award their own money only to students with demonstrated financial need, though a student is welcome to bring a National Merit Scholarship with him or her to any of these colleges to help defray the cost. Some schools are also concerned that the sole criterion for semifinalist status, performance on one two-hour multiple-choice test taken in the junior year, is a rather narrow definition of merit. Schools like the University of California and the University of Texas do not participate in the National Merit program, although they do award merit funds based on their own criteria. Additional details about the program (minus the concerns) can be found at www.nationalmerit.org.

Should You Prepare for the PSAT?

If you are a student likely to do well on a standardized test like the PSAT, it may be worthwhile to take the test seriously and do some modest test prep in advance. Some schools, particularly state universities like Iowa State University, University of Oklahoma, University of New Mexico, and Arizona State University, seek to attract high-performing students and actively court National Merit finalists with invitations to apply and automatic full tuition scholarships for those who do. Recognition through the National Achievement Award (for African Americans) program or the National Hispanic Scholars program can also lead to very generous awards at some schools.

While we find the idea of practicing for what is supposed to be a practice test a bit silly in isolation, in context it might make sense for a small percentage of students because of the potential scholarship money. Remember, though, that except in this narrow way, the PSAT has no bearing on the college admissions process and there is no reason at all to be anxious about it. For the vast majority of students, the PSAT is simply what it was originally intended to be: a practice test to give them an idea of their strengths and weaknesses early in their junior year so that they can prepare appropriately for the SAT itself.

TEST-OPTIONAL SCHOOLS

A growing number of schools no longer require any standardized tests, either the SAT or the ACT, for some or all of their applicants. Some schools exempt students who meet GPA criteria, while others require SAT or ACT scores but use them only for placement or research purposes. Still others offer students the option of submitting SAT Subject Test, Advanced Placement, or International Baccalaureate test scores, or of submitting a writing portfolio as an alternative.

These schools believe that they can make sound admissions decisions based on other information in a student's record. Bates College, one of the first test-optional schools, studied student records and alumni over a 25-year period and found no significant difference in the academic records of submitters and nonsubmitters. They also found no difference in success after graduation, except, not surprisingly, in standardized test scores for graduate school admissions. You may still benefit from submitting your scores if they are higher than average for a particular school, but the schools promise not to discriminate against you if you don't submit and will not assume you have low test scores. In fact, they feel that having a test-optional policy is attractive to students and gives their college a marketing advantage.

Some schools that are test optional for everyone include Smith College, Mount Holyoke College, Wake Forest University, DePaul University, College of the Holy

Cross, Lawrence University, and Bowdoin College. Other schools are test optional for at least some applicants; among them are the University of Nebraska, Lincoln, George Mason University, and Arizona State University.

Unless you are philosophically opposed to taking standardized tests or know that you are just a poor test taker, it is unlikely that you will apply only to test-optional colleges, though there are now enough such colleges that it is a feasible strategy. So you will probably end up taking tests like everyone else, wait to see what your scores are, and then decide where to submit them. A list of test-optional colleges can be found at www.fairtest.org. Be sure to check individual colleges' websites to confirm specific details and to check for updates. This is an area where changes happen quickly.

THE CASE OF SPECIAL ACCOMMODATIONS

The College Board and the ACT know that some students require special accommodations to overcome challenges that would otherwise impair their performance. Blind or visually impaired students are the most obvious example, but students with other kinds of physical impairments that make it difficult or impossible to complete the test in the standard way can also receive accommodations. With appropriate documentation submitted in advance to either testing agency, special arrangements can be made to address the student's needs.

Physical impairments represent just a small percentage of cases seeking such accommodations, however. Most special accommodation requests are for extra time to compensate for learning disabilities that would otherwise make it difficult for a student to perform up to his or her ability. Here too documentation of the learning disability satisfactory to the testing agency must be submitted well in advance of the test. ACT is reputedly stricter about granting accommodations than the College Board, though both require professional psychological testing. Accommodations can range from time and a half (the most common) to untimed testing, depending on the severity of the learning disability. Just as an exam in larger typeface may be provided to a student with visual problems, extra time accommodations for learning disabilities attempt to level the playing field for otherwise able students.

We will talk in detail about the process of obtaining testing accommodations in chapter 11.

THE SAT SUBJECT TESTS

As we noted earlier in this chapter, the College Board offers one-hour, multiple-choice subject matter tests in addition to the SAT ranging from Physics to US History. Like each of the three parts of the SAT, the SAT Subject Tests are scored from 200 to 800, though the average scores vary widely and are usually much higher than the 500 average for the SAT sections. About 150 colleges require or recommend that students submit scores from one or more of these tests, including many of the colleges that are selective by our criteria. As we noted earlier, some colleges allow students to submit ACT scores in lieu of both the SAT and the SAT Subject Tests in recognition of the content-based nature of the ACT.

Virtually all of the colleges requiring or recommending Subject Tests ask students to submit scores from two different tests; only Georgetown University currently recommends three, and even that is a recommendation, not a requirement. Be sure to check each school's requirements because some schools specify certain tests. For example, Harvey Mudd College, which specializes in science and engineering, currently requires Mathematics Level 2 and a science test. Pomona College specifies that the two tests must be in different subject areas, so you can't take US History and World History or Chemistry and Biology to satisfy its requirement.

Preparing for the Tests

As content-based tests, the Subject Tests are designed to measure a student's mastery of a specific subject. Studying and reviewing can result in big improvements. The major test preparation companies offer courses to prepare students for some of the Subject Tests and, of course, private tutors do this as well. Test prep books and software programs are also available. Low-cost options can work just as well as more expensive alternatives if a student is willing to put in the time and effort to use them.

On any given test date, students are allowed to take the SAT by itself or up to three Subject Tests. You cannot take the SAT and Subject Tests on the same day. When you do register for Subject Tests, you don't have to specify in advance which test or tests you are going to take, although you have to indicate how many you plan to take and pay the corresponding fee. Subject Tests are offered on all of the SAT test dates except in March, but foreign language and world history tests are offered on certain dates only. Check the College Board website at www.college board.org to find out for sure. The basic registration fee for the Subject Tests is

$23, plus $12 for each individual test. Fee waivers are also available as usual for these tests. If you have been approved for accommodations on the SAT by the College Board, the approval extends to the SAT Subject Tests as well.

When Should You Take the Subject Tests?

Students should choose their Subject Tests carefully and plan to take appropriate tests when the subjects are freshest in their minds. Most students take the Subject Tests at the end of their junior year. However, depending on your high school curriculum, you may want to take one or more a year earlier if you have the right preparation. For example, if you take World History as a sophomore and feel you have mastered the subject, it makes sense to take the SAT World History Subject Test at the end of your sophomore year rather than wait. You can get very useful information about the Subject Tests, including sample questions and information about the content areas covered on each test, on the College Board website. Read this information carefully and decide which tests would be the best ones for you, keeping in mind the requirements of specific colleges in which you have an interest.

As a final note, it is certainly possible to take three Subject Tests on the same day, but it can be a tough morning. You can spread out your testing if you plan far enough in advance. If you take more than two Subject Tests, the colleges that require only two say that they will consider only the two highest scores, though they will see all of them unless you use Score Choice.

A WORD TO PARENTS ABOUT STANDARDIZED TESTS

There is a lot of anxiety about the SAT and ACT. High school students sometimes feel that their future and their self-esteem depend on the outcome of one four-hour test taken on a Saturday morning. This is not healthy for them, and it is not true. Please help your children understand that the SAT and ACT are just tests, and flawed ones at that. Encourage them to prepare thoroughly and reasonably for the tests and to do their best, but try to keep standardized tests from becoming an obsession for you or them.

Some students dread receiving their scores for fear of disappointing their parents or, at the other end of the continuum, providing their parents with a reason to brag or embarrass them. Try to avoid both extremes.

CHAPTER 7

Deciding About Early Decision and Other Early Options

Although most students apply to college by January 1 of their senior year and choose from among their options once they receive their decisions the following spring, more and more are taking advantage of early acceptance programs. *Early acceptance* is an umbrella term for options that require applying to a college early in the school year, typically by November 1 or November 15, in exchange for an early response from that college, usually by December 15.

AN OVERVIEW OF EARLY ACCEPTANCE PROGRAMS

The programs offered by different colleges vary in important ways. Some, known as early decision (ED), commit you to attending if you are admitted. You can apply ED to only one college since acceptance is binding. Another approach, early action (EA), allows you to receive the college's decision by mid-December, just as with ED, but it lets you have until May 1 to make your final decision. Most EA programs permit you to apply EA to more than one college as well and even submit one ED application. A third type, generically known as restrictive early action (REA) or single-choice early action, does not commit you to attend if accepted but it does restrict you from applying EA or ED to other colleges, depending on the college's particular form of REA. If you feel you need a scorecard to keep all of this straight, you are not alone. And the rules can change from year to year.

Over 600 colleges offer at least one of these options. About 50 colleges have both EA and ED programs: University of Miami, Earlham College, Trinity University, Ursinus College, Spelman College, and Hampshire College are examples. About 60 colleges, including Smith College, Rollins College, Bowdoin College, Vanderbilt University, Gettysburg College, and Tufts University, offer only ED but have two different dates: ED I, with an application date around November 15, and ED II, with an application date around January 1. And a few even offer three options: Dickinson College, Colorado College, and Goucher College, for example, offer two ED dates as well as an EA option.

Early acceptance programs, and ED in particular, have engendered a good deal of discussion and controversy. In this chapter, we tell you what the debate is all about, guide you in sorting out the options, and help you decide whether an early acceptance program is right for you.

> There are so many early options to keep straight and choose from. I think the whole thing should be called "early confusion."
>
> PARENT OF A HIGH SCHOOL JUNIOR

THE PROS AND CONS OF EARLY DECISION

On the surface, the rationale for ED admissions programs is simple: if you have a clear first-choice college, you can express that preference by applying early and committing to attend if admitted. If accepted, you can bypass much of the drawn-out anxiety lasting into the spring that can accompany regular decision applications. If the college says no (a denial) or "we are not sure" (a deferral of the decision until the regular application cycle), you can still apply to other colleges by the regular cycle deadline, though it helps if you are prepared to submit those applications before you receive the news. Although some colleges have had early programs for decades, they have become much more popular in the past 15 years.

The Advantages of Early Decision for the College and the Student

Early decision is part of the marketing plan for a college. Although it may look as if it mainly helps students (and it does indeed help those who are successful), the advantages are mostly on the side of the college, and more and more so as early programs become more popular and more competitive.

Why Colleges Offer Early Decision

From a college's perspective, ED enrolls students who are exceptionally eager to attend. The college also gets a good start at assembling a well-rounded class, since it knows that each student who is accepted early decision will indeed enroll in the fall. There is no guesswork involved in the yield from the pool of early decision acceptances: it is 100 percent, unless a student must decline because of insufficient financial aid or some other unforeseen difficulty. This gives a college a head start on planning to fill the rest of the class in regular decision: geography, athletics and other special talents, and legacy numbers are all under control after the early round.

Early decision also reduces enrollment uncertainty for a college. It can help a college minimize the problems associated with overenrollment or underenrollment, since it is impossible to predict precisely the yield for regular decision admits. From a competitive standpoint, it takes desirable students away from rival schools.

Advantages for the Student

It is not news that the percentage of students accepted through ED is usually higher, sometimes much higher, than the percentage accepted during the regular cycle. Students and their counselors watch classmates with equivalent records sometimes have very different outcomes in the admissions process according to when they applied. As a result, the number of ED applications has gone up dramatically over the past 15 years, increasing at a faster rate than the number of applications overall. As more and more apply early, the acceptance differential is getting smaller, but it can still be quite real depending on the college.

A successful ED application can mean admission to a student's first-choice college and an end to the anxiety and uncertainty of the college admissions process by mid-December of senior year. The process appears to efficiently match students who want a given college with a college that wants them, so everyone wins. But as with everything else in college admissions, the situation is not that simple.

> "I just want to go to sleep until December 15th."
>
> "I've taken up praying. I don't even believe in God."
>
> "I'd sell my soul—if I still had one."
>
> "Either the best moment in life, probably better than sex, or the worst moment, even worse than death."
>
> STUDENT COMMENTS ABOUT EARLY DECISION AND EARLY ACTION POSTED ON AN INTERNET BULLETIN BOARD

The Major Problems with Early Decision

Critics of ED point out that it has become something it was never intended to be: an admissions strategy that appears to increase the chances of being accepted to a selective college for those who are savvy enough to make use of it. Some colleges have admissions rates two or three times higher for ED applicants compared with regular decision applicants, and they fill from one-third to almost half of their freshman classes from the early pool. As a result, the much larger pool of regular decision applicants ends up competing for fewer slots well after the much smaller group of early applicants has secured their place.

Some colleges, including Johns Hopkins University, the University of Pennsylvania, and Cornell University, have also been open in telling legacy applicants that their legacy hook will count only if they apply early, reinforcing the idea of early decision as a strategy. As we'll see in chapter 10, the same situation sometimes applies for recruited athletes: they are told that they will lose their hook, even their space on the team, if they don't apply early.

> For those applicants who have already decided that the University of Pennsylvania is their first college choice and who agree to matriculate if accepted, we encourage application under the Early Decision Plan. Children of alumni also receive some preference under this plan in accordance with standard University policy.[1]
>
> UNIVERSITY OF PENNSYLVANIA INSTRUCTIONS TO UNDERGRADUATE APPLICANTS FOR THE CLASS OF 2017

Critics argue that ED favors students who do not need financial aid and have access to a support system (counselors, well-informed parents) that will assist them in identifying a top-choice college by early fall of the senior year so they can submit their application materials by the November deadlines. Students with limited financial means, who disproportionately attend poorly funded and overcrowded public schools, are much less likely to meet these criteria than students from private schools or high-performing public high schools.

Students who are accepted ED also have potentially limited financial aid options. Although you can be released from an ED commitment if the college's financial aid package is inadequate, ED does not give students with significant financial need a chance to compare financial aid offers from several schools, and perhaps even obtain a more desirable package at one school based on the offer from another. In contrast, students who can pay the full sticker price of admission don't have this concern.

More Thoughts About Early Decision

Counselors cringe when they hear students say, "I want to apply early—I just don't know where," because it shows that students feel great pressure to make a choice, any choice, perhaps prematurely, to maximize their chances of admission to a selective college without adequate thought to the qualities of the college, except perhaps its prestige. Once students do pick a school and apply, the pressure builds, often intensely, up through the notification date. Students tend to think, often correctly, that an ED application is their best shot at their dream school. They greet acceptance with great joy, while they absorb denial and deferral, which are far more common outcomes, all too often with despair.

Everyone agrees that you should be absolutely sure of your first-choice college before applying ED because it is binding: you can't change your mind after being accepted. The best way to be sure, of course, is to learn as much as possible about colleges and visit them in person, ideally when they are in session and well before the ED deadline. To be a good ED candidate, you need to begin early, preferably by the spring of junior year, learning about ED options and deadlines. It also helps considerably to have the time and money to visit schools to see whether one emerges as a clear front-runner.

> I was surprised there was such a consistent result—that all of the colleges were favoring early applications. I was also surprised by the magnitude of the advantage.[2]
>
> CHRISTOPHER AVERY, PROFESSOR OF PUBLIC POLICY AT HARVARD UNIVERSITY AND COAUTHOR OF *THE EARLY ADMISSIONS GAME*

You will also have to have all your standardized testing done by October of your senior year. November tests may not arrive in time, even if you rush the scores to the college for a November 1 or November 15 application deadline. And you will generally have to have a solid first quarter (or first half of the first semester) in your senior year. Colleges may base their decision on grades only through junior year, although some will want to see how an early applicant is doing as a senior. If your school hasn't already sent first-quarter grades, such colleges may request them from your counselor before making a decision. The same is true for some colleges that use other forms of early acceptance (EA and rolling admissions), which we will discuss later in this chapter.

I didn't really know about early decision until I started hearing other kids talking about it in late October. They were all moaning about having to ask for letters of recommendation and worrying that the teachers wouldn't send them in on time. I couldn't see the point of all that drama, until someone explained to me that I might have a better chance if I applied early admission . . . like maybe if the college knew I wanted them, they would want me. So I started to feel pressure to "want" some place, but really I hadn't visited many, and the only place I really liked, I liked because my buddy was going there. I visited him once and we went to a cool party. I mean, maybe that means the atmosphere was right for me—you know, people I could get along with—but I don't know. And my parents flipped out when I said that maybe I'd just apply early decision to Jerry's school.

Anyway, I didn't apply early decision anywhere, so now it's March, and I'm getting awfully antsy because I don't know where I will be going in the fall yet. But that is better than picking a school for the wrong reason, getting in, and then having to go there because you applied early decision. I just wish I had gotten started earlier on the whole thing.

HIGH SCHOOL SENIOR

I wish I would have known how early early applications were due. It seemed as though the year had just begun and I was already applying for college.

COMMENT MADE IN THE SPRING OF SENIOR YEAR

EARLY ACTION IN DETAIL

In contrast to early decision, early action appears to offer a student the best of both worlds: no binding commitment but still an early response from a desired college. Early action has also been offered for many years.

How Does EA Differ from ED?

The major difference between EA and ED is that students accepted through EA can wait until May 1 to decide whether to attend; the acceptance is not binding. In the meantime, students are free to apply to other colleges through the regular process and can compare financial aid packages before making a final choice. Early action colleges have traditionally also allowed students to apply to other early programs—a maximum of one ED college as well as other EA schools.

Early Action with Restrictions

Some EA colleges do place restrictions, however, on the other schools to which you can apply. The most limiting are restrictive early action and single-choice early action (both terms are used) employed by Harvard University, Stanford University, Princeton University, and Yale University. Under these plans, you may not apply EA *or* ED to any other college (with a few exceptions, such as schools with nonbinding rolling admissions, discussed later in this chapter, or state universities with EA plans). In another form of restrictive early action, used by Boston College and Georgetown University, students may not apply ED to another campus, although they are free to apply EA elsewhere.

Keeping Your Commitment

Students who apply ED or EA with restrictions must honor the commitments of those application choices. Colleges typically ask students to sign a statement as part of their application indicating that they understand and agree to the terms of that program. Some require a parent and the student's high school counselor to sign the statement as well.

COMPARING EARLY APPLICATION OPTIONS

	Early Decision	Early Action	Restrictive Early Action
Binding?	Yes (except if financial aid is not adequate)	No	No
Allows comparisons of aid packages?	No	Yes	Yes
Allows other early applications	Yes (EA applications only)	Yes (EA applications and one ED)	Varies by college
Allows regular decision applications?	Yes (these must be withdrawn if the student is admitted ED)	Yes	Yes

Note: Be sure to check the instructions for specific colleges.

SHOULD YOU APPLY EARLY DECISION OR EARLY ACTION?

Early decision programs can work to your advantage if you (1) have a clear first-choice college that emerges after careful research, (2) don't need grades from the first semester of your senior year to bolster your academic record, (3) have the organizational skills and time needed to submit a strong early application, and (4) are not concerned about comparing financial aid offers. If you can satisfy all of these conditions and you are accepted come December 15, your college admissions process can conclude happily months before it otherwise would. Add the bonus of an increased chance of acceptance to begin with, and ED becomes something to seriously think about.

Early action, restrictive or otherwise, is more flexible, since an acceptance implies no commitment. An EA application is a good way to show "demonstrated interest" to a college. The admissions boost from an EA application will likely be smaller than you might receive from a comparable ED application, but you retain much more flexibility in your final decision making if you are accepted. You may still want to apply to a few other colleges you prefer more, but you can do so knowing that you have an acceptance in hand.

But an early application of either sort has a downside that we haven't yet discussed: the pressure to identify a single college for an early application can be intense. You end up thinking that there is only one college that is a "perfect fit" for you and that you must discover it and chase it with vigor. As more and more students apply early, however, more will be disappointed by denials or deferrals. For some students, the buildup has been so great and so much seems to be at stake that either of these last outcomes can be a major blow. Previously successful students lose perspective as they face, often for the first time in their lives, what they perceive as significant failure. In contrast, at regular decision time, your denials or wait listings will be buffered by some good news as well. Applying to several colleges also negates the idea of a perfect match: you see several colleges as a good fit. After all, why wouldn't you thrive at more than one college?

Not everyone gets into Ivy U, but even so it's not like the 5,000 students at Ivy U are the only ones who are happy with their college and will go on to success in life. While I eagerly hope for my deferral to turn into an acceptance, I know that I have to look at my other options as a definite possibility so my college experience is not haunted by the ghost of Ivy U.

COMMENT MADE ON DECEMBER 16 BY
STUDENT DEFERRED AT AN IVY LEAGUE COLLEGE

So where does this leave you? Well, it depends. If you have a first-choice college and satisfy the criteria for ED or EA we have noted, you may want to seriously think about applying early. If you would be a competitive applicant, there are clear advantages to doing so. But please remember what we said about the downside of early applications: don't let your enthusiasm for a college let you succumb to early acceptance syndrome—the belief that there is one, and only one, college where you can truly be happy. That is rarely, if ever, the case.

⊠ Is Early Decision Right for You?

☐ I have a clear first-choice college and am completely confident that it is a very good fit for me.

☐ I have done careful research about the college that supports my choice, including most of the following: visited in-person or on the web; studied the catalog, view book, and other material in detail; reviewed the college's profile in a big college guide; and talked with current or former students in person, through online chat, or e-mail.

☐ I will probably be comfortable with the financial aid that is offered to me and won't have to compare financial aid offers.

☐ My grades from first-semester senior year will not be significantly better than the rest of my record, and my first-quarter grades will be consistent or better than my previous work.

☐ I will have taken my standardized tests by October so that the scores will reach my early decision college in time for early review.

☐ My overall record places me within the admissible range for this college.

☐ I will be able to prepare and submit my application by the ED deadline, including letters of recommendation from my teachers and counselor.

☐ I know that ED candidates appear to get a boost in acceptance from this college.

☐ I would like to know for sure where I will be going to college as early as possible.

☐ I will do careful research on the rest of my college list and prepare applications to them in case I am deferred or denied in early decision.

☐ Although my early decision college is my clear first choice, I realize that I may not be accepted, and I know I will also be very happy and get a fine education at other colleges.

MORE THINGS TO CONSIDER

Much of what we have just presented changes frequently. As more students become aware of the early admissions boost, more are trying to take advantage of it. At the same time, some colleges are cutting back on the percentage of the freshman class admitted through the early cycle. It's like what happens when word starts to spread far and wide about a wonderful neighborhood restaurant that has always had tables available. The restaurant may need to start taking reservations that will be harder and harder to get as its reputation grows. The early admissions boost is decreasing and may eventually disappear at many schools.

But what others are doing or not doing shouldn't really matter. If you think a college is truly your first choice, whether there is an advantage to applying early shouldn't make much difference in your decision, as long as you are a competitive applicant and you meet the other criteria we have discussed. We also want to emphasize that even if you do apply ED or EA to your first-choice school, you should carefully consider where else to apply at the same time. December 15 is too late to decide on other colleges and begin your applications in the event #1 declines or defers your application.

Get Your Other Applications Prepared

One of the arguments often offered in favor of ED is that it can eliminate the need to complete additional applications. This just doesn't hold up in reality for a lot of students. Many regular decision applications are due January 1 or soon after. Starting new applications after December 15, during the holiday season, isn't an appealing option, especially after receiving a disappointing decision from a first-choice college.

Many students find themselves applying regular decision to their full array of college choices although they have an early application pending. If an ED application is successful, they must withdraw those additional applications. The extra effort and expense are written off as the cost of "insurance." Others complete their additional applications, but hold off on submitting them until they have heard back from their ED school. Either approach can work.

How to Handle Denial or Deferral

If you are denied early, you are done with that college. You cannot reapply in the regular round or ED II. They have decided that they know enough about you to make a final decision. If you are deferred from ED, you are released from your binding commitment. Then you are held in limbo for several months while the admissions staff reads all the regular applications. Finally, in late winter, you are considered again with the regular applicants who are roughly equal to you.

Many students see a deferral as a hopeful sign that they will be admitted in the spring. They submit letters with information about their first-semester grades (which must be sent when available), their latest extracurricular involvement, and their continued desire to attend the college. Some are admitted in the end, but most are not. It is good not to bank too much on a deferral. Sometimes a clear denial is a blessing in disguise: it allows you to move on and not risk being disappointed twice by the same college. Colleges vary a great deal in the proportions they deny and defer. Some deny no one in the early round. Others deny a great many. As regular applications continue to increase, the trend is toward denying more students in the early round so there are fewer applications to read at the end of the process.

Schools with Two Early Rounds

As we noted earlier, a number of schools have two rounds of early decision, ED I and ED II. The date for ED II often coincides with the date for regular decision applications, but of course the ED II applicants get their decisions earlier, usually by mid-February, and are committed to attending if they are accepted, just as in ED I. Colleges offering two rounds of ED say that they do this to give students more time to decide on a first choice. Although this no doubt helps many students, an additional reason for a college to have a second ED round is to receive applications from students denied or deferred on December 15 by another college. This approach gives both colleges and students two shots at making an early match. The ED II school will not know you applied early somewhere else.

LIKELY LETTERS AND EARLY NOTIFICATION

Colleges differ in the timing of their regular decision cycle notifications, with most notifying students between March 1 and early April in time for you to make a choice by May 1.

Greetings from Duke University! I am delighted to tell you that the Admissions Committee has reviewed your application, and I want to share with you the good news that you are one of a small group of particularly outstanding applicants to Duke this year, a remarkable accomplishment in a pool of over 31,500. Indeed, as long as you maintain the academic and personal standards reflected in your application, the Admissions Committee fully expects to formally offer you admission later this spring.

FROM A DUKE UNIVERSITY LIKELY LETTER FOR THE CLASS OF 2016

A Heads-Up on Admission

But a few students who apply regular decision get letters early—sometimes very early—that tell them that they are very likely to be accepted, even though it is not a formal letter of admission. Known in admissions circles as "likely letters," these early notifications allow a college to adhere to the letter of the official notification date while signaling to a select group of students that the college is especially interested in them.

Colleges hope that a likely letter will increase the chances that the student receiving it will accept the official offer of admission when it arrives later. Likely letters go to those the college is especially eager to recruit: athletes, members of underrepresented groups, and others who present with truly distinctive academic credentials. If you receive a likely letter, and only a very small percentage of accepted students do, you will be admitted unless you do something horrific, like get caught cheating or using drugs. It is tantamount to admission.

> Even in an applicant pool of 31,000 plus, some candidates are going to stand out to the highest degree. We're identifying those students who are going to have a lot of options when decisions roll in.[3]
>
> ERIC FURDA, DEAN OF ADMISSIONS AT THE UNIVERSITY OF PENNSYLVANIA, COMMENTING ON LIKELY LETTERS

Early Notification

Still other colleges, such as Swarthmore College, Williams College, and the University of Southern California, formally admit some regular decision cycle applicants a month or so earlier than others. Students do not apply for this kind of early notification. The college just decides. Yet another program is early evaluation. Wellesley College offers students the option of formally requesting an early assessment of the likelihood of admission. If you apply by January 1 rather than the regular deadline of January 15, you will receive a letter at the end of February that lists your chances for admission as "likely," "possible," or "unlikely."

The large majority of those accepted at colleges, however, receive their only notification on the previously announced date. Regardless of the timing of notification, all students who apply EA or regular decision have until May 1 to make a final decision.

THE ADVANTAGE OF THINKING EARLY EVEN IF YOU DECIDE AGAINST APPLYING EARLY

Many students habitually cut things close to the wire, and they extend that habit to the college application process. But even if you do not plan to apply early to a college, it may help to get your application in well before the deadline.

The most obvious example of the advantage of submitting an application well before a formal deadline can be found in schools that use rolling admissions. Some colleges read applications as they arrive rather than waiting until a fixed deadline when they can compare applications to each other. Used at many state universities and some private colleges, rolling admissions allows a college to accept qualified students until the freshman class is full. Clearly, in these cases, applying early is better than applying at or close to the deadline so that your application will be considered while there is still plenty of room.

But there are other advantages to getting your application in well before the deadline for any college. Even if you are applying regular decision to a college with a January 1 deadline, you can submit your application as early as you want once the applications are available. Of course, the college will not read it until your transcript, recommendations, and test scores have arrived as well. Getting your materials in early even if you want regular cycle review means that they will arrive earlier than the deadline crunch and be processed and acknowledged earlier (and be more likely to make it successfully to your electronic file rather than go astray). You will usually be able to check online to see if all parts of your application have arrived. These websites are notoriously slow, however, due to the volume of materials, and they may show something as missing when it simply hasn't been recorded yet. But if something does end up missing, you'll have lots of time to get a replacement sent.

Because admissions committees start reading complete files soon after the closing date, your application will be read by staff members who are fresh, not yet fatigued by the many hundreds of files they will read during the winter months. It's impossible to know, of course, if that will make any difference in the final decision, but it can't hurt. Getting applications in early also means that you can enjoy the holiday season with your family rather than spend it worrying about applications. We think you (and your family) will be glad you took this path.

AND HUMOR ALWAYS HELPS KEEP THINGS IN PERSPECTIVE

Mike Mills, former director of admission at Miami University of Ohio and now at Northwestern University, penned the following parody for the *Journal of College Admission*. We enjoyed it and hope you will too.

⊠ From an Application in the Future

Term applying for: Fall 2022_____   Spring 2023_____   Application Fee: $300

Applying for:

Priority Decision[1]_____   Regular Decision[2]_____   Precision Decision[3]_____

Division Decision[4]_____   Revision Decision[5]_____   Provision Decision[6]_____

Derision Decision[7]_____   Rescission Decision[8]_____

[1] Yes! Beyond the tangible benefit of earlier notification, I want to receive all other attendant (albeit ambiguous) benefits of applying under this plan. I also want to keep my options open while avoiding the stigma of applying under the Regular Decision plan.

[2] I want to keep all my options open, and I refuse to be a pawn in your silly admission game.

[3] This is exactly the school I'm looking for, and I will enroll if accepted.

[4] My parents and I fought long and hard over whether I should apply to this school, and it is your job to figure out who won.

[5] I like this school, but I may opt to attend a better school should I be admitted to one.

[6] I like this school and will attend provided you ante up with some significant scholarship dollars. I know you have the endowment to do it.

[7] I'm applying, but don't fool yourselves—you're definitely my back-up school.

[8] I'm applying, but I may and likely will cancel my application at some point in time.

Adapted from Mike Mills, "Applications We Hope Never to See." *Journal of College Admission*, Winter 2004, Number 182. Reprinted with permission. Copyright 2004 National Association for College Admission Counseling.

CHAPTER 8

Applying Well, Part I

The Application and the Essay

I f you've read to this point in *Admission Matters* you know it is important to do a lot of self-reflection and research before you begin applying to college. But once you have done that work and developed an appropriate list of good-bet, possible, and long-shot colleges, the next step is tackling the applications themselves.

You'll want to present your qualifications to college admissions committees in a way that will distinguish you from the many other applicants with similar credentials. In this chapter and the next, we will help you do just that. We'll look at the application process in general and guide you through writing your important personal statement and other essays, both long and short. In chapter 9, we'll continue with other parts of your application and tell you how to get strong letters of recommendation prepare an activities list that sets you apart, and shine in an interview. In chapter 10, we'll also have tips for athletes and for students with other special talents.

Preparing a strong college application takes work. There's no way of getting around that. A typical application asks many questions, and your answers tell a lot about your academic abilities, background, talents, and interests. Less obviously, your answers also send subtle messages about your degree of interest in a college and how much time and effort you have put into thinking about yourself. The best applications do both.

GETTING OFF TO A GOOD START

Although the competition for admission to selective schools is greater than ever before, the actual process of filing an application has never been easier. Almost every college now not only accepts but actively encourages electronic submission of applications. Some even waive their application fees if you submit online. Colleges use technology very differently in the application process, but the trend is clearly toward a paperless process where materials are submitted electronically and read from a computer screen.

Gone, fortunately for good, are the days when students prepared an application with a typewriter and a bottle of correction fluid. Many parents reading this may remember how hard the old-fashioned way was. It is a major advantage to be able to easily update and edit your application right up until you submit it. It can now be as complete and accurate as you can make it, without having to go through the agony of starting everything over because you forgot to include something or changed your mind about how to phrase an answer.

> I left my most important college application to the day before it was due. I planned to rework an essay I had written for a college that had an earlier deadline, so I wasn't too worried. After spending all day Sunday putting everything together, I was ready to submit my application electronically at 9:00 p.m. Then I realized the program cut off the last seven sentences of my essay. No matter what I did, I couldn't get the whole thing in. My mom looked at the essay, and we agreed that it would be really hard to cut. She suggested I look at the paper app— maybe it would fit in there. It did. I then spent the next two hours filling out the paper app by hand and doing cut-and-paste onto the form for my essay. It was after 11:00 p.m. when I finished. I had school the next day, but my mom mailed it for me and met the postmark deadline. I was accepted and am now a sophomore. But even I agreed I cut things too close. I could have really blown it.
>
> College sophomore

Fight the Urge to Procrastinate

Certainly completing a college application is not fun. It is hard to answer all those questions and distill yourself into little boxes of 200 words or 300 characters on a form. It also takes precious time, something often in short supply in senior year. And on top of it all, just thinking about college, as exciting as it may be, can make you nervous. *Where will I be next year?* you wonder. *Will I make friends? Will I be happy?*

The natural tendency in a situation like this is to put off dealing with it as long as possible. Our simple advice is DON'T. Do your research on colleges early, and begin the actual job of applying. Fight the urge to procrastinate. Everyone experiences it—including us, the authors of this book, as we tackled the job of preparing this revision and found it was tougher than we thought it would be. But procrastination never helps, and it can really hurt if it means that you assembled your college list hastily and it does not really fit your needs or that you rush to meet a deadline and do a sloppy job. Procrastination can result in missed opportunities, such as when your favorite teacher regrets that she won't have time to write your letter of recommendation because you asked her too late. It can mean less thoughtful (and usually more wordy) answers to questions, since you won't have time to carefully review and edit them, or benefit from feedback from others. Overall it can mean that you don't make your best case for admission.

The wise student starts early, makes a time line indicating what is needed and by when, and then just gets it done.

Neatness and Completeness Count!

The ease with which an application can be filled out online and submitted electronically can lead to carelessness in proofreading and failure to double-check everything for accuracy. We are all familiar with that problem in our daily e-mail. We just want to hit Send and be done with it. Resist the urge. Typos, omissions, and other errors can mar an otherwise good application. In particular, you want to avoid having your great response to the question about why you want to attend Hamilton College mention that you find the core curriculum at St. John's College exciting. Because Hamilton College has no core curriculum, the mistake is even more embarrassing. Errors of this kind, and worse, routinely happen when word processors are used to cut and paste from one application to another. Electronic applications make the process easier, but they can also make mistakes easier.

Mistakes can also happen when you are hastily filling out a lot of applications close to a deadline. An error-filled, incomplete application practically shouts, "I didn't take this application seriously." Why, then, should the

> "For years, parents, teachers, guidance counselors, school administrators, and members of the school board have been urging teenagers to abstain from sex or to use condiments."
>
> At least the student used spell check.
>
> ACTUAL SENTENCE FROM A COLLEGE APPLICATION REPORTED BY AN ADMISSIONS OFFICER[1]

college? So before hitting Submit, carefully proofread everything yourself and have a friend or parent proofread it as well. And then proofread it again. Sure, it's tedious, but why be sloppy when the outcome is so important to you?

Follow Directions

Be sure to read the application carefully and answer the questions that are asked, not other ones. In an effort to economize on work, you may want to recycle answers from one application to another. This is fine, as long as you make sure that the same questions are being asked and, as we just noted, you are careful to remove any specific references to the first college in your answer! This is especially important in switching from an early action or early decision application to a regular one, because you may have identified your first choice in your essay.

Following directions also means being aware of limits on the length of responses and the number of recommendation letters. We'll discuss how to approach these limits later in this chapter and in chapter 9.

USING THE COMMON APPLICATION

The Common Application is an application form accepted by more than 500 public and private colleges across the country. Although most participants are private colleges, public colleges are adopting it with increasing frequency. The Ohio State University, the University of Vermont, and Colorado State University are examples.

The Common Application was designed to simplify the college admissions process for students who would otherwise have to provide identical information in different formats to each college. Some schools that use it offer applicants a choice between their own form and the Common Application, but most now use the Common Application exclusively. A few private, selective colleges (for example, Georgetown University and MIT) still don't accept the Common Application, but the number is dwindling.

Using the Common Application can save you a lot of time, since you complete a single online application regardless of the number of schools to which you apply. Many Common Application colleges also require a Writing Supplement, however, that asks you to provide short-answer or essay-length responses to one or more college-specific questions. It is also the way to submit résumés, research papers, and graded assignments to colleges that specifically invite them. The Writing Supplement for a given school is submitted separately after the Common Application is submitted to that school.

Changes to the Common Application

Be sure to check the Common Application website, www.commonapp.org, for the list of participating schools as well as the application itself. For the 2013–2014 admissions cycle, the Common Application unveiled a major technological overhaul as well as some significant changes to its content. Probably of greatest interest to applicants are the essay prompts, which may now vary somewhat from year to year. The Common Application plans to announce the prompts for the next application cycle in March of each year, with the application itself being available on August 1. The prompts and instructions for 2013–2014 are found in Appendix B.

Students sometimes ask whether colleges that use both the Common App and their own form actually prefer their own form and if submitting the Common Application will imply that students are less interested in a college than they might really be. In fact, colleges that accept the Common Application pay a fee for the privilege. They also pledge to treat all applications, the Common Application and their own if they still have one, identically. Go ahead and use the Common App.

The Universal Application

Another type of generic application, known as the Universal College Application, is also available. Currently about 50 schools participate; forms and member colleges can be found at www.universalcollegeapp.com. Some colleges accept both the Common Application and the Universal Application, but most colleges on the Universal College Application list don't use the Common Application. If your college list contains one or more schools in this latter category, consider using the Universal College Application in lieu of or in addition to the Common Application, depending on the other colleges to which you are applying.

WRITING AN EFFECTIVE PERSONAL ESSAY

Many college application forms, including the Common Application, require one essay or personal statement. Some require more. In this section, we show you how to approach the essay as an opportunity for self-understanding, not just as a burdensome but mandatory assignment. Although colleges differ in the emphasis they place on the essay, it can always make a difference. Its importance may also vary for different students because of the strength of their credentials. At most schools where your grades and scores are at the top of that college's pool, a so-so essay won't be too damaging, but at the most selective schools, it always matters, since hardly anyone is admitted by grades and tests alone.

Why Do Colleges Ask for Essays?

Colleges see the essay as a way for you to personalize your application and give it life. Along with your letters of recommendation, your essay helps admissions officers differentiate you from many others with similar records. It is a chance to share something special about yourself that will help the reader conclude that you would make a wonderful addition to the next freshman class. It can also demonstrate to a college that you can express yourself effectively and persuasively in writing—a skill that is crucial for success in college. Harry Bauld, author of a delightful book on college admissions essays, sums up the essay as follows: "It shows you at your alive and thinking best, a person worth listening to—not just for the ten minutes it takes to read your application, but for the next four years."[3]

> What exactly do admissions officers want to know when they ask you to write the college essay? No matter which question, we are asking what is really important to you, who you are, and how you arrived where you are. The whole college application process is really a self-exploration, and the essay is a way to put your personal adventure into words.[2]
>
> DELSIE PHILLIPS, FORMER DIRECTOR OF ADMISSIONS AT HAVERFORD COLLEGE

The problem with advice like this is that it is hard to follow when you get down to the individual who is you. You realize that you should be honest, open, and tell the truth, but you also realize that you are trying to make a good impression on the readers. How can you do both? How can you avoid being stiff and impersonal, sort of like an awkward first date, as you try to make a good impression? How can you be sure you aren't making yourself too vulnerable if you admit you are not perfect? It's hard, but those are important questions to think about. In considering them, you are more likely to write a self-reflective and thoughtful essay. If you ignore the dilemma, you might err on one side or the other. Many students are so intent on being well perceived that they write bland, unengaging essays, thinking that as long as they are telling the truth, they are doing fine.

The Three Types of Questions

Sarah McGinty, a consultant specializing in workshops on writing college essays, points out that most college essays boil down to one of three types: some version of "tell us about yourself," some variety of "Why us?" in terms of college or career choice, or a "creative" question that asks you to reflect on some topic that seems

---

⊠ Sample Essay Topics

"Tell Us About Yourself" Essays

- "We honor the many different forms of diversity in our community. Your perspective is valuable because it comes from your life experiences, family background, and culture. Please tell us about yourself, how you plan to share your perspective with the Colgate community, and what you hope to learn from other members of the community." (Colgate University, 2012–2013)

- "Filling out college applications is time consuming and requires a lot of thought. Let's go back to a time when learning was a pure joy. Please tell us your favorite childhood book and why." (Kalamazoo College, 2012–2013)

"Why Us?" Essays

- "What about Scripps College has inspired you to apply?" (Scripps College, 2012–2013)

- "Reed is a unique and exciting college experience. Discuss the reasons that you believe Reed would be an appropriate place to continue your education." (Reed College, 2012–2013)

"Be Creative" Essays

- "'A man cannot be too careful in the choice of his enemies.' (Oscar Wilde). Othello and Iago. Dorothy and the Wicked Witch. Autobots and Decepticons. History and art are full of heroes and their enemies. Tell us about the relationship between you and your arch-enemies (either real or imagined)." (University of Chicago, 2012–2013)

- "Why did you do it?" (Tufts University, 2012–2013)

---

only tangentially related to the college admissions process, if at all. McGinty emphasizes that regardless of the form of the question, each is trying to get information about you.[4] What you choose to write tells the reader a great deal about how you think, what your life experiences have been, and what you value.

Selecting a Topic

In writing your essay, focus on yourself, not on what you think colleges want to hear. Who are you? What makes you tick deep inside? What do you want them to know about you? Think about the qualities you want to convey, and then think about how to represent those qualities in your answer to the question. Ideally, your essay should illustrate your points through personal example rather than simply state them; the old advice still holds: show; don't tell.

A Good Essay Tells a Story

Many good essays are essentially stories, based on a personal experience. Storytelling comes naturally to us, more easily than essay writing. The trick is to make it lively and interesting to read. You want the reader to think, "I would like to get to know this person." Or: "She sounds as if she would be a fun student to teach or have in a dorm or on a team." The problem is that you are so close to yourself that it is hard to see how a benevolent stranger reading your essay might view you.

Admissions readers like their work. Nobody does it for the money or the glory. They also like teenagers, and they are open-minded enough to realize that they come in different shapes and sizes and think differently. Trusting your reader to be interested and positive is reasonable. She is not an enemy to be tricked or a gullible target to be wowed. She may be young enough to clearly remember high school herself, or she may have teenage children of her own. Treat admissions officers as human beings, and they will respond in kind.

Common Themes

The standard admissions prompts, on both the Common Application and elsewhere, are purposely very broad to encourage freethinking. Certainly when students write about a piece of literature, they tend to use something familiar, such as the Bible, Shakespeare, or *The Great Gatsby*. Or if they write about a person, they are likely to choose a grandparent or a famous person like John F. Kennedy or Martin Luther King Jr. These choices are fine, IF you have an original approach to the subject. But it doesn't hurt to choose something off the familiar path as long as the choice matters to you personally. It is even all right to write about a book or music that the reader might not be familiar with, as long as you explain why it matters to you. Writing about Charlemagne or an Edith Wharton novel doesn't do any good if it doesn't reflect your ideas and self.

Not surprisingly, certain themes appear often in college application essays. Among them are "How My Summer Trip to _____ Changed My Life," "Winning [or Losing] the Race [or Game, or Election]," or "The Death of My Beloved _____." These topics, and other common ones, are not necessarily bad. In fact, there are almost no bad topics, just weak essays. A weak college essay tells the reader little about what makes the writer an interesting, unique person. The more common your essay topic is, the greater your burden is in writing something different from what the large number of other applicants tackling the same topic are writing.

Looking Inward

A topic more unique or personal to you, no matter how small it may be, is often easier to make distinctive and interesting. Fine essays have been written on topics as simple as a weekly walk with an aging grandparent, working with young children in a summer camp, and cooking a meal for a special friend. In fact, given the tremendous volume of applications at most schools, there are probably few truly uncommon topics any more. Searching for one is likely to be frustrating because you can never know what someone in Spokane or Savannah is writing about. So don't worry about it.

One counselor we know challenges students to write about the time they saved someone from drowning at the beach and made the six o'clock news as a hero. Since this never happened, they naturally look puzzled. "Look," he says, "you are a normal teenager who has led a normal life with no great tragedies, thank goodness, and no Nobel Prize at sixteen either. You have to write about something in your mundane everyday life. The solution is to look inside yourself, not out 'there,' for a topic."

What to Avoid

Some topics, though, are best avoided altogether, no matter how distinctive your approach. You should almost always avoid writing about sexual experiences, rape, incest, or mental illness. Don't write to express your pain. We feel a little differently about very controversial political and social issues such as abortion. Just be careful that you come across as a person of thought, not just conviction, which means that you have considered opposing arguments and are not an ideologue who knows the truth and doesn't want to hear any opposition. If you can't tell the difference, pick something less sensitive to write about. You don't know who your readers will be, and it is foolish to write about a topic that may make a reader uncomfortable.

Be sure, though, that you answer the question that is asked, not some other one. Although the questions are all asking about you, directly or indirectly, they vary in how they frame their inquiry. Your essay should address the question the way it is asked. An essay written for one prompt can often be reworked to fit another one, however, so you may be able to use a good essay in different ways for different colleges, saving you time and effort. Just be sure to modify your essay carefully each time you reuse it. This is particularly true of the supplements asking why you like a particular college, as we mentioned earlier. Although you might want to major in biology at each college, you will want to show that you know that one college has a research facility at the seashore and another has a forest.

> My son's girlfriend was hanging around the house bemoaning the fact that she had nothing to write about in her essay. I said, "But you like reading. You like the classics. I remember how upset you were when other kids said they didn't like *Jane Eyre*." I knew if she wrote about books, her essay would show real passion.
>
> FORMER WRITING TEACHER WHO KNOWS THAT MANY HIGH SCHOOL STUDENTS DON'T ENJOY THE CLASSICS

⌧ Essay Don'ts

- Don't write an essay that any one of a thousand other seniors could write, because they probably will (*and are probably doing just that at this very moment*).

- Avoid writing an essay that might embarrass or annoy the reader. While you definitely must risk something personally to write an effective essay, the risk should not place a burden on the reader. *Don't confess something too personal that you haven't completely worked through in your own mind. Any risk you take should not make the reader uncomfortable.*

- Don't try to sell yourself. Rather than persuading the college that you are great, just show them who you are, what you care about, what the pivotal points in your life have been so far. *Remember you are just a high school senior who puts his shoes on one at a time like everyone else. You are also a person, not a box of corn flakes. You are not "packaging" yourself. This is one of the worst metaphors in the admissions field, and we are embarrassed that some writers and counselors don't see anything wrong with "packaging" yourself. The difference between presenting and packaging yourself is a subtle one. It can be hard to tell when you are going too far in the latter direction, but you must be aware of the possibility.*

- Don't try to write an "important" essay—the definitive statement on the Middle East, American race relations, or climate change. These essays tend to come across as much more impersonal than the authors intend. *Honestly, what do you have to say about the Middle East or climate change that they haven't heard before? But perhaps a relative served in the army in Iraq, or you are a leader of your high school's environmental club. It is the personal connection that counts, not whether you are on the "right" side of an issue. Don't assume the reader shares your views either. You are entitled to an opinion, but be sure it is a reasoned, thoughtful one, even if you take on a hot-button issue like religion, abortion, or gay rights. Colleges are places of debate and the exchange of ideas; admission officers want students with different views as long as they are intelligent, reasonable, and civil.*

- Don't set out to write the perfect essay, the one with huge impact, the one that will blow the doors to the college open for you. Think instead of giving the reader a sample of yourself, a slice of the real you, a snapshot in words. *Remember, essays don't often have that kind of impact. They are just one personal piece of a bigger file. Remember also that you can't put everything in your life into 500 words. You have to select, you have to figure out what is most important, and you have to leave out some things that you like and that you would like them to know. Then you have to make it "sing."*

Source: Annotated in italics and adapted with permission from "What Not to Do and Why" by William Poirot, former college counselor, in 100 Successful College Application Essays, New York: Penguin, 2002. Copyright © The Harvard Independent.

What Kind of Help Is Appropriate?

Colleges expect that the essays you submit with your application are your own work. They ask you to sign a statement to that effect on the application. This doesn't mean that you can't brainstorm ideas for the essays with your family, friends, teachers, and school counselor. Nor does it mean that you can't get comments from others once you have written a draft. In fact, most professional writers go through several drafts and get comments and reactions from others along the way. It makes good sense to write a draft, put it away for a few days, and then revisit it. William Zinsser, author of *On Writing Well*, says that there is no such thing as good writing, only good rewriting.[5]

Almost by definition, a first draft is going to be rough, so give yourself enough time to get some feedback. Your English teacher or high school counselor can be especially helpful in making suggestions about your essays because they are professionals who evaluate writing for a living and have seen many essays over the years. They also observe natural boundaries when it comes to students' writing. They know when to stop and how to let the student's voice stay intact.

Parents can sometimes lose sight of this and set about trying to rewrite their child's essays. Although help with brainstorming and editing is good, wholesale rewriting is not. It can hurt much more than help. It can rob a student of his distinctive voice—something that admissions officers really want to hear—and signal that the parent doesn't think the child can do the job himself. The important point, however, is that the end product should be your own work and sound like you, not someone else two or three times your age, no matter who it is.

Pay Attention to the Shorter Essays

The typical application includes one or two 500 to 650-word essays and a few questions to be answered in a paragraph or less. Many students focus all their effort on the long essays, leaving the shorter ones to the very end when they are rushed and trying to meet a deadline. In fact, shorter questions are important as well, because both short and long essays give the reader insights into who you are.

Pay attention to the shorter questions, and edit and proofread them just as you would the long essays. Colleges using the Common Application may ask for a short paragraph on an extracurricular activity or work experience as part of their Writing Supplement. This can be a challenge since you have to be very stingy with words. Although it is probably not as important as your main essay, everything counts in the end, so take it seriously and try to give it some flair and personality.

Colleges may also include a "Why X?" question where they ask how their individual college appeals to you. You should respond very carefully to these questions. Colleges ask them for a reason, even if you don't like them. They are trying to assess your motivation and your thoughtfulness. A good answer shows that you have carefully researched the college and thought about what you would get from it, as well as contribute to it. A vague answer shows lack of real interest or homework.

Admissions staff members are naturally experts on their own colleges. Don't tell them things that are obvious or just not very interesting: Boston University is in Boston, for example, and you love Boston! A good answer may never mention Boston; it discusses something specific about Boston University that reveals something interesting about you. Boston University is only the apparent subject of the essay, and you do have to write about why you like the school, but YOU are the real subject, so your essay has to be distinctively about yourself. How can you tell? Well, try to imagine your best friend who is also applying to Boston University. Perhaps he likes the same aspects that you do. But he is a different person, so his answer should tell them who he is and differ significantly from yours.

Colleges know that students tend to get the most advice on the longer essays, so they think you are less likely to get heavy editing on the shorter pieces, which might seem fresher, more direct. Even short answers about your favorite music, movie, or a current event say something about you. Everything counts.

Do I Have to Count Every Word?

Applicants often wonder how strictly they need to adhere to a word limit. The Common Application specifies an essay of 250 to 650 words, which is about one to two and a half pages of double-spaced print. The word limit on both the upper and lower ends is strictly enforced.

Writing clean, stylish prose is an art you can master. We have worked with hundreds of students on their essays, and it is rare that a 700-word essay cannot be trimmed to 650 words or less and be strengthened in the process. So be aware of your essay's length and its effect on the reader. At the University of California, two essays are required, and a limit of 1,000 words total is specified and enforced. Some schools, however, may have soft limits—essays with suggested lengths that are not enforced by the technology in the electronic application. In these cases, you have a bit more leeway, but it is important not to go overboard. This is not the place to display your feisty, rebellious side. Be aware also that application may allow you to enter a longer-than-average essay but will truncate it before it can actually be submitted. To avoid this, be sure to print preview your electronic applications before submitting them.

Steps to a Successful Essay

We conclude this section with some tips that will help you write great essays. The Resources section at the end of this book lists some excellent books that focus exclusively on writing the college essay. We've given you a good start here, but we encourage you to consult one or more of these sources if you would like more detail about essay writing:

- Brainstorm either by yourself or with others about the personal qualities that you hope to convey in your essay. Look deep inside yourself. Who are you? Who are you becoming? What have you learned in your short life?

- Read the essay topics carefully. Which one grabs you? What would be fun to write about?

- If you have a choice of topics, select one that allows you to speak in your own voice and tell a story about yourself.

- Be sure to show by example, not just tell. Use details, even names of other people like your teacher, boss, or teammate if you mention them. You want the reader to imagine being there with you.

- Try to avoid the passive voice. When in doubt, cut extra words. Don't write a conclusion or moral at the end, like: "What I learned was . . ." The essay is short enough that it should contain its moral. You are not writing one of Aesop's fables. Think about making it easy and fun to read, not just expressing yourself. You have an audience.

- Set your essay aside for a couple of days, and then revise it. Think carefully about who you want to ask for advice. Ask your English teacher or counselor or both to read and comment on your essay. Your parents will probably be eager to read it as well.

- Incorporate the best suggestions into another draft. Set it aside again for a couple of days again, and then reread it, changing it until you are reasonably happy with it. You cannot write a perfect essay, so at some point, you have to let it go.

- Proofread your essay carefully. Then have someone else proofread it too. Why take a risk with preventable mistakes?

AN IMPORTANT TO-DO LIST

It is often said that the devil is in the details. The last thing you want to happen is for your thoughtful, carefully prepared case for admission, including a terrific essay, to be sabotaged by minor details. We offer this list to help you keep track of all those little things that can make a big difference. In chapter 9, we discuss other parts of your application besides the essay, but we suggest that you take a quick look at this list now. When you are ready to apply, review it again carefully, and then double-check it several times along the way to be sure you have covered all the bases:

- **Keep close track of all deadlines; they vary from college to college.** It is easy to forget when things are due when you have multiple applications and so much going on at school and at home. Develop a time line that will work for you, and then follow it to be sure everything gets done (and sent) on time.

- **Be sure to spell your name exactly the same way on all of your application materials, SAT or ACT registration, and any correspondence.** If you use your middle initial, use it every time on every form for every college-related purpose. Get into the habit of doing this right at the beginning and avoid the hassle of having three copies of every college mailing arrive at your house or test scores or recommendation letters that go astray. If your social security number is required, be sure you enter it correctly each time.

- **Make sure your e-mail address reflects your maturity.** Save Imtoosexy@ hotmail.com for communication with your friends, and get another address, from a reliable provider, for your college applications. Don't laugh; they do notice. And while we are on the topic of maturity, be sure that your postings on Facebook, YouTube, or similar websites don't contain things that would embarrass to you. You never know who may get access to them and at what point.

- **Keep a copy of everything you send in, including online applications and other written and e-mail correspondence.** Make sure you submit all parts of the application, along with the application fee if one is required, by the indicated deadlines. Don't wait until the last minute to file; unanticipated problems can happen near the deadline. When filing electronically, check online to see that all parts of your application, including any supplements, have been received.

- **Give all those who are writing recommendations for you, teachers and your counselor, everything they need to submit them on time.** If your school uses Naviance or the Common Application system to send supporting materials, everything may be transmitted electronically. Check with your guidance office for its requirements, and be sure to follow directions carefully, including any deadlines your high school may impose. Arrange to pay for the transcripts that colleges typically require if your school requires payment.

- **File your financial aid forms promptly, even if you and your parents have to estimate the previous year's figures.** Chapter 12 discusses financial aid and typical deadlines. Be sure to check the specific deadlines for each school to which you are applying. Keep copies of everything you use to fill out the forms. You may need to produce them later.

- **Ask the College Board or ACT, or both, if you took both tests and want to report both, to send your scores to your chosen colleges.** The College Board and the ACT give you score choice and will send only the scores you ask them to send. Each gives you a limited number of free score reports if you provide the names of the colleges at the time of testing or shortly after. Later reports can be purchased online, by mail, or by phone. Be sure you send your test results in time. Allow at least three weeks for regular delivery of scores. You can pay for rush delivery, but it is expensive and unnecessary if you plan ahead, except for November scores if you apply early. This is your responsibility, not your high school's, even if it put your scores on your transcript. Colleges consider those scores unofficial. The scores you report for yourself on the Common Application or other applications are unofficial as well. The colleges require official scores, sent by the testing agencies, in most cases.

- **Be sure to check e-mail regularly and keep all correspondence you receive from your colleges after you apply.** Some may come by regular mail, but most will come via e-mail. Read everything carefully and respond as appropriate. You will probably get a password to access the status of your application online, as well as the final decision. Keep your password in a safe place and, just as important, remember where you put it.

- **Check the status of your application about three to four weeks after everything was sent.** It can take quite a while for everything to get where it needs to be, and information is not always immediately posted online. If a college doesn't have a website where you can check your application's status, be patient. They will contact you if something is missing. It drives them crazy to get hundreds of anxious phone calls. You can always get something in late if it is actually missing, and it won't hurt your application.

- **Stay alert for phone messages or e-mail from alumni interviewers if your colleges offer such interviews.** Read the college material to see whether you have to formally request an interview (and by what date) or if you will be contacted automatically (and when). If you do not hear from someone in the time frame indicated, call or e-mail the admissions office. Be proactive. We'll talk more about the interview process in chapter 9.

- **By mid-January, request that your high school send your fall semester grades to each college that requires them as part of the regular decision application process or to a school where you were admitted early.** Colleges typically require a midyear report from your high school. Some high schools send a new complete transcript; others submit the new grades right on the form itself. The midyear report form also invites the counselor to note any significant additions or changes to the applicant's academic, extracurricular, or character record. This is a place where good news can be added or problems noted.

- **If you have a new major honor or accomplishment after you apply, send a note or e-mail to the admissions office (with your name and birthdate clearly indicated at the top) asking that this information be added to your file.** But don't add something insignificant. It can make you look as if you are trying too hard and won't help your case.

We turn now, in chapter 9, to the remaining parts of your application.

CHAPTER 9

Applying Well, Part II

Recommendations, Interviews, and Activities

As we discussed in chapter 8, essays are an important way colleges learn about students beyond their grades and test scores. But many colleges go beyond what you tell them in your essays by asking for letters of recommendation, gathering information about extracurricular activities and honors, and requiring or recommending interviews. In this chapter, we discuss how to make the most of each of these opportunities to let colleges learn about you. Along with your essays, they are your chance to personalize the process and help you stand out from the crowd. In chapter 10, we provide special advice for athletes and students with other special talents.

GETTING GREAT LETTERS OF RECOMMENDATION

While many schools, mostly public colleges, do not require or even accept letters of recommendation as part of the application process, most colleges that do ask for them require or recommend one or two letters from teachers and an official secondary school report, usually prepared by a school counselor or, in some cases, another school administrator. Along with your essay, these letters can make your application distinctive. Especially valuable are anecdotes that bring a paper file to life—one admissions dean referred to applicants' files as her "flat friends"—and transform numbers into a real person. Admissions officers also welcome context: descriptions of special challenges you have faced and overcome, an explanation of erratic grades or other unusual aspects of your record, and an evaluation of you relative to classmates, among other things. All of this helps the admissions officer develop a fuller picture of you and distinguishes you from many others with similar stats.

Whom Should You Ask to Write?

Although you obviously have no direct control over what your counselor or teacher writes in a letter and you probably have no choice about your school counselor, you can increase the chances that your teacher letters will be helpful in making your case for admission by asking the right teachers.

Ask Teachers Who Have Taught You Recently

Ask teachers who have taught you recently, in eleventh grade, if possible. The tenth grade is usually a bit too far back, and the twelfth grade is probably too fresh, especially if you are applying early action or early decision. A senior-year teacher may not have a lot to write about yet, even if you are very enthusiastic and doing well. Teachers who have taught you in more demanding courses, honors or Advanced Placement for example, if you have taken them, are good choices. They can testify to your ability to do more challenging work over a full year or semester. That is another reason not to use a tenth-grade teacher if you can avoid it: the work is usually not as advanced.

What Fields Should They Be From?

Focus on academic teachers from English, history, math (including computer science), science, and foreign language. Colleges consider these academic solids. Sometimes a college will be very specific about the letters it wants to see. MIT, for example, asks students to send one letter from a math or science teacher and one from a humanities or social science teacher. This is rarely mandatory elsewhere, but it would make sense to ask a math or science teacher for any college where you hope to major in one of those fields. Journalism, art, music, or drama might be very important to you, and even be a centerpiece of your main essay, but in general you should not use these teachers for a required teacher reference unless a college specifically asks you to do that as part of an application for a special program in that field. Otherwise have that teacher write a separate, optional letter if your schools will accept it, as many, but not all, will.

Ask Teachers Who Know You Best

Students sometimes have a difficult time deciding which teachers to ask for a letter of recommendation. The most helpful letters are those written by teachers who know you the best—not necessarily the teachers who gave you the highest grades, though it is nice if both are true. A well-written letter of recommendation should include specific examples of your contributions and achievements. Like a good personal statement, it should show by example rather than simply tell. A teacher who sees you as an active and thoughtful contributor to class discussions can more easily provide specific examples about you.

Of course, your teachers will say good things about you: 99 percent of recommendations are entirely positive. Who among your teachers has seen you at your best? Where did you shine? Did you write a great paper? Did you do extra work voluntarily or independent research? Help other students with their work? Add to the class energy? That is the teacher you should ask.

Some schools with strong college guidance programs provide training for teachers in writing effective recommendations. Most schools, however, leave it up to the teachers to figure it out for themselves. Given that reality, savvy students seek out teachers who seem particularly thoughtful, know them well, and are themselves strong writers.

How Should You Approach a Teacher?

Writing letters of recommendation is part of a teacher's job, but they can do it well or carelessly. It can be hard to know how enthusiastic a teacher will be when the time to write your letter arrives. You should approach your teachers early—at least one month before a letter is due, ideally more—especially if they are popular teachers who get lots of requests.

Tell your teachers that you plan to apply to colleges that include letters in their review process and ask whether they feel they know you well enough to write a supportive letter of recommendation. The number of colleges doesn't matter; they only have to write one letter and then submit it electronically to the schools through the Common Application, Naviance, or other electronic means. If your school doesn't provide this service, they can simply copy their recommendation multiple times and send their letter by regular mail. The response you want to hear is an enthusiastic, "Sure," "Yes," or "Of course!"

If you sense any hesitation, including a time constraint because a teacher is very busy, pick up on the cue. Thank the teacher for considering your request, but indicate that you'll be happy to ask someone else. A reluctant letter writer may not provide a helpful letter, so just move on to another teacher if you can. You should have a good idea of which teachers have seen you doing your best stuff in their classes, so the hope is that you won't have this problem.

What Your Recommenders Need to Know

School counselors need as much information about you as possible to write an effective letter for the secondary school report, and you can help them gain that background. Many schools have students fill out a multipage form that provides teachers and counselors with information about their college plans, extra-curricular activities, grade point average, standardized test scores, intellectual interests, hobbies, and other general background information that present their personal strengths. Your letter writers will use this form, so be sure to complete it accurately and thoroughly. If your high school does not provide the kind of form we are describing, you can use the one in Appendix C (and found at www.admissionmatters.com) or make up one of your own.

What Your Teachers Will Be Writing About

Your teachers may rely less on the form than your counselor will, since their job is simply to describe you in class, but it can still provide them with helpful context about you, especially if personal circumstances have affected your academic performance. Teachers only have to be experts in what you have achieved in their classes and related activities. If they know you play soccer or sing in the chorus, that's great, as long as it is based on their personal knowledge of you. But they don't have to repeat your activities, your grades, or test scores, because that will be found elsewhere in your file. In a sense, the admissions staff is working for their college's faculty, who want to enjoy teaching you. The main point of a teacher recommendation is to give the college an idea of you as a student.

You may want to supplement the general school form with specific details to help teachers refresh their memory of you in the classroom. Tell them how much the class mattered to you: What did you learn that you didn't know before? How has it changed your perspective on what you want to study? What have you done to follow up on this class, even if another class in that subject is not available? In other words, help the teacher help you by providing qualitative information and context for your experience in their class that they might not know about. You can't tell them what to write, of course, but they will appreciate the help, and their letter should benefit from your thoughtfulness.

If you are curious about what your counselor and teachers will be asked to write about you, you can see representative forms in PDF format on the Universal Application website at www.universalcollegeapp.com. With the Universal App and the Common App, each person writing a letter for you prepares just one that is shared with all the schools to which you apply. Colleges generally ask for much the same information, so a teacher or counselor can usually use the same content for all of your recommendations, even for schools that don't use the Common App or Universal App.

Waive Your Right to See the Letters

The Family Educational Rights and Privacy Act, known as FERPA, gives students the right to see their permanent college record after they enroll in a college unless they voluntarily waive that right. The Common Application and other applications provide a place for you to waive your right to see the letters that will be written on your behalf. Failing to sign the waiver could signal to both your high school teacher or counselor and colleges that you distrust your recommenders. If that is so, do not ask them to write for you in the first place. Otherwise sign the waiver in all cases. Since the passage of FERPA in 1974, most colleges destroy recommendations anyway, so there is little point in reserving access to them.

How Many Letters Should You Submit?

Most schools that require letters of recommendation ask for one or two letters from teachers. Sometimes a college offers students a chance to submit an optional recommendation from a coach, employer, or someone else who knows the student well, in addition to the required letters. A few colleges— Davidson College and Dartmouth College, for example—even ask for a letter from a peer.

When Should You Submit an Extra Letter?

Consider sending an extra letter only if someone could share valuable information about you that might not otherwise get into your file. This could be the drama or debate teacher you have worked with closely, or someone outside the school setting entirely who can describe another side of your personality or achievements. Ideally the writer makes it clear that he or she knows you well and has specific examples or anecdotes to back that up. But don't worry if you don't have someone who fits this bill. Most applicants, including most of those who are accepted, don't submit an extra letter.

Most, but not all, colleges will accept an extra letter or two from people with something fresh to say about you. Extra letters may have to be sent by regular mail rather than be transmitted electronically, depending on the college. If a school accepts extra letters and uses the Common Application, those letters may be submitted electronically. If you are submitting an extra letter to a school that does not accept them electronically, be sure that the writer includes your full name and birthdate, and your ID number if one has been assigned to your application, prominently at the top of the letter so that it can be added to your file.

Be Careful Not to Overdo It

Resist a letter-writing campaign, however. Weaker students sometimes try to pad their applications with multiple letters of endorsement. This can make it look as if you are trying too hard. The reader might wonder, "Why can't he stand on his own two feet like everyone else?" Application readers hate fluff—extra stuff that clogs up a file and takes time to read through but doesn't add anything of substance in the end. They are always tired during the reading season. Don't risk annoying them.

The only really helpful letters are from people who know you well and can add real substance to your file. A letter of support from a prominent alum of the college, your uncle's lawyer who met you once years ago, or the nice neighbors you babysat for so responsibly will have little or no impact. Limit your extra letters, if you send them at all, to one. Sometimes less is actually more.

The Secondary School Report or Counselor Letter

As we mentioned earlier, many colleges also require a letter from your counselor— the secondary school report (SR). You should give your counselor the same background information that you prepare for your teachers. In fact, it is more important for your counselor because counselors are expected to cover more ground in their letter than your teachers, so the more your counselor knows about you, the better. In addition to asking for a letter similar to the teacher letters, the SR asks your counselor to rate the rigor of your program relative to that of your classmates and provide an overall evaluation of you as a student, including class ranking if available. (Don't worry if your high school does not rank; more and more schools have eliminated rank.)

What If My Counselor Doesn't Know Me Well?

Colleges know that counselors in large public high schools often cannot get to know their students well, even if they try, simply because caseloads are enormous. They see this when they visit high schools, so their expectations for the level of detail in such letters are realistic. In contrast, letters from high school counselors at independent schools, some of whom are former admissions officers themselves, are often extremely detailed, even flowery. One admissions reader called this language "private school prose" or "glosh," meaning that it was sticky and sweet to touch, like molasses. The point is that admissions officers read files in the context of the high school, including the workload of the counselor, the school's curriculum, and its demography. They are trained to be fair.

Nevertheless, a detailed letter can still help, so you should get to know your counselor as well as possible. This is especially important if aspects of your record or background would benefit from explanation. For example, if your first-semester grades in your junior year suffered because of a serious illness, be sure your counselor knows. Your counselor can explain your situation only if he or she has this information. Or if you have a learning disability that was only discovered recently and your record shows a positive jump because you are now studying more effectively due to accommodations, the counselor needs to know this too if you are comfortable having her mention this in her letter. (This is optional, but we think it is usually a good idea to disclose this information. We discuss this further in chapter 11.)

The Special Case of Disciplinary Infractions

On both the Common App SR and most school forms, your counselor must indicate whether you have ever been suspended in high school, and if so, why.

Obviously it is best if your counselor can truthfully answer no. If the answer is yes, it is absolutely crucial that you disclose this information yourself as well in a thoughtful, contrite way that demonstrates that you have learned your lesson well and that the incident is unlikely to recur. Do not think of concealing an infraction. Honesty here is paramount. It is rarely the end of the world if the incident is honestly reported, but a cover-up is usually worse than the crime. It helps, of course, if it happened early in high school and you can demonstrate a clean record over a long period of time since then.

SHINING IN YOUR INTERVIEW

Schools vary widely in the importance placed on interviews. As we briefly discussed in chapter 2, some colleges require an interview as part of the admissions process, some make it optional, and some don't offer it at all. Just how important are interviews anyway, and how should you view them?

If a college doesn't offer interviews—most public universities don't use them, for example—then obviously interviews play no role in the admissions process. But what if they are offered? Our best advice is to take advantage of an interview, prepare for it, and take it seriously. But don't expect it to carry too much weight in the final outcome.

The Difference Between Informational and Evaluative Interviews

Interviews fall into two main types with different purposes: informational and evaluative. You need to ask a college which type it offers. Interviews are also just good experience. Inevitably you will be interviewed later in life: for scholarships, graduate school, and jobs. Learn the ropes now.

The Informational Interview

In informational interviews, colleges provide applicants with personalized information about their program that would interest you. The main goal of informational interviews is simply recruitment—having applicants feel there is a human face to the college and getting them excited about enrolling. They are usually offered by local alums who volunteer to help their alma mater, but they can be offered on-site at the college as well, sometimes by admissions staff but often by current college students. Informational interviews let you ask lots of questions and learn more about a college. Notes are rarely kept from these sessions, although the fact that you participated in one will likely become part of your file.

> We would be delighted to sit down and talk to you, but you should know that our interviews are strictly informational. They are not required and have no bearing on admissions decisions (we mean it).[1]
>
> WILLIAMS COLLEGE ADMISSIONS WEBSITE

The Evaluative Interview

Evaluative interviews are trickier. Here the college is upfront about saying that the results of the interview will be part of your admissions file. Evaluative interviews may be strongly encouraged or merely optional, and they may be offered at the college by admissions staff or college seniors specially trained for the task, or locally by alums in your home area. Many colleges with very large numbers of visitors have cut back or eliminated on-site interviews because of the volume, leaving the task of conducting interviews to alumni volunteers located across the country. The alum who interviews you can be a recent graduate or one who graduated long ago. Although the interview may be described as evaluative, you will still have ample opportunity to ask questions. You should come prepared with some good ones and use this opportunity to make a good impression.

What Are They Looking For, and How Much Will It Count?

The variability among interviewers—admissions staff, seniors, and, especially, alums—can make it difficult for colleges to place great weight on interview results, even when they are evaluative. Alums do this for fun and to give something back to the college beside money because they enjoyed their college experience. At selective colleges, alumni interviewers frequently complain that the applicants they are most excited about are often denied admission. This simply reflects the reality that there are many more strong applicants than available spots and that an evaluative interview usually plays only a very small role in the final decision.

For colleges that consider demonstrated interest, participating in an interview can be a plus. Therefore, we encourage students to take advantage of the opportunity to interview if possible. Some schools, like Pitzer College and Wake Forest University, for example, strongly encourage interviews and provide multiple ways to have them with an admissions representative, from on-site interviews to telephone or Skype discussions to even one-way video uploads at Pitzer. Regardless of who is doing the interview or where it takes place, expect the experience to be positive, warm, and friendly, not an interrogation. Almost always it will be.

A written evaluation becomes part of a student's file after an evaluative interview. While specifics will vary from college to college, the following categories will give you a good sense of the kind of information a college hopes to gain from an admissions interview:

- *Why is the student applying?* Is the student knowledgeable about the college and able to express why she thinks it might be a good fit for her?

- *What are the student's intellectual qualities?* Does he demonstrate curiosity, depth, creativity, or breadth of awareness? Has he challenged himself? How would he contribute to the college intellectually?

- *How has the student demonstrated commitment and personal motivation outside the classroom?* Does she have the potential to make a positive, significant contribution to the college community outside the classroom?

- *How does the student exhibit character and personal qualities such as initiative, responsibility, resilience, and maturity?*

⊠ Some Frequently Asked Interview Questions

1. What are you looking for in a college? What attracts you to this college?

2. What are your top two extracurricular activities, and why do you like them?

3. What sort of challenges have you faced in your life so far?

4. What is your favorite subject in school, and why?

5. How would you describe yourself to a stranger?

6. What is your favorite pastime?

7. How did you spend last summer, and how did you grow from it?

8. Can you name a book you have read that left a lasting impression?

9. What have you enjoyed most about high school?

10. Do you have any questions I can help answer?

How to Approach Your Interview

The admissions office may describe its interview as evaluative or informational or both, or might make no distinction at all. Your interview may take place in a college admissions office with an admissions rep or trained student, at a hotel, at your school with a visiting rep, or in a coffee shop or private home with an alum. Regardless of how it is done, there are some general guidelines to follow.

> After my interview, the interviewer said he wished he had told me from the beginning that it was only an informal conversation so that I wouldn't be as nervous. That meant he thought I was nervous. That means I rambled and did poorly. Been reading articles on how to handle college rejections the whole night yesterday.
>
> STUDENT WHO THINKS THE INTERVIEW IS MORE IMPORTANT THAN IT REALLY IS

Arranging the Interview

Colleges vary in how they set up interviews. You are always responsible for setting up interviews on-site at the college or with visiting admissions reps. You need to check college websites for information about how to sign up for an on-site interview if those are offered, as well as watch for information about opportunities to meet with a visiting rep. Alumni interviews are different. Some schools will contact you soon after you have submitted your application to arrange an alumni interview. Others will wait for you to contact them, either before or after you have applied, by phone or through a website, depending on the school.

Some colleges have to limit the number of interviews they can offer due to the pressure of high numbers of applicants and not enough on-site staff or alumni in an area. You should research this for each college, either through the website or by calling the college admissions office. Interviews at a college are more available in the summer, but the admissions office can be very busy in August, the prime family vacation month. In some cases, interviews are available on-site as early as spring break of the junior year. Before you leap at the first chance, though, ask yourself how much you know about the college and how ready you are for an interview. It might be better to wait for an alumni interview back home in the fall if they are offered.

Colleges typically limit interviews to one per student, so choose the kind you prefer if you have an option and must pick one.

Timing

Regardless of where your interview will be held, be on time. It is okay to arrive at an admissions office early to get settled, but don't arrive early at an interview in someone's home; just be there when you are supposed to be. Expect the interview to last about 45 minutes, plus or minus 15 minutes, depending on the interviewer and how the conversation goes, unless you have been told otherwise. The first part of the interview is the most important. We interview others for our work, and in talking as well with college alumni interviewers, we have found a consistent pattern: early impressions stick. The first few minutes can set the tone for the rest of the interview, so go into it alert and focused.

Dress

Dress neatly and look presentable—no jeans, sneakers, or flip-flops—but you don't need to dress up for the occasion either. If the interview is in an admissions office, it is fine for your parent to wait in the outer office for you while the interview takes place. If someone drives you to an interview at an alum's home, be sure he or she can take you home promptly after the interview. You don't want to have to awkwardly hang out in the interviewer's living room while you wait for your ride. Most schools now recommend that alumni conduct interviews in public places, like a coffee shop, to reduce the discomfort of being in someone's living room and reduce liability issues, so this may not be an issue for you.

> Somebody I interviewed once said he wanted to major in accounting. I said, "You know, that's not a major at Harvard." It went downhill from there.
>
> HARVARD ALUMNI INTERVIEWER

What Will You Be Asked?

In preparing for an interview, think about how you would answer the most likely questions like those shown in the box. You may be asked different questions, but thinking about how you would answer these will help calm you. Don't try to memorize your answers, though, since memorized answers can come across as stiff and awkward, and maybe not even relevant to the specific question. Instead, think about how you would answer questions like these so you can go into the interview feeling confident regardless of what you are asked.

Asking Your Own Questions

Have several prepared questions ready to ask when given the opportunity (and you will always get the opportunity). It is perfectly all right to have a note card with you to remind yourself of your questions. Interviewers understand that you may be nervous. They want you to be comfortable and as relaxed as possible. Make sure that your questions are not obvious and purely factual or could be readily answered by looking at the catalog, website, or application materials, such as, "Do you have an engineering program?" or "Is there separate housing for freshmen only?" Questions that show you have read the material provided by the college and thought about it are the best kind, as are questions that ask the interviewer to explain how something like the housing or advising system works. You could ask the interviewer what the high (and low) points of her own experience at the college were, how the college has changed since she graduated, and how the college changed her life.

After the Interview

When the interview is over, thank the interviewer for her time and ask for a card or otherwise write down her name and e-mail or postal mail address. A short thank-you note or e-mail sent after the interview is a nice gesture.

⊠ Interview Checklist

☐ Make sure you have the exact details of the interview time and location, and arrange reliable transportation. If something goes wrong and you are late, don't blame the interviewer. Just apologize for the misunderstanding or for the delay.

☐ Carefully review the material you have about the college (online and paper) to make sure you know about its programs and special features.

☐ Think about your answers to possible questions, including the most important one: "Why are you interested in this college?"

☐ Prepare your own thoughtful questions about the college to ask your interviewer.

☐ Dress neatly and appropriately for the setting. Dressy clothes are not necessary, but avoid jeans and shorts.

(continued)

Interview Checklist (*continued*)

☐ Shake hands when you meet the interviewer, and try to maintain eye contact throughout the interview.

☐ Try to relax and enjoy the conversation.

☐ After the interview is over, thank the interviewer for taking the time to speak with you. Shake hands again, and ask the interviewer for a business card or other contact information.

☐ Send a short thank-you note in the next few days. A written note is nice, but e-mail is fine too.

Above all, keep the interview in perspective. We have provided a lot of advice on the topic because students are often nervous. Just remember that the interview is a small, and certainly not the most important, part of your application.

HIGHLIGHTING WHAT YOU'VE ACCOMPLISHED

As we discussed in chapter 2, extracurricular activities, community service, and work experience are important ways for students to demonstrate their passions, initiative, and leadership skills. Most application forms, including the Common Application, provide space for you to list each of your activities, the grades when you participated in them, and the number of hours per week and weeks per year you spent on them. Applications typically also ask you to include any positions held, honors earned, or athletic letters awarded for each activity, as well as a very brief description of the activity. Colleges are seeking insight into how you spend your time outside the classroom as well as the extent of your involvement in various activities.

This information is important, so be sure to give careful attention to this part of the application. Be careful with abbreviations. In general, avoid them and spell out the name of the organizations to which you belong.

Most students find that they can convey their activities and degree of involvement in the spaces provided on the application. Sometimes, though, students find the space too limiting. Their activities may be unusual or their involvement difficult to convey in the format and space provided. In this case, you might prepare a supplementary activities list or résumé to accompany the information presented on the application itself.

If the basic application meets your needs, however, don't feel you have to produce a separate activity sheet or résumé. In fact, in general colleges discourage the use of a separate résumé, although some accept one and provide information about how to include it, usually as an upload. If no information is provided, you

---

⌧ Activity Sheet Format

A separate activity sheet gives you the flexibility to organize your information as you want and to present detail where it would be helpful. We provide suggested categories below. You can decide to include some categories as is, combine others, and omit those that are not relevant to your situation. Limit the details to a couple of sentences or a short paragraph at most.

Categories to Consider

    Extracurricular activities (includes athletics)

    Awards and honors

    Hobbies and special interests

    Summer activities

    Work experience and internships

    Community involvement

Be sure your activity sheet has your name, address, and birthdate at the top. Arranging information in columns makes it easy to follow. The format below (we've included a sample entry) works well for most categories, although you'll need to modify the headings somewhat for a couple of them.

Extracurricular Activities

Activity	Grade (9, 10, 11, 12)	Hours per Week/ Weeks per Year	Description
French Language and Culture Club	10, 11, 12	5/40	Secretary (11); president (12). Led development of foreign language semiannual newsletter at high school

can print one out and submit it by regular mail, along with a note asking that it be added to your application. If you do prepare a résumé, keep it short—one or two pages maximum. Use the extra space you now have to write a brief description of your involvement in each activity if it is not obvious from its name; bullet points work well and can save space. Just be sure it is compact, neat, and well organized. Listing every debate tournament or equestrian competition you have placed in is tempting, but overkill. Once again, less is more.

Athletes who want to play varsity sports in college as well as students with exceptional talents in the arts that they wish to have evaluated as part of the college admissions process are special cases. While most high school athletes and student artists and performers will treat their involvement in the same way as other activities, those with exceptional talent will want to take advantage of opportunities to highlight their abilities in a more focused and intensive way. Chapter 10 is devoted to these special situations.

THE CANADIAN AND BRITISH/IRISH DIFFERENCE

In chapter 4, we introduced the idea of studying abroad to obtain your undergraduate degree. If you are interested in exploring this option, it is important to know that the application process differs in some significant ways from what we have described for colleges in the United States. For example, you would apply by specific program to British and Irish universities and most universities in Canada, although on Canadian application forms, a major may be called "undetermined or undeclared."

Need-based aid from universities is rarely available for international students, although FAFSA-supported loan programs are usually portable. An international student can apply for merit aid, however, particularly in Canada. Merit scholarships usually require a separate application. The United Kingdom (UK), Ireland, and Canada all allow students to work on and off campus both while at university and after graduation, but the details vary, and there are restrictions.

Application deadlines vary and can be as early as October 15. Some, however, are quite late, even after the May 1 date by which you must reply to US colleges. The late dates can make them attractive options for US students who get off to a late start or who want additional college options. Admissions offices are aware of the US May 1 reply date and generally notify you of your decision before that date if you apply in midwinter or before. An exception is the British conditional acceptance, which might require you to achieve certain scores on AP or IB exams taken near the end of your senior year. Since you wouldn't get those scores until the summer, you would treat a conditional acceptance in the same way as a wait list (see chapter 14 for information about wait lists in general).

Applying in Canada

Your application to schools in Canada will be evaluated on the basis of your transcript, grades, and test scores. Ontario has one central application for all universities in the province, available at www.ouac.ca, but in all the other provinces, you apply directly to a specific university. All universities need your official high school transcript and score reports sent directly to them by your school and the testing agency. Your first-semester senior-year grades are the most important, and since there are generally no early application options, decisions are made only after the university has received them. Many universities base their decision on junior- and senior-year grades, converting US grade scales to Canadian equivalents, and they may rely on standardized test scores more than many US schools do.

Canadian universities generally do not require essays as part of their application, although there are some exceptions, like the University of British Columbia and Queens University, and most do not require recommendation letters. Many universities do ask for short essays on applications for merit scholarships. Some programs require a letter of intent addressing your interest in that program, reasons for applying, and how the program relates to your personal and professional goals; a résumé of volunteer and work experience and extracurricular activities may also be requested.

Be sure to check each website for application requirements by specific program. With a few exceptions, Canadian universities do not seem as selective as the most selective American schools, largely because they are not yet part of the frenzy of increasing numbers of applications that we discussed in chapter 1.

Applying in the United Kingdom

The universities of the UK (which includes England, Wales, Scotland, and Northern Ireland) use the UCAS (Universities and Colleges Admissions Service) online application, available at www.ucas.com. A few universities also accept the Common Application. With the UCAS, you may apply to as many as five university programs for one fee by January 15 (or submit up to four medicine, dentistry, or veterinary medicine undergraduate applications by October 15). Some art schools have a later deadline. You may not apply to both Cambridge University and Oxford University, each of which has a deadline of October 15 as opposed to the general deadline of January 15.

Oxford and Cambridge have additional complex requirements, often including separate examinations in your subject and an interview. Sometimes these are available in the United States, especially on the East Coast, or by Skype. Some programs in other universities also require an interview or other supplementary materials; as always, check the university websites. No university sees where else you have applied, and all make their decisions simultaneously and independently. You are expected to have taken AP, IB, or SAT Subject Tests relevant to your program, particularly for the English, Welsh, and Northern Irish universities, since the British education system is exam driven.

Some universities have extended deadlines for North American students as explained on their websites, and the UCAS has an extended deadline of June 30 for non-UK students. A word of caution: the extended deadline is useful for applications to English, Welsh, and Northern Irish universities only if you know that your program still has openings. On the other hand, the less specialized first-year curriculum of Scottish universities, as we will discuss following, may make them more accessible even in June.

The UCAS has five sections, four requesting information about you and the fifth being an essay of roughly 600 words. It also requires one school recommendation that you will be able to read online once it has been uploaded by the writer. You will make your case to all five programs identically in this one essay. The essay should address your reasons for choosing the programs you're applying to and all related education and experience. You should allow no more than one-fourth of the essay for describing your other interests and experiences, if those are requested, showing especially how they relate to your proposed course of study and your potential to succeed in a demanding program.

The University of St. Andrews website describes the role of the essay at selective British universities: "Most of our applicants will be well qualified so decisions on who will receive offers [of admission] will often be determined by the quality of the Personal Statement." Further on, it states that the essay "should give the Admissions Officer(s) a picture of someone who is interested in the subject area for which you have applied and who has the motivation and potential to do well in a university environment."[2] Unlike their American counterparts, British admissions faculty are almost exclusively focused on your academic preparation for the specific course of study you have chosen, with little emphasis placed on nonacademic factors except as they may relate to your ability to succeed in the program you have chosen.

You must specify a subject you want to study, and, except at Scottish universities, you will be admitted for that subject and no other. So the British system is both simpler and more restrictive in some ways. It is also very difficult to change majors. You must be certain you know what you want to study and that the universities you are applying to have an approach to the subject that you are comfortable with. In Scotland, however, universities respond to your application by admitting you to a Faculty (of Arts, of Science, and so on) within which your subject is taught. For most subjects, the Scottish system allows you to change the emphasis or subject of your degree as you progress through your first two years.

Unlike American publications that rate entire colleges, the UK public evaluation system rates individual majors at colleges using many criteria, among them student satisfaction (including teaching quality) and research quality. The most popular publication presenting rankings information is the *Good University Guide*, published by the *London Times* and available through the UK site for Amazon.com at www.amazon.co.uk. As with all other rankings, you should approach them with considerable caution, but in trying to learn about UK universities from a distance, they can be helpful.

Applying in Ireland

With the exception of universities in Northern Ireland, which use the UCAS, American students apply for Irish undergraduate courses directly to each university. Information about Irish education, how to apply to Irish universities, and links to all undergraduate institutions may be found at Education in Ireland, www.educationireland.com and at the Irish Universities Association, www.iua.ie.

Irish universities distinguish among Irish, EU, and non-EU applicants regarding requirements and applications processes. While essays are not always required for non-EU applicants, some applications provide space for a supporting statement. For non-EU students, both University College Dublin and University College Cork require a personal statement and two academic recommendations.

Trinity College Dublin requests additional information in support of your application, including two recommendations and, for US and Canadian applicants, at least two SAT Subject Tests in addition to the SAT or ACT. As always, check the website of each university for specific requirements.

YOU'VE FINISHED YOUR APPLICATIONS. WHAT'S NEXT?

Completing your applications is a major milestone in the college admissions process. Although you may still have a few things left to do (for example, checking on the status of your application and registering for interviews), as well as submitting financial forms and scholarship applications, the bulk of the work is now behind you. Take a deep breath and celebrate!

If you have built your college list well, you will have at least one and probably several good choices come April. Now you can return to being a fully engaged student, keeping your grades up, and participating in meaningful extracurricular activities. You should enjoy these last few months of high school. It has been a long haul, and you're almost there. But don't take it too easy. Colleges will see your final grades in June!

CHAPTER 10

Making the Most of Your Special Talents

Well before actually applying to college, student athletes, visual artists, and performers need to prepare to showcase their talents if they want them to be considered part of the admissions process. Athletes need to determine the level of their talent and decide whether to apply to colleges that offer athletic scholarships or to seek out being recruited at schools that might like them to participate in intercollegiate athletics without a scholarship. Visual artists need to prepare a body of work to submit in a portfolio. Performers need to prepare for auditions. The spring or summer before junior year of high school is not too early to begin for many of you. Athletes aspiring to play certain high-profile Division I sports like football and basketball should start even earlier as, lamentably, recruiting is now reaching to sophomores. Artists, especially performers, need to research the options available to them and continue to develop the skills required by the programs they are considering.

THE STUDENT ATHLETE AND ATHLETIC RECRUITMENT

As we noted in chapter 2, athletic talent can be the biggest hook of all when it comes to admission at a selective college. If you are an exceptionally strong athlete and want to play in college, your athletic talent may give you a big boost when you apply, and it might result in a sizable athletic scholarship at schools that offer them, in addition to any need-based aid for which you are eligible. This is the dream of many college-bound athletes, although the reality is quite different for most.

The Truth About Athletics Scholarships

You may have heard for years that athletic scholarships will reward all your hard work in your sport, but this is not true at all colleges, for all sports, and under all circumstances, as we will explain later. In fact, only about 2 percent of high school athletes receive athletic scholarships to play in college, and many colleges don't offer them at all. Of the scholarships that are awarded, only a small percentage are full scholarships, usually limited to sports that draw large, paying crowds, mainly football and basketball. But the good news is that the opportunity to participate in athletics in college is available to just about any student athlete who seeks it. The key is finding the right athletic fit; the nature and level of involvement will vary greatly from student to student.

The Structure of College Athletics

As a prospective college student athlete, you need to have a working under-standing of how college athletics is organized. There are two main national athletic associations for colleges. By far the better known is the National Collegiate Athletic Association (NCAA), whose teams appear on national television and are closely watched by ardent followers all over the country. The National Association of Intercollegiate Athletics (NAIA) has fewer participating schools and is less well known, but it includes hundreds of smaller colleges.

NCAA Division I

The over 1,000 colleges in the NCAA are divided into three divisions. Division I (D-I) houses the most athletically competitive programs; with 18 exceptions, all offer athletic scholarships. The Big Ten schools are all D-I, as are Stanford, the Ivy League colleges, those in the Southeast Conference, and many others. The eight Ivy League schools are among the 18 D-I schools that do not offer athletic scholarships.

NCAA Division II

Division II (D-II) schools, which offer some scholarships, are less competitive both athletically and academically than most D-I schools. They tend to be regional universities like the University of Wisconsin, Parkside, and California State University, Chico, as well as private colleges that draw students primarily from their geographical region. In terms of level of athletic competition, D-II schools tend to be in the middle between D-I and D-III.

NCAA Division III

Division III (D-III) schools tend to be more selective academically than D-II schools and usually, but not always, less competitive athletically. Like the Ivy League, they offer no athletic scholarships. Liberal arts colleges like Bowdoin College, Amherst College, and Linfield College are in Division III. So are a small number of research universities like Emory University, New York University, and Carnegie Mellon University. D-III coaches want to win just as much as the well-publicized D-I schools do, and some D-III teams are perennial competitors in national championships. A few D-III schools have one D-I sport, like ice hockey at Union College and Clarkson University, and can offer scholarships in that sport.

More About NCAA and NAIA

Most of the 287 smaller colleges in the NAIA have athletic scholarships. A complete list of NCAA membership by division can be found at www.ncaa.org, and NAIA colleges are listed at www.naia.org.

What You Need to Consider

If actively participating in your sport in college is important to you, you will need to determine the level of competition that is right for you given your athletic talents, and you should consider the fit, that is, whether your skills will have you in action or on the bench at each school you have in mind. It is important to make this assessment as realistically as possible, seeking honest advice from your high school or club coach.

You also need to understand the time commitment to practice, team travel, and competition schedules, which will have an impact on your academic work at college. D-I and D-II programs are the most demanding of your time, D-III less so. Learn more about what would be expected of you if you were a team member. Considering time commitments is always important, and it is especially so if your level of talent might result in your being admitted to a school that would otherwise be a big academic stretch for you. We all know student athletes who stopped competing in their sport at highly demanding colleges because of academic pressures. Balancing college sports and college-level academics requires significant time management skills and a strong drive to succeed at both.

Be Sure to Register with the NCAA or NAIA

Be sure to register with the NCAA Eligibility Center at www.eligibilitycenter .org by the end of your junior year to ensure your eligibility if you plan to play in Division I or Division II or with the NAIA Eligibility Center at www .playnaia.org if you plan to play in one of those colleges. The registration fee can be waived for eligible students; ask your school counselor if that might apply to you. Student athletes who plan to apply only to D-III colleges do not need to register.

Both the NCAA and the NAIA determine eligibility using a combination of grade point average and test scores, available on their websites, and the NCAA also includes tightly defined amateur status in its eligibility requirements. Your high school should be registered with them, and for the NCAA, it should have core courses approved; you should verify that your course schedule will include the required number of approved core courses during high school. You can view the list of approved courses offered at your school through the NCAA Eligibility Center website. This is an area where it is good to do some planning early.

Take the SAT or ACT early as well, usually by December of your junior year, so that you have time to prepare if you need to retake it and will have scores to send to coaches when you have your first contact with them. To give yourself more options in terms of admissibility, plan to retest at least once in the spring unless your scores are exceptionally high.

How the Recruiting Process Works

At many colleges, the admissions office gives coaches a specific number of slots to fill with their highest-priority recruits. They can submit additional names, but those athletes won't get priority from the admissions office beyond the merit of the rest of their nonathletic credentials. The problem for most recruited students is that they rarely know in advance where they rank on a coach's list. It is okay to ask, however, and an honest answer can be helpful. Coaches like to use generalities, like, "I will give you my full support," or, "I can see you playing for us right away." These comments sound encouraging, but they may be misleading because the coach may put you near the bottom of the list despite his or her apparent enthusiasm. Listen carefully to what a coach is saying, and try to get as much specific information as you can about where you stand.

Coaches have to recruit more students than they need, since they have no guarantee all will remain interested in their school and eventually enroll. Another problem for recruits is that the coach may not know their full potential talent pool until late in the recruiting season. A student who is high on the list at an early stage may be bumped down by talented late arrivals.

> Dealing with college coaches in the fall of your senior year is flattering but nerve-wracking. A coach may call and write every week, insisting that you're the 6'2" center she needs for her basketball team . . . but you don't know how many other 6'2" centers she has on her call list as well, and she only needs one for next year. If you delay, and another of those players commits, your phone will go stone cold, and you'll never even know what happened.
>
> COLLEGE FRESHMAN HEAVILY RECRUITED TO PLAY WOMEN'S BASKETBALL

How Coaches Know You Will Be Admissible

As we noted earlier, being a recruited athlete is the most powerful hook in college admissions. However, colleges are under great pressure to ensure that their student athletes succeed academically and graduate with their peers, which prevents them from recruiting athletes who fall far from the usual admissions standards.

The Ivy League, for example, maintains its own academic standards for eligibility, called the academic index (AI), a complex calculation that takes into account grade point average and test scores. The AI is computed for each prospective athlete. (The Resources section at the end of the book contains a link to a site that will show you how to compute your own AI.) The basic premise behind the AI is that the academic credentials of recruited athletes overall and individually should not deviate too much from the credentials of their classmates.

An acceptable AI places an athlete in a group, or "band," at one of four levels, with very few places in the band with lower credentials and more places in the bands with higher academic credentials. The goal is to have the bands balance

> A young athlete at my child's private school was superb in her sport. An Ivy League coach showed intense interest and encouraged her application so forcefully that the private school's counseling staff thought it was a done deal. The girl was denied early decision. Turns out that the coach was new and inexperienced, and had encouraged the girl without checking with admissions to see if she had an admissible profile. She didn't make the Ivy League grade for athletic recruits.
>
> MOTHER OF TWO ATHLETIC RECRUITS

out to the required AI for the group overall. This is very different from the minimum eligibility standards established by the NCAA or the NAIA.

While their admissions processes give a big boost to athletes on a coach's list, Ivy League colleges have agreed to accept common constraints on just how big that boost can be. Many D-III colleges like those in the New England Small College Athletic Conference use a banding process similar to the Ivies. A number of other colleges have established constraints as well.

Getting Noticed by the Coach

All college coaches are always looking for athletic talent. Sometimes that talent comes to their attention when high school students are nationally ranked in their sport, receive sports-related honors, or a coach sees them play in summer camps or showcases. Coaches keep track of such students with an eye toward actively recruiting them when it comes time for college admissions. Most students, though, have to take steps to bring themselves to the attention of a coach and be the one who makes the first contact. Either way can get you a spot on a coach's recruiting database.

Be Proactive

Talk to your high school or club coach about your level of ability early in your junior year or even before, depending on your sport. Use that information to begin your college search early so that you can identify colleges that both meet your academic and social needs and can also offer the opportunity to play your sport at the right level for you. You can estimate whether your 50-meter freestyle is fast enough to swim on a college team by looking at the team statistics; you can figure out whether a college is likely to need a new freestyler by checking graduation dates of the swimmers to see when a slot will open up. Targeted research will help you identify a good athletic fit as well as a good academic fit. Your coach will also have good suggestions.

Reach out to college coaches by the end of your junior year if you are not contacted first and provide relevant athletic and academic statistics. Many schools have websites where prospective athletes can express interest in participating in a particular sport. If a school does not have a website like this, send the coach an e-mail expressing interest and include basic academic and athletic information. In either case, the coach will probably send you a questionnaire in response, which you should complete and return immediately. Depending on the sport, athletes may also include a YouTube link with highlights of their performance in games or competitions that makes it easy for a coach to take a quick look without the hassle of putting a DVD into a player.

Stay in contact. If you don't hear back from a coach after a reasonable period of time, resend your note: coaches get a lot of inquiries, and some slip between the cracks. If you don't hear back after two tries, though, that coach is probably not interested. Just accept that and move on.

If you participate in a regional summer showcase, a holiday tournament, or a summer sports camp, alert the coach at the colleges you are interested in. Coaches routinely scout championships and venues like these. We strongly suggest that you also ask your high school or club coach to contact the college coach at those schools to discuss your ability and potential.

Recruitment Guidelines

The NCAA sets rigid guidelines that govern the recruitment process. Strict rules govern when and how often a coach can contact a prospective athlete, as well as what can and cannot be reimbursed if an athlete comes to campus for an interview. The rules ensure that eager coaches do not overwhelm young athletes, and now that the pressure of athletic recruiting has reached into sophomore year of high school in some sports, the concern is heightened. You can find the guidelines that govern the sport and the division you are interested in at the NCAA website noted above, and you should also check the websites of the schools you are interested in to investigate further the policies of those schools or their athletic divisions. By and large, the rules bind the coaches more than the students, but you should know what they are just to be safe.

Official and Unofficial Visits

D-I and D-II coaches may invite athletes to visit campus at the school's expense; these are known as "official visits." Schools can offer only a limited number of official visit invitations, and students may accept a maximum of five such invitations. Getting an official visit invitation indicates pretty serious interest on the part of the coach. Regulations prevent D-III coaches from paying for such visits, however. You can visit, but at your own expense.

During a visit, your time on campus will be focused on the athletic program, but ask to go on a regular admissions tour, sit in on the information session, and visit a class if you have not already done so. You can also ask the coach about coaches' interaction with the admissions office at that college and whether the coach would advocate for you. The coach can also answer questions about where you stand on his or her list, which slots are likely to be open on the team, and what kind of academic support is available from the athletics department. This is your opportunity to investigate policies about vacation time training, graduation rates for athletes, and time commitments during the season and off-season. Assess this information as realistically as possible.

Making the Commitment

If you are successful in the process in D-I or D-II in any sport and are offered an athletic scholarship, full or partial, that you wish to accept, you may be asked sign a National Letter of Intent (NLI), contractually binding you to that college for one year. The date on which you would sign it differs from sport to sport. (Information about the NLI can be found by searching for NLI at www .ncaa.org.) Many, but not all, schools that offer athletic scholarships participate in the NLI program. Neither the offer nor your signing the NLI, however, is an absolute guarantee of admission. It would be very surprising if the coach and the admissions office were not in agreement, although it occasionally happens.

If you are not offered an athletic scholarship or are being recruited at a D-III school that does not offer scholarships, college coaches will sometimes say that they will guarantee you a place on the list they submit to admissions only

> Recruiting puts some kids under tremendous pressure to apply ED. Most coaches told my daughter that the only influence they had was in the ED cycle—if she waited and applied regular decision, they could not help her. I don't know if that was the truth, or just a ruse so that the coach would know which students were serious enough about the college to merit further attention.
>
> PARENT OF A HEAVILY RECRUITED ATHLETE

if you agree to apply early decision. Accept the offer only if you know you want to attend that school and will be happy there. Do you want your whole choice of a college to revolve around sports? If not, placement on the coach's list may be no bargain if the school itself does not excite you. You might be injured and unable to play, or your sport might be eliminated for budget reasons. In such cases you would want to have chosen a college you love. Remember that the point is to be in control of your own decisions as much as possible.

Become Knowledgeable About the Process

The NCAA website provides a wealth of information about athletic recruiting. The *Guide for the College-Bound Student Athlete*, found on the site, is worth downloading. You and your parents should read it carefully and scour the rest of the site so that you will know what to expect and what is expected of you. Recruiting is an intricate dance, with coaches casting as wide a net as possible to ensure that they recruit the best possible athletes for the slots they need filled on their teams, and athletes trying to position themselves well to ensure the best outcomes in terms of acceptance, athletic scholarships, and participation in their sport. Recruiting can be as different for each sport as the sports are from each other. Check the NCAA website for the specifics.

A Word About Gender

In 1972, Congress passed Title IX of the Education Amendments series, guaranteeing women and girls equal opportunities in all aspects of education, including athletics. Although there continues to be considerable debate about its impact on men's athletics, there can be no question about its impact on women. The success of US women in the 2012 Olympics has been attributed to the changes wrought by Title IX.

So what does this mean for athletes applying to college? For women, it means more athletic opportunities and more athletic scholarships. If the college has a football team, with its large number of players, it needs to fund a similar number of female athletes in varsity programs. In sports like track and swimming, for example, the NCAA allows more scholarship support for women than men so that colleges can achieve gender equity when it is thrown out of balance by the budget needs of the football team. The bottom line is that the athletic hook for women has never been stronger.

If You Are Not Recruited

Depending on the sport and division, a strong athlete who is not recruited may be able to play as a walk-on to the team once he or she is admitted through the regular admissions process. Coaches keep an eye out for likely talent, and you may be invited to try out for the team as early as during the admissions process if you have alerted a coach to your interest in the sport. And even if a coach has returning and recruited athletes, plus a few invitees, you may also be able to try out successfully as a walk-on, especially at the D-III level, once you arrive on campus if you have maintained your training. Some sports like rugby or crew may even have slots for an athletically inclined novice regardless of level.

In addition, you may enjoy playing on club or intramural teams and find the competition rewarding and the time demands much more workable. A strong athlete who can lead less talented or experienced teammates is also a gift to the community. Love of sport is not only about level of competition, as many volunteer coaches attest.

College Life for Student Athletes

A student athlete really has two jobs, but any dedicated high school student athlete already knows this. It is crucial that you balance these jobs, choosing a college that fits your academic readiness and at which you can also engage in your sports at a level that develops your talent appropriately. Many D-I and D-II schools have academic support for their athletes, who may be putting in 20 to 30 hours a week in practice and competition commitments. Athletic department advisors work with coaches to ensure that student athletes have the tools they need to succeed academically as well as athletically. At D-III schools and colleges as selective as the Ivy League, the support might be less structured and more a matter of suggestion. As you research colleges, ask about the scope of athletic commitment and how you will be supported academically, especially during your sports season.

OPTIONS FOR THE STUDENT ARTIST

Whether you are a visual artist or a performer, a writer or a composer, an aspiring critic or a stage technician, you share a common element with the entire range of student artists: many choices about what kind of degree in what kind of program in what kind of college. Many liberal arts colleges and research universities have strong arts programs as part of their regular curricular offerings. In addition, a number of schools specializing in the performing and visual arts offer degrees in the arts as part of an arts-focused liberal arts program. And some highly specialized schools, known as conservatories or art schools, have as their sole mission the training of professionals at the highest level.

Some of you may be interested in showcasing your talent as part of the overall college application process, even though you are not planning an academic focus on the arts once you are enrolled. We'll have tips specifically for you at the end of this section.

What Degree Do You Want to Get?

Students interested in studying the arts can choose among several types of degrees that vary in their degree of professional focus.

Bachelor of Arts

The bachelor of arts (BA) in a college with strong arts programs can give you training in your art as well as a broad liberal arts education in which you also take courses in other academic areas. For example, you might take History of the Middle East alongside Arabic majors, zoology with biology majors, or Shakespeare with English majors. You could even choose to double major in something quite different from your art. Studio art majors who add a biology major may seek a career in scientific illustration, for example, or combine art with computer science and work in electronic game development. Some colleges have scholarships like the Filene Music Scholarships at Skidmore, which require you to continue taking lessons and participate in campus ensembles but not that you major in music.

Bachelor of Fine Arts and the Bachelor of Music

The bachelor of fine arts (BFA) and the bachelor of music (BMus or BM), on the other hand, are more focused and have more arts course requirements, and therefore usually preclude a double major. While you might take about 35 to 50 percent of your course work in a BA arts major, the percentage of course work in the arts increases to about 70 percent in a BFA, BMus, or BM program.

The BFA and BMus are offered by some liberal arts colleges as well as by art schools or conservatories, as well as by music or art schools or departments within large universities. Admissions offices at these schools look for solid academics as well as outstanding artistic talent, but they focus primarily on your ability in art or music.

Where Should You Study?

Students interested in majoring in the arts have a wide range of colleges to choose from, depending on the kind of educational experience they are seeking and their level of talent.

Liberal Arts Colleges and Universities

Liberal arts colleges and large universities offer a traditional college experience with sports teams and a full range of extracurricular activities. Some, like Oberlin College and Lawrence University, combine a liberal arts college and a separate conservatory on one campus, each distinct but with the advantage of linkage to the other. Both offer a five-year dual-degree program where a student can get both a BA in a field other than music and a BFA or BM in the conservatory. Schools like these also offer a music major in the liberal arts college, music lessons and classes for nonmusic majors in the college, and opportunities for highly qualified liberal arts students to perform in college music organizations. Sometimes dual-degree programs are available through neighboring institutions, as at Brown University with the Rhode Island School of Design.

Some universities, like the University of Michigan and Stony Brook University, have strong music departments that are part of their arts and sciences offerings. Depending on the university, the department may offer the BA or the BM, or sometimes both. Schools of visual and performing arts can also be a formal division of a larger university, like the College of Visual and Performing Arts at Syracuse University, the School of Visual, Media and Performing Arts at Brooklyn College, and the Tisch School of the Arts at New York University.

Cross-registration between a liberal arts school and an arts school also expands the possibilities if you seek a BA but want a more intense arts education as part of the experience: a Columbia University or Barnard College student can take courses at the Juilliard School, for example, and a Mills College student at the

California College of the Arts. You have lots of options in this range, but you need to decide ahead of time which option you want; the application process is different for each.

Professional Schools in the Arts

Unlike the programs just described, a music conservatory or art school focuses intensely on training arts professionals. The training can be broad or very specific but includes at least some liberal arts requirements if the school offers a bachelor's degree. An art school may offer a wide range of specialties, including two- and three-dimensional visual art, architecture, and a range of crafts. It may require a foundation year to explore broadly in the visual arts, or it may specialize in one area like design or architecture. A theater or film program may require the study of all the related disciplines or offer specialized programs in one or another aspect of the art. Some music conservatories focus on classical music, others on popular music; still others include classical and jazz but not other contemporary forms, which may be the focus of still other conservatories. Compare the more classical Curtis Institute of Music to the more contemporary Berklee College of Music to understand the breadth of the field. You will need to define your own priorities and investigate each program and what it offers.

> At a traditional liberal arts school, one can also take a broad range of academic classes and choose to either double major or minor in an academic subject and as well as major in dance. Those opportunities are usually quite limited in conservatory or BFA programs.
>
> PARENT OF A DANCER REFLECTING ON AN ADVANTAGE OF A LIBERAL ARTS PROGRAM

> Since practically every college/university has a theater major, we found it very helpful to look at the course catalogs online. You very quickly can see what they offer—whether it's more of an overview, a very academic approach, lots of hands-on experience, or a combination of academics and training classes.
>
> TIP FROM A PARENT ABOUT HOW TO NARROW THINGS DOWN

Finding the Right College for You

Begin with your teachers. Your art, dance, theater, or music teacher knows your work and has seen your potential. Ask for suggestions about colleges and programs. Go to one of the Performing and Visual Arts College Fairs sponsored by the National Association for College Admission Counseling to talk with representatives from art schools, conservatories, and college arts programs around the country; ask about both their programs and their special requirements. You can find the date and location of the nearest fair and the colleges that will be represented at www.nacacnet.org.

No matter what role the arts might play in your future, it may help to participate in summer arts camps and programs, especially during the summers after sophomore and junior years. Not only do these programs help you build your skills and define yourself as an artist, but you are also immersed in a community of artists much as you would be in a college music program or a conservatory, and you can see whether you really like this intensity and community feeling. In addition, your teachers there are professionals who may well teach in college and conservatory programs and even be involved in admissions at their home institutions.

If visiting colleges is important in general, visiting a conservatory, art school, or arts program is doubly so. Seeing the work produced, and learning what the studio facilities, performance spaces, and practice rooms are like and when they are available to students, are invaluable since you will be spending much of your time in those places surrounded by people producing that kind of work. Meeting the faculty and speaking with current students introduces you to the intense artistic community that will be yours for (at least) four years. Music students should also arrange for a lesson before their campus visit if possible. You should try to visit early during your junior year so that you have plenty of time to shape your college list and prepare the portfolio or audition material that will be an important part of your application.

> Auditioning for a music school is all about finding the right teacher, more important than the name brand of the school. Visiting in person is a must if at all possible, and do your best to get a lesson with the teachers in your instrument.
>
> ADVICE FROM MUSIC GRADUATE

An Overview of the Application Process

You should begin the process early, especially if your application will require auditioning. Art schools and programs tend to have later deadlines to allow for inclusion of senior work in the portfolio, but they also have specific requirements for the portfolio and some offer early decision. If you are applying to performance programs, whether theater, dance, or music (or musical theater, which encompasses all three), you may have two deadlines: one for scheduling the audition and one for the actual application. Some colleges require that you submit an application before submitting a portfolio or requesting an audition.

In fact, if you are applying to a performing arts program in a large university or a liberal arts college, you may have two applications: one to the college itself and one to the performing arts program. You must be accepted at both to enter the arts program.

> My daughter has decided to major in dance and wants to pursue a BFA. Yikes! I am overwhelmed with the amount of time we will have to spend in the next few months getting ready for college auditions and applications.
>
> MOM WHO REALIZES ARTS APPLICATIONS TAKE A LOT OF WORK

Portfolio and Audition Requirements

No matter whether you are a visual or performing artist, you need to scrutinize the portfolio or audition requirements of each college, as well as any other supplementary requirements. College and program websites have detailed information. You can provide a web address where schools can see your work. For visual artists, including those in theater design and tech, some colleges require CDs or a PowerPoint presentation or have a SlideRoom portal to which you upload your images. Performing artists may need to prepare prescreening audition tapes to submit on CD, DVD, website, or a web portal on the college website. As always, read the instructions of each college carefully, and follow them exactly. If you have any questions, call or e-mail the admissions office.

Résumés and Recommendations

A common requirement for all artists is the résumé. This summarizes your experience, giving the years you studied each aspect of your art, where you studied, the names of your teachers, any awards or honors, and any special programs or course work. Musicians, dancers, and actors would provide their repertoire; visual artists would list any exhibitions.

You will be asked to provide a recommendation from a teacher who knows your artistic work well. Earlier in *Admission Matters*, in discussing letters of recommendation, we noted that colleges generally require recommendations from teachers in core academic subjects like English, foreign language, mathematics, science, and social studies. Artists are an exception: all artists should have a solid recommendation highlighting their artistic achievements and promise. Art schools, conservatories, and arts programs require it, and you would be at a severe disadvantage if you apply without it. Ask for a letter from an art, music, theater, or dance teacher as an extra recommendation if the application does not specifically request one. This may need to be sent separately from the electronic submission of the rest of your application.

Your Statement of Purpose

Other common requirements involve discussing your work, whether in an interview or in an essay or artist's statement. Be prepared to address your creative process, your challenges and successes, and your vision. Talk about the artists you enjoy, the music that speaks to you, the performances that delight you, the role art plays in your life now and as you imagine your future. Martha Graham once said, "A vitality, a life force, an energy, a quickening, that . . . is translated through you into action, and because there is only one of you in all time, this expression is unique." Introduce your admissions readers to your uniqueness.

The Visual Arts Portfolio

First, read the requirements from all the colleges you're applying to, including deadlines both for applications and scholarships. Requirements vary from school to school and may have specific and unique assignments, like a home test or a self-portrait or selections from your sketchbook. Most colleges requiring portfolios list what kinds of work they suggest you include on their website. If you have questions, call the college. Most admissions offices are happy to help applicants know what to include (and not to include) in their portfolios.

Assembling Your Work

Gather your work from the past two years, lay it out, and determine which pieces speak to your ability and potential. Ask your teacher to review your work with you for an objective critique. What is required that the work you have already done does not cover? That is your task for senior year. Overall, you need to present 10 to 20 pieces. It is wise to include some that show the range of your interests and skills as well as your personal focus. If your school does not have a strong arts program, consider a continuing education or summer course in portfolio development at an art school or local college.

Students interested in applying to visual art programs requiring portfolios should begin enrolling in advanced art courses during eleventh grade to allow ample time to create enough artwork from which to create a portfolio. Attending a summer or precollege arts program the summer before twelfth grade is an excellent way to not only create more portfolio-ready work, but also to see whether attending an intense BFA arts program is a good fit. It is much easier to create an excellent portfolio when you have 30 to 50 or more works of art to choose from when narrowing to the final 12 to 20 portfolio images.[1]

BARRY BEACH, INDEPENDENT COLLEGE CONSULTANT AND FORMER DIRECTOR OF ADMISSIONS AT OREGON COLLEGE OF ART AND CRAFT

National Portfolio Day

A number of portfolio day events around the United States and Canada sponsored by the National Portfolio Day Association provide an opportunity to take your work to be reviewed by any of about 50 US and Canadian art schools and programs. Participating colleges are nonprofit, regionally accredited, and nationally accredited through the National Association of Schools of Art and Design.

Because of large crowds, plan to come early and decide which colleges to seek out first to increase the likelihood that they will indeed be able to speak with you before the end of the day. The schedule and list of art schools can be found at www.portfolioday.net. In addition, most colleges of art provide a portfolio review when you visit their campus if you have scheduled it in advance. This can be an excellent way to get feedback from colleges to which you are most interested in applying.

Documenting Your Portfolio

When you have assembled your portfolio, you need to photograph it. You can have this done professionally or do it yourself with a good camera, excellent lighting, and a neutral background. Most portfolios now are presented electronically rather than on slides, but the same guidelines apply: photograph each piece separately, using a neutral background and good lighting (some say that outdoor light is best). The piece should fill the camera frame, and three-dimensional work should be photographed from several angles using lighting that helps define edges or textures. While uploading your files, each image should be numbered, identified with your name, the title (if any) of the work, the date it was done, its medium, and its dimensions. If you send slides, check to be sure that the colleges to which you are applying will accept them. Label them and send a separate typed description sheet of the portfolio along with it. Be sure to keep master copies of any slides or CDs that you send.

Notes for Abroad: United Kingdom

If you are applying to a British college of art and design, you need to prepare a very different portfolio. Most of these art schools are interested mainly in process: they want applicants to present their creative ideas from inception through development and encourage students to submit their most recent work even if it is unfinished. They value the interview in particular because they can talk with you about your creative process and artistic goals. These schools also emphasize including the sketchbook to show your exploration of ideas, techniques, and media.

For Writers and Filmmakers

If you are interested in film or writing, including screen writing, you also need to scrutinize the portfolio requirements of the various programs and follow them carefully. An artist's statement will certainly be required and a résumé of your experience. You may be asked to submit visual materials by DVD or hyperlink or write a 10-page review or analysis of some aspect of cinema; some programs accept a wide range of creative material, both written and visual.

Required materials for filmmaking programs vary widely, from only visual information to only written information. While most film programs at colleges of art want a visual portfolio, film programs at liberal arts colleges or universities often review writing samples only. Application requirements can range from photographs or a short film clip to a full film with script or storyboard (or both) to just a script. There is usually a 10- to 20-minute time limit for film, but sometimes as little as five minutes. Samples of screenwriting or other creative writing should be about 10 pages, but many BA and BFA programs in creative writing do not require portfolios or do so only during a student's freshman or sophomore year. Students interested in theater tech and scene or costume design also need to submit a portfolio of their work. Whenever a portfolio is required, college websites have detailed information on what is required and often have helpful suggestions about how to meet the requirement.

The Performing Arts Audition

Auditions are a critical part of the application process for actors, singers, dancers, and musicians. Sometimes they are all that really counts. The general application process parallels that of your peers, but scheduling and preparing for auditions start early. Auditions can be scheduled as early as October and are most commonly given in January and February of your senior year either on campus or in central locations around the country.

Six music conservatories currently use the Unified Application for Music and Performing Arts Schools to help students avoid having to submit common information many times on different applications: the Boston Conservatory, the Manhattan School of Music, Mannes College New School for Music, the

New England Conservatory of Music, the Oberlin Conservatory of Music, and the San Francisco Conservatory of Music. Other programs use different applications.

Plan Your Schedule

First, consider how many auditions you can do in a day; we advise limiting yourself to one, with the possible exception of acting. Theater auditions are usually relatively short, but musical theater, because it involves acting, singing, and dancing, takes much more time. Music auditions sometimes involve sight-reading or music theory tests, as well as specific prepared (and often memorized) performance pieces. Dance auditions may involve dancing in class groups as well as solo. Before you start to schedule, check the college websites for precise information on the audition. Consider your energy as well as time; auditions can be draining.

If you have researched college options carefully and made your college list, you are ready to map out the audition schedule. Scheduling is like assembling a puzzle: you start with one piece, and arrange other pieces around it, sometimes rearranging until it all fits. Some colleges do not schedule an audition until they have received your application, and others may want to prescreen you from a CD, DVD, or uploaded onto a website or a dedicated portal; always check the college website for precise information. Make a spreadsheet with deadlines and requirements. If you must schedule two auditions in one day, be sure to get a time frame from the first college so you have plenty of time to get to the next one. The earlier you can plan out and arrange your audition schedule, the better. College websites provide detailed information about current audition requirements and guidelines. You should be able to get all the information you need by late summer or early September, if not earlier, with very specific guidelines for your instrument, monologue and song selection, or dance techniques.

Theater Auditions

For actors, over two dozen colleges offer centralized theater auditions during the first half of February through Unified Auditions in New York, Chicago, Las Vegas, and Los Angeles, so students can travel to one location and audition several times over the course of a day or two. However, since musical theater demands that you be an artistic triple threat, your audition may well last all day. Colleges not affiliated with Unified Auditions may also be auditioning on the same schedule in those locations. Other colleges usually offer audition slots around the country on

> My son auditioned at fourteen schools and applied to two nonaudition schools. We had very large pieces of white butcher paper taped to his bedroom walls—one was a matrix of all the schools, spaces for scores/transcripts, recommendations sent, audition scheduled, etc. This helped us see at a glance what was left to do at any given time. We kind of turned his bedroom into a "war room," which sometimes it felt like the process was.
>
> THEATER MOM

specific dates as well as on their own campuses. Different conservatory programs often require different kinds of monologues, so be sure to ask what kind of monologues to prepare for each school. At the audition you may be asked to modify your monologue performance in one or two different ways; an audition also usually includes some discussion with the evaluators about the craft of acting and your own experience. They want to see how teachable you are. These are, after all, educational institutions. At some colleges, the audition can involve callbacks.

Music Auditions

Music auditions usually encompass a general information session, ear-training and music fundamentals or theory exams, and about 20 minutes of actual performance following limited warm-up time, ideally but not always in a dedicated practice space. They may take place on the college campus or at locations around the country. Some colleges allow an off-campus audition only if the student lives more than a few hundred miles away. Both on-campus and off-campus auditions may be videotaped for further faculty review. When colleges require a prescreening process, they review recordings submitted on CDs or a digital audition portal before scheduling an audition, and many require at least a partial application. Early audition options at some colleges allow you both to stretch out the audition scheduling and build audition experience before the intensity of January and February.

Dance Auditions

Dancers usually participate in two different technique classes and present a short solo, either a repertory piece or original choreography, and also interview with faculty. Because you will be dancing, expect a dress requirement. You might be asked to dance en pointe, so don't hang up your toe shoes prematurely. If you submit a DVD instead of auditioning live, requirements are clear and specific, and they usually cover a range of ballet and modern. You may also be asked to include an oral statement about your goals in dance. All of this, and any variations to it, is available on college and conservatory websites.

Showcasing Your Artistic Talents as Part of a General Application

What if you are not interested in applying to an arts program, but want to bring your artistic ability to the attention of an admissions committee? As we discussed in chapter 2, colleges seek to build a freshman class with students who will contribute in many different ways, including through their involvement as artists. One way to make admissions committees aware of your talent, of course, is to include your participation in the arts in the activities section of the Common Application, as well as other applications that ask about extracurricular involvement. However, students with a deep commitment to the arts as well as notable talent can do more to ensure that colleges consider their talent in the admissions process.

How and What Should You Submit?

Some colleges do not consider this kind of information as part of their admissions review, but those that do can differ in the approach they take to obtaining and using it. Colleges that use the Common Application may ask students to submit arts-related material through a SlideRoom portal integrated with the Common App. Others colleges, both those that use the Common App as well as those that don't, may have their own forms and process for submission that may or may not involve SlideRoom. Procedures vary from college to college, so you have to check carefully to see how each one handles submissions for your specific art form— dance, music, theater, or visual arts.

Unlike conservatories and art schools, many colleges do not provide detailed information about what to include in your submission, so you will need some help deciding how best to present yourself as an artist. As you assemble your art or plan your audition for taping, your teachers will be your best resource. Arts teachers have done this themselves and have seen many students through the process. Another resource is the information on portfolios and auditions provided on the websites of conservatories and arts schools.

How Is Your Submission Reviewed?

Although your submission may be sent first to the admissions office, the relevant academic department generally reviews it, so there may be an earlier deadline to compensate for the extra processing time. The admissions office will then receive a professional assessment of your supplementary material from its own faculty. When the evaluation comes back to the admissions office, it is entered into your file and is considered part of the overall application.

If the evaluation indicates exceptional ability in a given area, your talent may serve as a significant admissions hook, especially if it is in short supply at the college. If the evaluation of your work isn't particularly strong—if, for example, you are just good, not great, at the piano—it won't hurt you since you cannot be faulted for trying, but it probably won't help either. A small number of schools discourage the submission of supplements unless the student's level of talent is very high; these colleges include this advice along with their submission instructions.

If you have any questions about how to submit evidence of your talent, call or e-mail the admissions office. The website will often give you the name of a specific contact person for arts-related questions. The earlier you do this the better, since it often takes a good deal of time to prepare your portfolio or audition materials. Although planning ahead is a good idea for everyone, it is especially important if you want to make your artistic talent part of the application process.

CHAPTER 11

Students with Special Circumstances

Students with disabilities, homeschoolers, and those planning to transfer each have special considerations in their college search and selection process. If you fall into one or more of these categories, you'll find key information in this chapter to help answer the many questions you no doubt have.

STUDENTS WITH DISABILITIES

Do you receive or have you been offered accommodations in high school such as extended time on tests, extra help keeping on top of assignments, large-type books because of a vision problem, or the option to leave class for brief periods of time without needing permission because of a medical condition? If so, you are far from alone. About 10 percent of students who plan to enroll full time in colleges and universities in the United States meet the federal definition of *disabled*, making them eligible to receive various types of accommodations from their high schools. You are probably familiar with the terms *504* and *IEP* if you belong to this group.

What Is the Definition of *Disability*?

The federal government considers you to have a disability if you have a medical or psychological condition that substantially limits a major life activity like walking, eating, concentrating, learning, and so forth. Some disabilities, like those that affect mobility or vision, are usually fairly obvious. Others, like learning disabilities, attention deficit hyperactivity disorder (ADHD), psychological disabilities, and some medical conditions, are not. They are considered hidden disabilities. All, however, qualify you for certain legal protections if the condition meets the criterion of impairing a major life activity.

When students with a federally defined disability prepare to apply to college, the first question they (or their parents) often ask is whether the disability should play a role in the decision about where to apply. Following soon after is the question of whether the disability should be disclosed to colleges at all before the student is accepted. Then, if the answer to the second question is yes, the next question is how to do this in the most positive way. The answer to all of these questions, as you will see, is, "It depends." There is no one-size-fits-all answer because students have widely differing disabilities and accommodations. This section is designed to help you figure out the answers that work for you, including how to request appropriate accommodations on the SAT or ACT if needed.

The Most Common Disabilities

The most common diagnoses that lead to accommodations in high school are learning disabilities—a broad, umbrella-type category that includes such things as dyslexia, processing speed problems, and dysgraphia—and ADHD. To simplify the discussion, we focus here on accommodations for these disabilities, although much of what we have to say can be adapted easily for students with physical disabilities that affect mobility, vision, or hearing, as well as for students with psychiatric disorders and other medical conditions.

Before we discuss the specifics of college selection and application, we first want to share some background information to help you better understand the differences in the federal laws that apply when you are in high school and the laws that apply once you enroll in college. The differences are important because the services offered by a particular college may differ, sometimes greatly, from what you have come to count on.

What Laws Apply in High School

The Individuals with Disabilities Education Act

The Individuals with Disabilities Education Act (IDEA) is a federal law, passed in 1975, designed to help students from preschool through high school who have disabilities that require special education services. Depending on the nature of the disability, the help provided can be extra time on tests, tutoring, more frequent breaks, testing in a quieter environment, orally administered exams, or other kinds of assistance, in addition to special classes or modifications to the regular curriculum. The law requires that the appropriate services for each eligible high school student be provided free of charge and that they be documented in an Individual Education Plan (IEP) or other intervention plan that is evaluated every three years.

The goal of IDEA is student success. A student with a disability who can nevertheless function adequately in a regular classroom without any additional educational support would generally not qualify for services under IDEA because he has demonstrated that he can be successful without them.

Section 504

A second route to help for students with disabilities is Section 504. Section 504 is part of the Rehabilitation Act of 1973 that prohibits discrimination against a student whose "physical or mental disability substantially limits one or more major life functions such as . . . seeing, breathing, learning, and walking." The law entitles students to appropriate accommodations so that they can access educational programs and activities. Unlike students covered by IDEA, students do not have to be eligible for special education services to be covered under Section 504. These accommodations include access to medication during the school day, use of a school elevator, and extra time on tests for students with a specific reading disability.

Different Laws Apply in College

The benefits of IDEA end when a student graduates from high school. Replacing it is the Americans with Disabilities Act, or ADA, a far-reaching law passed in 1990, that applies to both institutions of higher education and businesses.

The Americans with Disabilities Act

The ADA requires colleges and universities to provide students with reasonable accommodations to ensure that they are not being discriminated against because of a disability. The IDEA emphasizes student success; the goal of ADA is to level the playing field and ensure that all students have appropriate access to educational offerings. Whereas IDEA deals with entitlement programs, the regulations of the ADA are civil rights protections, just like Section 504.

Student Success Versus Student Access

This difference in approach between student success and student access is very important to understand, particularly for students with learning disabilities or ADHD. Some colleges provide the basic access services mandated by the ADA, while others go beyond—in some cases, well beyond what is minimally required. Each student needs to determine what he or she needs to be successful and then seek out colleges that will provide the appropriate level of support in addition to the many other qualities that make a school appealing.

Some Important Questions to Ask Yourself

Students who have received accommodations in high school for learning disabilities, ADHD, or any other disability, whether in conjunction with special education services or not, should continue the honest self-assessment begun in chapter 4. Along with your family, you should ask yourself additional questions to help you understand the role your disability and accompanying accommodations play in your education. The greater the role or impact of the disability, the more important it will be to find schools that will meet your needs as they relate to the disability. *The K&W Guide to College Programs and Services for Students with Learning Disabilities or Attention Deficit/Hyperactivity Disorder* is a valuable resource by two experts in the field that provides an extensive list of questions for a self-assessment that applies to all students with a diagnosed disability regardless of what it is.[1] These are some of the most important ones to ask:

- What is the nature of my disability, and when was it first diagnosed? When were my last diagnostic tests given?
- What is my level of performance in high school?
- Am I enrolled in college-prep courses, modified courses, special education courses, or a combination?
- What accommodations have been approved for me, and which ones do I use and need?
- What are my academic strengths and weaknesses?
- What are my long-term goals, and are they realistic?

With answers to these questions in hand, you and your family will be in a better position to evaluate colleges and the disability services they offer. It won't surprise you to know that colleges will be interested in this information if you choose to share it with them.

Categories of Disabilities Support

Colleges and universities vary widely in the nature and extent of the support they provide students with disabilities, but each can be placed in one of three broad categories. Knowledge of these categories will help you find colleges that best meet your needs.

Tier One or Basic Support

Most colleges provide what is often referred to as *basic support*, or Tier One support. Basic support meets the federal mandate that requires reasonable accommodations for students with disabilities who provide the appropriate documentation of those disabilities. They are sometimes referred to as limited or self-directed programs.

> My son was diagnosed with ADHD his senior year in high school. Because he was very smart and his dad and I helped keep him organized and on track, we did not consider ADHD assistance when he picked a college. That was a big mistake.
>
> MOM OF SON WHO EXPERIENCED DIFFICULTY BUT EVENTUALLY GOT THE HELP HE NEEDED

The law requires that each college have a staff member responsible for ensuring that appropriate accommodations are provided for students who submit adequate documentation. Tier One support provides accommodations such as extended time on tests, large-print materials, and access to text-to-speech software. At a Tier One school, the disabilities service office generally provides a student needing extended time on exams with copies of a letter to give to each of his or her teachers explaining the need for such accommodations and asking that they be provided. The student would be responsible for answering any questions a teacher might have and in general for self-advocating in the process, with the support of the disabilities service office. There would likely be no monitoring of the student's academic progress by staff trained in disabilities issues, and it is not likely that trained staff would be available to provide additional disabilities-related support if needed, although there are exceptions. The advising, support, and tutoring services provided would be similar for all students on the campus.

Many students find that the minimal level of disability support provided at Tier One is all that they need to be successful in college. It generally works quite well for students who have strong self-advocacy and time management skills and have performed well in high school, as many hard-working students have.

Tier Two or Coordinated Services

Tier Two support goes beyond the minimum required by law and provides specialized services beyond basic accommodations to students who submit adequate documentation of their disability. Another common term for Tier Two support is *coordinated services*. In addition to providing basic accommodations, Tier Two support can include special tutoring at no cost to the student, special skills classes, and remedial classes where needed.

A Tier Two support college typically has at least one certified learning disabilities specialist on staff to help students develop strategies to meet their individual needs. Tier Two programs typically require students to be proactive in requesting services, and monitoring of student progress, if provided, would be modest. Coordinated services work well for students whose high school performance has been solid but who might need help effectively managing their time as well as in requesting accommodations.

Tier Three or Structured Programs

The highest level of disability support is known as Tier Three, or *structured programs*. Structured programs offer the most comprehensive set of services designed to support students with learning disabilities or ADHD. They are also sometimes called *proactive programs*.

These programs have staff with specialized training in learning disabilities and related areas and offer an extensive array of services, including, but not limited to, diagnostic services, special counseling and advising, special courses and tutoring, and a wide array of specialized aids such as text-to-speech or speech-to-text software and note takers. Staff closely monitor the progress of each student and recommend changes to the program as needed.

Tier Three schools often charge an additional fee for these special programs over and above regular tuition, and students typically have to submit a separate application to the program beyond the application for general admission to the school. One of the best-known programs in this category is the SALT program at the University of Arizona, with almost 600 students participating out of an undergraduate body of about 31,000. Each participant is assigned a learning specialist with whom he or she meets weekly on matters ranging from self-advocacy to time management, as well as help from tutors on assignments and subject matter areas. Landmark College in Putney, Vermont, is another example. It is a two-year college exclusively for students with ADHD or learning disabilities.

Structured programs can work well for students who have relied heavily on accommodations in high school and are unlikely to succeed without more extensive support that may include assistance in effectively managing their time. Close monitoring of student progress can be very important to head off problems before they become overwhelming. Structured programs are also very helpful for students with weaker self-advocacy skills.

Choosing Colleges That Meet Your Needs

An excellent resource to begin your search with once you have determined the kind of disabilities support that will meet your needs is *The K&W Guide*, which gives detailed information about support for students with learning disabilities or ADHD at over 350 colleges and universities, ranging from well-known four-year universities to community colleges around the country. College websites also provide information about the disability services and programs that are offered for students with learning disabilities or ADHD and other disabilities. A good place to start is to search for "disability services." Colleges that offer a wider range of services and programs tend to make information about those services readily available on their website, although you may have to explore a bit to find where it is located.

> I encourage all students to "own the process" and be in the driver's seat. These decisions should be your dreams as long as you have done your "homework." Keep your family on your team, your priorities in order and enjoy the journey.[2]
>
> MARYBETH KRAVETS, COAUTHOR OF *THE K&W GUIDE*

Once you have narrowed your list of schools, visiting them can give you valuable information. Make an appointment to visit the disability services office and talk to the person in charge. Those offices typically work independent of the admissions office so you need not worry that your visit will be associated with your future application unless you choose to mention it in the application. It is also a good idea to ask about what kinds of documentation the office will require if you enroll and wish to access services. Tier Three programs ask for recent documentation as part of your formal application to the program. Colleges offering

Tier One and Tier Two levels of support ask you to submit documentation after you are admitted. Knowing what will be required in advance of enrollment will help you be prepared.

Should I Disclose My Disability on My Application?

Families often wonder whether it is to a student's advantage to disclose a disability on a college application. The decision is almost always a personal one, since colleges are not permitted to ask a student about disabilities or needed accommodations on the application. The only exceptions, of course, are those programs specifically designed for students with such disabilities. Structured programs like SALT typically require students to submit two applications—one to the college and the other to the structured program itself. In these cases, the disability is an important part of the application.

But what about disclosing in general? Sometimes students feel that their need for accommodations may disadvantage them relative to other applicants or that they don't want their disability to be highlighted on their application when they are considered for admission. The choice about whether to disclose is really up to you. It can actually be to your advantage to disclose your disability (perhaps in the section for "Additional Information" on the Common Application or on other applications) if any of the following situations applies to you:

- Your grades (or your test scores) are lower because of the disability.
- Your disability was identified later in high school, and your grades have improved significantly since.
- Your disability has affected the classes you pursued in high school, for example, you have not taken a foreign language, or you regularly take study skills courses that most other students do not take.
- Your disability has had an impact on the nature and extent of your involvement in activities outside the classroom.

Disclosing will help admissions officers put your application into context and answer the questions that would naturally arise in their minds when they are reading your file: "Why did her grades go up so much in sophomore year?" "Why are his test scores so low relative to his academic performance?" It is generally better to provide the answer yourself rather than have admissions officers guess the reasons. Colleges are forbidden by law from discriminating against you in the admissions process because of your disability, and learning disabilities and ADHD are now so common and so commonly disclosed that admissions officers are very familiar with them. In fact, disclosing can actually help you if you have shown the personal qualities, such as determined hard work, self-advocacy, and insight, that colleges want to see in general, and in particular for students with learning disabilities.

A special case has to do with certain medical and psychiatric disorders since they frequently affect a student's academic record and other aspects of high school life. Sometimes disclosure of a medical condition, whether physical or psychiatric, is unavoidable due to facts on the transcript, such as a medical withdrawal. You should stress the extent of your recovery, hopefully complete, and your confidence in taking on college life. Again, insight, maturity, and thoughtfulness will go a long way. We caution against disclosing too much detail, as it is not really necessary at this point.

Standardized Testing—Accommodations and More

Students with diagnosed disabilities of all types that warrant accommodations may seek them from the College Board (for the PSAT, SAT, SAT Subject Tests, and Advanced Placement Tests) and from the ACT (for the ACT). Detailed information about the process for obtaining accommodations on tests administered by the College Board may be found at www.collegeboard.com/ssd/student/. Information for the ACT may be found at www.actstudent.org/regist/disab/.

> Because the A.D.A. is outcome neutral, we are not looking to maximize a student's performance so that they can do the best they can. We are looking to provide equal access.[3]
>
> SUSAN MICHAELSON, MANAGER OF TEST ACCOMMODATIONS, ACT

Start Early

Both the College Board and ACT have comprehensive review processes that can take several weeks, so it is important to seek accommodations early so that they can be approved and in place when you need them. The most frequently requested accommodation is extra time, usually time and a half, but accommodations can include frequent breaks, a separate testing site, testing over multiple days, large-print materials, use of a computer for the essay, and others. Some accommodations are offered at the regular test site, but other types may require in-school testing at another time. The College Board and ACT do not flag or annotate test scores obtained with accommodations, so colleges cannot tell whether you had extra time.

What You Need to Request Accommodations

The process of obtaining accommodations is easiest when a student has had appropriate assessments at a school that have led to an IEP, 504 plan, or school accommodations plan that is currently in force. In these cases, the student's counselor or another person designated by the school can submit the request for accommodations through separate online systems for the College Board and the ACT. If the evaluation is too recent to have an IEP in place or if one was never developed, you must typically make the request by mail using forms accessible through the College Board and ACT websites. Parents sometimes submit these themselves, or they may seek the help of the guidance office.

The response from the College Board or ACT typically comes as a letter to the student, indicating approval of accommodations (and detailing the specifics), a denial, or a request for additional information before a decision can be made. Families need to time their request for accommodations so that they will be approved and in place at least a week before a test date to ensure that there will be time for the appropriate arrangements to be made. Once a student has received approval for accommodations from the College Board, those accommodations may be put into place on all College Board tests, including SAT Subject Tests and AP tests.

After You Have Been Accepted

Whether or not you have disclosed your disability on your application, once you are accepted, we encourage you to contact the disabilities services office if you have not done so already to find out what kinds of documentation are required to be eligible for accommodations.

The process varies from school to school, so get this information as soon as you can. In general, most schools require testing done within the past three years, and any IQ test must use the adult version (as opposed to the version for children). For many students, this will likely mean retesting at their own expense if they do not have the appropriate test results available. Sometimes, though, your family may be able to arrange for the testing through your high school if you would otherwise be retested in tenth or eleventh grade. Schools often administer the adult version of the IQ test if requested and if the student was on schedule to be tested. Advance planning can potentially save time and a lot of money.

TIPS FOR HOMESCHOOLERS

Over the past 25 years, homeschooling has become an increasingly popular option for American families. Homeschoolers are very difficult to count, but a recent National Home Education Research Institute study estimated that over 2 million students are homeschooled in the United States. If you are reading this section, you are probably one of them.

Families homeschool for many reasons; the most often cited are concerns about school environment, a desire to provide religious or moral instruction, and dissatisfaction with the academic instruction available in other schools (including a wish to provide a more challenging curriculum). Young athletes competing and training internationally, young artists performing around the globe, and students with serious health issues are also among the homeschooled. Whatever the reason or reasons, you and your family have chosen homeschooling. Despite the proliferation of online college courses and even some graduate programs that can be done entirely online, however, like most other homeschoolers, you probably still prefer the idea of a traditional college education. Very few opt for homeschooling beyond high school.

Colleges Welcome Homeschoolers

The good news is that colleges have become much more receptive to homeschooled applicants than they were even a decade ago. Most colleges now have considerable experience evaluating the credentials of homeschooled students, and many have developed formal admissions guidelines and policies for homeschoolers. Suggestions about how to proceed

> One quality that we look for in all of our applicants is evidence of having taken initiative, showing entrepreneurial spirit, taking full advantage of opportunities. Many of our admitted homeschooled applicants have really shined in this area.[4]
>
> MIT ADMISSIONS WEBSITE

that fit almost any college are found on some college websites themselves. We suggest you search for Home-Schooled Applicant Guidelines at Stanford University or the University of Florida, for example. Homeschool Admission Guidelines at Claremont McKenna College and Homeschool Applicants at Lawrence University also provide some good examples.

Similarities and Differences

As you approach the college application process, we advise you to try to emulate the approach and research of a regular high school applicant as much as possible. Everything we have said in *Admission Matters* about self-inquiry, visiting colleges, writing essays, preparing for standardized tests, and deciding on a balanced list of colleges applies to homeschoolers as much as to regular students. On several points, however, the experience of homeschoolers does diverge significantly, and special care needs to be taken to be sure that you will have the strongest possible applications.

Grades and Transcripts

Colleges like to see grades, but they mean something only in a comparative context. Even in a regular high school, all A's don't help much if half the class gets all A's. Similarly, if you are the only one in the class and your parents are your teachers and give you all A's, it is hard for a college admissions officer to use that information to compare you to other applicants, even other homeschoolers. Colleges do want you to have taken a broad array of courses in high school, including laboratory science and foreign language. While they may grant you some flexibility because you followed your passion for ornithology for a year but didn't take a basic biology course, or read nothing but Greek and Celtic mythology without a regular English class, you may look unbalanced and, worse, unprepared. Basically you have to think about meeting the college halfway.

It can help if you have supplemented your homeschooling with some regular courses from a high school, community college, or online program—anything that allows the college to evaluate your record relative to other applicants. Students who have used the full high school diploma curriculum and teacher support of a distance learning school like Laurel Springs School or the Oak Meadow School may well find that the organization itself functions as would a high school in terms of transcript and recommendations. The same is true of public virtual schools and academies in a number of states.

Test Scores

With less capacity to evaluate your grades, standardized testing is often more important for homeschoolers than it is for regular applicants. It seems to fly in the face of the purpose of homeschooling, which celebrates individuality above all else, to emphasize standardized tests, but SAT Subject Tests and Advanced Placement (AP) tests in particular can help a college evaluate your mastery of your curriculum. Even if your colleges do not normally require them, taking SAT Subject Tests in several areas can strengthen your application, and many colleges recommend taking them. Some students prepare for and take AP exams to demonstrate the rigor of their course work. You would have to contact a local high school several months in advance to register for AP exams, since they are offered only in high schools.

Recommendations

Is your mother your "school counselor"? Can she write an objective letter on your behalf that will be persuasive to a college admissions officer? This can be difficult, but most colleges will want something like that. Anything you can do to supplement your file with recommendations from others not related to you who have taught you will help. Here, courses taken at a high school or community college, or even from a private tutor, can be especially valuable. Claremont McKenna College also requires an extracurricular recommendation for homeschoolers, preferably written by a nonfamily member who knows you in the context of your larger community: a coach, employer, or clergy member, for example. Consider adding such a letter even when it is not explicitly required.

Activities

Stereotypes die hard, but some people, including some admissions officers, believe that homeschoolers have few friends and don't socialize well. There is no basis for this, of course, but it is important to be aware of it early in your high school years. You should make a concerted effort to be a normal teenager, to get out and do things in the community. It is not important what you do, and the admissions office will understand that you didn't have a school band or yearbook to belong to, but it is good to show energy, commitment over time, and some social experience that suggests you get along well with your peers.

Interviews

While we think it is a good idea for all students to take advantage of an interview with an admissions officer or alumni interviewer, we strongly recommend that home-schooled students have an interview if one is available. In fact, some colleges require that homeschoolers interview as part of the application process. An interview gives you an opportunity to talk about your experience as a homeschooler, discuss your aspirations, and display your social and communication skills firsthand.

Record Keeping

Parents: Keep good records of your child's education from ninth grade on, including what textbooks you used, what books your child read for English, and what special projects she worked on. Special projects are an advantage for homeschoolers, who can demonstrate more easily than regular high school students that they can pursue projects on their own and take responsibility for their own education. Colleges like this ability, but they want details. Explaining why you and your family chose to homeschool, how you went about it, and how you feel about it now will all be important elements of your personal essay and other parts of your application.

The Importance of Starting Early

We cannot stress too strongly that you need to be proactive much earlier than regular high school students in finding out what specific colleges will want from you in terms of a transcript, required course work, testing, recommendations, a portfolio, and the like. Most colleges want to see an explanation of the reasons for homeschooling and a comprehensive overview of your curriculum, including descriptions of the courses taken and the books used in those courses. Each college is likely to be different, however, even if their applications look the same. A call to discuss requirements with an admissions officer at each college you are interested in is a good idea. You have to take the application process just as seriously as anyone else, and perhaps even more so since you lack the normal sources of information found in a high school counseling office.

MAKING A CHANGE: HOW TO SUCCESSFULLY TRANSFER COLLEGES

The largest number of students who transfer colleges have planned it from the beginning when they enrolled in a community college with the idea of completing the requirements for transfer to a four-year college in two years. Students choose to attend a community college for many reasons: financial, personal, or because they need to demonstrate that they can succeed in college-level work to gain admission to a four-year college of their choosing. Others choose to enroll immediately after high school in a four-year college that accepted them, while also intending right from the beginning to transfer at the earliest opportunity to a school more to their liking. Still others find that the school where they first enroll turns out not to be such a good fit after all. Sometimes students want to transfer for very tangible reasons. Perhaps the cost of tuition, fees, and living expenses turns out to be too great a burden despite some financial aid, or perhaps family circumstances force you to move closer to home. Maybe you have developed an interest in an area of study not offered by your current school, or you have found the academic demands of the school to be too great (or not challenging enough).

Other reasons are less tangible. Some students find that they are lost in the big university they thought would be exciting with a big stadium full of devoted fans on six Saturdays in the fall. They decide they would be more comfortable at a smaller school. Others may find that the small school they loved at the outset now feels too small, and they decide to seek a bigger school. Some find the student climate (or the actual climate!) uncomfortable at their current school. Others feel homesick and just want to be closer to home.

Much of what you have already read in this book applies to transfer students because the process is very similar to the freshman process, but with some twists. In this section, we discuss the similarities and differences and help you decide whether transferring makes sense for you. If you conclude the answer is yes, we'll advise you how to move forward.

How Transfers Help Colleges

Many colleges like to admit transfer students because they are generally a bit older, are more mature, and bring a seriousness of purpose with them when they enroll. Transfer students have also been put to the test by their previous college, so a college does not have to predict whether a student will do well in college since transfer students have an actual college track record that they can evaluate. Transfer students also help colleges fill gaps in their enrollment from students dropping out, stopping out, or transferring themselves.

Here are some important points about transferring to keep in mind:

- Colleges vary greatly in how many transfer students they admit. Some of the most selective colleges are even more selective for transfer admission since they have so few open spots to accept these students.

- Students generally transfer at the end of either their first or second year. Most schools want a student to be enrolled for at least two years of credit in order to award a bachelor's degree from that school.

- State universities often have articulation agreements with community colleges in the state to ease the transfer process for students. Students who meet grade point average requirements in a set of general education courses may be guaranteed admission.

- Schools will vary in how much weight they place on standardized tests and your high school record in the transfer admissions process. That weight may vary depending on whether you transfer after one or two years. The later you transfer, the less weight they will carry. In some cases, they might not matter at all. So if your high school record and test scores were modest, be sure to check in advance with the college where you are thinking of transferring to see what they will ask for.

- Applications are generally due by February 1 or March 1, although some may be earlier or later.

- Decisions are generally made later than for freshman admission, by May 1 or June 1.

- Colleges vary widely in how much financial aid is available for transfer students.

Is Transferring Right for You?

The decision to transfer from one four-year college to another is complex. Most decisions made to transfer after two years tend to be well founded. By that point, students have a good idea of what their current school does and does not offer, as well as the advantages and disadvantages of transferring. Assuming a student has a clear, realistic view of the options, submitting transfer applications can be a good choice.

More problematic are decisions to transfer after one year, which means that students often decide to transfer in their first semester of college. Since applications are due in late winter or early spring, you generally need to begin the process early in the second semester. Is that really enough time to know if a college is a good fit for you? Earlier in the book, we discussed how there are no perfect colleges, but that there are plenty of colleges where a student will be perfectly happy. Have you looked beyond any immediate problem like an incompatible roommate or a couple of teachers you may not be too excited about? Have you joined clubs or gotten involved in activities that interest you? If you find some of your classmates in freshman classes unengaged, have you gone to a professor to see if you can get involved in research? (Yes, freshmen can do research. Professors like them because they will be around a long time.) If you are having academic difficulties, have you sought help from the academic support services center or your teachers or teaching assistants?

> When I applied to college, I was wait-listed or denied at my top schools. So I went to Big State U. determined to transfer ASAP. But I didn't transfer. I found that the honors programs, opportunities to know professors, and the undergrad research made what I thought was going to be my "back-up back-up school" my dream institution.
>
> STUDENT WHO HAD PLANNED TO TRANSFER BUT DECIDED NOT TO

If you are considering transferring after one year for these or any other reason, we encourage you to talk to others about it. A good place to start is the advisor you were likely assigned when you started school. Some schools assign an academic advisor as well as a peer advisor, a junior or senior specially trained to help first-year students. Talk to one or both or to the dean of students or someone in that office. Talk to your parents. The problem may resolve itself with a bit of time.

One student we know went back to talk to his high school counselor after one semester at college. The college was too small, he said; there was just one party each weekend—always the same party, it seemed. The counselor volunteered to help with the transfer process if he wanted to pursue it, but he never heard from the student again until the end of his junior year. The student said he was now very happy at his college. When the counselor asked what, in retrospect, had been wrong freshman year, the student replied, "I was a freshman."

How Colleges Evaluate Transfer Applicants

Many colleges that use the Common Application for freshman admission use the Common Application adapted for transfer students if they accept transfers. The questions for transfers are very similar to the ones asked of freshman applicants with three main exceptions. Those exceptions give insights into how the transfer process differs from the one you may have experienced the first time around.

Your Grades in College Courses

Although your grades and the courses you took in high school were likely the most important factors in your admission to college as a freshman, your college academic record will now be the most important factor in another college's decision whether to admit you as a transfer student. You will be asked to report your current college courses or those you have taken during the current academic year, as well as submit a transcript from each college you may have attended.

Certainly many schools will review your high school transcript and test scores, especially if you are transferring after just one year in college, but your college record will receive careful scrutiny. One college we know counts the high school record as roughly two-thirds of your academic record if you are a first-year transfer and only one-third if you are a second-year applicant. Some colleges publish the minimum college GPA a student must have to be considered for admission as a transfer. Meeting the minimum, however, may not be enough, especially if a college receives many more transfer applicants than it has room for. And those in admissions know that some colleges grade more strictly than others, just as high schools do.

Colleges with open admissions or very lenient admissions policies are good options for transferring for students who find their current academic environment too demanding and whose college grades have suffered as a result. Selective colleges, in contrast, want to see evidence of strong academic performance.

Your Reasons for Wanting to Transfer

The second difference between the Common Application for freshmen and transfers is a required prompt for your personal essay. You will be asked to provide a statement that addresses your reasons for transferring and the objectives you hope to achieve. The strongest transfer applicants have a compelling, mature reason for wanting to transfer.

The answer is easy, of course, if you are completing a two-year degree and now want to pursue a bachelor's degree: you need to transfer in order to achieve your educational goals. In other cases, you have had more time to contemplate your educational direction. You have probably thought a good deal about a major. Your application is no longer simply about going to college. You may find that you cannot pursue a newly discovered academic interest at your current school because no major is offered or that your school doesn't have many small seminar-style classes or enough opportunities for undergraduate student research in which you thrive, or that the sport or other activity you wanted to pursue has been discontinued or is undersupported. There can be lots of compelling reasons for wanting to transfer schools.

Staying Engaged

The third difference between the freshman and transfer application is the time period for which you will be asked about your activities. Instead of grades 9, 10, 11, 12, and postgraduate, you will be asked to list extracurricular and work experiences just for grades 11 and 12 as well as freshman, sophomore, and junior years of college, if applicable. In other words, colleges are interested in how much you have become involved at your current college.

This means that even if you enter as a freshman intent on transferring at the first opportunity, you should still get involved in the life of your school as soon as you can. Being involved may even lead to a change of heart about transferring. Through that community service project or club sport, you may find your niche. But even if that doesn't happen, that activity will strengthen your transfer application. Colleges want transfer students who will be engaged, contributing members of the campus community, and the best predictor of future engagement is your most recent level of activity.

Activity itself is usually enough. College freshmen and sophomores are rarely editors of the school paper, presidents of the student body, and captains of sports teams as they may have been as high school seniors. If you attend a large state university, it may be harder to get involved significantly at the outset. Your transfer colleges will understand this, so don't force yourself to be active simply because you want to transfer. Just get involved in something you like.

Why Are You Interested in Our College?

Many schools that accept the Common Application for transfers also require students to complete a supplement with questions that often focus on the student's area of academic interest as well as on the by-now-familiar question, "Why are you interested in our college?" Sometimes you will find these two combined into one big question: "How will our college help you achieve your academic goals?" Notice the word *academic*.

Here, as in the freshman application, you should explain as specifically as possible why a particular college would be a great fit. Especially at schools with very low transfer admit rates, generic answers about "outstanding reputation" or "wonderful facilities" will not help you. Schools want to know that the few transfer spots they have will go to the students who will most benefit from them. A thoughtful, insightful response to the "how" or "why" question can help make the case that you are one of them. So you need to do some research on the college. Who are the leading professors in your prospective field? What courses do they teach? Why is this subject exciting to you?

Letters You Will Need

Public universities that accept community college students or other transfer students after two years generally do not require any letters of recommendation to support the transfer application. In fact, if you have prearranged the transfer through an articulation agreement—a contract that spells out what courses you have to take and what grades you have to achieve to be admitted to a specific college—your transfer process will be simple, smooth, and predictable. Even if you don't have an articulation agreement in place, you still probably won't need any letters of recommendation as part of your application.

If you are applying to private colleges as a transfer, however, you may need one or perhaps two letters from college instructors, one from a college dean or other official, and perhaps even a secondary school report from your high school. Each college sets its own requirements regarding the forms and letters it wants to see for a transfer application, so you have to check each school to be sure that you submit what each one asks for.

If your college classes are large and you don't feel you know any instructors well enough to ask for a letter, consider asking a teaching assistant in a discussion section. It is much better to get a detailed letter from someone who knows your work than a perfunctory letter from a distinguished faculty member who doesn't know you at all. You don't want your letter to say, "I don't know Joe Smith, even though he received an A in my large lecture class." Many schools also designate a specific person to write the official "school letter" that many colleges require. Be sure to find out how this is done at your current college by making a timely inquiry at the office that deals with student advising. This varies at different schools, so we can't tell you specifically where to go to get this information, but it should be easy to find. Don't feel bad about asking a teacher for a recommendation to transfer. You are not criticizing his or her teaching; you just want to move on. You are not the first to do so, and most will gladly help you.

Interviews and Visits

College visits can help you decide if a particular school is right for you as a transfer student, just as visits during high school can help students applying for freshman admission. Colleges that accept large numbers of transfer students may even have special programs for transfer students. If you can attend one, we encourage you to do so, since you may pick up tips that will helpful for your application.

Some schools offer on-site interviews for potential transfer students as well. They can be especially helpful for students who have had a major gap in their education as a result of military service or other reasons. A transfer interview generally focuses on your reasons for wanting to transfer and how you have grown since you first applied to college. While you will no doubt be asked about your experience at your current school, avoid being overly negative about it. Focus instead on what you have learned from the experience and how you will benefit from the opportunities at your new college. Careful review of the transfer information section of college websites is critical to be sure that you have met a school's requirements.

CHAPTER 12

Paying the Bill

Most families would probably agree that one of their biggest concerns during the college admissions process is the cost. This chapter is devoted to helping you pay that bill. The good news is that for many students, the cost of tuition, fees, room, and board posted on the college website is not what the student actually pays. Although no one pays more than the "sticker price," many students pay less, sometimes much less, depending on the family's financial situation and the campus's financial aid policies. The not-so-good news is that financial aid can be complex and confusing to those unfamiliar with how it works, and in some cases it is disappointing.

In this chapter, we will help you understand the two major types of financial aid and when they are awarded. We'll show you how you can roughly calculate how much aid you might expect to receive and the ways it may be packaged, and we'll explain why the actual amount may vary depending on a college's financial aid policies, practices, and resources. We'll also share our thoughts about the role of financial considerations in developing a college list and making a final decision. If your family can easily cover the cost of your education, you can skip this chapter. Otherwise it will pay for everyone to read it carefully.

> Financial aid allowed us to send our daughter where she wanted to go, a private school in the East. With three children, we couldn't have done it without that help. Financial aid really helped our middle-class family.
>
> PARENT OF COLLEGE SOPHOMORE

KEY CONCEPTS FOR UNDERSTANDING FINANCIAL AID

There are two major categories of financial aid: need-based aid and merit aid.

Need-Based Aid

Need-based aid as we will discuss shortly, is awarded to families to help them cover the difference between what the college calculates they can pay and the actual cost of attending a particular college. Colleges use formulas that consider current income, assets, family size, number of children in college, and other considerations to determine the amount a family can pay. With need-based aid, needier students applying to a given college usually receive more aid than more affluent students who would normally pay more on their own. Need-based aid comes in several forms: grants that do not have to be paid back, loans that do, and work-study jobs.

Merit Aid

Merit aid is different. It is essentially a tuition discount that a college offers to encourage a student to attend. Occasionally the size of a merit award may be tied to a student's financial need, but most often merit awards are independent of need and can be awarded to any student a college would really like to have attend, using whatever criteria the college wishes to apply. Some schools award both need-based aid and merit aid, but a small number of schools, including many of the most selective, provide only need-based aid.

Sources of Funding

Two major sources provide the funding for financial aid: the federal and state governments and the colleges themselves. Outside scholarships that students apply for directly from businesses, organizations, and foundations are also a source of funds, but in terms of total number of dollars available for financial aid, they are a very small piece of the pie.

As we will see, the differences between need-based aid and merit aid, the type of aid awarded, as well as the sources of funding can influence your choice of where to apply and ultimately which college to attend. But we are not there yet. First, we need to show you how the process works.

HOW COLLEGES DETERMINE YOUR FINANCIAL NEED

Need-based aid is financial assistance awarded on the basis of a family's demonstrated need. Demonstrated need has a simple definition: it is the difference between the cost of attending a particular college (including tuition and fees, room and board, transportation, books, and personal expenses) and what a family is expected to pay for such costs (the expected family contribution, or EFC for short). A family's EFC theoretically remains a constant while the demonstrated need will change according to the cost of a particular school.

The Principle Behind Need-Based Aid

Need-based aid is designed to reduce or eliminate financial need as a barrier to attending college. Determining what a family can afford, however, is not left up to the family, for obvious reasons. Colleges use formulas that provide an objective way of measuring how much a family can reasonably contribute to a child's education. An underlying principle is that students and parents have the primary responsibility to pay for the cost of a college education, up to their ability to do so, before receiving need-based financial aid. Need-based aid is meant to supplement, not replace, the family contribution.

> I thought we would qualify for need-based aid, but the calculations showed we didn't. It was probably just wishful thinking on my part.
>
> PARENT DISAPPOINTED BY THE RESULTS OF THE NEED ANALYSIS

Forms and More Forms

All applicants for need-based financial aid who are US citizens or permanent residents, regardless of where they live or where they are applying, must complete

---

⚑ The Key Equation for Financial Aid Based on Need

Cost of attendance (tuition and fees, room and board, books, personal expenses, travel)
— Expected family contribution
_____

= Financial need

---

the Free Application for Federal Student Aid (FAFSA). Beyond this, the forms you'll need to submit will depend on the colleges to which you are applying and your home state. Some schools require another form known as the CSS PROFILE from the College Board or an institutional form that the college itself prepares and administers. Supplementary forms may be required for particular students such as those with separated or divorced parents, those whose parents own their own business, or those who do not need to file taxes. Finally, many schools require that federal tax forms be submitted as part of the financial aid process or that the FAFSA be updated using the IRS Data Retrieval Tool that we will briefly discuss later in this chapter.

The Free Application for Federal Student Aid (FAFSA)

The FAFSA is a need analysis form that all colleges use to calculate the EFC to determine eligibility for federal financial aid. It is also used to determine eligibility for most state-based aid, many private awards, and institutional-based aid at many colleges.

What Is Included in the FAFSA Formula?

The FAFSA uses the family's taxed and untaxed income and assets, with various exclusions. For example, it excludes untaxed social security income and does not consider the equity of the family's primary residence. In the case of separated or divorced parents, it does not take into account the income and assets of the noncustodial parent, but if the custodial parent has remarried, the income and assets of the stepparent are included in the calculations. For federal student aid purposes, the custodial parent is the parent with whom you lived the most during the past 12 months. The FAFSA asks about the size of the family, the age of the parents, and the number of household members currently in college, and it assumes a certain basic level of household expenses. Calculation of need using the FAFSA is known as the *federal methodology.*

> I didn't find the FAFSA as daunting as some people said it would be. It's time consuming, but it's not difficult. You need to gather all your records and your tax returns in one place. From there on, it's pretty straightforward.
>
> MOTHER OF AN APPLICANT

When Should You File the FAFSA?

The FAFSA can be submitted between January 1 of the year a student plans to start college and June 30 of the following year. (For example, the 2014–2015 FAFSA can be submitted between January 1, 2014, and June 30, 2015.) It requires detailed information from the parents' and student's federal income tax return for the previous calendar year, current asset information, and the list of colleges to which a student is applying.

It is a good idea to file the FAFSA as early as you can, even before your tax returns are completed. Most schools have priority due dates, some as early as January 15, and some schools award aid based on first filed, first awarded. The FAFSA allows you to estimate the numbers that will appear on your tax return. You submit the FAFSA online at www.fafsa.ed.gov. You can also file by paper form, but it is far preferable to use the online version, especially if you need to amend the estimates when you have the final figures from your tax returns. The online version is easy to use and gives you immediate feedback about any errors you may be making in entering your data. Confidentiality is assured.

The Student Aid Report (SAR)

After your FAFSA is filed and processed, you should get an e-mail (sent to the e-mail address listed as the student's e-mail address on the FAFSA) with a link to your online Student Aid Report (SAR), indicating your expected family contribution based on the federal methodology. It can take three to four weeks to get your response if you submit your FAFSA by mail or do not list an e-mail address on the FAFSA, but only a few days if you submit it online and include a student e-mail. Be sure to review your SAR carefully for any errors and correct them immediately. Copies of your SAR are sent electronically to the campuses you designate on the form. For the online version, only 10 schools can be listed at a time. After the first 10 have been processed, you can return to the application, delete the original schools, and add the remaining schools you are applying to if there are more.

College Scholarship Service PROFILE

Approximately 250 colleges, mostly private, require financial aid applicants to complete an additional application, the College Scholarship Service PROFILE, or, more colloquially, the PROFILE. Colleges use this form to determine aid eligibility for college-based resources. Some states and a number of foundations and other groups that award special scholarships also require the PROFILE. It is longer, more complex, and more detailed than the FAFSA. Here the colleges are dealing with their own money, and they want to see a full portrait of the family's finances. The College Board, the administrator of the SAT, also administers the PROFILE. Information about the application, a list of schools that require it, and the online form can be found at www.collegeboard.com.

What the PROFILE Considers

The PROFILE considers all the sources of income and assets used in the FAFSA and asks for additional information such as the net value of the family's primary residence, amount of parental funds in the name of siblings, and amount of untaxed social security benefits received for all family members, excluding the student applicant. For separated or divorced parents, schools using the PROFILE usually also require the noncustodial PROFILE, which considers the income and assets of the noncustodial parent. These additions generally increase the expected family contribution where applicable.

On the other side of the ledger, the PROFILE calculations consider some of a family's expenses such as medical and dental costs and the need to save for the college costs of younger siblings. A need calculation using the PROFILE is known as the *institutional methodology.*

The PROFILE Is Customized for You

Unlike the FAFSA, for which everyone files the same application, the PROFILE is customized for each family with additional questions that vary depending on the colleges a student lists when registering for the PROFILE. Individual colleges can choose from among a large number of supplemental questions dealing with things such as the cash value of life insurance plans or the value of 529 College Savings Plans established for the student by someone other than their parent.

How and When to File

The PROFILE can be submitted only online. Unlike the FAFSA, which, as its name suggests, is free, students pay a fee to register for the PROFILE and then a fee for each college to which the results are sent. The registration fee is $9, with an additional charge of $16 per college. The PROFILE is available October 1 for that year's application cycle. Students who apply early decision (ED) may need to submit the PROFILE by the ED application deadline in order to receive a financial aid award if they are admitted. Others will have later submission dates that vary from school to school. As with the FAFSA, you usually complete the PROFILE with estimated numbers. After it is submitted, you cannot make changes to the PROFILE except to add more schools. You can then make changes to the numbers for those schools. Colleges themselves will update the numbers after they receive tax forms from your family.

WHAT FORMS WILL YOU HAVE TO FILE?

The good news is that the FAFSA, PROFILE, and any state forms do not have to be submitted separately to each school; you simply list the colleges that should receive the information, and the processing agency sends the forms electronically. However, you need to keep careful track of which forms your schools request. For example, the University of Virginia requires the FAFSA, PROFILE, signed copies of student and parental federal income tax forms, and an institutional form titled the Parent and Student Signature Page. The University of California asks its applicants to submit the FAFSA and California residents to complete a form called the Cal Grant Verification Form. Required forms vary from school to school, beyond the FAFSA and PROFILE.

Be Sure to File on Time

It is critical to keep track of submission due dates. If you plan to apply early action (EA) or ED, colleges will typically ask you to submit the PROFILE or their own institutional form soon after the application deadline and then follow up with the FAFSA after it becomes available on January 1. Sometimes colleges that do not use the PROFILE will give you the option of submitting it if you are applying early so that they can provide an estimate of your financial aid package if you are accepted. A FAFSA-only school that uses the PROFILE for a student applying early will still be running the numbers according to the federal methodology, however. The school is simply gathering the numbers off the PROFILE (since the FAFSA is not yet online) but is not using the institutional methodology to determine aid.

Getting your forms in as early as you can is always wise. Aid can be limited for late applicants, and some schools will not award college-based funds if they receive an application after the due date.

The Verification Process

Verification is a process to ensure the accuracy of financial aid information submitted on the FAFSA. Verifications are conducted because of possible errors, inconsistencies, or other anomalies. The comments section of the SAR (which you need to review online after submitting the FAFSA) will tell you if your file has been selected for verification, and if so, the college you choose to attend will ask you to submit a verification worksheet. You'll also be asked to use the IRS Data Retrieval Tool that allows a family to go back into the FAFSA and automatically upload their actual tax numbers from their submitted tax return using an IRS database. If your file is chosen for verification, it does not mean that an error has been made. The verification process is simply a double check for possible errors.

GETTING AN ESTIMATE OF YOUR FINANCIAL NEED

Regardless of where you are in the college admissions process—years away or right in the middle of it—it is a good idea to do a quick preliminary analysis to determine how much your expected family contribution might be.

Using a Financial Aid Calculator

You can use online calculators at any time to get a ballpark estimate of your EFC. The Department of Education has established a website, www.fafsa4caster .ed.gov, to provide you with an early estimate of your eligibility for federal financial aid. But of course this covers only federal financial aid, not other possible funds from a college. The BigFuture website, www.bigfuture.org, also has a helpful and easy-to-use calculator to estimate what your EFC will be using either federal or institutional methodology, although individual schools may follow their own guidelines in interpreting the PROFILE calculations. No matter which calculators you use, make sure your numbers are accurate. The calculators are only as good as the numbers you enter into them. (Later in this chapter, after our discussion of merit aid, we will look at another type of calculator, the net price calculator, which can give you information about your family's estimated out-of-pocket cost at each of the colleges you may be considering.)

⊠ Differences Between the PROFILE and FAFSA Calculations of Expected Family Contribution

- The PROFILE includes the net value of the family's primary residence. Net business value is also included. The FAFSA does not include home equity of the primary residence or business value if the family is the majority owner and the business has fewer than 100 full-time employees.

- PROFILE schools usually require the completion of the noncustodial PROFILE and thus include information on the income and assets of a noncustodial parent. The FAFSA does not ask for this information.

- The PROFILE collects information on private elementary and secondary school tuition, medical expenses, and so on and allows the campus-based financial aid officer some discretion in evaluating special financial circumstances. The FAFSA does not ask for these costs, although you can write a letter explaining such costs directly to the school, which may consider them.

- Although it does not go into the calculations, the PROFILE asks the amount that parents have in retirement accounts. In addition, any funds a student has in retirement accounts must be listed and will be included as a student asset. The FASFA does not ask for this information.

- The PROFILE includes additional child tax credit, earned income credit, untaxed social security benefits received for all family members except the student applicant, tuition and fees deduction, and the amount of foreign income exclusion. The FAFSA does not include these amounts.

- The PROFILE asks for the breakdown of the income numbers listed on the federal tax forms and will add back in any losses, such as capital loss or loss from rental property. The FAFSA simply uses the adjusted gross income.

Differences Between FAFSA and PROFILE Calculators

You and your family may be pleasantly surprised to learn that your expected family contribution is lower than you thought it would be. Other families, however, may find that they are expected to contribute more than they had planned. In general, the need analysis formula for the institutional methodology calculates the expected family contribution slightly more favorably than the formula FAFSA uses.

However, the PROFILE may also calculate a higher EFC, meaning less need, because it includes income and assets specifically excluded from the FAFSA. For example, a family with substantial home equity or a noncustodial parent with significant financial resources may find that the EFC is considerably higher using the institutional methodology. So a lot depends on specific family circumstances. If a school requires both the FAFSA and PROFILE and if the EFC is higher on the FAFSA than the PROFILE, a school will typically use the EFC as calculated by the FAFSA.

WHAT GOES INTO A FINANCIAL AID PACKAGE?

The financial aid that a student typically receives from a college is made up of different kinds of assistance from federal, state, and college-based resources. The particular combination you receive is known as your financial aid package. Need-based financial aid packages usually have three parts: grant funds, work-study funding, and student loans. Grants and scholarships are considered gift aid because they are essentially free money, while work-study funding and student loans are often referred to as self-help. In addition, most schools expect that the student can work during the summers, earning approximately $2,000 each summer that can be contributed toward college costs.

Grants

Grants are awards you don't have to repay. Some schools use the term *scholarship* rather than *grant* to refer to some need-based awards of this type, but *grant* is the common term. They are tax free when used to cover the cost of tuition, fees, books, and supplies. (Many other types of scholarships are awarded for reasons other than need; we will discuss these in the section on merit aid later in this chapter.) Need-based grants come from three primary sources: the federal government, state governments, and college resources. Currently there are two major need-based federal grant programs:

- *Pell Grants* range from $600 to $5,550 a year for 2012–2013 depending on need. In recent years, about 90 percent of Pell Grant recipients have had family incomes below $50,000.

- *Federal Supplemental Educational Opportunity Grants (FSEOG)*, currently ranging from $100 to $4,000 per year, are awarded to students with exceptionally high need. Pell Grant recipients have priority.

Work-Study

Work-study programs provide the opportunity for a student to apply for a part-time job on or near campus. Students are paid at least minimum wage, receive a paycheck every two weeks, and usually use the funds for their personal expenses. Most work-study programs are subsidized by the federal government, which provides approximately three-quarters of the funds. Often the work can be related to a student's area of study or involve community service, although not all jobs meet one of these criteria. Freshmen typically work about 10 to 15 hours a week when classes are in session, a load that is quite manageable for most.

Loans

Loans are borrowed money that must be repaid with interest. Both students and parents can take out financial aid loans, and the federal government may subsidize student loans. In addition, some schools offer their own loans. For a subsidized loan, the government, or college, pays the interest while the student is in school, and repayment begins only after the student graduates, leaves school, or drops below half-time enrollment. The standard repayment period for a federal loan, once it begins, is 10 years. We describe several federal loan programs below. The figures cited are current as of our publication date, but are of course subject to change. You can find updates at www.admissionmatters.com.

- *Perkins loans* (to students) are fixed-rate, low-interest loans (currently 5 percent) offered by participating schools to students with financial need. The federal government subsidizes these loans by paying the interest while the student is in school and for nine months after graduation. When repayment begins, you repay the loans directly to the college or a third-party processor. The maximum Perkins loan is currently $5,500 per year.

- *Subsidized federal direct loans* (to students) are awarded on the basis of financial need and as of July 6, 2012, have a fixed interest rate of 3.4 percent. These loans are also known as Stafford Loans. The government pays the interest while the student is in school and for six months after graduation. The maximum that can be awarded is $3,500 for a freshman, $4,500 for a sophomore, and $5,500 for a junior or senior.

- *Unsubsidized federal direct loans* (to students) are available to students independent of need, and the government does not pay the interest while the student is in school. The current interest rate is fixed at 6.8 percent. The student may defer payment of the principal (until after graduation, withdrawal from school, or going below half-time status), but unless the interest is paid while the student is in school, it will accrue and be added to the principal. The total of subsidized and unsubsidized federal direct loans may not exceed $5,500 for freshmen, $6,500 for sophomores, and $7,500 for juniors or seniors.

- *PLUS Loans* (parent loans to undergraduate students) allow parents to borrow up to the total cost of education for each child, minus any student financial aid that is awarded. The current interest rate is fixed at 7.9 percent, and the loan is unsubsidized, but payment may be deferred while the student is in school. To be eligible, parents do not need to have a high credit score, but they must not have adverse credit (for example, bankruptcy or foreclosure in the last five years).

How Is Your Package Put Together?

Grants and scholarships are clearly the most desirable source of funding, since no extra work is required and they do not need to be repaid. Most colleges, however, include some form of self-help (student loans, work-study, and a student summer work expectation) in a financial aid package. The proportion of the aid package that is self-help and the amount of need that is met vary.

Colleges with exceptionally large endowments can usually guarantee to meet full demonstrated need and afford to award a large portion of the package as grant aid. As of 2013, roughly 50 of the wealthiest colleges have pledged to eliminate loans from financial aid awards for some or all of their accepted students. However, with over 2,200 four-year, nonprofit colleges in the United States, that means that loans remain an important part of most financial aid packages. Loan burdens are attracting a lot of media attention, and one rule of thumb is that students should not graduate owing more than their anticipated first year's salary.

In general, when awarding money from programs they administer but do not fund (i.e., federal programs), colleges give priority to the neediest of the able. When awarding money from their own funds, colleges give priority to the ablest of the needy.[1]

ANNA AND ROBERT LEIDER, AUTHORS OF *DON'T MISS OUT: THE AMBITIOUS STUDENT'S GUIDE TO FINANCIAL AID*

When you receive your aid award, the components of the package will be listed separately, and you will be asked to accept or reject each item if you choose to attend that college. If the package is inadequate or less than another one you have received, you or your parents can ask the financial aid office to review your case for possible adjustment. We'll talk more about how to approach this in a later section of this chapter.

WHY NEED-BASED PACKAGES CAN DIFFER FROM COLLEGE TO COLLEGE

You may be surprised to learn that your aid offers will differ, sometimes by a sizable amount, even at colleges that promise to meet the full demonstrated need of all admitted students. Although all colleges must use the FAFSA to compute the EFC expected family contribution for federal financial aid, they may use the PROFILE or their own form to determine need for college-based institutional aid. Colleges have considerable flexibility in how they award their own funds.

Colleges That Meet Full Demonstrated Need

Schools that use the PROFILE and guarantee to meet full demonstrated need run the numbers in various ways. For example, many put a cap on how much home equity goes into the calculations, but the level of the cap may vary from school to school. Other schools may exclude home equity completely even though it is included on the application. Some colleges give consideration to the cost of a sibling in private elementary or secondary school; some make an adjustment for the cost of living in high-cost areas such as New York or San Francisco; some exclude money received from a relative; and so on. These differences often result in differences in the size of need-based financial aid packages.

Colleges That Do Not Meet Full Need

The majority of schools, however, cannot guarantee to meet the full demonstrated need of all students. When a school does not meet a student's full need, this will leave a gap, or unmet need. Some schools award financial aid based on a combination of need and merit. Before these schools award college-based funds, a student must demonstrate a certain level of merit based on grades, rigor of courses taken, test scores, and so on. A student with high need and high merit might have her full need met from a combination of federal aid plus need-based aid from the college. Another student with high need may be admitted and receive only federal aid, because his merit standing is not outstanding enough to receive need-based college aid. Other schools may award grant aid for all admitted students up to a certain percentage of their demonstrated need. Some schools award aid using a combination of the two methods. It can get complicated pretty quickly.

Professional Judgment

Colleges also have some flexibility in determining the final EFC—more with institutional methodology than with federal methodology—based on the special circumstances of a particular family and the professional judgment of the financial aid staff. A family can write to a college financial aid office explaining nondiscretionary extenuating circumstances: the need to support a family member not living in the home, a parent's loss of job, tutoring cost for a younger sibling, and the like. Using professional judgment, a financial aid officer can decide whether to consider these circumstances. While many schools will review such a letter before an award is made, some schools prefer that special circumstances be handled through an appeals process. In the latter case, they would base the financial aid award on the numbers as submitted, and then the family would appeal.

Summing Up

Colleges have different guidelines for how they use the numbers, and financial aid administrators can exercise discretion in awarding aid. Some colleges guarantee to meet full need, but demonstrated need may be calculated differently from one school to another. Other colleges cannot guarantee to meet full need and often leave a gap, or unmet need. However, a college that is eager to recruit a particular student may offer a higher total award or a higher percentage of grant money in the total package, making it more desirable to the recipient.

Unfortunately, you can't know exactly what your aid will look like, in either amount or type of aid, until you have your offer in hand. However, the net price calculators we discuss later in this chapter can help since they are designed to take into account the financial aid policies of each individual school. Since these are still relatively new, only since 2011, there is much debate about just how well they do this, but they certainly provide information that you would not otherwise have.

WILL YOUR NEED FOR FINANCIAL AID AFFECT YOUR CHANCES FOR ADMISSION?

As we mentioned previously, only a small number of private colleges have the financial resources to admit students without regard to need and then to meet their full demonstrated need. These colleges are "need blind" in admissions and "full need" in their financial aid policies. Most of them direct all of their available financial aid, with the exception of athletic scholarships where offered, to students demonstrating financial need.

Need-Aware Policies

All colleges would like to be able to guarantee to meet full need and be need blind; that is their goal. However, most have limited financial resources. Some colleges guarantee to meet the full demonstrated need of admitted students but have policies that are need aware or need sensitive in admissions. These colleges have sufficient resources to make most, but not all, of their admissions decisions independent of financial aid considerations.

Those affected by need awareness are usually only a small portion of the applicants, and you can't know if you will be one of them. If you apply to a need-aware college and do not need financial aid, you may enjoy a small admissions advantage over someone with a similar record who needs substantial aid. This is especially true if you are a borderline candidate. Colleges that cannot afford to offer full support to all of their students will offer the support they do have to the most compelling students in their applicant pools. But the admissions advantage associated with being able to pay the full cost of college is usually quite small—not anything to count on if you have it or to fret about if you don't.

Carleton College, Tufts University, Macalester College, and Wesleyan University are among the schools that guarantee to meet full need but, with great reluctance, are currently need aware to some extent. Policies can change, however, based on a college's financial situation. All four of these colleges had been fully need blind for many years until they could no longer afford to be, reflecting changes in both the amount of financial aid funding available and the increased demand for it in a challenging economy.

How Can You Determine a School's Policy?

Read the information about a college's financial aid policies carefully. You can usually find this information posted on the web along with other admissions-related information. If a college states that it meets the full need of all admitted students but doesn't state that it has a need-blind policy, it probably admits some percentage of its freshman class on a need-aware basis.

On the flip side, many colleges will be need blind in their admissions policy but don't commit themselves to meeting the full need of those admitted. At these schools, many students will find a gap between the college's financial aid award and what they actually need to attend. These students have been accepted without regard to their need, but their need is not met in full. That gap, or unmet need, has to be filled somehow if they choose to attend that college.

HOW MERIT AID WORKS

More and more colleges, especially those seeking to build their reputations or the quality of their student body, are offering aid that is not based on need. Known as merit-based aid, these awards are often given to students in recognition of particular abilities, talents, or other criteria. Recipients may also have financial need, but need is not the basis for the award. Merit awards, as we noted previously, are often referred to as scholarships.

I talked to several parents who had not considered private schools because they thought the cost was prohibitive. Well, that's not always true. The most selective schools don't give merit aid, but others do. We were really fortunate that our kids were high achievers and worked hard in high school. They got a lot of merit-based aid.

MOTHER OF FAMILY NOT ELIGIBLE FOR NEED-BASED AID WITH TWO CHILDREN IN PRIVATE COLLEGES

Why Do Schools Award Merit Aid?

Colleges have learned that a merit aid scholarship of $5,000 or $10,000 can encourage students with little or no financial need to accept an offer of admission. This kind of "tuition discounting" can raise a college's yield. A large merit scholarship, often a full ride, extended to a student with an outstanding record may result in a "catch" for the college—an academic superstar whose presence can raise standards and contribute positively to intellectual life on campus. The size of merit awards and the criteria for receiving them vary widely from college to college, as well as within a given college, when they are offered. Some schools that offer merit awards automatically consider all applicants for them, although they may set an earlier application deadline for those wishing to be considered. Other schools have additional applications for their merit awards.

Some public research universities like the University of Oklahoma and Iowa State University, as well as some private colleges, have pursued this approach by aggressively targeting National Merit finalists (see chapter 6 for more information about the National Merit Scholarship Program). These students may receive a generous scholarship from those schools if they apply and inform the National Merit Scholarship Corporation that the university is their first choice. National Merit finalists usually have stronger academic profiles than the typical enrollee at such an institution and thus are seen as very desirable prospective students.

> We want kids who are good at dancing, who are good at collecting butterflies, who are good at basketball. At the point where we have the capacity to attract students with the magnetism Harvard does, we'll be happy to follow Harvard's [need-based] policies.[4]
>
> STEPHEN TRACHTENBERG, FORMER PRESIDENT OF GEORGE WASHINGTON UNIVERSITY

The Merit Aid Controversy

Non-need-based financial aid is a controversial topic in higher education. The wealthy and most selective colleges argue that all of their aid should be need based to ensure that financial need is not a barrier for students. They see no reason to offer aid to families that do not qualify for need-based aid. Other colleges want to give scholarships to academically talented students with no financial need, while still awarding most of their aid to those with demonstrated need. This may divert money from some needy students, but it raises the profile of the college overall. They sometimes claim that in raising the school's academic reputation, merit aid leads to larger donations and more financial aid in the future. The debate over the two approaches to aid is sure to continue and in fact shows signs of intensifying as colleges compete for students with special qualities they seek and as the demand for need-based aid grows.

SEEKING OUTSIDE SCHOLARSHIPS

While colleges themselves are the largest source of scholarship dollars, there are other sources as well.

Awards from Businesses and Organizations

Scholarships sponsored by organizations, foundations, and businesses are awarded to students for a variety of reasons: academic achievement, talent, writing competitions, significant community service, and overcoming of hardship. Local Rotary Clubs and Lions Clubs, for example, award scholarships to high school students in communities across the country, and some large corporations offer scholarships for their employees' children in addition to National Merit Scholarships.

These awards are typically paid directly to a college to offset the cost of attendance. The amounts very widely, from a few hundred dollars to several thousand. Most are fairly small, maybe $1,000 or less, and are one-time awards, but even those can add up to make a difference. Local scholarships typically have fewer students competing for them than the big national awards like the Gates Millennium Scholars awards, Coca-Cola Scholars awards, and the various scholarships funded by the Toyota Corporation. Hence, the chances of winning one are generally higher.

State Scholarships

Although there are no federal merit scholarships for undergraduates, a number of states have their own merit scholarship programs that vary in generosity and how they can be used. HOPE scholarships, for example, cover full tuition at any state-supported institution for all Georgia students having a minimum GPA or higher. The Florida Bright Futures Scholarship Program has several options for students who choose to stay in state for college, one of which covers 100 percent of tuition and fees at

> We encouraged our kids to apply for community-based scholarships. They are easier to get because you're only competing against people from your own local area.
>
> PARENT OF STUDENT WHO APPLIED FOR LOCAL SCHOLARSHIPS

public or private institutions for Florida high school graduates meeting certain academic and community service criteria. Although most state scholarships apply only to in-state institutions and sometimes to a particular campus, others are more flexible and can be applied anywhere a student chooses to attend.

Awards Cannot Exceed the Cost of Attendance

Federal law requires that financial aid not exceed the cost of attendance. Thus, if a student receives an outside scholarship in addition to a full need-based package that contains federal aid, the college must reduce the aid package by the amount of the scholarship. Colleges are usually willing to substitute the scholarship, dollar for dollar, for all or part of the self-help components of the aid package rather than the gift aid component. This means that although a scholarship will not increase the total amount of your aid package or reduce the expected family contribution, it can make your package more desirable. If the college has awarded aid leaving a gap, or unmet need, an outside scholarship is usually first applied to the gap. Colleges vary somewhat in their policies with regard to the treatment of outside scholarships, so you should ask the financial aid office of each college that admits you how an outside scholarship would affect your package.

Should You Use a Scholarship Search Service?

High school seniors and their parents often receive letters from businesses offering to help the student find or apply for outside scholarships. These letters may look very official and suggest that the student and family must participate in a special program to find out about scholarship opportunities. It is easy to see why such businesses exist. A service that promises to ferret out thousands of dollars in awards in return for a fee of a few hundred dollars may seem like a good investment. But is it?

Financial aid experts generally agree that no family needs to pay for help finding scholarships. At best, these services provide information about funding programs that are already in the public domain. At worst, they may be shady businesses that defraud or exploit vulnerable families. The Federal Trade Commission cautions families to be aware of the following approaches that can signal a scam:

"The scholarship is guaranteed or your money back."

"You can't get this information anywhere else."

"I just need your credit card or bank account number to hold this scholarship."

"You've been selected by a 'national foundation' to receive this scholarship."

"You're a finalist"—in a contest you never entered.

Most financial aid, whether federal, state, or college funded, is awarded through college financial aid offices after you've applied, completed your FAFSA and any other required need analysis forms, and been accepted. Information about private scholarships is readily available, for free, from many sources. The counseling office at your high school is the first place to look. Counselors are a particularly helpful source of information about scholarships awarded by local businesses and community organizations, in addition to national programs. Several websites, which make their money through advertising rather than fees, also provide good information about scholarship opportunities. Two sites definitely worth exploring are www .finaid.com and www.fastweb.com.

I'm not saying there aren't people out there who are legitimate private counselors [for aid], but we try to direct families to where they can get help without spending unnecessary dollars.[5]

DALLAS MARTIN, PRESIDENT OF THE NATIONAL ASSOCIATION OF STUDENT FINANCIAL AID ADMINISTRATORS

⌧ Questions to Ask Colleges About Financial Aid

- Does the college meet the full need of all admitted students?
- Is this college need blind or need aware?
- Does the college offer merit aid, or does it offer need-based aid only?
- How will an outside scholarship affect my financial aid package?
- Assuming my need remains the same after freshman year, will the composition of my financial aid package change?
- What are the academic requirements for continued financial aid?

FINANCIAL AID AND YOUR COLLEGE LIST

Especially in times of financial uncertainty, parents and students need to talk openly and honestly about how much they, as a family, are willing to contribute to the cost of college through current income, savings, and borrowing. A college may calculate that a family can contribute $10,000 a year to a student's education, but the family may be either unwilling or unable to contribute that amount.

Thinking About Financial Aid Before You Apply

There are many uncertainties in financial aid (both up and down), and it is important to have a good idea as to how financial aid is run at the schools you are considering applying to. Perhaps your parents are divorced, and one parent says he or she will not contribute to your college costs, yet the schools you are applying to expect a contribution from both biological parents. It is good to know information such as this when you are compiling your college list. It is also very important to know if the schools you are applying to do not guarantee to meet full need and if a gap may likely be left.

In addition, if you are worried about your family's ability to comfortably handle their expected family contribution, it would be wise to include at least a few colleges that you could afford and, of course, where you have a good chance of admission. Think of them as your financial good-bet colleges, which can provide some much-needed security. These often include public universities in your home state because of relatively low in-state tuition. It is very important to have a good selection of colleges, not only in terms of being admissible but also in terms of possible financial aid. When awards arrive in March and April, you want to have choices where the financial aid is workable for you and your family.

Considering Regional Compacts

Students interested in public universities in states other than their own should look carefully at whether their state participates in an educational compact with neighboring states that might result in a substantial discount on out-of-state tuition. Both the size and terms of the tuition break will vary, and not all schools and programs in a given region may participate, but the educational compacts are worth investigating. There are four: the Academic Common Market in the South, the Midwestern Higher Education Compact, the New England Board of Higher Education, and the Western Undergraduate Exchange. Putting the name of a compact into Google will take you to the appropriate website for more information.

Maximizing Your Chances of Receiving Merit Aid

College-based merit aid is a bit of a wild card in the financial aid equation. If a college offers such aid, that's great, but it can be hard to predict your chances of getting it or how much you might receive. As a general rule, colleges award their most generous merit aid to the students they most want to attract. This means that all other things equal, you are more likely to get a sizable merit award at a school where your academic credentials place you in the upper quartile of those who are applying than you would at a school where you were a borderline admit.

Two pieces of information about each school are generally readily available: its admissions profile and its merit aid policies and practices. You can maximize your chances for merit aid by looking for schools that are both generous with merit aid and where you would likely fall in the top quartile of the

incoming class. The BigFuture website, www.bigfuture.org, shows whether a college offers merit aid and how much they offer, and it provides fairly current information about each college's admissions profile as well.

Another useful website is www.meritaid.com. It is worth checking out the colleges you are interested in to understand their practices. If a college offers merit awards and your record is strong compared to that of an average freshman at that school, you're a good prospect. The stronger your record, the better your chances of getting a merit award. We encourage you to consider this when you build your college list, but don't let it drive all your decisions.

Using the Net Price Calculators

A net price calculator is an online tool that will give you an estimate of your family's out-of-pocket cost, or net price, for one year at any college you are considering. All colleges that award federal financial aid, which is almost all of them, are now required by the federal government to post a net price calculator on their website. Some are located right on the main financial aid web page, while others are a bit harder to locate.

The idea behind the calculator is simple. It starts with the sticker price for one year of school, which includes direct charges for tuition and room and board, as well as indirect costs for books and supplies, transportation, and personal expenses. After you enter your financial information into the net price calculator, it estimates the amount your family would be expected to contribute to the cost of attending college—your expected family contribution or EFC.

Next, the calculator evaluates your financial and sometimes your personal characteristics using the criteria specified by the college. The result of that evaluation is the amount of grant and scholarship aid you are likely to receive from that college if you are admitted.

The difference between the sticker price and the total amount of grant and scholarship money is the net price to the family. Options to pay the net price consist of student loans, work-study (if awarded), and the parental contribution (this could include the EFC, parental loans, and any unmet need).

A net price calculator allows you to compare the actual out-of-pocket cost for different colleges in light of their financial aid policies. Of course, no calculator can tell you exactly how much grant and scholarship money you may receive, any more than a calculator can tell you whether you will actually be admitted to a college. But a calculator can give you some insight into what students like you would likely receive in the way of grants and scholarship were they to be accepted. Remember that special circumstances will be handled on a case-by-case basis by each school once you apply.

⊠ Net Price Calculation

> Cost of attendance
> − Grants and scholarships awarded
> ─────────────────────────────
> = Net price to family

The BigFuture website has a useful tool that lets you use the net price calculators of many different colleges using data that you enter into the system just once. If you are interested in colleges that do not participate in this College Board service, you will have to enter your information into the individual calculators on their websites to get your net price estimate. The US Department of Education site at www.collegecost.ed.gov takes you directly to the net price calculator of any college.

EVALUATING AID AFTER YOU'VE BEEN ACCEPTED

Once you have your award packages in hand, comparing financial aid offers can be an important part of your decision-making process. As we noted earlier, financial aid packages can vary widely, not only in the total amount of aid offered but also in the individual components. Financial aid awards also differ in how they present the information, so you should put them into a common format before you begin. The Financial Aid Comparison Worksheet in Appendix D and at www.admissionmatters.com will help you do this.

Is the Cost of Attendance Realistic?

Take a careful look at the total cost of attendance for each school. Is it realistic, or does it omit or underestimate some key expenses such as travel home? Another worksheet, in Appendix E and at www.admissionmatters.com, lets you compare how colleges estimate cost of attendance. Since the cost of books, incidentals, and travel is a key factor in determining your financial need, an unrealistically low figure will mean that you might have additional expenses that are not covered by your financial aid package.

Evaluating the Package and Net Cost

Carefully compare the total cost of attendance and the total amount of your aid packages as well as the components. The total amount of aid is important, but so is the composition of the package. All of this is relevant for estimating the total cost of the college. When completed, Appendix D will show you the breakdown as well as the total amount of each aid package. You should compare not only the amount of gift aid offered, but also the total amount of out-of-pocket costs the family must absorb. This may include the expected family contribution, student loans, work-study, student summer contribution, and any amount of gap, or unmet need.

Two schools may offer the same amount of total aid, yet one may offer a much higher percentage of the package as grants that do not have to be repaid. From a purely financial perspective, assuming the cost of attendance is the same at the two schools, the package with a higher percentage of gift aid is more desirable. As we saw earlier, the total cost of attendance minus grants and scholarships is the net cost to the family. Colleges offer loans and work-study to help pay the net cost.

Beyond the First Year

Be sure you know each college's policies on financial aid for subsequent years. Almost all schools will require you to reapply for aid each year by submitting the required forms. Even if the amount of aid will remain the same (assuming no change in your family's financial circumstances), will the package change? Are scholarships renewable, and if so, what does renewal require? Will packages in subsequent years contain a higher percentage of self-help aid? You should consider all these questions as you review your financial aid offers.

> Too many parents jump quickly into negotiation mode, trying to play one school's offer against another's. If they sense you are just trying to get a better deal and you are treating it like a car, even if there's flexibility on their end, they're not likely to show it.[7]
>
> STEPHEN PEMBERTON, PRIVATE COLLEGE CONSULTANT

Appealing Your Offer

Students and parents often ask if they can appeal a financial aid offer. Although most colleges resist negotiating revised packages, they are usually open to reviewing their offer in light of new information. You may, in fact, be able to work out a more favorable package at a given college based on changes in your family's financial situation or a possible error in how your financial information was interpreted. You should appeal your financial aid offer diplomatically and without any hint of arrogance or entitlement.

> We have been open about our willingness to review financial aid awards to compete with certain private institutions for students admitted under the regular decision plan. Unlike most institutions, the university states these principles openly to those offered first-year admission under the regular decision plan. While early decision students are not eligible to participate in this aid review process, we will meet their full demonstrated need as calculated by the university.[8]
>
> CARNEGIE MELLON FINANCIAL AID REVIEW POLICY

Adjustments to reflect new circumstances or clarification of previously submitted information are the easiest ones for colleges to accommodate. Perhaps your mother's hours have been reduced, or the college did not adequately consider the expense of caring for your elderly grandparents. You or your parent should respectfully ask the financial aid office to review your package, making clear the basis for your request and your sincere interest in attending the college. You'll be asked to put your request in writing, and you may be asked to document your circumstances.

Will Colleges "Match" Another Offer?

It's more difficult for colleges to make adjustments based on offers from other colleges, although some openly invite it. Other schools not only do not invite requests for adjustments based on other offers; they simply won't do it. As a general rule, though, a college is more likely to increase your offer based on one from another college if it routinely competes with that college (or aspires to compete with it) for students.

A highly selective college, for example, will be more inclined to match a package offered by another highly selective college rather than a package offered by a less selective school. Cornell University and Dartmouth College, for example, explicitly state that they will match the financial aid award from another Ivy League school. But a school that offers only need-based aid will not make an adjustment based on a merit offer from a less selective school. In addition, a college may be more likely to increase its financial aid offer if you have exceptional academic qualifications or other talents relative to its overall pool of admitted students. In this case, it is better to be a big fish in a small pond rather than a small fish in a big pond.

> A number of elite privates give substantially different packages depending on how much they want you.[9]
>
> MORTON OWEN SHAPIRO, FORMER PRESIDENT OF WILLIAMS COLLEGE

ANOTHER WORD ABOUT EARLY DECISION

In chapter 7, we noted that one of the major criticisms of ED programs is that they commit students to attend a college without giving them a chance to compare financial aid packages. Since packages can vary significantly, especially when merit awards are involved, ED can be a risk if you hope to maximize your financial aid offer.

Students whose families do not have special circumstances (which can cause aid awards to vary), do not have home equity (which different schools can view differently), and who are applying to a school that guarantees to meet full need may have the least to be concerned about when applying early. Colleges able to meet the full need of accepted students will provide packages to cover the total cost of tuition, room and board, and other expenses. Those with special circumstances or those who are applying to schools that do not meet full need must accept that colleges vary in how they define need and how they propose to meet it. Early decision, but not EA, may be unwise if they want to compare aid packages.

You do not lose all flexibility, however, if you apply ED. You may still request that a college reconsider your ED financial aid package if the award amount is genuinely insufficient for you to attend. Colleges do sometimes make adjustments, and if the package does not meet your need, you can decline the offer and continue with regular decision applications to other colleges. But you cannot hold on to your ED aid offer until April and then decide to attend if it turns out to be the best award.

PLANNING AHEAD WHEN YOUR CHILD IS YOUNG

This chapter has discussed financial aid issues that families face in a student's senior year. At that point, a family's income and assets are usually a given. But what if you are reading this book when your child is much younger? What can you do to prepare for the financial responsibilities of a college education? We want to mention briefly some important but often overlooked points about saving for college. More detailed advice on the topic can be found on financial aid websites and in books on financial planning. Laws and practices can change quickly, however, so it is important to seek the most current information at the time you are making your plans:

- It may be advantageous to save money for college in a parent's name rather than in the student's name. Currently, federal and institutional need analysis formulas "count" parental assets at a much lower rate than student assets. Saving money in the parents' name also keeps it under parental control until it is needed. But parental income is usually taxed at a higher rate than children's income, so you have to estimate the relative pros and cons.

- Every state has 529 College Savings Plans, and they are worth a careful look. Although contributions are after-tax, they grow tax deferred in the parent's name. When used for postsecondary qualified educational expenses, earnings are currently tax free at both the federal and state levels. In addition, some states provide income tax deductions for all or part of the contributions of the donor.

- Education IRAs (Coverdell Education Savings Accounts) are another good way for some families to save for college expenses. Contributions are nondeductible, but earnings accumulate tax free and remain tax free if they are used for college. Coverdell ESAs can also be used for qualified elementary and secondary educational expenses. There are annual contribution limits, as well as limitations based on income.

Some observers have complained that financial aid policies do not encourage families to save, since savings reduce the amount of aid for which a student is eligible. Although it is true that a small percentage of nonretirement savings (over an asset protection amount) will reduce the amount of financial aid your child may receive, you have no guarantee far in advance about which colleges will accept your child or what their financial aid polices will be at that time. It doesn't make sense to spend down your assets just in the hope your child may receive a generous scholarship in the future.

The more money you can save toward a college education, the greater your student's flexibility in choosing colleges and in dealing with the vagaries of financial aid. In addition, it is far preferable to have savings to help pay for college costs rather than to depend on loans, which in the end will cost much more than paying upfront. Those who can and do save are in a very real sense making an investment in their children's future—one of the best long-term investments a parent can ever make.

CHAPTER 13

Advice for International Students

I f you are reading this chapter, you are probably one of the many high school students born and usually educated outside the United States who plan to apply to American colleges and universities as freshmen each year. Now more than ever before, schools in the United States welcome applications from international students and value the important contributions they will make to their new academic communities.

Although the information in the rest of this book applies to you as much as to American students, as an international student you need additional information to be a successful applicant. You need to understand why the American admissions process is so different from that of other countries and how that affects your application, what additional information international applicants need to provide to colleges, and how American admissions offices respond to applications from international students.

This chapter builds on the information in earlier chapters to provide more specific detail and emphasis on issues that pertain to you. Not all of this information applies to all countries equally, but when it is relevant to your country, be sure to make a note of it. We cover some important background information first and then consider specific details for your application. At the end of the chapter, we will briefly discuss other special circumstances, such as undocumented students and foreign nationals educated in the United States.

THE ADVANTAGES AND DISADVANTAGES OF BEING AN INTERNATIONAL APPLICANT

International students bring new perspectives and experiences to campus life and are therefore highly sought after by colleges that want to provide a more global education for their American students. Colleges know that students learn from their peers as well as from their professors, and international students greatly enrich the diversity of the educational experience, inside and outside the classroom. Colleges also have financial incentives to increase their population of international students. A growing number of families from around the world are willing to pay the full cost of an American education at a time when many American families are finding it difficult to do so. The rise in international applicants and enrollments has been a real bonus for American colleges, who see this expanding market as an opportunity to balance their budgets with full-pay students from overseas and to increase the global awareness of their campuses at the same time.

On the other hand, some countries, including China and India, send many more students to the United States than others, so these students may find themselves competing with their compatriots for a limited number of places at some universities. And if an international student has significant financial need, few colleges can provide all of the necessary financial support since US government financial aid is not available to noncitizens. As a result, a student from one of the countries sending the most students to the United States who also needs substantial financial support may be at a serious disadvantage. Later in this chapter, we will discuss ways to approach the college selection and application process that may help you deal with these challenges if they apply to you.

WHAT ARE COLLEGES LOOKING FOR?

In many countries, university admission is by national exams or university entrance exams, with little else required. The American admissions process is more complex. For one, it varies from college to college, or from state to state for public universities, and involves

Education in the United States is not centralized nationally as it is in many countries, so it's important to note that admission requirements will vary greatly from one university to another.[1]

STACEY KOSTELL, DIRECTOR OF ADMISSIONS, UNIVERSITY OF ILLINOIS, URBANA-CHAMPAIGN much more than exams. We encourage you to read chapter 2 again, carefully, and note the importance not only of the high school academic record, or transcript, but also of the various other elements in American college applications.

Engagement Beyond the Classroom

Unlike most other universities around the world, American colleges and universities see themselves as communities. More than institutions with just classes and labs and libraries, they have orchestras, sports teams, debating societies, theaters, newspapers, and some activities you may have never heard of. All of this is meant to enrich your educational and social growth. Students learn structured competition through participating in or supporting college athletic teams and are enriched by student-powered arts, whether they actively contribute or just observe. Student organizations provide opportunities for leadership, and community service provides a chance to help off-campus organizations and serve the local population. The dynamism of an American college community is itself an education.

As a result, the application process goes beyond determining your readiness to do academic work at a high level and seeks to identify how you will contribute to the whole college community. By asking for personal statements or essays, the college wants to evaluate you as a unique individual who will participate in the community not only in classes but also in residence halls, on teams, and in any of the many activities that make up campus life. Applications ask about your activities beyond the classroom because they want to know how your various skills and talents will enrich their campus. As you apply, be sure to present your various skills and talents outside the classroom as well as in school; American colleges are interested in *all* you can bring to their campuses.

> When applying to schools in the United States, don't try to "Americanize" your application by focusing on your trip to the United States or even your participation in out of class activities prevalent in the United States. It won't help differentiate you and may make your candidacy less appealing.[2]
>
> SETH ALLEN, VICE PRESIDENT AND DEAN OF ADMISSIONS AND FINANCIAL AID, POMONA COLLEGE

International Status as a Hook

In chapter 2, we described the hooks that help a student stand out in the applicant pool. International status can be one of those hooks, especially for students who come from a country or part of the world that is not well represented in the student body. Some countries send large numbers of their students to the United States for a college education, as we noted earlier, and colleges can choose carefully among those applicants. But just as a student from Wyoming is a rarity in the Northeast United States and a rural Alabaman unusual in California, so a qualified English speaker from countries that rarely send students to the United States is sought after as a major addition to the diversity of the student body. To get a sense of geographical diversity at various schools, look for recent class profiles on college websites. Most of them indicate how many states and how many countries are represented in the incoming freshman class for that year, and some list the states and countries that students come from.

> Since colleges and universities seek international students who will contribute both inside and outside the classroom, applicants should definitely highlight in their admission applications what they will bring to the campus academically, culturally, and socially.[3]
>
> JAMES MONTOYA, VICE PRESIDENT OF HIGHER EDUCATION, THE COLLEGE BOARD

For most international students, the factor that can distinguish them from their peers in their home country, as well as from most American applicants, is their political or cultural awareness of their country and its place in the world. In some cases, it may be enough today to be an Iraqi, an Afghan, a Palestinian, an Israeli, a South African, a Venezuelan, or an Egyptian. To have lived through the past few years in any of these countries is to be indelibly marked by the turmoil in these regions. It might be harder to make being from New Zealand, Sweden, or Switzerland as compelling. Still, there is something interesting about every country. That indeed is the task: to make yourself appealing and distinctive to the admissions officer who reads applications from your part of the world.

HOW WILL YOUR APPLICATION BE REVIEWED?

Every admissions office has at least one officer responsible for international applications. Just as admissions officers read applications from different parts of the United States where they visit high schools and give presentations, an admissions office with large numbers of international applicants may divide up the applications to allow officers to develop special knowledge of certain countries or areas. Many colleges now send their admissions officers to different parts of the world to recruit students, visit schools, and keep current with education abroad.

There is a knack to reading files from Singapore, India, France, Brazil, or China, so the admissions officer for each country must have special expertise. These applications are much more different from each other than New York applications are from Florida's or California's. If additional information is needed to evaluate an application from a remote part of the world, these officers can and do consult with colleagues at other universities and with members of their own faculty.

For the most part, international admissions reflects the same pattern of factors that is used in evaluating applications from the United States. Colleges use the same documents, in roughly the same order of importance: grades and rigor of course work, standardized tests, the student's writing, extracurricular activities, recommendations, and special talents, including music and athletics.

Yet as an international student, you are also evaluated through an international lens: Is there a standard national curriculum in your home country so that all students take essentially the same courses? What are grading practices and standards? Does your school (or the country in general) put little emphasis on extracurricular activities, or are these carried out away from schools, as, for example, in private sports clubs? Is community service not yet widely undertaken? Does your school have an idea of what American colleges want to see in a recommendation? (The French, for example, are notoriously stinting in giving praise. An admissions officer must know this and factor it in.) Of course, some international students attend American-style or international high schools abroad with Advanced Placement (AP) and International Baccalaureate (IB) curricula that are familiar to admissions officers. Those applicants also have teachers and counselors who write American-style recommendations that are detailed and personal.

WHERE SHOULD YOU APPLY?

Be sure to read chapter 4 very carefully, and consider the differences among the various kinds of colleges in the United States as compared with your home country. A liberal arts education—breadth of study across the humanities, arts, social sciences, and sciences and mathematics, as well as specialization in one or more of those areas—is the main educational philosophy in American higher education at the undergraduate level, more so than professional training in fields like engineering, architecture, or business, although these are popular too.

Offered at research universities, liberal arts colleges, and other kinds of colleges as well, a liberal arts curriculum enriches your intellectual experience by prompting you to consider issues from the viewpoint of various disciplines. It may surprise you that most American undergraduates begin college without having decided on a major field of study. Not only is that acceptable, but it encourages students to explore fields unavailable to them in high school before they commit to a major field of study.

Students and parents are often concerned that the college a student attends be known and respected in their home country, which sometimes leads them to apply only to extremely selective colleges or colleges whose name includes known geography—a state or city or region. In some countries, lists circulate of the 10 or so universities recommended for a wide variety of majors and, given the difficulty of researching institutions in a foreign country in another language, these lists have credibility with families struggling to distinguish among the thousands of American institutions. These lists are not reliable or sufficient sources of information, but they do succeed in funneling students into a few colleges and thereby increase the level of selectivity for those students. We suggest you consider some alternative approaches that we describe below.

Start at Your Counseling Office, Which May Be Online

If your school has counselors, teachers, or administrators knowledgeable about American college education, you have an excellent resource to help you. But if not, the Internet offers abundant support. Begin with the BigFuture website, www.bigfuture.org, and the International Student Resources pages assembled by the National Association for College Admission Counseling at www.nacacnet.org. Also visit the website of EducationUSA, a global network of more than 400

It is difficult to overestimate the help and support I got from the EducationUSA Advising Center. The center was my first and primary source of information about the American educational system. The books, magazines, and Internet access at the center proved extremely useful, and the staff assisted me very much in achieving my goals.[6]

International student from Ghana

advising centers supported by the Bureau of Educational and Cultural Affairs at the US Department of State. At www.educationusa.state.gov, you can find information as well as the nearest advising center. EducationUSA centers also host college fairs at different locations around the world, where admissions representatives from various colleges come to meet students. If you attend such a fair, bring a translated transcript, test scores, and a résumé of your extracurricular activities to share with college representatives.

If college fairs do not come to your city and arranging to visit American campuses is not realistic, the Internet can provide good substitutes. You can visit virtual college fairs, as described in chapter 5, each month or even after they have taken place by accessing the archives at www.collegeweeklive.com. Virtual campus tours are offered on many campus websites and also at www.youniversitytv.com and www.campustours.com.

Read the Catalog

An often overlooked but very helpful source of information is the college catalog, available on almost every college's website. Look for general information about the educational philosophy of the college, also called its "mission," as well as specific information about graduation requirements, the requirements for completing any majors you might be interested in, course offerings, and so on. Information about admissions requirements is also there, but probably easier to find on the admissions page of the college website. College admissions offices welcome contact from prospective students, so you shouldn't hesitate to e-mail questions about anything not covered on the websites, in view books, and in catalogs.

Check the Basics

As you research colleges, be sure that each college you are interested in is accredited, meaning that the American educational community has certified its academic quality. You can check accreditation status through the US

Department of Education at www.ope.ed.gov/accreditation. To check that a college has been approved by the US Student and Exchange Visitor Program, check with its database, SEVIS (Student and Exchange Visitor Information System), at www.ice.gov/sevis. You can also use the SEVIS site to access Study in the States, a new online resource designed to help international students navigate the process of obtaining an appropriate visa.

Some Thoughts on Agents and Consultants

Some American colleges hire agents overseas to recruit international students. Although these agents may help with the application process, their allegiance may be divided between helping you and recruiting for those specific colleges since they are usually paid by both the colleges and your family. If you are working with an agent, you should ask whether the agent also recruits for any universities. Because commercial recruitment agents representing specific universities do not ensure unbiased information about the full range of American higher education opportunities, EducationUSA centers do not partner with them. The use of agents is very controversial in the United States and is the subject of heated discussion in the admissions profession. Some educational placement agencies may claim that they can guarantee college acceptance, the I-20 (certificate of eligibility for a student visa), or a student visa. They can do no such thing: only colleges grant acceptances, only colleges issue the I-20 form, and only the US State Department can issue a student visa.

Independent educational consultants are another resource, if available in your country, and are not paid by colleges. Some consultants based in the United States work successfully with students overseas through e-mail and Skype. A good consultant should work with you and your family to consider the full range of educational possibilities, should make no promises of admission, and should serve as a guide as you prepare your applications. Do your own research to assure yourself that you have explored widely and have all the facts you need, and be sure to take charge of your own applications.

By adhering strictly to the ethical standards of providing unbiased and comprehensive information, EducationUSA equips foreign students to find the U.S. institutions that are right for them while enabling U.S. institutions to enroll qualified foreign students.[7]

NATIONAL ASSOCIATION FOR COLLEGE ADMISSION COUNSELING

THE ROLE OF STANDARDIZED TESTS

Standardized testing plays a lesser role in American college admissions than it does in most other countries, but it can be an important factor in admissions to any college that requires SAT or ACT scores. Sometimes students can take this to mean that every school break should be devoted to studying for the SAT or ACT, but in fact, colleges would prefer to see you spend part of the summer either doing an unpaid internship to explore career choices or volunteering in the community.

Some selective colleges require students to send all of their test scores if they have taken a test more than once; others allow students to choose the test scores they wish to submit, and still others don't require students to take these tests at all. A word of caution on test optional: some test-optional colleges require scores for merit scholarships, others for certain programs only, and some for all international students. We always recommend that you check with each college. We also encourage you to reread chapter 6 for information on how these tests are used.

The SAT and ACT are not available everywhere and at all times. At this writing, students in mainland China who do not attend authorized international schools must take the SAT elsewhere, and usually take it in Hong Kong. The March SAT is not available anywhere outside the United States, and the September administration of the ACT is limited to the United States and Canada. The ACT website warns, "Not every country has established test centers, and not all test centers are scheduled for every test date." So after you discover which tests you must take, find out where and when you can take them. It is advisable to plan far ahead.

If both tests are available, compare them carefully. Some international students find that the ACT's format is more approachable for nonnative speakers of English, but not all agree. If neither test is offered in your country, colleges that require testing will find it more difficult to evaluate your application but may consider it nonetheless. It would serve you best to take one of the tests if at all possible. Even if a college is test optional, international students should submit their scores because scores from the American tests provide a familiar benchmark for admissions officers.

TESTS TO SHOW PROFICIENCY IN ENGLISH

Colleges want to be sure that students can do challenging academic work in English. Some may admit students who are less proficient in English but then require that they first complete an English transition program, or bridge program, where the students must improve their English skills before being admitted to the college's regular academic program.

Colleges determine an applicant's level of English fluency in a number of ways, many of which apply to American students as well: the quality of writing on the application, grades in English courses, a recommendation from an English teacher if provided, living in an English-speaking country, and, of course, standardized tests like the SAT, ACT, AP, IB, and state exams in other countries if they are in English. Colleges vary widely in how much importance they place on any one of these factors.

The TOEFL and the IELTS

Colleges also rely on special tests for international students.

The TOEFL

Best known among these is the TOEFL (Test of English as a Foreign Language), a four-hour test given almost exclusively over the Internet, usually at Sylvan Learning Systems offices around the world. It is also available in mainland China, while the SAT is not. It frequently appears with the acronym iBT (Internet-based test; the paper-based test, or PBT, is being phased out and increasingly unavailable).

The TOEFL is a different kind of standardized test from the SAT and ACT. It changes the questions as the student goes through the test. If you get a right answer, the next question is a little harder. If you miss one, it gets a little easier. The test is scored instantly, except for the mandatory writing sample and the recorded speaking segments, with a scale from 0 to 120 points. A score of 80 or higher or even 100 or higher is required for admission to some selective colleges. The international section of admissions pages on a college website should provide minimum TOEFL scores. If it doesn't, that's a good question for the admissions office. Check to see how the minimum is specified: by total score only or by total with minimum subscores.

The IELTS Alternative

A similar test, the IELTS (International English Language Testing System) was developed at Cambridge University in England and has made considerable headway among US colleges. It is most popular in India and Pakistan, where many students apply to British universities as well as American ones. It is a two hour and 45 minute test, with a speaking component conducted by a live examiner and is scored on a 1 to 9 scale.

The Choice May Be Yours

Many US colleges accept either one, but you need to check with a particular college to be sure. Again, you are usually required to achieve a minimum score, as with the TOEFL. The TOEFL is clearly the market leader and the test more US colleges are comfortable with. The Educational Testing Service, the organization that administers the TOEFL, has a tool for comparing a TOEFL and an IELTS score on its website, www.ets.org. Both tests have taken on increased importance because of concern about widespread fraud in the writing of applications from overseas.

> TOEFL and IELTS results help admission staffers determine whether a candidate's level of English language proficiency will be a barrier to their academic progress as an enrolled student. It is in the candidate's best interests to take one of these tests to eliminate any question about whether or not their proficiency is high enough to ensure academic success.[8]
>
> MICHAEL STEIDEL, DIRECTOR OF ADMISSION, CARNEGIE MELLON UNIVERSITY

Exemptions from Taking the TOEFL or IELTS

If you are an international student who has studied in the United States for three or more years, you may not be required to take the TOEFL or IELTS. The same is true of international students who have studied at an American or English-speaking international school. Nevertheless, you should verify this with each college; some selective colleges require very high scores on the Critical Reading section of the SAT to waive the TOEFL requirement for an international student.

You may want to offer TOEFL or IELTS scores anyway to enhance your application. The verbal sections of the SAT and ACT are designed for native English speakers, whereas the TOEFL and IELTS are designed for students who speak English as a second (or third or fourth . . .) language and therefore can highlight your English skills more positively. Many selective colleges recommend taking the TOEFL for this reason, because the TOEFL gives them more detailed information about your English ability. In some cases, a strong TOEFL score can replace a weaker SAT Critical Reading or ACT Reading score in a college's admissions deliberations. In any case, "it's value added to an application," according to one admissions officer from a highly selective school. International students who have studied in English for high school might also consider taking an SAT Subject Test in their own language, if available, to demonstrate literacy skills in their native tongue.

GETTING THE APPLICATION COMPLETED

Deadlines

Be aware that the American application process begins many months earlier than it does in most other countries. Standardized tests should be taken during your junior year, so you have time to repeat a test if needed. The application forms themselves may be filled in as early as August 1 of the year before you plan to begin college and are usually due at some point between October 15 to March 15 of your senior year; the exact deadline varies from college to college. Deadlines generally apply to all students, international or not, but some colleges may have restrictions for international applicants. Always check the websites of the individual colleges for the most accurate information.

Transcripts and Official Documents

All colleges require an official transcript of your course work and grades, sent directly from each high school attended. You may also need to provide a photocopy of your current valid passport. Other required or recommended documents may include diplomas, school certificates, and results of national examinations. If not in English, these must be sent with a notarized or certified translation, possibly accompanied by an evaluation of the education credentials by an approved service that specializes in converting foreign educational information into US equivalencies. College websites describe their requirements and recommendations and designate approved service companies so that you will know how to proceed. Boston University, for example, states that "all documents written in a foreign language must be accompanied by a notarized English translation. Please note that both documents are required—the original in your first language and the English translation."

Just as with American students, admissions offices scrutinize the transcript to assess the level of difficulty of your courses and how you have performed in each class. To ensure accuracy, colleges can hire experts to verify the authenticity of foreign transcripts and credentials. Your English grades will hold special interest, since as an international student, you need to show definitively that you are not only ready for college work but are ready to do it in English.

Even American students need to be reminded that an offer of admission is conditional on successfully completing senior year; the high school is required to send a transcript with all final grades and the date of graduation before a student can begin classes at college. If the final grades are not equivalent to those submitted with the application, the college could respond with anything from a harsh letter to academic probation to cancelling the student's acceptance. For many international students accustomed to admission by test, this is shocking—almost unbelievable. Believe it.

Extra Forms for International Students

International students need to submit more forms than do their American counterparts, as well as more information generally. If you are studying in a non-American school system, you will need to make sure that your school's curriculum and grading system are described in English. If your transcript is being sent by an approved translation and evaluation service, this information should be included. A school official will usually be asked to provide some additional information about you, such as predicted scores on secondary leaving examinations, if offered. Testing requirements may be more extensive, as we have just discussed. Some colleges also require international applicants to submit statements of financial support, which we discuss later in this chapter.

Essays and Statements

Each applicant is unique, and it is that singular person whom the college wants to hear, in his or her own voice. In fact, the application essay or essays are often called the "personal statement" for just this reason. As an international student, you offer unique perspectives and should be confident in sharing them. Each country is interesting, and each citizen of that country has something interesting to say about it. Each country has a culture, a history, a literature, and some relationship with the United States,

> The essay is such an important part of your application. Take the chance to show that you've got something extra.[9]
>
> INTERNATIONAL STUDENT FROM SOUTH KOREA

hostile or friendly. Every student can find something to write about that will bring that culture to the fore in the application.

This is not essential, of course. An international student can write about sports just as an American can, but an Indian student writing about cricket, a Spanish student writing about basketball, or a Japanese student discussing baseball can express something cultural in addition to their love of the sport. Global warming may be global, but it is different in Bangladesh and Russia than in the American heartland. It is the quality of the essay that matters most, not the subject alone, and your ideas and experience should always be central.

When Help Is Not Appropriate

In the American classroom and in the admissions process, it is assumed that all writing submitted is the student's own original work. Admissions officers are experts at detecting the touch of writers who are several years (or decades) older than 18. They also have access to the essay portion of the SAT and ACT to compare the timed writing there with the more polished application prose. Essays crafted with too much outside help have been an issue for years, from applicants everywhere.

We may seem to be overstating the problem of fraud in essay writing, but it is because we understand that in some cultures, especially those where admission to university is determined solely or mainly by examinations, application essay writing and the like can be routinely outsourced to hired hands and is perfectly ordinary behavior within that culture. Each culture defines acceptable behavior in its own way, but a student entering a different culture is moving to different academic assumptions and protocols, as well as different modes of courtesy and behavior. This begins with the application process itself.

The American admissions process demands that the student be the sole author of the application. This is an important discussion to have with any agent or counselor who may be working with you. Any suspicion that someone other than the student applicant has created any part of the application may result in a dismissal of the application.

Sending the Application and Supporting Documents

It is wise to submit applications over the Internet to ensure timely arrival. In fact the Common Application accepts only online applications. Even if a school accepts a paper application, it may waive application fees if it is submitted online. Check the admissions page of each college website for specific information. If you must mail your application or any other documentation, be sure to keep copies of everything and, if at all possible, arrange for confirmation of delivery. Many colleges require that you set up an account on their website so you can check the status of your application, know what materials have been received, and even read your admissions decision at the end of the process.

Recommendations

Most colleges require a secondary school report, a general recommendation letter by a school counselor or administrator, and require or recommend one or two teacher recommendations. In many countries, this is unheard of. Many international students report that the administrator or teacher they approached has asked them to write the recommendation for the school official's signature. This may be tempting, but do not write such a letter yourself. Provide the administrator and teachers with a list of your courses and grades, your other activities, and a description of the purpose of the recommendation. Dartmouth College provides helpful guidance that applies to just about any college. It says:

> The written evaluation from your counselor that is included in your Secondary School Report is one place where we will start to look for a better understanding of both your intellectual engagement and your interactions with others beyond the classroom. Your counselor will provide us with a perspective on your experience within your school (and perhaps beyond school) . . .
>
> We use the Teacher Evaluations to help us understand what you are like in the classroom or at the lab bench and to learn a little bit about your approach to learning. While it's fine to choose a teacher who may know you both in and out of the classroom, the real focus of a teacher evaluation should be on your intellectual engagement in class.[10]

To make this process even more challenging, the letters must be written in English or accompanied by a translation, and sent directly to the colleges or uploaded to the Common Application or other online application site. On the Common Application, or the recommendation form, you will be asked to "waive your FERPA right," which is the right granted by US law to read your application file once you arrive on the campus of your college. No matter how tempting it might feel to see what your file contains (if, indeed, the college has kept it), we strongly urge you to waive this right so that letter writers have the power of unfettered honesty. It also shows the college that you trust your recommenders.

Interviews

Not all colleges offer interviews. When an interview is available, by all means accept the opportunity. It may be conducted in person by an admissions officer or a graduate of the college, or by Skype or telephone. Interviews may be conducted in part to assess your proficiency in English, but interviews can also be less about language and more about getting to know you better. Rereading the section on interviews in chapter 9 will be helpful preparation for interviewing.

PAYING FOR YOUR EDUCATION

For most international students, the opportunity for an American undergraduate education depends on having the financial resources to afford the tuition, living expenses, and other costs. The amount of financial aid for international students is not growing, and only a handful of American universities practice need-blind admission for international students and meet full demonstrated need as well. (We defined these terms and others important to understanding financial aid in chapter 12.)

Why? The reason is very simple and entirely based on economics. It is US government policy to support the college enrollment of domestic low-income students, even if the amount of aid may not meet their full need. This does not apply to international students. Aside from their families, the only source of financial assistance most of them have is the American college they will attend.

Colleges That Offer Aid to International Students

As of this writing, the only colleges in the United States that admit international students

Some colleges offer aggressive scholarship programs for international students. Others have very limited aid for internationals. Some offer merit aid to international students. Others are need-based only. It can vary widely from campus to campus, so check the financial aid and international student sections of college websites for specific information about each college in which you have serious interest.[11]

CHRIS HOOKER HARING, DEAN OF ADMISSION AND FINANCIAL AID, MUHLENBERG COLLEGE need blind and meet full demonstrated need are Harvard University, Yale University, Princeton University, Dartmouth College, MIT, and Amherst College. And, of course, these schools are already swamped with applications from both American and international applicants.

Still, many other colleges do offer substantial, if partial, financial aid to international students. A list of colleges offering financial aid to international undergraduates, including the number of students receiving awards and the average amount, can be found by putting "Douglas Thompson Financial Aid" into Google. The list is prepared periodically by Doug Thompson, an honored veteran admissions dean, now retired, and is the most up-to-date resource of its kind. It currently includes 152 public and private colleges and universities from all over the United States.

Apply Widely

Don't be put off if the school cannot meet your full demonstrated need. Every college would like to do so, but they just don't have the financial resources to afford it. But they still have financial aid available, and only the students who apply for it get it. If you limit yourself to the few schools listed above, you may be missing out on other opportunities. A student who needs aid must apply widely and consider colleges that are less well known to their compatriots but that have a record of providing financial aid to international students.

As usual, the Internet is a good place to start. Both the International Student Resources page at the National Association for College Admission Counseling at www.nacacnet.org and the Library page at the Overseas Association for College Admission Counseling at www.oacac.org have useful links, including a link to the Douglas Thompson financial aid listing. Three other websites can also help:

- NAFSA: Association of International Educators, www.nafsa.org
- EduPass, www.edupass.org
- International Student Network, www.internationalstudent.com

Be careful not to succumb to offers from unscrupulous agencies promising scholarships: they are easily identified because they ask you for money first. Real scholarship agencies are free of cost to applying students.

Forms and More Forms

Students seeking financial aid from a college may be able to use the College Board's form, International Student Application for Financial Aid, but may also need to complete a college-specific form. Sometimes international applicants for financial aid are also asked to use the same forms as domestic applicants: the Free Application for Federal Student Aid (FAFSA) or the CSS PROFILE, or both. As always, check with each college for its policy.

Most important, either when they apply or on accepting an offer of admission, all international students need to provide proof that they have the financial resources to attend the college. In order to obtain the document that allows you to apply for a student visa for study in the United States (the I-20), you and your family must submit evidence that you can pay for the full cost of your first year of study. The financial support needs to be sufficient to cover tuition, books and supplies, room and board, health insurance, travel, and daily essentials. Each college will help you determine the proper amounts.

One commonly used form is the Certification of Finances. You can access this form and the International Student Application for Financial Aid through the Overseas Association for College Admission Counseling website. There are alternative forms, like the Affidavit of Financial Support, used by individual colleges and available from colleges themselves. You will need bank account records and/or records of other assets to fill out the forms. Colleges may also request original documents.

Some Additional Points About Finances

Several caveats and qualifications are appropriate at this point. First, on the plus side, some colleges include Canadian and Mexican students in their American need-blind admissions policy as a kind of good neighbor relationship with these strategic American allies. This can help you if you are from either one of these countries. On the minus side, some schools have very little or no money for international transfer students, and at some you cannot apply early decision if you need aid since those colleges want to evaluate all international applicants together in the regular admissions round. Schools can change policy at any time.

Enterprising students sometimes hope to work while attending college and thereby earn enough to pay the costs of their education. Because of the stipulations of the student visa, international students have very limited employment options in the United States, none of which can provide enough income to fully fund a college education or significantly supplement partial financial aid. We caution you against planning to pay for your education in this way.

SPECIAL CIRCUMSTANCES

Undocumented Students

Although not formally considered international students, undocumented students raised and educated in the United States face special challenges when pursuing higher education. Although they can attend college, they are not eligible for federal financial aid and may not be eligible for state aid. The situation is in flux.

At this writing, legislation, sometimes called the Dream Act, has been proposed in Congress to offer undocumented students a path to citizenship. It has not yet been passed, although a 2012 program of deferred action partially addresses the issue. In California, the California Dream Act passed in 2011 allows children of illegal immigrants who graduate from California high schools to receive state financial aid. In-state status at public colleges and universities varies from state to state. Georgia and South Carolina currently even prohibit undocumented students from attending some or all public universities in those states.

Since you don't have a social security number, you will need to fill out college applications without it. Do not invent one, and be assured that the FERPA law protects the privacy of the information contained in your application and financial aid forms. Even if information about your citizenship or immigration status is requested, you do not need to provide it, and you should not. Sometimes online forms make it difficult to leave some items blank; if so, print out the form if possible or obtain a paper application, fill it out by hand, make a copy, and mail it in.

Undocumented students need to investigate the implications of their legal situation at every college, begin their search early, and seek help from teachers, counselors, community organizations, and older students who have traveled this road themselves. The FinAid website at www.finaid.org provides excellent initial information on financial aid and state support for undocumented students. Put "undocumented" in the search box at this site to go directly to this information.

Who Counts as an International Student?

Universities define an international student as someone who is neither a US citizen nor a documented permanent resident of the United States. International students may have had their entire education in the United States and may speak excellent English, but they are still international students. Similarly, an American citizen may live abroad, even since birth, may have dual citizenship, and may be educated in another country's school system but would not be considered an international student officially and certainly not for purposes of financial aid. What are the implications of these special situations for college admissions?

An international student educated in the United States would apply just as an American would, but with the addition of forms providing proof of financial support. TOEFL or IELTS scores could be helpful if your SAT or ACT verbal scores are low. A Subject Test in your first language, if available, would support your academic skills in your native language.

As an American citizen educated overseas, you might need to describe the local educational system if you are studying in a local school or a non-American international school. You might confront some of the challenges we described earlier about getting teacher recommendations and a secondary school report. If your SAT or ACT verbal scores are at the low end of a college's midrange of scores, taking the TOEFL or IELTS might be recommended even though English is your first language.

Your internationalism is of great interest to an admissions office and may boost your chance of admission if you can effectively articulate the value of having lived in two cultures, or even more in some cases. An international student living and educated in the United States can bring a unique perspective to that experience, as can an American student living and educated abroad. We urge you to display that perspective in one of your application essays.

THE BIGGER PICTURE

International students have been coming to American colleges and universities for a long time, but their number has more than doubled over the past three decades, with a greater percentage coming as undergraduates. The number of Chinese students alone has more than doubled over the past five years.

But internationalization is not a one-way street. While studying abroad, whether for a summer, semester, or year, was once merely an option for some Americans, many colleges now emphasize it as a priority. Some, like Suffolk University, St. Lawrence University, Colby College, and Colby-Sawyer College, have programs abroad for a subset of their entering freshman class each fall; students at Goucher College are now required to earn at least some academic credits abroad before they graduate.

International students today are members of a large community of young people from all over the world who have left the predictable culture and academic norms they have grown up with to explore new cultures and new expectations. We hope the information provided in this chapter will make your transition to education in the United States a little smoother.

CHAPTER 14

Making Your Decision After the Colleges Make Theirs

U p to this point, *Admission Matters* has focused on the process of choosing colleges and preparing strong applications. We now want to shift to the end of the process and discuss how to approach the choices you and your family will have to make once you receive the colleges' decisions.

For students applying early decision (ED) or early action (EA), closure may come quickly. Colleges usually notify students mid-December (or mid-February, for those pursuing ED II options offered by some colleges). Many colleges with rolling admissions, most often public universities such as the University of Pittsburgh, Indiana University, and the University of Minnesota, also provide fast turnaround in just a few weeks or less. But students applying regular decision (including those deferred from an early cycle) may not get all their decisions until the middle or end of March. Ivy League colleges are usually among the last to announce their decisions, observing a common notification date (and time: 5:00 p.m. Eastern) in late March or the beginning of April.

> Getting in doesn't mean life's doors are now open to you without effort and drive. Being rejected doesn't mean your dreams are suddenly and forever dashed. Sure, celebrate or mourn a bit, but then realize that the truly important stuff—the love of family, the support of close friends, the desire to learn and explore—really hasn't changed at all.
>
> PARENT REFLECTING ON THE NOTIFICATION PROCESS

HOW WILL YOU BE NOTIFIED?

Whether you submitted applications early or during the regular cycle, both hope and anxiety naturally rise for students and parents as the notification date nears.

Most colleges notify students electronically, either through e-mail or via a website, to speed up the process and reduce uncertainty about when decisions will be received, since regular mail can be unpredictable. Colleges that post their decisions online typically announce the precise date and time when this information will be available. At the appointed hour, thousands and sometimes tens of thousands of students across the country sit tensely in front of their computers checking for the final outcome. A small number of colleges still mail their decisions.

> Early Action and Early Decision letters should arrive next week. We feel that it is very important for students to treat other members of the community, and themselves, well—no matter what the results. Students who are admitted should consider the feelings of those who may not have been admitted or who have not applied early. Intense displays of happiness in public are not the most advisable behavior. Conversely, no one expects a student who did not get admitted to be happy about that. But intense public displays of anguish also can be a burden to others. We recommend that students try very hard to receive the decisions off-campus.
>
> POSTING ON PRIVATE SCHOOL WEBSITE IN EARLY DECEMBER

THE SPECIAL CASE OF EARLY DECISION

The wait for an early answer is often an emotionally intense time. By the very nature of the process, the student has made a major investment in a college as their "top choice." A lot seems to be riding on the outcome. When the outcome is a happy one, students and families are elated. When the outcome is unfavorable, they can be severely disappointed, even if they knew it was a long shot.

Students can easily get caught up in their own feelings and forget that their friends and fellow students are dealing with their own concerns over the admissions process. We encourage everyone to save overt bursts of emotion, whether shrieks of joy or tears of disappointment, for a private setting. Some schools discourage students from using on-site computers or cell phones to access admissions results for just this reason.

I applied early action to Harvard. That's where my sister goes, but I didn't get in. The decision came on Wednesday, and I was pretty upset for a couple of days. By Friday, I was OK. Then the weekend came, and I just kind of forgot about it. Just because I didn't get into Harvard doesn't mean that there's anything wrong with me. It also helped that my sister had been rejected by Princeton and Yale. That showed me how random things could be. The other thing that really helped was that those who did get in did not run around screaming, "Oh, I got in early. My life is great!" That would have made it much worse for those of us who didn't get good news. Everyone was really respectful of everyone else. A lot of terrific kids got rejected or deferred. It was like "Join the club." We kind of shared the pain.

HIGH SCHOOL SENIOR

⋉

We also urge parents to respect their children's privacy for decisions received at home, whether they arrive by e-mail or regular mail or are posted on a college's website. Some students may want family members present. Faced with possible disappointment, however, some prefer to be alone to absorb the decision. Parents should take their cue from their child and be there, literally or figuratively, to support him or her regardless of the outcome. If the news is disappointing, parents should try not to add to their child's burden with displays of anguish or anger. This applies not only for the early acceptance cycle but also for the regular cycle notifications that come later.

Accepted!

If your early application is a binding one, your acceptance brings your college search to an early, happy conclusion. If your notification does not include financial aid information, it will follow shortly, and if the offer adequately covers your need, you are expected to submit your intent-to-enroll form and deposit by the deadline indicated, usually within a few weeks. You must also withdraw all other pending applications. Other than some unforeseeable family catastrophe, unmet financial need is the only legitimate grounds for not attending a college that admits you under binding ED.

Financial Aid and Early Decision

If your financial aid package provides less money than you will need to attend, contact the financial aid office immediately to explain the situation in detail and respectfully request that your financial aid package be reviewed. Perhaps something can be worked out. Remember, though, that the difference between what a college believes a family needs and what the family feels it needs (sometimes known as "felt need") may not be totally reconcilable. The family, however, makes the final decision about whether the ED financial aid package will allow the student to attend.

Financial aid issues aside, colleges primarily rely on an honor system to enforce the binding agreement, since they cannot legally force you to attend against your will. School counselors also enforce the rules. Some selective colleges using ED share their acceptance lists as a way to police compliance with the binding policy. If your name were to show up on two ED admit lists, you would be in trouble with both schools and both of them could withdraw their acceptance. Students who are not released from their binding commitment and choose not to enroll at their ED college may find some other doors closed to them. The vast majority of students admitted ED, however, never even remotely think of not attending their chosen college, or if they do, the buyer's remorse passes quickly.

The Early Action Acceptance

An EA acceptance can also bring your college search to a happy ending. But under the terms of EA, you have until May 1 to formally accept your offer. If your EA school is clearly your first choice, it is courteous (although certainly not mandatory) to withdraw other applications from the regular decision process and not submit any new ones (especially if financial aid is not an issue). The reason is simple: the more applications in the college pipeline, the lower the percentage of applicants whom a college can accept. If you know for sure where you will be going in September, share your good fortune by giving your fellow students (locally and nationally) a better chance for a regular decision admission at a college they would like to attend.

But an EA acceptance need not end your college search. You may be interested in other colleges as well and want more time to make a decision. You may also want to see what your other financial aid packages look like when you receive other acceptances in the spring. In that case, you'll have to wait until you receive your regular cycle decisions. You can do so, however, knowing that you already have an acceptance from a school you would happily attend.

Denied or Deferred

Many early applications end happily, but a lot do not. As more and more students seek the advantage of applying early, colleges have to deny or defer more of them to leave room for regular cycle admits. Colleges differ in their approach to dealing with applicants they do not accept. Some, like Georgetown University, defer all or most of them, denying only those who clearly don't meet the qualifications for admission. A deferred application is considered again along with the applications submitted during the regular cycle. Other colleges prefer to make hard decisions sooner rather than later, denying many qualified candidates whom they know would be denied in the regular cycle anyway, and deferring just a small percentage who look seriously competitive for the final round. Vanderbilt University, for example, does not defer anyone who is not admitted ED.

As early applications continue to rise, the trend is to deny more students in the early round rather than fewer, partly to ease the burden of the admissions staff during the winter. The continued growth in the regular cycle applicant pool makes it harder to read all the files if there are too many deferrals to be read again in the winter. Colleges that deny a student during an early cycle do not allow them to resubmit their application for the regular cycle for the same year. The problem with an early application denial is that it is usually the only response you receive, and it's at holiday time. A student has usually applied to only one college early, so those denied have no compensating acceptances to ease the blow. But a denial does not mean that you weren't a strong applicant or that you weren't qualified to attend. It simply means that the admissions staff decided not to admit you—nothing more and nothing less—and that your application will not be considered further. Given the vagaries of the college admissions process, it is best to accept the decision and move on.

Despite your natural disappointment, this may be a blessing in disguise as a reality check. This is a good time to reassess your college list one more time, trim some of the most difficult ones, and perhaps add a possible or good-bet school to balance your list. If you follow our advice, you will have your other applications ready to go or already submitted.

WHAT YOU CAN DO IF YOU ARE DEFERRED

Students who find themselves deferred still face uncertainty about the final outcome, and it is hard to predict the chances for admission during the regular cycle. Statistically the odds are not very high. The regular pool is likely to be large and strong, and the admissions staff feels an obligation to treat the regular applicants fairly. The admissions office may tell you in your letter how many applicants were deferred. If not, they may tell you if you call and ask. You can also see whether your high school counselor can find out from the admissions office how close you came to admission. Some colleges will provide this information, and it may help you assess your chances in the regular cycle. But if you can't get this information, don't worry. Just knowing what your chances are isn't going to increase them.

Increasing Your Chances

It is natural to continue to hope, even more so when this was your first choice. The first instinct it to ask, "What can I do to increase my chances of admission after being deferred?" First, take a deep breath. Is this still your first choice? You are now released from your binding commitment to enroll. You can play the field again. Think about it. It may be a relief. Second, accept that while there is still hope, there is not a great deal you can do now to improve your chances. You should, however, write a letter reaffirming your strong interest in the college. Asking your high school counselor to send a similar note of support with your midyear grades is also appropriate. If you have received any significant new honors (this is rare, of course) or participated in any noteworthy activities since you first applied, you should tell the college this as well.

Finally, finishing the fall semester with a strong record can only help. During the regular cycle, unlike the early review, colleges will see your fall semester grades, and high grades can help you. In fact, that may be one reason you were deferred: they wanted to see your semester grades.

It is wise to assume that your chances of being admitted during the regular cycle are the same as if you had first applied regular decision. No more and no less. Major changes in your file are fairly rare after December, and you can never count on a deferral converting to an offer of admission. There are lots of other fine colleges out there. Do not mourn your loss for very long.

Being Prepared for Any Outcome

Be prepared whatever the outcome. Because most early application outcomes are unpredictable, students applying early must have a well-developed list of additional schools waiting in the wings with applications ready to go (or, if you are proactive, well organized, and impatient, already sent out by the time a decision arrives on December 15). Depending on how good a chance you believed your early application had to begin with, it can be psychologically quite deflating to be denied or deferred. You want to avoid, if possible, having to complete new applications when your confidence has been shaken.

Don't Get Discouraged!

Above all, don't get discouraged! Try to remember that the outcome depends not only on your submitting a strong application, but also on factors outside your control, such as the quality and number of the other early applications that year. It also depends to a great extent on the priorities of each admissions office that year. All of these are out of your hands. Focus on what you can control. If you have prepared your college list wisely, you will have good choices at the end, regardless of the early outcome at one college.

WHEN IT IS YOUR TURN TO DECIDE IN THE SPRING

Mid-December, as intense as it may be, is just a dress rehearsal for the spring when the regular admissions cycle results start arriving. This time, many more students are waiting for responses from even more schools—and everything is drawn out over a longer period. But now, after waiting several months to hear their decisions from colleges, students and families once again can make their own decisions.

Choices Can Be Tough to Make

The process of making a final decision to attend a college will vary, not surprisingly, from student to student and from family to family. A lot depends not only on personality and decision-making style but also on the specific choices. A student admitted to his top-choice school with sufficient financial aid or no need for aid has a pretty easy decision to make.

Other students may have several desirable choices, with financial aid sometimes weighing heavily in the final decision. Because many highly selective colleges offer only need-based aid or very little merit aid, less selective colleges can compete for strong students by offering attractive merit aid packages, sometimes half or even full rides, which go beyond calculated need. It can be hard to turn down a good school that offers a free or almost free education in favor of one, no matter how attractive and prestigious, that would cost your family much more. Many students, particularly those who do not qualify for need-based aid, find merit aid attractive in the end.

Revisit Your Priorities

Sometimes students facing a difficult decision find it helpful to make a list of pros and cons for each college. We suggest revisiting the priorities that emerged when you completed the questionnaire at the end of chapter 4. Thinking through what is really important to you is critical, now more than ever before. Your priorities may have changed over the past few months. Now that you know your choices, prestige may no longer play such an important role because the high-prestige schools turned you down. Or you may have a better idea of the major you want to pursue because a senior-year course has changed your academic direction. Or you may be more willing to go farther from home, or you may feel more comfortable not needing to do this. All of these are valid factors to consider.

You may, however, prefer to bypass lists and go with gut instinct. Both approaches can work, and in fact, elements of both may work best of all. The selection priorities will be different for each person, but make sure they are sound. One young man we know likes to plan ahead. Characteristically, he took a long view in choosing to attend a particular Ivy League college. "Thirty-five percent of legacy applicants get in," he said. "If I say yes to Ivy U, I'm saying yes for my children; I'm saying yes for everyone down the line." Had this been a major factor in his decision (it wasn't), he would have been on shaky ground. No one knows whether legacy preferences in admission will even exist in 25 years, let alone whether his children would even want to attend Ivy U.

Make a Decision by May 1

Colleges ask that students declare their intentions, one way or the other, by May 1, the widely observed candidate reply date. It is courteous to respond as soon as you have made your decision—not only to the college you plan to attend but also to the others you are turning down. All colleges admit more students than they have room for because they know some will go elsewhere. As we'll see in a later section, your decision not to attend a college may open up a spot for a student on the wait list. The earlier a college can determine it has space, the sooner it can send the happy news to someone else.

> What I did was flip a coin, and wherever it landed, I tried to decide how I felt about that. Every time it landed on College X, I got a gut feeling that I wasn't going to feel comfortable on that campus.
>
> SENIOR WHO DECIDED TO ATTEND COLLEGE Y

DEALING WITH DISAPPOINTMENT

While many students look forward to choosing a college in April, others are disappointed. If you are admitted to only one or two good-bet colleges and denied or wait-listed by the others, you may not be excited by any of the choices. It isn't fun to be told no by a school you were really enthusiastic about. When several say no, it is even harder. Remember, though, what we emphasized in chapter 3: many factors in the college admissions process are beyond your control and have no bearing on who you are as a person. Realizing how uncertain the outcome can be at some colleges can make it easier to accept each outcome gracefully.

> My parents knew I was nervous, so they sat me down and said, "Look, you've done everything you can do." But when the rejections came in, I still felt like every mistake I'd made in the last four years of high school was coming back to haunt me.[1]
>
> HIGH SCHOOL SENIOR

Even students with several acceptances may find themselves uncomfortable as they second-guess whether they made the right choices to start with. Having

---

I applied early decision to Elite University although I didn't really think I'd get in. It was a big stretch for me, but you never know. I was rejected, which made me unhappy, but then I got over it. What was hard was getting rejected later at less competitive schools. I could have gotten into those schools without working so hard. People who played a lot and weren't so serious about school got in there, too. I really wanted to have that happy acceptance thing, when I would open the mail and jump up and down and call my mom to tell her the great news. I missed that. But I learned that if you don't get in where you want to go, it's not the end of the world. I'm not a religious person, so when people say everything happens for a reason, I'm like, "Yeah, well." But I think in this case, everything did happen for a reason. I'm really happy here.

COLLEGE FRESHMAN

---

become a reality, suddenly none of the colleges looks that good, and some students start to wonder whether they should have "aimed higher."

Remind Yourself That There Are No Perfect Colleges

These reactions are normal. It is important to move beyond that first shock of rejection. Dwelling on the negative, as well as what-ifs, slows that down. All colleges, no matter how highly rated or well regarded, have faults. And all colleges, even the most humble by most measures, have good points. If you have done your research carefully at the outset, your choice will be a good one no matter what you choose. In fact, the college itself does not make the crucial difference in your future contentment; rather, it is your degree of commitment to your own education. The choice is your first step of that commitment.

One young woman we know was denied by all colleges except her one good bet. Although disappointed, she took a positive approach. Ten weeks into her freshman year, she enthusiastically reported how happy she was with her college, even though she had no choice. She loved her classes, her new friends, and the college itself. Each year many thousands of students have similarly happy endings after a disappointing March.

The Transfer Option

Remember also that choosing a college is not an irrevocable act. Students can and do transfer after freshman or sophomore year. Some students transfer from their first-choice schools, even an ED school, and some from their good bets. Doing well in the final semester of high school and during your freshman year will boost your transfer odds, although some colleges may be as selective for transfer students as they are for freshmen. And not all colleges accept transfers. We don't recommend choosing a college as a springboard to transferring to another one. This is a recipe for being an unhappy freshman. You should find the good points of your college and vow to make the best of it. If it doesn't work out, then you can think about transferring, but first give your college an honest try. We discuss the transfer process at greater length in chapter 11.

SPRING ADMITS

Inundated with more good applicants than they can accept, some colleges have found a creative solution so they can admit a few more students each year: they offer a group of students the opportunity to enroll as freshmen starting in the spring semester rather than in the fall. A college can do this because it knows that some students will not return for spring semester. Students withdraw due to health, adjustment, financial problems, or poor academic performance, and a few seniors usually graduate early. The spots opened up by the departures create space for students willing to start midyear.

Colleges offering spring admission encourage students to use the fall semester well, either through course work at another college or other enriching activities. Middlebury College and the University of California, Berkeley, have offered spring admission for many years. Middlebury calls their spring arrivals "Febs" for the month of February, when the spring semester starts. The University of Southern California, Brandeis University, and Wheaton College (Massachusetts), as well as a number of other colleges, now offer spring starts as well. A few schools offer students a first semester overseas: for example, Skidmore College in London, Colby College in Dijon, France, and Northeastern University in several countries.

> The scary thing is that no one in our family, adult or child, has the slightest clue which school would be best. They all have pros and cons. Sometimes I think it might be a relief to get rejections from all but one to avoid having to make these incredibly difficult decisions.
>
> A PARENT AT DECISION TIME

The disadvantage of a midyear start is obvious: you don't get to experience the first exciting semester of college life with your future classmates. On the plus side, though, after just a few months you will join them when you would not otherwise have had a chance. You usually don't apply for spring admission; if a school cannot accept you for the fall but expects to have room in the spring, it will tell you in your admissions letter. Middlebury asks on the application if you would like to be considered for spring admission so you can express your willingness. They look for outgoing, flexible students who will adjust easily when they arrive in February.

TAKING ANOTHER LOOK

Most colleges host special admit days or weekends in April before the May 1 Common Reply Date. Even if you have visited a college before, going to an admit program can be fun and a good way to get a feel for the campus. It can be especially useful, of course, if you have not visited before.

Finally, the pressure is off, and you can enjoy being courted with tours, receptions, panels, and faculty lectures. Everyone realizes that the campus is at its best on this special day or weekend, but you'll still get to know the campus better because you can meet so many students, including your potential classmates.

Normally students must pay the cost of travel to admit programs. In some cases, though, a campus may be particularly eager to recruit a student and will offer to pay all or some of the expenses up to a certain dollar limit. This applies mostly to underrepresented minorities or students from low-income families. If you are not offered financial assistance but find that the cost of travel is a hardship, consider asking the admissions office whether the campus can help with your travel costs. They may say no because of budget limitations, but it cannot hurt to ask.

Admit programs, especially when you stay overnight, give you a good chance to talk to current students about what the college is really like, as well as get a sense of who might be joining you in the freshman class. It is worth rereading the section on college visits in chapter 5 to refresh your memory of what to look for. Some colleges also encourage parents to attend and even offer special programs for them (although no dorm housing!), and all colleges welcome them regardless of whether formal events are provided. It's fine to accompany your child to an admit weekend; just be sure you give him or her lots of space.

> I want to look at the academics and which college really fits my academic goals the most. Visiting becomes more important. Getting a feel for the people that go there. Making sure that they're compatible. Do I want to live in New Jersey? In Southern California? How much of a stretch do I want from my current lifestyle?
>
> SENIOR TRYING TO MAKE A DECISION BETWEEN TWO VERY DIFFERENT BUT EXCELLENT COLLEGES

REVISITING FINANCIAL AID

If your financial aid offers are disappointing, reread the section on how to request reconsideration near the end of chapter 12. Once you have all your acceptance and financial aid offers, you may want to make your top-choice college aware of any offer that is significantly larger than theirs if the differences in the aid packages may affect your final choice. Also tell them of any changes in your financial situation that might increase your eligibility for aid. Courteously requesting a financial aid review to see whether anything more can be done is both appropriate and smart. Be prepared, of course, for a negative answer.

A college can more easily make adjustments when new information or a new interpretation of existing information results in a calculation of greater financial need. They can sometimes make adjustments even without such new information as the result of a second careful look, but these cases are less common, and this might happen only for the applicants the college is most eager to enroll. However, don't expect a college that offers only need-based aid to adjust its package to offset a merit scholarship at another college. At the same time, don't let a no discourage you from continuing to consider the college as an option if you are excited about the college and it is within financial reach, even with less than an ideal aid package.

HOW WAIT LISTS WORK

A wait list consists of applicants who were not admitted outright but are notified that they will be considered for admission if space becomes available later in the spring. What should you make of a letter that essentially puts you in limbo?

Being placed on a wait list means that your file will be considered again if the college has fewer acceptances than it anticipated when it mailed offers of admission. On the basis of experience, they calculate an estimated yield. Then they wait, usually, but not always, until after the May 1 deadline to see how many students have sent in their deposits. Because of competition for good students, colleges know that some of their wait-listed students are likely to be wait-listed at other comparable colleges. So they may even take students from the wait list before May 1 to get a head start on their rivals. Sometimes they may admit wait list students in stages: 20 prime candidates before May 1 and 30 more on May 10, when they have a firmer fix on the yield. The process is very similar to the way airlines fill their planes. It is common to overbook a plane, since some passengers will be no-shows. If empty seats remain when the plane is ready to leave, those seats can be filled by standbys who know that they may or may not get a seat but have been patiently waiting.

I was put on the wait list. The dean sent me a very nice letter that said, "After long and careful consideration, the admission committee has decided to place your name on the waiting list . . . I congratulate you on your fine record of accomplishments which deserve a much more fitting recognition than I can provide right now. I hope you will remain interested in our college and that you will choose to hold a place on our waiting list. I also hope that I may ultimately have a chance to offer you a place in our entering class."

Accompanying the letter was an attachment stating that about a thousand students were placed on the wait list, that about 300 to 400 were expected to remain on it, and that over a 10-year period, the average annual number of acceptances from the wait list was fewer than 30. At least they were upfront about how tough it would be.

WAIT-LISTED STUDENT

⊠

If more students accept admission than planned, the college may have to increase the number of freshmen in each residence hall room, convert student lounges into bedrooms, use trailers or motels for temporary housing, or drastically cut the number of transfer students who will be offered admission that spring. All of these have happened many times at various colleges. Estimating yield is very hard to do. One enterprising campus we know purchased smaller furniture when it found it had to house three students in rooms meant for two. And of course, if a college finds itself in an oversold situation, it does not take anyone from the wait list.

Who Goes on the Wait List?

Over the last few years, wait lists have gotten longer as colleges find predicting yield more difficult. This reflects, for the most part, the increasing number of highly qualified candidates who apply to an increasing number of selective institutions. A wait-list decision can mean that a candidate was fully qualified to attend and would indeed have been admitted if only there were room. It can also be a gentle way for a college to say no to a weaker candidate it finds difficult to deny outright for other reasons, such as a legacy applicant. And as we saw in chapter 1, a few colleges place even exceptionally qualified candidates on the wait list if they think the student might receive and accept an offer elsewhere.

Because of a combination of all or some of these factors, many wait lists are as big as or bigger than the size of the entire freshman class. The "Principles of Good Practice" of the National Association for College Admission Counseling say that each college should tell you how many applicants have been placed on the wait list for your year and for each of several previous years, along with the number on the wait list eventually offered admission, but you may have to ask for this information.

The number admitted from a wait list can vary greatly, from zero to low single digits to several dozen or more. It all depends on the ability of a college to accurately predict its yield in the first place. The importance of predicting yield is one reason colleges like ED so much and why some colleges consider demonstrated interest in making their admissions decisions. Both policies give them a better advance idea of their yield.

The domino or trickle-down effect from wait lists can be disruptive to colleges. As students are admitted from the wait list at College A, other schools that those students had accepted now find themselves with empty spots that they in turn fill from their wait lists. And so on down an invisible ladder. A college with a full class on May 1 may have space on May 15 after losing some students to other colleges. The sequence can take a while to work out, often into June or even later.

> I didn't like being wait-listed. It felt like a consolation prize. Why would they wait-list so many people when clearly they're letting in very few? It seemed so pointless.
>
> SENIOR WHO WAS WAIT-LISTED BY HARVARD UNIVERSITY AND DECLINED TO REMAIN ON THE LIST

> It is a great way to shape the class and meet our institutional priorities. Maybe we could use a few more artists or a few more math or science researchers.[2]
>
> DICK NESBITT, DIRECTOR OF ADMISSION AT WILLIAMS COLLEGE, REFERRING TO THE WAIT LIST. FOR THE CLASS OF 2015, WILLIAMS OFFERED 1,352 STUDENTS A SPOT ON THE LIST AND EVENTUALLY OFFERED ADMISSION TO 14.

Steps to Increase Your Chances of Acceptance from the Wait List

A letter notifying you that you have been placed on the wait list includes a postcard or an electronic reply link asking whether you wish to stay on the list. What should you do? No single answer fits everyone. Don't fall into the trap of automatically thinking that the college that didn't take you at first is automatically better than any that accepted you. It was just a different admissions process. Usually, depending on the school, fewer than half of those placed on a wait list opt to remain. If your other college choices are more attractive to you, why remain on the wait list? But if the wait-list college is still an appealing option, you may want to accept the offer, even knowing that your chances for being accepted later are low. You should also inquire about a college's policy regarding financial aid for students admitted from the wait list. In some cases, aid is not available for wait-listed students. You have to ask. You still need to send a deposit to a college that accepted you by the May 1 reply deadline.

Wait Lists Are Usually Unranked

Although airline standby lists are ordered so passengers can assess their chances of getting a seat, wait lists are usually unranked. This means that openings are not filled from the list in any prearranged order. There may some broad groups ranked in tiers, but the college usually won't tell you which group you are in. They don't order the wait list because they don't know who will stay on it, ordering it would be a lot of extra work, and they don't know what the composition of the final class will be by gender, geography, or major interest. They want to retain the flexibility to add whom they want to balance the class. So as openings occur, a college may examine its whole freshman class along geographical, gender, racial, and many other dimensions and use the wait list to fill any perceived gaps. Someone who came close to admission during the regular review cycle will not necessarily be chosen from the list because he or she doesn't fit the college's need at this time.

> I tell my wait-listed kids to put their wait-list schools out of their mind and pick one where they have been accepted because chances are pretty good that they will go there. If they find out later that they've won the lottery and got admitted, that's great. But they need to start forming new attachments. I also encourage parents to foster that attitude.
>
> INDEPENDENT COUNSELOR

When and How Will You Hear?

Usually there is little movement from a wait-list until colleges have a clear indication of their yield from those already accepted, and that generally doesn't happen until after the reply deadline. Mid-May through early June is thus the busiest time for wait-list notifications. Wait-listed students who are accepted are usually notified first by phone, followed by written confirmation, with a two-week, or sometimes much shorter, deadline for reply. If you tell the caller you are no longer interested (and that is okay even if you agreed to stay on the wait list a month earlier), the college will move on to another wait-listed student and repeat the process. Sometimes a college will call the high school counselor to see if the student is still interested. At this point, they

⊠ What Can You Do If You Are Wait-Listed at Your Top Choice?

- Return the reply postcard or send an electronic reply indicating you want to remain active on the wait list. It is okay to remain on more than one wait list.

- Write a letter to the dean of admissions and let him or her know that you are still very eager to attend. Include any significant new information since you last wrote: grades, awards, and so forth. Again, it is rare to have a lot to add at this point, other than your enthusiasm for the school. If it is your clear first choice, say so upfront. But, ethically, you cannot say this to more than one college.

- Ask your counselor to call or write to the admissions office conveying your enthusiasm and his or her support for you.

- Consider sending an additional recommendation or letter from a teacher or another person who knows you well. But don't overdo it to the point that it looks like a campaign.

- Carefully select a school from among those that have admitted you, and send in your deposit.

- Recognize that most students placed on the wait list at many colleges, especially selective ones, are not ultimately admitted. Once you have taken the steps indicated above, put the wait list out of your mind and focus on the college you will probably attend in the fall. By the time you are admitted from a wait list, you might be very happy with your May 1 choice and want to stick with it. Telling a college where you were wait-listed that it is your first choice is not binding like ED.

want 100 percent yield on wait-list offers and try to nail these down in advance. It all happens very quickly and without warning. Most selective colleges officially close their wait lists by the end of June and release those who have not been accepted. Many have very little activity from the wait list after Memorial Day.

Reemphasize Your Interest

If you decide to remain on a wait list, it is wise to discuss your continued interest in the college with your high school counselor. Tell your counselor whether the college is your first choice. Your counselor may be able to help your cause by contacting the college and conveying support for you as well as your

> Colleges are looking for a 100 percent yield from any students they take off the wait list, so they are going to be looking for commitment. The key is for students to demonstrate as much honest interest as they can and say that if offered admission, they will definitely enroll. They are the students the admissions office will most likely look at first.
>
> — Experienced high school counselor

enthusiasm for the college. A letter from you expressing your interest as well as any new accomplishments may be helpful. Don't rely on your counselor to do this for you. But again, movement from the wait list at a selective college is a long shot at best. Don't let hope of admission, which could even come well into the summer, spoil your excitement about college. Sometimes you need closure, even if it means deciding to attend a college lower on your list, instead of the emotional limbo of staying on a wait list for what feels like forever. You know yourself best: be sure to weigh the wait-list option carefully before deciding what to do.

In any case, remember to send your intent-to-register form, along with your deposit, to your preferred college from among your acceptance options. If you subsequently decide to join a college that accepts you from the wait list, you will need to send a deposit as well to that college. You will forfeit the deposit you made to the first school, but it may be worth it if you end up where you really wanted to go. Some deposits are quite large, even close to $1,000 in one case we know, to encourage you to stick with your first school.

DEPOSIT ETHICS

Students are expected to send a deposit to hold a spot at only one college by May 1 and any time thereafter. Holding more than one spot, known as double depositing, deprives others of the potential opportunity to move from a wait list. If you are offered a spot from a wait list and accept, you'll have to inform the first college you accepted of your change in plans as quickly as possible. A phone call usual isn't enough—they want something in writing. Your letter doesn't have to be long; a simple note informing the college of your new plans is sufficient. This happens all the time, so don't be bashful or embarrassed about your change in plans.

It is important to notify the college quickly. The place you release may then generate an opening for a student on that school's wait list unless the school is oversubscribed, continuing the cascading effect. Double depositing is unethical, and if either college finds out, you can lose your place at both colleges. It is tempting, we know, to think you can buy some time to consider your choices a little longer, but you must resist.

SHOULD YOU CONSIDER A GAP YEAR?

Most students who have finished the college admissions process in good spirits are eager to put it all behind them and look forward to college life in the fall. But maybe you are different.

Perhaps you've sent in your deposit to a great college, but are starting to feel that you need an extended break from school. Foreign travel to strengthen your language skills, full-time volunteer work for a cause that really matters to you, or work in a field for which you have passion are all attractive ways to spend a year before you start college.

> I am not suggesting the gap year as a viable alternative to a great safety school, but if your heart isn't in it, maybe you should take time to rethink where you want to be (and how you want to get there) rather than attending a college you aren't excited about simply because they accepted you.
>
> STUDENT WHO DECIDED TO TAKE A GAP YEAR

Or maybe the college admissions process didn't work out as well as you had hoped, and you can't get really excited about any of your options. Rather than settle for a college that you truly feel doesn't suit you, you may want to use the next year to strengthen your record in various ways and reapply to college.

Or maybe you didn't apply to college at all, knowing that you needed to strengthen your record before you would be a successful applicant. Your goal now is to figure out how best to do that.

All of these are great reasons to consider a gap year. Colleges know that students who take a gap year usually arrive on campus with greater maturity and interesting experiences to share with their classmates, so a gap year can be a win-win affair—great for the student and great for the college.

Gap Year After You Have Been Admitted

Although most colleges will happily review a student's request to take a gap year before enrolling, a few colleges even actively encourage recently admitted students to consider one. Most notably proactive about a gap year is Harvard University. For over 20 years, the letter of admission to Harvard has included a paragraph suggesting that students consider the option of taking a gap year, noting that Harvard wants them to avoid arriving on campus burned out from an intense high school experience. Of course, Harvard (and any other college) would be in trouble if large numbers of students took them up on the offer, but about 50 to 70 do each year out of its freshman class of about 1,700. Other schools report a similar proportion of students choosing a gap year.

Requesting a Gap Year

Typically students must submit a formal request for a gap year that outlines how they plan to spend their time. Most schools are very flexible but want to see evidence that you are going to put your time to good use: being a coach potato won't impress them, and enrolling full time in a degree-granting program at another college is usually not allowed, though a college course here or there should be fine. That still leaves a lot of wonderful options.

For nearly two generations we have encouraged students to consider deferring entrance for a year. Many students have done so, finding their varied experiences extremely rewarding and their subsequent college careers greatly enriched. If you would like to defer, please inform us of your intention by logging in to the online response website to register your deferral.

FROM THE HARVARD UNIVERSITY ACCEPTANCE LETTER FOR THE CLASS OF 2016

You will also usually be expected to submit your deposit to secure your place in the freshman class entering the following year, as well as sign a document indicating that you do not plan to apply to other colleges during your gap year. If you end up changing your mind partway into your year, you should notify the college that granted the gap year of your change in intentions.

Timing Your Inquiry and Request

It is best to raise specific gap year plans with a college after you have been accepted but before the May 1 Common Reply Date. If a college does not approve your request, you will still have other options if taking a gap year is critical to you. Be sure to ask before you deposit.

It can also be helpful to inquire early in the application process about a college's gap year policy if you think you might want to consider a gap year. In particular, you need to know that some public colleges and universities may not be gap year friendly and may require you to reapply for the following year if you choose to do a gap year. The official policy of the University of California, for example, is that students must enroll in the semester for which admission is granted; enrollment at a later date requires another application. But even within the University of California, each campus is free to interpret this policy as it wishes, and individual decisions may vary based on circumstances.

Taking a Gap Year with a Plan to Apply for the Following Year

If you plan to take a gap year without making a commitment to attend a specific college the following fall, you just have to decide to do it. No college has to give you permission. It is just as important, though, to have a good plan in place to help you achieve your goal of strengthening your record for future college admission.

Consider the following pragmatic advantages of a gap year:

- If you are not satisfied with your SAT or ACT results, you can retake the tests to raise your scores. You may have more time for preparation and be more familiar with the tests.

- If you had a good senior year, you may have more and stronger options for recommendations, since your twelfth-grade teachers will now have known you for a full academic year.

- If you are taking Advanced Placement or International Baccalaureate courses in your senior year and do well, those test scores, along with your senior-year grades, will be part of your record.

- Your gap year activities may make you a more interesting or distinctive candidate for admission and give you a great topic for your personal statement, even if you have just a few months of experience before submitting your applications.

- A successful gap year can help address any academic, personal, or extra-curricular weaknesses in your record and allow you to demonstrate your maturity and readiness for college.

The Postgraduate Year Option

A small percentage of students seek to gain these advantages through a formal postgraduate (PG) year at a private high school, most commonly located in the Northeast. Some programs are available as boarding only, which means that you would have to live on campus, while others are day programs. Athletes who want to improve their academic record while continuing to play their sport at the high school level often choose a PG year. The full array of extracurricular activities, courses, test prep, and college counseling is available in such programs. Tuition can be expensive, however, rivaling the cost of tuition at some colleges. Many PG programs fill up early, and others may still have room right before school begins in the fall.

The Self-Directed Gap Year

The vast majority of students seeking to apply to college the following year choose a self-directed gap year. Through careful time management (always an important skill), a student can prepare for standardized tests if needed, enroll in community college classes if there is a need to demonstrate that he or she is able to do college-level work, or engage in a meaningful gap year experience similar to that of a student already admitted to his or her dream college. Be careful, though, about the number of credits you take at a community college if you decide to go that route. Some colleges limit the number of credits you can complete elsewhere if you want to apply as a freshman as opposed to a transfer student. The Resources section at the end of *Admission Matters* includes references that will give you ideas about ways to spend your gap year.

Things to Do to Ensure a Smooth Gap Year

Regardless of the form of your gap year, be it PG or self-directed, we strongly recommend that you talk with your high school counselor and teachers whom you would like to write on your behalf and let them know your plans as soon as possible. And then stay in touch with them. They won't need to do anything right away, but you don't want them to be surprised when you "invite" them to write on your behalf through the Common Application in the fall. And when you are ready to ask for their letters, we suggest you write each of them a note updating them on what you have been up to during your gap year.

You will also need to do careful research into colleges that will be a good fit for you across the range of selectivity. Unless you are doing a PG year, you probably won't have easy access to a high school counselor, so you will have to do more on your own. You will be fine using the many online tools available as well as carefully rereading this book. An independent counselor may also be helpful if you feel you need additional guidance personalized for your situation.

A WORD ABOUT SENIORITIS

Senioritis typically strikes students in March or April after seniors receive their college acceptances, sometimes earlier. For those accepted early, it may hit in mid-December, but for most others it attacks in mid-April. (Wait-list status may retard it.) Teachers know to expect senioritis, but they dread it nonetheless. Students start performing significantly below their pre-infection levels: homework is late and tests are taken without much studying. High school no longer seems to matter very much since the big hurdle is over.

We encourage you to avoid falling victim to this disease. We'll review several reasons—perhaps one or more will resonate with you. First, colleges accepted you on the explicit condition that your performance for the remainder of the year will remain at its prior level. Your admissions letter says this clearly. It is easy to ignore that cautionary paragraph at the bottom in the moment of joy of being accepted, but colleges mean what they say. The last official part of your college application process is having your final transcript sent to the college of your choice at the end of the school year. Colleges review these in the summer to identify any marked departures from previous performance, or even changes in the courses you said you were going to take in the spring.

If your grades have dropped dramatically, colleges will send letters of varying degrees of harshness asking for an explanation and quickly. A serious decline may result in a more strongly worded letter threatening that your admission is in jeopardy. Colleges reserve the right to put conditions on your enrollment (requiring summer school classes, for example), or they may even rescind your admission entirely if your performance deteriorated drastically or if you dropped demanding courses without good reason. True, the drop in grades has to be pretty striking and without mitigating conditions for an offer of admission to be withdrawn, but a college can and will do this in serious cases. All of this is foreseeable. Frustrated counselors compare these students to trains running down a track out of control. Their warnings are frequently ignored. Why risk everything that you have worked so hard for?

Your high school record will be with you forever. Although your grades in high school may not matter much once you have entered college, you may want to transfer to a different college later. A weak record in the second half of senior year will not help your case. Finally, and maybe most important, continuing your best effort shows respect for your parents, your teachers, your counselors, and especially yourself. Show your appreciation and maturity by continuing to be a good student. Almost everyone will cut you a little bit of slack—just don't abuse it.

CELEBRATE AND ENJOY!

With your college choice now behind you, you can enjoy the remaining weeks of high school. You can look forward to the senior prom, graduation, and, increasingly common, an alcohol-free all-night party or trip for the entire senior class. Make the most of this time to cement the bonds with your classmates. Some of them may turn out to be lifelong friends. Others will be people you will see only at class reunions every five or ten years. Over time, you will remember most of them fondly, even if they aren't close friends now. One of us attended her first high school reunion a while back, having missed the others, and can personally attest that this is true.

CHAPTER 15

What Matters Most

Advice to Parents and Students

We wrote *Admission Matters* to help families navigate the college admissions process. We wanted to show you how the role of the student and the role of the parent are complementary yet different and provide you with the information and practical advice you need to work together to achieve a good outcome.

In this final chapter, we offer some parting thoughts that summarize and capture the heart of what this book is about. It may be helpful to read this chapter more than once as you go through the college admissions process. It is easy to get caught up in the whirlwind and lose perspective, but this chapter will remind you what matters most. The chapter is divided into two parts. The first part is for parents; the second part is for students. Like the rest of the book, you should read not only the part intended for you but the other part as well. We think everyone will benefit.

SOME PARTING THOUGHTS FOR PARENTS

What your child will remember long after the college admissions process is over is how you supported him or her.

He or she will be your child for the rest of your lives. This year is a tiny portion of your overall time as parent and child. Keep that in mind as you think of imposing your own ideas or detaching completely from the process. Above all, don't do anything that might impinge on your future relationship. Whatever seems so important at this moment really isn't so crucial in the long run. Earlier in this book, we mentioned a parent who steamed open his child's newly arrived SAT scores when she was away at camp. It was a long time ago, but both parties remember it to this day. Don't do it!

It can be hard to accept that your almost grown child has ideas and preferences that differ significantly from your own. This is especially true when it comes to college choice because so much seems to be at stake. Your child may want to experience a different part of the country; you may want your child to be close to home (or vice versa). You may feel an education at a liberal arts college is best; your child may be looking forward to the excitement of a large research university (or the reverse). The list goes on and on. The bottom line is that although your child should respect your views and may ultimately embrace them, the final choices—where to apply, what to put in the application, and where to go after acceptance—should be the student's.

Ideally, you want to be able to look back after the final college choice is made and savor the knowledge of having provided emotional and practical support for your child that contributed to a successful outcome. It may take your child a while to appreciate your good intentions and acknowledge your contribution. That too is part of being a parent, and you should be used to it by now.

The parent's role is to support, advise, and listen, except when it comes to money.

You can support your child in the college admissions process in many ways: sharing your own thoughts and experiences; encouraging research into colleges, including visits where feasible; and providing useful feedback and organizational support. But you need to realize that your child must own this process. It is the student, not the parent, who is applying to and ultimately attending college.

It is critical, however, that you be up front about financial considerations. As you have read in chapter 10, colleges use a complex formula to determine your financial aid packages and thus the expected family contribution, the amount they believe a family should be able to pay to help support their child's education. This is rarely the amount that parents are eager to pay. Doing some early calculations and being frank about what you are prepared to contribute financially to your child's education is imperative to avoid misunderstanding and disappointment later on. This is not as easy as it sounds. Most parents keep their family finances and discussions of big expenses to themselves. This may have to change now. Most teenagers, we have found, are realistic and understanding if you treat them as intelligent adults. They know that these are tough times economically. They understand you have a mortgage or rent to pay, younger siblings you have to put through school as well, a retirement plan that may not be as flush as it was during earlier boom times, or jobs may be (or have been) lost. Trust them; they will respond.

This is not the time to live vicariously through your child, however tempting that may be. Try not to use college admission as validation of your parenting skills.

Most parents of high school seniors are forty years old or older. Participating in the process with their child allows them to reexperience, or perhaps experience for the first time, a uniquely American rite of passage. However, if you catch yourself saying, "We're applying to college," you may be overly involved. Even the most confident children may fear they will disappoint a parent if they do not get into their parent's alma mater or dream college(s), or if they do less "well" than a superstar older sibling. Wise parents try not to inadvertently contribute to that fear by their words or actions. A parent recently told a counselor at the end of the year that the family "was resigned to settling for College C" after the child was not admitted to two super-selective schools. Although the child had four other choices that most students would have been thrilled about, the outcome was a letdown for them. How could the child not think that she had disappointed her parent? The good news is that this young woman is enjoying College C very much anyway. Things have a way of working out.

Parents sometimes lapse into the belief that all of their parenting efforts over the past 18 years will be held up to scrutiny during the admissions process. The parents of a student accepted by one or more prestigious colleges have "done a good job," while parents of students who apply to less prestigious institutions or who are denied by brand-name colleges didn't do their job quite as well. Put bluntly, these inferences are ludicrous, but they frequently lie just under the surface. The bumper stickers and T-shirts that proclaim "Proud Mom of a Yalie" put them into words. So does the seemingly endless supermarket checkout line and carpool chatter about where Suzie has applied early, or where Amit got accepted. All of this sends subtle messages that put teens under great pressure and promote values that are at best superficial and at worst actually harmful. A wise parent learns to be upbeat even when the news is disappointing and modest when the news is good. Think of the difference between, "My child got into X," and, "My child is going to get a fine education at Z."

Remember that at many first-rate institutions with reasonable acceptance rates, your child can get a fine education and be happy.

Most people know surprisingly little about the amazing array of institutions of higher education in the United States. One counselor challenges audiences to see if they collectively can name more than 300 colleges. If they come up short, they have to pay him. If they go over 300, he has to pay them. Nobody takes him up on the challenge. Try it for fun. See how many you can come up with without a guidebook. Most parents can name a few local colleges, most of the Ivy League and their peers, and some schools whose football games are televised nationally, but that's about it.

As part of the college admissions process, you can support your child by learning about colleges you may not be familiar with and helping your child realize that a successful college experience is the result of a good fit between a college and student—and that while there is no perfect fit, many good ones are possible. Many wonderful colleges accept a much higher percentage of their applicants than those considered very selective. By all measures, these colleges offer an education that is every bit as good as and maybe even better than some highly selective, brand-name institutions. Helping your child explore options and supporting his or her choices can be immensely rewarding.

Help your child with organizational matters, and be a good sounding board and editor during the application process—but don't do the work for your child.

The process of applying to college can be daunting. There are forms galore, short and long essays to be written, score reports and transcripts to be sent, and lots more, all by looming deadlines. When asked what they would do differently if they had a chance to start over, many high school seniors say that they would have started the whole process earlier and procrastinated less. Procrastination is a normal human reaction in face of an unappealing task, say, writing a will or paying taxes. But it is just a bad habit, not a sin. And it can be foreseen. With your greater adult experience, you can encourage your child to get started early and keep track of what has been done and what remains to be done. Some teens resent this; they have always been able to complete their work by deadlines, so they are convinced they can do the same now. The problem, though, is that college applications are probably much more complex than any task they have undertaken before, and more hangs in the balance. College deadlines are also more stringent and inflexible than those usually imposed in high school.

Students should be encouraged to organize their materials and set deadlines for themselves. If your child decides to apply early action or early decision, he or she will probably have to get everything together by November 1 or November 15—a very early date indeed, especially if he or she starts preparing them on October 1. What kind of help can you provide? Proofreading of applications and help with essay ideas and constructive criticism can be very helpful (just be aware that your efforts may not be enthusiastically welcomed!). Resist the urge at all costs to rewrite the application yourself, however, even if your child seems willing or even eager for you to do that. Admissions readers get pretty good at telling an authentic student voice from one that has been doctored in a major way by adults.

You can also assist with organizational matters if you have those skills and your child welcomes the help. You can register your child for the SAT, for example; it's your credit card, after all. It is fine for you to get the maps from Google for the college trip, as long as you don't pick the colleges too. Make the organizational tasks easier and less time-consuming for your child, so he or she can devote energies to the hard parts. Of course, some teens enjoy these organizational tasks because they're easy to do and yield a sense of progress. Offer to help, and let your child decide.

Model ethical behavior and integrity.

Our children learn many lessons from us, including those we never explicitly teach. Children learn by observing others, and the most powerful role models are parents. The pressure to do everything possible to ensure "success" in college admissions is powerful, even if it means compromising their integrity along the way. Don't give in to this temptation. The college admissions process is a major opportunity for parents to model ethical behavior and integrity for their children. Use it accordingly.

Don't offer inappropriate help with the application itself ("editing" an essay to the point of essentially writing it yourself, for example), and don't permit your child to seek it elsewhere (paying someone to write the essay). Similarly, discourage any tendency toward exaggeration of activities or accomplishments. Admissions officers look for consistency between what students have written about themselves and what teachers and counselors say about them. Why take a risk by embellishing too much?

But getting caught in a fabrication is the least of the reasons to encourage honesty in the application process. Our society has too many people who believe shaving the truth is not only okay but also the smart thing to do. Young adults need to know that their integrity is their most precious asset. Parents can reinforce that lesson through their actions and advice.

Everyone wants to be accepted for their own efforts and for who they really are. Allow that for your children. You don't want them to arrive freshman week and think, "I'm not the person who was on my application. This school doesn't want the real me."

Accompany your child on college visits, but stay in the background.

As we have said before, probably the best way for a student to get the feel for a college is to visit it. Where possible, encourage your child to visit a number of campuses, perhaps in conjunction with vacation, and go along if you can. Going to some nearby colleges of different sizes can help give your child an idea of the kind of college she might be interested in. When it comes time to look seriously at colleges, you can help schedule tours and encourage your child to have an interview if one is available. But remember that the visits are for your child's benefit. Encourage, and perhaps even do so strongly, but let your child make the final call about whether to visit a given campus.

Help your child make realistic choices.

One of the major themes of this book is that admission to selective colleges can be quite unpredictable. Your child can have a wonderful record yet be denied at a given college, while a classmate with a weaker record is accepted. You never learn why, but in the end, it doesn't matter. If you understand the difficulty and uncertainty of selective college admissions, you can help your child consider a good range of colleges. This means you have to keep your own vicarious ambitions to yourself as much as possible.

If your child is interested in a super-selective college and would be a competitive applicant, he or she should certainly apply. But your child should understand that admission to colleges that select less than 20 percent of their applicants is a long shot for almost everyone simply because of the numbers. After the final decisions arrive, support your child by sharing the disappointment at the denials and the joy over the acceptances. Model poise over the former and humility for the latter. Every parent knows that if the worst thing that ever happens to your child in life is being denied from a college at the age of 18, then they will have a long and happy life. If the family carefully made the list at the outset, your child should have a happy outcome regardless of the particular decisions.

Be supportive as your child makes his or her final choice.

When the decisions arrive, your child may be elated or disappointed or somewhere in between. Give him or her space to sort it out and make the final decision. Offer your perspective where appropriate, but remember that within the boundaries of financial constraints and family responsibilities, the choice is your child's, not yours.

Rejoice with your child.

Regardless of the outcome, express your love, and let your son or daughter know how proud you are of the young adult he or she has become. Savor the moment!

SOME PARTING THOUGHTS FOR STUDENTS

Parents want the best for you and want to help. Let them, within boundaries.

Although parents differ widely in their knowledge, abilities, and resources, almost all want to help a college-bound student however they can. Be gracious and communicate with your parents so that they can help appropriately. The trick is to define boundaries for what is helpful, what is intrusive, and what is counter-productive. Each family is different, so you'll have to work this out together with help from this book.

Parents can sometimes make great suggestions about colleges to consider. They can also be your companions on trips to see colleges in person. And they can sometimes be good editors, proofreaders, and clerical assistants, depending on their skills, as you prepare your applications. The more you both know about the college admissions process, the easier it will be to agree on what form their help should take. Encourage them to be partners with you. If they see you taking charge maturely, they will be much less likely to feel that they have to be constantly on your case.

Recognize that launching a child to adulthood is emotionally difficult for many parents—help them get through it.

Sending a child off to college is bittersweet for many parents. They share your delight at your prospects for a wonderful future, but at the same time they inevitably feel a sense of loss. The child they have loved and nurtured for 18 years is now a young adult, ready to leave home for a new life in which they will play a much less prominent role. Try, even briefly, to put yourself in your parents' place. Something as simple as an occasional heartfelt "thank you" in response to help that is offered can make all the difference to a parent struggling with a changing role.

Share something about the high school scene with your parents. Most know surprisingly little about the pressures at school, and they are often unaware of the many discussions about college that go on between you and your friends. If you help your parents understand the environment you operate in every day, they will appreciate why your experience of the college admissions process may be very different from theirs.

The most important part of the college admissions process is choosing schools that you think will be a good match. Be as honest as you can with yourself about your interests, preferences, strengths, and weaknesses as you consider colleges.

A recurring theme throughout *Admission Matters* is that a successful college experience is all about fit—finding a college that is a good match for you. The most important and probably hardest part of the process is self-assessment—an honest self-evaluation of your interests, preferences, strengths, and weaknesses. The next toughest part is doing the necessary research to find colleges that you like based on your self-assessment. Part of that match includes a determination of the likelihood of acceptance. You want to be sure to have a range of colleges on your list so that you are more likely to have a good outcome.

Make all your choices first choices.

The idea is to be sure that you will be happy to attend any of the colleges to which you apply. This includes the good-bet applications as well as the long-shot ones. Joyce Mitchell, a high school counselor who has written her own book on college admissions, has made the "first choices" rule a cornerstone of her advice to students.[1] It is good advice. Because you cannot predict the response from long-shot colleges, having several first choices, including at least one that is a good bet (and also a financial good bet), virtually guarantees a happy outcome. You should use the first choices rule even if you apply early decision, since it may not work out.

Don't procrastinate.

When high school seniors are asked what they would do differently if they could relive their college application experience, the most common response is, "I would start earlier and not procrastinate." Procrastination is a normal reaction to a stressful process. But it really does make things worse. Leaving applications to the last minute invariably means rushed decisions, mistakes, and potentially missed opportunities, not to mention needless stress. Establish a reasonable time frame for your efforts, setting deadlines for yourself along the way. Having and meeting deadlines will also reduce stress on your parents. Do this for them, as well as for yourself.

Get and stay organized, keep everything together, and make copies of everything you send in.

The college application process is complicated. Brochures and college view books arrive by the dozen early on, and e-mails flood your in-box. Later, multipart applications have to be completed, recommendations and transcripts requested, and financial aid forms filed. Adding to the complexity is the fact that different colleges have different requirements and deadlines. Staying on top of it all can be a real challenge, but it is a challenge that is important to meet. A simple filing system in a cardboard box is all that you need, along with a record of each school's requirements and deadlines that you can check off as you meet them. And be sure to make a copy of everything you send in, even online applications. Colleges rarely lose materials, but you don't want to take any chances. Starting over when you thought you were done is no fun.

Talk to your friends, but remember that each person is different.

Peers can be wonderful sources of information. For example, a friend may return from a trip to another part of the country excited about the colleges he saw and open your eyes to new possibilities. But a good choice for one person, even a good friend, may not be a good choice for you. When someone offers an opinion of a college, whether good or bad, try to find out what's behind it. Get to the facts, then see how those facts fit with your own needs. And respect the choices of others. A good-bet college for one person may be a possible or even a long-shot for another.

Enjoy your senior year. College applications are important (that's why you are reading this book), but they should not be allowed to take over your life.

College admissions can easily become the focus of your senior year. There is so much to do, and so much seems to be at stake. But the senior year in high school should also be special in other ways—sharing adventures with old friends, enjoying a fleeting year of being top banana, and beginning to enjoy the freedoms that come with adulthood. Balance is key. A wise student takes the college application process seriously but doesn't let it overwhelm everything else. If you approach things calmly, rationally, and in a timely way, you can achieve the dual goals of having an array of fine college choices and a senior year filled with wonderful memories.

End the college admissions process on a high note.

When the final decisions from colleges come in, you get to decide. Do so carefully. Your choice may or may not be the one you hoped or thought you would make when you began the process, but if you have followed our advice, it will be a good choice. Celebrate with your family and friends, and begin to plan for your new life as a college student (but remember you still have to successfully complete your senior year).

Thank your teachers and counselors again for writing letters for you and tell them where you got in and didn't. Visit them to say "hi" when you return home over winter break during freshman year, or send them e-mails if you can't see them in person.

Above all, thank your parents for all they have done and still do for you, and tell them that you love them. Do this along the way, but especially when the process is over.

Appendix A
College Research Worksheet

(Make copies of this form and complete one for each college you are seriously considering.)

Name of School _____ Location _____

Admissions Phone and E-mail _____ Campus Website _____

Testing Requirements (circle all that apply):

Required: SAT   ACT   ACT Writing   SAT Subject _____

Recommended: SAT   ACT   ACT Writing   SAT Subject _____

Optional: SAT   ACT   ACT writing   SAT Subject _____

Freshman Class Profile:

GPA: % in the top 10% of class _____ % in the top 20% of class _____

    % in the top 50% of class _____

applications _____   % admitted _____

early applications _____   % admitted _____   % of class filled early _____

SAT: mid-50% math _____   mid-50% critical reading _____   mid-50% writing _____

ACT: mid-50% composite _____

Total # undergraduates _____   Total # students on campus _____

Academic Profile:

Circle one: Research University   Liberal Arts College   Other _____

Majors of interest to you: _____

_____

(continued)

Academic Profile *continued*

Curriculum requirements (general education, senior thesis, etc.): _____

_____

Special programs of interest (honors program, arrangements with other colleges, etc.):

_____

_____

Overall impression of academic pace and rigor: _____

_____

Other: _____

_____

Campus Life

Campus Housing: Guaranteed for ____ years

Details (process for assignment, housing options, % living on campus):_____

_____

_____

Characteristics of Student Body (single sex, geographic and ethnic diversity, liberal/
conservative, etc.): _____

_____

_____

Social Life and Activities (% in sororities and fraternities, intramural and club sports,
recreational facilities, clubs of special interest, etc.): _____

_____

_____

_____

Other:_____

_____

Special Interests

Intercollegiate Athletics: Your sport: _____ NCAA Division or NAIA: _____

Coach's name and contact info: _____

Arts, Music, or Special Academic Focus:

Area: _____ Contact: _____

Area: _____ Contact: _____

Other: _____

_____

Financial Aid Policies

Circle all that apply: Guarantees to meet full demonstrated need   Offers merit aid

Need-blind admissions   Need-based aid only

Financial Aid Deadlines: FAFSA _____   CSS PROFILE _____   Other(s) _____

Application Process

Circle all that apply: College specific form   Pre-application

Common Application   Common Application Supplement

Application Deadlines: Early action _____   Early decision _____

Regular _____   Rolling _____   Fee _____

Interview: Required   Optional   Not offered

Details: _____

_____

Other Notes: _____

_____

Appendix B
Common Application Essay Instructions and Prompts, 2013–2014

Instructions: The essay demonstrates your ability to write clearly and concisely on a selected topic and helps you distinguish yourself in your own voice. *What do you want the readers of your application to know about you apart from courses, grades, and test scores?* Choose the option that best helps you answer that question and write an essay of no more than 650 words, using the prompt to inspire and structure your response. Remember: 650 words is your limit, not your goal. Use the full range if you need it, but don't feel obligated to do so. (The application won't accept a response shorter than 250 words.)

- Some students have a background or story that is so central to their identity that they believe their application would be incomplete without it. If this sounds like you, then please share your story.

- Recount an incident or time when you experienced failure. How did it affect you, and what lessons did you learn?

- Reflect on a time when you challenged a belief or idea. What prompted you to act? Would you make the same decision again?

- Describe a place or environment where you are perfectly content. What do you do or experience there, and why is it meaningful to you?

- Discuss an accomplishment or event, formal or informal, that marked your transition from childhood to adulthood within your culture, community, or family.

Copyrighted and reprinted with permission of The Common Application.

Appendix C
Sample Student Information Sheet
for Letters of Recommendation

In order to write a recommendation letter for you, counselors and teachers need information that will be used solely and confidentially for that purpose. You benefit when they are able to provide a comprehensive academic and personal report. Read this entire form before you begin to fill it out to prevent yourself from entering duplicate information. Take your time, and answer each question thoughtfully. You'll need to have this same information for your college applications, so it will help you later as well. When you have completed the form, prepare a packet for each person from whom you have requested a letter that contains the following: the copy of the form and all attachments; for colleges that do not use online recommendations, the recommendation forms and a stamped and preaddressed envelope for each college; and a listing of due dates. Packets should be submitted to your recommendation writers at least four weeks before the first due date.

Please print neatly or type your responses. You may attach separate sheets as needed.

Student Name _____ Nickname (if any)_____

Phone_____ E-mail _____

1. Test Score Information

ACT

Date _____ Verbal _____ Math _____ Sci _____ Read _____ Writing _____ Comp _____
Date _____ Verbal _____ Math _____ Sci _____ Read _____ Writing _____ Comp _____
Date _____ Verbal _____ Math _____ Sci _____ Read _____ Writing _____ Comp _____

SAT

Date _____ Critical Reading _____ Math _____ Writing _____
Date _____ Critical Reading _____ Math _____ Writing _____
Date _____ Critical Reading _____ Math _____ Writing _____

SAT Subject Test Date _____ Subject _____ Score _____
SAT Subject Test Date _____ Subject _____ Score _____

SAT Subject Test   Date _____   Subject _____   Score _____

SAT Subject Test   Date _____   Subject _____   Score _____

Future Test Dates for SAT _____   SAT Subject Test _____   ACT _____

AP or IB Test   Date _____   Subject _____   Score _____

AP or IB Test   Date _____   Subject _____   Score _____

AP or IB Test   Date _____   Subject _____   Score _____

AP or IB Test   Date _____   Subject _____   Score _____

AP or IB Test   Date _____   Subject _____   Score _____

2. Do your test scores and grades accurately reflect your academic potential? _____
   If not, explain why. _____
   _____
   _____

3. Attach a copy of your transcript (for teacher recommendations only—your counselor already has your transcript). List any college courses taken during high school that are not included on your transcript.

   Course _____   Where taken _____   Year _____

   Course _____   Where taken _____   Year _____

   Course _____   Where taken _____   Year _____

4. Attach a brief list of your extracurricular activities and achievements; academic honors and awards; hobbies, special interests, or talents; community service activities; and work experience.

5. Attach a copy of your draft college personal essay if it is completed, or answer, "What sets you apart as an individual?"

6. Ask your parent/guardian or a friend to write an anecdote that describes your character and attach it to this form. This should be about one paragraph long.

7. Where were you born? If not in the United States, at what age did you move to the United States? _____

8. Do you speak more than one language? If so, list and indicate fluency.
   _____

9. With whom are you living? Circle: Mother Father Both parents Other

10. Will you be the first person in your immediate family to attend college?

_____

11. Please tell us about your family. List your siblings, providing name, age, current school and grade level, degrees, and/or occupation. _____

_____

_____

_____

12. Parents' or guardians' occupations and highest level of education completed

Father/Guardian Occupation _____ Education level/degree _____

Mother/Guardian Occupation _____ Education level/degree _____

13. Do you have any significant travel experience? Describe, including dates.

_____

_____

_____

14. Have you ever been suspended from school during 9–12 grades? _____

If yes, when and for what reason? _____

15. Is there any significant, unique, or unusual experience, situation, or involvement that you want to share? _____

_____

_____

_____

16. List three adjectives that you feel best describe you and explain why.

_____

_____

_____

17. List the colleges to which you are applying and the reason you are interested in attending. If you plan to apply early decision (ED) or early action (EA) please indicate that next to the name of the college.

College_____   Reason _____

College_____   Reason _____

College_____   Reason _____

College_____   Reason _____

College_____   Reason_____

College_____   Reason_____

College_____   Reason_____

College_____   Reason_____

Please feel free to attach any other information that you believe would be helpful to those writing on your behalf.

Appendix D
Financial Aid Comparison Worksheet

Name of College _____ _____ _____ _____

Cost of Attendance _____ _____ _____ _____

Financial Aid Package

Grants/Scholarships _____ _____ _____ _____

Net Price to Family _____ _____ _____ _____

Loans _____ _____ _____ _____

Work-Study _____ _____ _____ _____

Total Financial Aid _____ _____ _____ _____

Expected Family Contribution (EFC)

Student Contribution _____ _____ _____ _____

Parent Contribution _____ _____ _____ _____

Total _____ _____ _____ _____

Unmet Need (If Any) _____ _____ _____ _____

Appendix E
Cost of Attendance Worksheet

Name of College   _____ _____ _____ _____

Tuition and Fees   _____ _____ _____ _____

Room and Board   _____ _____ _____ _____

Books and Supplies _____ _____ _____ _____

Personal Expenses _____ _____ _____ _____

Travel   _____ _____ _____ _____

Total   _____ _____ _____ _____

College Preparation Time Line

This college preparation time line covers key points in the college preparation process. The specifics will vary depending on both you and the counseling program at your high school. Use this time line as a preview of what is to come and as a general guide, but be sure to supplement and refine it with information provided by your counseling office and the colleges to which you will be applying.

In preparing the time line, we have assumed that you will begin thinking seriously about college admissions by your junior year. If you are one of the many students who waits until senior year, we have a special senior-year fall semester time line designed especially for you. You'll find it at the end of the time line.

FRESHMAN YEAR

Although no special focus on the college application process is needed during freshman year, the following steps are good preparation for success in general:

- Take challenging courses in academic solids: English, foreign language, mathematics, science, and social studies.
- Study hard.
- Explore extracurricular activities both inside and outside school to find those that interest and excite you.
- Read as much as you can.

- Plan summer activities that will enrich you in some way: summer school, work experience, family travel, and so forth. Don't be a couch potato.
- At the end of the year, begin a permanent record of your extracurricular and volunteer activities, academic honors and awards, and so on.

SOPHOMORE YEAR

In your sophomore year, continue taking challenging courses and developing your extracurricular interests and talents. It is also a time when a number of students take on part-time jobs. Families may begin thinking about college in more concrete terms. Some high schools begin a formal program of college orientation in the sophomore year, but most do not.

All Year

- Study hard in a challenging curriculum.
- Continue your involvement in extracurricular activities; look for opportunities to assume leadership roles.
- Consider volunteer activities.
- If you work part time, be sure you keep on top of your academics.
- Save samples of your best papers and work in the arts (if applicable) for potential later use.

Fall

- Consider taking the PSAT or PLAN (or both) for practice.
- Seek help from your teachers early if you experience academic difficulties.

Winter

- PSAT and PLAN results arrive in December. After reading the information that comes with your scores, consider meeting with your counselor to discuss steps you might take to address your weaker areas.
- Plan a challenging program of classes for your junior year.

- Begin to make plans for summer activities that will be enriching (for example, paid or volunteer work, classes, travel).
- Register at school for May Advanced Placement tests if appropriate.

Spring

- If your family will be traveling over spring break, consider including a trip or two to colleges that may be of interest to you.
- Consult your counselor and register for SAT Subject Tests if appropriate.
- Update your record of extracurricular activities, awards, and so on that you began at the end of freshman year.

Summer

- Reap the benefits of your earlier planning for a productive summer. Continue to read.
- Some students who are interested in qualifying for the National Merit Scholarship Program prepare for the PSAT that they will take in October.

JUNIOR YEAR

Junior year typically marks the start of the college selection process. Junior-year grades play an especially important role in college admission, so a focus on academics is very important. By junior year, most students have identified the extracurricular areas in which they have the greatest talent and passion, although new interests can develop.

All Year

- Study hard in a challenging curriculum.
- Continue involvement in extracurricular and volunteer activities and seek leadership roles as appropriate.
- If you work part time during the school year, make sure to continue a strong focus on your academics.

- Continue to save samples of your best papers and work in the arts (if appropriate) for potential later use.
- Students interested in athletics at the Division I and Division II level should talk to their coaches and explore eligibility requirements on the NCAA website, www.ncaa.org.

Fall

- Buy a copy of a "big book" college guide such as the *Fiske Guide to Colleges*. It will be a useful resource to you over the next eighteen months.
- Take the PSAT in October.
- Study hard in your classes. If you experience academic difficulty, seek help early.
- Complete the "Determining Your Priorities" questionnaire at the end of chapter 4 to help you decide what to look for in a college.
- Many colleges send representatives to high schools in the fall. If your school allows juniors to participate, consider attending sessions that are of interest to you.

Winter

- PSAT results arrive. After reading your score report, talk to your counselor about steps you can take to improve your performance on the upcoming SAT or ACT as appropriate.
- Become familiar with the differences between the ACT and SAT and decide which one(s) you will take. Register for winter or spring SAT or ACT tests or both. February is a good month to take the ACT for the first time; March is a good month for the SAT.
- Winter is a good time to prepare (using a book, software, or courses) for standardized tests.
- If you have not already met with your counselor to begin discussing college selection, do so now.
- Explore search engines like the ones at BigFuture, SuperMatch, and College Navigator.
- Register at your school for May Advanced Placement tests.

- Choose challenging courses for your senior year.
- Make plans for an enriching summer. Once again, consider travel, course work, volunteer or paid employment, workshops, or clinics that match your interests.

Spring

- Continue to develop your college list, ideally in consultation with your counselor.
- Start a filing system to help you keep all your college materials organized.
- Consider using the spring break to visit colleges.
- Register for and take spring SAT Subject Tests as appropriate, depending on the requirements of the colleges that are of interest to you. Register and take the SAT or ACT (or both) as appropriate.
- Request materials from colleges that interest you.
- Attend a college fair if one is nearby.
- If you want to be a varsity athlete in college, contact the coaches at the schools that interest you if they have not already contacted you.
- Consider visiting colleges over the summer, and plan these visits early.
- Continue to meet with your counselor as you develop your short list.
- Update your record of extracurricular activities, awards, and so forth.

Summer

- Reap the benefits of your planning for an enriching summer experience, whether it involves work, travel, study, or other activity.
- Visit colleges as appropriate to help refine your college list.
- Consider getting a head start on the college application process by brainstorming about or actually drafting a personal essay.
- If your applications will require a portfolio or audition tape, get started on it now.

SENIOR YEAR

The senior year is the busiest in the college selection process. Some students choose to apply early and need to have a completed application ready to go by

November 1 or 15. In general, students should have their college list identified by mid-November so that they can submit their rolling admissions and regular decision applications by the deadlines without being rushed.

All Year

- Study hard in a challenging curriculum. Colleges will receive your fall grades if you apply regular decision, and may ask for quarter grades if you apply early decision or early action.
- Part-time work is often a part of senior year. Again, be sure to maintain an appropriate focus on academics.
- Continue involvement in extracurricular and volunteer activities and leadership roles as appropriate.

Fall

- Visit additional colleges if time and circumstances permit. Arrange overnights and on-campus interviews where feasible and available.
- Meet with college representatives who are visiting your high school, and attend a fall college fair and college nights to get more information.
- Use net price calculators to get estimates of out-of-pocket costs at different colleges.
- Finalize your college list in consultation with your counselor. Decide if an early application is right for you.
- Be sure to check and make note of all deadlines for each of the colleges on your list.
- Register and take fall SAT or ACT tests if necessary. Be aware of deadlines if you are submitting an early application and want a fall test administration to be part of your application.
- Ask teachers for letters of recommendation at least one month before the first letter is due.
- Finalize your essays, having carefully edited them with the benefit of appropriate input from teachers and parents.
- Submit applications by the required deadlines, double-checking that all parts are complete.

- Arrange to have standardized test scores and high school transcripts sent to colleges by their deadlines.

- Participate in alumni interviews as appropriate if applying early.

- If applying early, receive your decision by December 15. If admitted, congratulations! If not, move on. If you haven't yet submitted your regular decision applications, do so right now. Consider an early decision II application, if appropriate, to another school that is very high on your list.

- If you will be applying for financial aid, begin the process of learning about the FAFSA and CSS PROFILE, as appropriate, and ask your parents to gather the information needed to complete them. Start your scholarship search.

Winter

- If deferred when applying early, write to the college and express your continued interest in attending.

- Submit any remaining applications as well as financial aid and scholarship forms.

- For both deferred and regular applications, send significant new information regarding accomplishments and awards, if any, to colleges.

- Ask your counselor to send a midyear report to colleges.

- Participate in alumni interviews as appropriate.

- Keep focused on your academic work.

Spring

- Decisions may arrive as early as February or as late as early April.

- Take advantage of "admit" programs in April, if possible, to learn more about the colleges that have admitted you.

- Carefully consider and compare your financial aid packages and consider requesting a review if a package is not adequate for your needs.

- Make your final decision about where you want to go, and submit your deposit by May 1. Notify the other schools that you will not be attending.

- If you are wait-listed, decide whether to remain on the wait list. Be sure to make a deposit by May 1 at a school where you have a firm acceptance. If you decide to remain on a wait list, write to the admissions office conveying your enthusiasm, as well as any new information. Ask your counselor to do the same.

- Enjoy the remainder of your senior year!

WHAT IF YOU ARE BEGINNING YOUR SEARCH IN SENIOR YEAR?

A lot of students put off serious thinking about college until the fall of their senior year. Maybe you are one of them. While we don't recommend that approach, don't worry—you can make up for lost time if you use the time you do have wisely and to your best advantage. Once you get to January of your senior year, you'll be in sync with your classmates who started their college search much earlier. The following special fall senior year time line will help you get going:

- Begin using the college search engines at BigFuture, SuperMatch, and College Navigator to develop a list of colleges that meet your criteria.

- Make sure you have already taken (or are registered to take) the SAT or ACT and SAT Subject Tests if they are likely to be recommended or required by the colleges to which you may be applying. If you can't complete certain tests in time, you will need to focus on the many colleges that do not require them.

- Read chapters 4 and 5 of this book carefully, and fill out the Determining Your Priorities questionnaire to help you identify your preferences. Meet with your counselor as soon as possible to discuss colleges that will meet your needs.

- Talk to friends, family members, and classmates about colleges they may recommend.

- Do careful research on the colleges that emerge from your data-gathering efforts. Study college websites.

- Watch for visits by college representatives, evening programs, and nearby college fairs. Use them to gather additional information.

- Visit colleges on your list if you have a chance, taking advantage of high school vacations. But don't worry—you'll have another chance to visit in the spring after you are accepted and before you must make a decision.

- A good application takes time to prepare, especially if it requires a special essay or other custom responses. Keep this in mind as you decide where to apply.

- Make sure that your college list has an appropriate range of colleges: good bet, possible, and long shot. Check back with your counselor before you finalize it.

- Ask one or two teachers whether they would be willing to write letters of recommendation on your behalf if letters are needed for the schools you are interested in. Talk to them as early as you can in the fall semester once you determine that your probable colleges require or recommend such letters. Tell them that you will give background information about yourself once you have your final college list and application forms. Make sure they have at least three to four weeks to write their letters.

- Be aware that early action and early decision applications are generally due by November 1 or November 15. You may not have enough time to do a careful job of selecting a college and preparing a strong application by that date. If you are rushed, don't do it. Some colleges have a second early decision due date in mid-December or early January. This works better for late starters.

- Make sure you know all of the deadlines (preapplications, applications, financial aid, test scores) for the schools you choose. Be sure to release your SAT or ACT scores to colleges on your list.

- Prepare your applications carefully and thoughtfully, and don't forget to proofread everything well. Have someone else help you proofread as well.

- Ask your parents to begin gathering necessary information for financial aid applications.

- Use the Common Application whenever possible to save time and effort. Apply online everywhere you can.

Glossary

Academic Index
A calculation based on standardized test scores and class rank (or equivalent) that Ivy League colleges use to ensure that athletic recruits have academic records that exceed a minimum threshold.

ACT
Short for ACT Assessment. A standardized college admissions test that is an alternative to the SAT.

Advanced Placement (AP)
A program coordinated by the College Board whereby high schools offer college-level courses with specific curricula in a large number of academic fields. Participating students have the option of taking an AP exam at the end of the course to demonstrate knowledge and potentially earn college credit.

Award letter
Financial aid terminology for the document sent to a financial aid recipient that indicates the amount and type of aid.

Candidate reply date
Postmark date by which a student must notify a college about his or her intention to enroll. May 1 is the standard date for students admitted regular decision.

Class rank
The student's place in his or her class based on a rank ordering of students by grade point average.

Common Application
A standardized application form accepted by over 500 colleges. Some colleges also require a school-specific supplement.

Consortium
Several colleges that join together in a cooperative arrangement that allows students to take courses and use library facilities on each campus.

Core curriculum
A group of specially designed courses in the humanities, arts, social sciences, and sciences designed to give students a strong foundation in general education.

Cost of attendance
Financial aid terminology for total educational costs: tuition, fees, books, supplies, room and board, incidentals, and travel home.

CSS PROFILE
Abbreviation for College Scholarship Service PROFILE. A need assessment form administered by the College Board that some schools use to determine eligibility for institutionally based financial aid.

Deferral
A decision by a college to delay a final response to an early action or early decision application until the regular decision cycle.

Deferred admission
A decision on the part of an admitted student to wait until the following academic year to enroll.

Demonstrated need
Financial aid terminology for the difference between the total cost of attendance and the expected family contribution to the student's education.

Double deposit
Unethical practice of sending deposits to hold places at two or more colleges while deciding between them.

Division I, II, and III
National Collegiate Athletic Association (NCAA) groupings of colleges for purposes of athletic competition.

Early action (EA)
An application typically submitted by November 1 or November 15 in exchange for a decision by December 15 that does not bind the student to attend if admitted.

Early decision (ED)
An application typically submitted by November 1 or November 15 in exchange for a decision by December 15 that commits the student to attend if admitted.

ETS
Abbreviation for Educational Testing Service, the organization affiliated with the College Board that prepares, administers, and scores the PSAT, SAT, and Advanced Placement tests.

Expected family contribution (EFC)
Financial aid terminology for the amount of money a family is expected to contribute to a student's education based on a methodology that considers income, assets, and other expenses.

FAFSA
Abbreviation for Free Application for Federal Student Aid. Used to determine eligibility for federal financial aid.

Federal methodology
The calculation of expected family contribution to the cost of college using the Free Application for Federal Student Aid.

Financial aid package
Total amount and types of aid a student receives from federal and nonfederal sources.

Gift aid
Financial aid terminology for the grant portion of the financial aid package that does not have to be repaid or earned through work.

GPA

Abbreviation for grade point average. An overall average of a student's grades.

Hook

A special quality that gives a student an edge in the admissions process over others with similar academic qualifications. Hooks may include athletic ability, legacy status, exceptional talent, having a parent with the ability to make significant donations, or being part of an underrepresented minority group.

IB

Abbreviation for International Baccalaureate. A special high school diploma awarded to students who complete a rigorous academic curriculum of special courses and perform satisfactorily on a battery of nationally normed tests corresponding to that curriculum.

Institutional methodology

Expected family contribution to the total cost of education as calculated through the CSS PROFILE or other form that is institution specific.

Liberal arts

An academic program that includes the sciences, social sciences, languages, arts, mathematics, and so forth; distinguished from professional programs that are focused on specific careers such as engineering, business, and nursing.

Need analysis

Financial aid terminology for the determination of the expected family contribution to college expenses based on the family's financial situation.

Need-aware (or need-sensitive) admissions

Admissions process that considers a student's ability to pay in the final admissions decision.

Need-blind admissions

Practice of reviewing an applicant's file and reaching a decision on admission without regard to the student's ability to pay.

Pell Grant

Federal grant to students from low-income families.

PLAN

A short version of the ACT that is typically taken by high school sophomores.

PLUS Loans

Abbreviation for Parent Loan to Undergraduate Students. A loan taken out by a parent that is not subsidized by the federal government.

PSAT

Abbreviation for Preliminary SAT. A short version of the SAT that is typically taken in the fall by high school juniors as practice for the SAT and as a qualifying test for the National Merit Scholarship Program.

Regular decision

Application process that involves applying by a late fall or early winter deadline in exchange for an admissions decision the following spring.

Rolling admission

A process by which colleges review and make decisions about applications as they are received. The application cycle usually opens in the early fall and may extend into the spring or until the freshman class is filled.

SAT

The most widely taken standardized test for college admission. SAT is the full name—it is not an acronym.

Self-help

In financial aid terminology, the loan and work-study portions of a financial aid package.

Single-choice early action

A type of early action plan that places restrictions on the student's ability to apply early action or early decision to other schools.

Stafford Loan

Low interest loans to students.

Student Aid Report (SAR)

Official notification from the processing center that gives the results of the need analysis calculated from the Free Application for Federal Student Aid.

Student search
Mechanism for colleges to receive the names of potential applicants based on interests, grades, and so forth. Students taking the SAT and ACT are invited to participate when they take those tests. Colleges purchase the names and addresses of students meeting certain criteria and use them for targeted mailings.

Subsidized loan
A loan for which the US government pays the interest while the student is enrolled in school.

Transcript
Official record of a student's courses and grades. Colleges usually require an official transcript, sent directly from the high school, as part of the application.

Wait list
A group of students held in reserve through the late spring after a college makes its admissions decisions. If openings occur, students on the wait list may be offered admission.

Work-study
A component of need-based financial aid in which the student works part time in a campus or other job that is supported by government or institutional funding.

Yield
The percentage of students offered admission to a college who subsequently enroll.

Resources

The resources listed here provide additional information on selected topics covered in *Admission Matters*. We've chosen some web resources and a few books that we think do the job well, although we have not attempted to provide an exhaustive list, since there is a lot of duplication of information.

This list is a dynamic one as new materials appear and others become outdated or unavailable. Check our website at www.admissionmatters.com for additional resources, as well as updates and changes.

GENERAL ADMISSIONS INFORMATION

www.collegeboard.org: College Board site that contains useful information about all aspects of college search and selection, as well as test preparation and registration. BigFuture can be accessed through this site or directly at www.bigfuture.org.

www.nacacnet.org: Site of the National Association for College Admission Counseling, geared primarily to high school and college counselors, but with a section for students and parents with helpful information.

www.princetonreview.com: Princeton Review site with a lot of free information about the college admissions process, including test preparation. The site also sells test preparation courses and materials.

www.fairtest.org: Contains a list of more than 850 colleges and universities nationwide that admit a substantial number of students without regard to SAT or ACT scores.

www.campustours.com: Site with links to virtual campus tours at hundreds of campuses.

College Unranked: Ending the College Admissions Frenzy, by Lloyd Thacker (Cambridge, MA: Harvard University Press, 2005): Edited volume containing excellent advice on keeping the admissions process in perspective.

REFERENCE GUIDES TO COLLEGES

See the College Board BigFuture and Princeton Review sites in the previous section. Each contains detailed profiles of individual colleges as well as a search feature that identifies colleges meeting criteria entered by the user.

http://nces.ed.gov/collegenavigator/: College Navigator sponsored by the US Department of Education. The site contains a database of thousands of schools that allows search by location, program, and degree offerings.

www.usnews.com/education: Site provides free, limited access to the *U.S. News* database used to generate college rankings. Although we do not favor the use of these rankings, the data used to generate them can be helpful. The full database can be accessed for an annual fee.

www.utexas.edu/world/univ/: Site provides links to the home pages of four-year colleges and universities throughout the United States. The links can be sorted by state or alphabetically.

Barron's Profile of American Colleges, by Barron's Educational Series: Updated periodically but not annually. Contains profiles of over 1,650 four-year colleges that are rated according to degree of competitiveness. Includes free access to Barron's web-based college search engine.

College Handbook, by the College Board: Updated annually. Contains profiles of all 3,800 four-year and two-year colleges in the United States. Tables show policies and outcomes for early decision, early action, and wait list applicants.

The College Finder, by Steven Antonoff (Westford, MA: Wintergreen Orchard House, 2008): Helpful lists of recommended programs by major, sport, and many other categories.

NARRATIVE AND EVALUATIVE GUIDES TO COLLEGES

www.ctcl.org: Site that originated with *Colleges That Change Lives* by Loren Pope but that has expanded to include a few other institutions as well. Contains lots of good information about college selection.

www.collegeprowler.com: Student-generated evaluations of colleges.

Colleges That Change Lives: 40 Schools That Will Change the Way You Think About Colleges, by Loren Pope and Hilary Masell Oswald (New York: Penguin Books, 2012): Descriptions of 40 lesser-known but excellent liberal arts colleges.

Fiske Guide to Colleges, by Edward Fiske (Napierville, IL: Sourcebooks, 2013): Updated annually. Contains profiles and personal descriptions of more than 320 popular colleges and universities.

Insider Guide to the Colleges, Yale Daily News Staff (New York: St. Martin's Griffin, 2012): Updated annually. Contains profiles and personal descriptions of more than 330 colleges and universities.

INSIDER ACCOUNTS

These are best viewed as a window into the admissions process at highly selective institutions rather than as a how-to guide to gain admission to them.

The Gatekeepers: Inside the Admissions Process of a Premier College, by Jacques Steinberg (New York: Penguin, 2003): Describes the author's experience observing an admissions cycle at Wesleyan University.

Creating a Class: College Admissions and the Education of Elites, by Mitchell Stevens (Cambridge, MA: Harvard University Press, 2009): Describes the author's experience observing the admissions process at Hamilton College.

SPECIAL FOCUS GUIDES

www.ajcunet.edu: Site sponsored by Jesuit colleges.

www.hillel.org: Site of Hillel, the Foundation for Jewish Campus Life.

www.womenscolleges.org: Official site of the Women's Colleges Coalition.

www.blackexcel.org: The College Help Network for African American students.

www.usafa.af.mil: Site of U.S. Air Force Academy.

www.usma.edu: Site of U.S. Military Academy (West Point).

www.usna.edu: Site of U.S. Naval Academy.

www.usmma.edu: Site of U.S. Merchant Marine Academy.

www.cga.edu: Site of U.S. Coast Guard Academy.

African American Student's College Guide: Your One-Stop Resource for Choosing the Right College, Getting in, and Paying the Bill, by Isaac Black (Hoboken, NJ: Wiley, 2000): Advice for African American students.

TEST PREPARATION

www.collegeboard.org: Information and preparation for the PSAT and SAT. The site can be used for online test registration for the SAT.

www.ACT.org: Information and preparation for the PLAN and ACT. The site can be used for online test registration for the ACT.

www.number2.com: Free SAT and ACT test preparation.

www.ets.org: Information and preparation for the TOEFL (Test of English as a Foreign Language). The site can be used for online test registration for the TOEFL.

www.ielts.org: Information and preparation for the IELTS (International English Language Testing System). The site provides a downloadable registration form and instructions for registering for the IELTS.

The Official SAT Study Guide with DVD, by the College Board (Princeton, NJ: College Board, 2009): Official test preparation guide to the SAT.

The Real ACT with CD, 3rd ed. (Albany, NY: Peterson's, 2011): Official test preparation guide to the ACT.

ESSAY WRITING

On Writing the College Application Essay, 25th Anniversary Edition: The Key to Acceptance at the College of Your Choice, by Henry Bauld (New York: Collins Reference, 2012): A former Ivy League admissions officer provides tough and funny advice on coming up with the best essay possible.

The College Application Essay: All-New Fifth Edition, by Sarah Myers McGinty (Princeton, NJ: College Board, 2012): Contains excellent advice on writing effective essays.

ADVICE FOR ARTISTS

www.npda.edu: Site of the National Portfolio Day Association, a group of accredited arts colleges and university art departments that are members of the National Association of Schools of Art and Design.

College Guide for Performing Arts Majors: The Read-World Admission Guide for Dance, Music, and Theater Majors, by Carole J. Everett (Albany, NY: Peterson's, 2009): Guide to programs in music, arts, theater, and dance.

College Guide for Visual Arts Majors, by Peterson's and Sandra Reed (Albany, NY: Peterson's, 2009): Guide to programs in fine arts, graphic design, architecture, media arts, or any of the many other art disciplines.

Creative Colleges: A Guide for Student Actors, Artists, Dancers, Musicians and Writers, by Elaina Loveland (Belmont, CA: Supercollege, 2010): Contains profiles of more than 200 art, drama, dance, music, and creative writing programs.

ADVICE FOR ATHLETES

www.ncaa.org: Website of the National Collegiate Athletic Association. A must-read for those interested in varsity athletics at colleges and universities that belong to the NCAA.

www.naia.org: Website of the National Association of Intercollegiate Athletics. Important for those interested in varsity athletics at colleges and universities that belong to the NAIA.

http://www.nytimes.com/2011/12/25/sports/before-athletic-recruiting-in-the-ivy-league -some-math.html?pagewanted=all: Article that discusses how the Academic Index is calculated and used.

Reclaiming the Game: College Sports and Educational Values, by William Bowen, Sarah Levin, James Shulman, and Colin Campbell (Princeton, NJ: Princeton University Press, 2005): Analysis of the role of athletics in the admissions processes at Ivy League and selective liberal arts colleges.

The Student Athlete's Guide to Getting Recruited: How to Win Scholarships, Attract Colleges and Excel as an Athlete, by Stewart Brown (Belmont, CA: Super-college, 2011): Guidance on choosing an NCAA division and handling the recruitment process.

SPECIAL CIRCUMSTANCES

www.E4FC.org: Site of Educators for Fair Consideration. Provides information for undocumented students.

www.nilc.org: Site of the National Immigration Law Center. Provides information for students concerned about immigration status.

College Opportunity and Access Guide, by the Center for Student Opportunity (Naperville, IL: Sourcebooks, 2011): Guidebook for first-generation college students.

K&W Guide to Colleges for Students with Learning Disabilities or Attention Deficit Hyperactivity Disorder, 11th ed., by Marybeth Kravets and Imy Wax (New York: Princeton Review, 2012): Profiles the services for learning disabled students at over 300 colleges.

Life After High School, by Susan Yellin and Christina Cacioppo Bertsch (Philadelphia: Jessica Kingsley Publishers, 2010): Offers advice and support to students with disabilities and their families, before and during the transition to life after high school.

And What About College? How Homeschooling Leads to Admissions to the Best Colleges and Universities, by Cafi Cohen (New York: Holt Associates, 2000): Resource for homeschooled students about the college search and the documentation they need in the application process.

FINANCIAL AID

www.bigfuture.org: Site (click on Pay for College) for information on the FAFSA, CSS PROFILE, net price calculators, and expected family contribution calculators.

www.fafsa.ed.gov: Federal site for FAFSA (Free Application for Federal Student Aid). If you are applying for need-based aid, visit this site. You can complete the FAFSA online.

www.fafsa4caster.ed.gov: Federal site that lets families get estimates of their expected family contribution without actually submitting the FAFSA.

www.fastweb.com: General site with terrific scholarship search, as well as expected family contribution calculator.

www.finaid.org: General site with lots of information about all aspects of financial aid.

http://studentaid.ed.gov: Comprehensive government site with information in English and Spanish.

Scholarship Handbook 2013: All-New 16th Edition (College Board Scholarship Handbook), by the College Board (Princeton, NJ: College Board, 2012): Provides information on private, federal, and state funding sources of financial aid.

Getting Financial Aid 2013: All-New Seventh Edition (College Board Guide to Getting Financial Aid), by the College Board (Princeton, NJ: College Board, 2012): Advice on all aspects of the financial aid process.

Secrets to Winning a Scholarship, by Mark Kantrowitz (CreateSpace Independent Publishing Platform, 2011): Advice on finding and applying for private scholarships

INTERNATIONAL STUDENTS

www.nafsa.org/Explore_International_Education/For_Students/: Site of the Association of International Educators with pages for US students studying abroad and international students studying in the United States, including resources for financial aid.

www.edupass.org: Site for international students that calls itself "The Smart Student Guide to Studying in the U.S.A." Provides information on every topic about studying and living in the United States.

International Student Handbook 2013, 26th ed., by the College Board (Princeton, NJ: College Board, 2012): Information on 2,900 colleges, including TOEFL requirements, financial aid, housing availability, and other services.

Learn in the United States: The International Student's Guide for Applying to American Colleges, by Ryan Byrne and Gayle Byrne (Kindle, 2011) (electronic version only): Guide to understanding the total international student application process from exploring the US educational system to securing a visa.

GAP YEAR

The Complete Guide to the Gap Year: The Best Things to Do Between High School and College, by Kristin M. White (San Francisco: Jossey-Bass, 2009): Comprehensive guide to 200 gap year programs.

www.interimprograms.com: Site for the Center for Interim Programs gap year counseling service. Contains helpful, free articles.

STUDYING IN CANADA, THE UNITED KINGDOM, AND IRELAND

www.aucc.ca: The official website of the Association of Universities and Colleges of Canada, in English and French. Links to all Canadian universities, programs of study, and information about tuition, enrollment, job trends, and quality assurance.

www.ucas.ac.uk: The basic guide and application site universities in the United Kingdom. Provides information on majors and applying, with advice for students, parents, and counselors.

www.iua.ie: Website of the Irish Universities Association, with links to the seven major Irish universities. Information about courses, application processes, visas, quality assurance, and accommodation.

Times Good University Guide, by the Times (New York: HarperCollins, updated annually). Available for purchase at amazon.co.uk. Authoritative guide to higher education programs at all universities in the United Kingdom.

Notes

CHAPTER ONE

1. S. Cohen, "College Admission Tougher Than Ever," *Forbes*, April 5, 2012, http://www.forbes.com/sites/stevecohen/2012/04/05/the-fat-envelope-please-college-admission-tougher-than-ever/.

2. J. Moses, "The Escalating Arms Race for Top Colleges, *Wall Street Journal*, February 5, 2011, http://online.wsj.com/article/SB10001424052748703555804576102523244987128.html.

3. V. de la Torre, "High Anxiety for Students Awaiting College Admissions Letters," March 27, 2012, http://articles.courant.com/2012–03–27/news/hc-college-acceptance-letters-0328–20120327_1_acceptance-letters-college-bound-high-school-seniors-ithaca-college.

4. D. Marcus, "When Parents 'Too Invested' in College Admissions Make Their Children Anxious," *New York Times*, October 8, 2012, http://thechoice.blogs.nytimes.com/2012/10/08/when-parents-too-invested-in-college-admissions-make-their-children-anxious/.

5. "More Students in Limbo as College Wait Lists Grow," *Portland Press Herald*, May 2, 2012, http://www.pressherald.com/news/college-admissions-wait-list-grow-bates-maine.html.

6. J. Worland, "College Applications Increase Stress," *The Harvard Crimson*, March 30, 2011, http://www.thecrimson.com/article/2011/3/30/college-students-school-admissions/.

7. *Knocking at the College Door: Projections of High School Graduates* (Boulder, CO: Western Interstate Commission for Higher Education, 2012).

8. B. Mayher, *The College Admissions Mystique* (New York: Farrar, Straus and Giroux, 1998), 28.

9. G. Casper, letter to James Fallows, editor of *U.S. News and World Report*, September 23, 1996, www.stanford.edu/dept/pres-provost/president/speeches/961206gcfallows.html.

10. Graduation rate performance measures the difference between a school's six-year graduation rate for a given class and the predicted rate for that class based on characteristics of the students as entering freshmen and the school's expenditures on them.

11. President William Durden, letter to the Dickinson College community, September 7, 2001, www.dickinson.edu/news/usnews2001.html.

12. L. Bollinger, "Debate over the SAT Masks Trends in College Admissions," *Chronicle of Higher Education*, July 12, 2002, B11.

13. R. Toor, *College Confidential: An Insider's Account of the Elite College Selection Process* (New York: St. Martin's Press, 2001), 2.

14. G. Goldsmith, cited in G. Golden, "Glass Floor: Colleges Reject Top Applicants Accepting Only Students Likely to Enroll," *Wall Street Journal*, May 29, 2002.

15. S. Dale and A. Krueger, "Estimating the Payoff to Attending a More Selective College: An Application of Selection on Observables and Unobservables," *Quarterly Journal of Economics* 117 : 1491–1528.

16. Ibid. S. Dale and A. Krueger, "Estimating the Return to College Selectivity over the Career Using Administrative Earning Data," Princeton University Industrial Relations Section, working paper 563 (February 2011).

17. Stacy Dale, personal communication, May 2004.

18. A. Krueger, cited in D. Leonhardt, "Revisiting the Value of Elite Colleges," *New York Times*, February 21, 2011.

19. D. Davenport, "How Not to Judge a College," Scripps Howard News Service, September 9, 2003.

20. S. Lewis, cited in A. Kucsynski, "Best List for Colleges by U.S. News Is Under Fire," *New York Times*, August 20, 2001, C1.

CHAPTER TWO

1. G. W. Pierson, "Historical Statistics of the College and University, 1701–1976" (1983), www.yale.edu/oir/pierson_original.htm.

2. E. Duffy and I. Goldberg, *Crafting a Class* (Princeton, NJ: Princeton University Press, 1998), 35.

3. Williams College, "Apply," November 12, 2012, http://admission.williams.edu/apply/highschoolprep/coursework.

4. David Erdmann, personal communication, January 2004.

5. D. Gould, cited in R. Shea and D. Marcus, "Make Yourself a Winner," in *America's Best Colleges* (Washington, DC: *U.S. News and World Report*, 2001).

6. S. McMillen, "In Admission, How Do You Separate the Wheat from the Wheat?" *Chronicle of Higher Education*, June 27, 2003, B13.

7. F. Hargadon, "Advice from the Inside," in Harvard Independent Staff (Eds.), *100 Successful College Application Essays* (New York: New American Library, 2002), 6.

8. S. McGinty, "The College Application and Issues of Access," January 12, 2005, www.nacac.com/miatpa.sarahmcginty.pdf.

9. P. Marthers, "Admissions Messages vs. Admissions Realities," in L. Thacker (ed.), *College Unranked: Affirming Educational Values in College Admissions* (Portland, OR: Education Conservancy, 2004), 79.

10. C. Deacon, cited in E. Craig, "GU Defends Use of Legacy Admissions," *Hoya*, April 16, 2004, 1.

11. T. Parker, cited in M. Klein, "Bill Aims to Increase All College Opportunities," *Amherst Student*, November 12, 2003, 1.

12. D. Golden, *The Price of Admission: How America's Ruling Class Buys Its Way into Elite Colleges—and Who Gets Left Outside the Gates* (New York: Three Rivers Press, 2007).

13. W. Bowen and S. Levin, *Reclaiming the Game: College Sports and Educational Values* (Princeton, NJ: Princeton University Press, 2003).

CHAPTER THREE

1. The descriptions of the Wesleyan admissions review process are drawn from J. Steinberg, *The Gatekeepers: Inside the Admissions Process of an Elite College* (New York: Penguin, 2003). Confirmed as current as of 2012–2013 through personal communication with Nancy Hargrave Meislahn, dean of admission and financial aid.

2. J. Merrow, transcript of Inside College Admissions, broadcast on KVIE, November 15, 2000, www.pbs.org/merrow/tmr_radio/transcr/.

3. Shawn Abbott, personal communication, January 2004.

4. D. Cattau, "Parents Need Not Apply," stropngweb.com, August 14, 2004.

5. M. Rubinoff, personal communication, November 2012.

6. Independent counselor cited in R. Worth, "For $28,000 You'll Get . . . ," *New York Times*, September 24, 2000, sec. 14WC, 8.

7. M. Jones, "Parents Get Too Aggressive on Admissions," *USA Today*, January 6, 2003, 13A.

CHAPTER FOUR

1. Michael Tamada, personal communication, April 2004.

2. *Academic Advising Highly Important to Students*, Noel-Levitz, https://noellevitz.com/documents/shared/Papers_and_Research/2009/AcademicAdvisingHighlyImportant09.pdf.

3. E. L. Boyer, *The Undergraduate Experience in America* (New York: Harper and Row, 1987); E. L. Boyer and P. Boyer, *Smart Parents Guide to College* (Princeton, NJ: Peterson's, 1996).

CHAPTER FIVE

1. E. Fiske, *Fiske Guide to Colleges* (Naperville, IL: Sourcebooks, 2013); *The Insider's Guide to the Colleges* (New York: St. Martin's Griffin, 2012).
2. J. Greenberg, personal communication, October 2012.
3. Trinity University, "Admissions Criteria," November 12, 2012, http://web.trinity.edu /admissions-and-financial-aid/how-to-apply/first-year-students/admissions-criteria.

CHAPTER SIX

1. L. Bollinger, "Debate over the SAT Masks Perilous Trends in College Admissions," *Chronicle of Higher Education*, July 12, 2002, B11.
2. College Board, http://press.collegeboard.org/sat/faq, October 18, 2012.
3. C. Jencks and D. Reisman, *The Academic Revolution* (Garden City, NY: Doubleday, 1968), 281.
4. R. Zwick, *Fair Game? The Use of Standardized Tests in Higher Education* (New York: RoutledgeFalmer, 2002), viii.

CHAPTER SEVEN

1. University of Pennsylvania admissions website, Applying Early Decision, http:// 316841-web1.admissionsug.upenn.edu/applying/early.php.
2. C. Avery, A. Fairbanks, and R. Zeckhauser, *The Early Admissions Game* (Cambridge, MA: Harvard University Press, 2003).
3. Eric Furda in S. Sweifler, "Penn Reaches Likely Candidates Through Video," *Daily Pennsylvanian*, March 14, 2011, http://www.thedp.com/article/2011/03/penn_reaches _likely_candidates_through_video.

CHAPTER EIGHT

1. Susan Hallenbeck, former dean of admission at Hood College, personal communication, January 2004. She reported that the student was admitted after giving everyone a good chuckle.
2. D. Phillips, "The Question of the Essay," in G. Georges and C. Georges, *100 Successful College Application Essays* (New York: New American Library, 2002), 12.

3. H. Bauld, *On Writing the College Application Essay* (New York: Collins Reference, 2012), xviii.
4. S. McGinty, *The College Application Essay, Fifth Edition* (New York: College Board, 2012).
5. W. Zinsser, *On Writing Well* (New York: HarperCollins, 2006).

CHAPTER NINE

1. Williams College, "Visit, November 12, 2012 http://admission.williams.edu/visit/thevisit/interviews.
2. University of St. Andrews, "Overview: UCAS Applications Process," November 12, 2012, www.st-andrews.ac.uk/admissions/ug/apply/.

CHAPTER TEN

1. B. Beach, personal communication, November 2012.

CHAPTER ELEVEN

1. M. Kravets and I. Wax, *The K&W Guide to College Programs and Services for Students with Learning Disabilities or Attention Deficit/Hyperactivity Disorder*, 11th ed. (New York: Princeton Review, 2012).
2. M. Kravets, personal communication, October 2012.
3. S. Michaelson, in A. Moore, "Accommodations Angst," *New York Times*, November 4, 2010.
4. MIT Admissions website, http://mitadmissions.org/apply/prepare/homeschool.

CHAPTER TWELVE

1. A. Leider and R. Leider, *Don't Miss Out: The Ambitious Student's Guide to Financial Aid* (Alexandria, VA: Octameron, 2000), 42.
2. H. Rawlings, cited in "Rawlings-Led Group Affirms Commitment to Need-Based Financial Aid," *Cornell Chronicle*, July 12, 2001, 1.
3. E. Houston, Oberlin Admissions Blog, April 16, 2012, http://blogs.oberlin.edu/applying/selection_process/need_sensitive.shtml/.
4. S. Trachenberg, cited in M. Bombardieri, "Needy Students Miss Out," *Boston Globe*, April 25, 2004, A1.
5. D. Martin, cited in S. Teicher, "Not Enough Financial Aid? Seek Counseling," *Christian Science Monitor*, April 26, 2004, 13.
6. Muhlenberg College, "The Real Deal on Financial Aid," October 20, 2012, http://www.muhlenberg.edu/main/admissions/realdeal.html.

7. S. Pemberton, cited in Teicher, "Not Enough Financial Aid?"

8. Carnegie Mellon, "Navigating College Financial Aid," October 26, 2012, http://admission.enrollment.cmu.edu/pages/financial-aid.

9. M. O. Shapiro, cited in J. Russell, "Top Applicants Bargaining for More Aid from Colleges," *Boston Globe*, June 12, 2002, A1.

CHAPTER THIRTEEN

1. S. Kostell, *U.S. News* Education Blog, September 14, 2011, http://www.usnews.com/education/blogs/college-admissions-experts/2011/09/14/what-are-some-tips-for-international-students-applying-to-us-colleges.

2. S. Allen, "Tips on American College Admissions Essays, from a Veteran Dean, India Ink Blog," *New York Times*, January 11, 2012.

3. J. Montoya, *U.S. News* Education Blog, cit. September 14, 2011.

4. Lewis & Clark College, "International Students and Scholars," November 11, 2012, www.lclark.edu/offices/international/alumni_profiles/.

5. EducationUSA, "Your Steps to USA Study," November 11, 2012, www.educationusa.info/5_steps_to_study/undergraduate_step_1_research_your_options.php#top.

6. Ibid.

7. National Association for College Admission Counseling, "International Student Resources," October 26, 2012, www.nacacnet.org/studentinfo/internationalstudentresources/pages/default.aspx.

8. M. Steidel, personal communication, November 2012.

9. EducationUSA, "Your Steps to USA Study."

10. Dartmouth College, "Teacher Evaluations," October 27, 2012, www.dartmouth.edu/admissions/apply/first-year/teacher-recommendation.html.

11. C. Haring, in Unigo Expert Network, October 26, 2012, www.unigo.com/expertnetwork.

CHAPTER FOURTEEN

1. Student cited in M. Coomes, M. "Life After the Letter," *(Louisville) Courier-Journal*, May 5, 2004, D2.

2. D. Nesbitt, cited in J. Lee-St. John, "Getting Off the College Wait List," *Time*, May 5, 2008.

CHAPTER FIFTEEN

1. J. Mitchell, *Eight First Choices: An Expert's Strategies for Getting into College* (Belmont, CA: SuperCollege, LLC, 2009).

About the Authors

Sally P. Springer, associate chancellor emerita at the University of California, Davis, is a psychologist with more than 30 years of experience in higher education as a professor and university administrator. She is the coauthor of *Left Brain, Right Brain* (W. H. Freeman, 1998), which was honored by the American Psychological Foundation for contributing to the public's understanding of psychology. It has been translated into seven languages and appeared in five editions. Her second book, *How to Succeed in College* (Crisp Publications, 1992), is a guide for college freshmen. She received her bachelor's degree summa cum laude from Brooklyn College and her doctorate in psychology from Stanford University, and has served on the faculty of both Stony Brook University and the University of California, Davis. She has been a volunteer admissions reader for the Davis campus and is a member of the National Association for College Admission Counseling and the Western Association for College Admission Counseling. For the past six years, she has provided one-on-one college admissions guidance to families as an educational consultant through Springer Educational Consulting. She is a Professional Member of the Independent Educational Consultants Association and serves as a member of its Committee on Education and Training. She has personally taken the college admissions journey twice, with her son and her daughter.

Jon Reider is the director of college counseling at San Francisco University High School, an independent 9–12 high school. Before that, he served as an admissions officer at Stanford University for 15 years, rising to the post of senior associate director of admissions. He has two degrees in history, including a doctorate from Stanford, where he taught in a freshman humanities program for 25 years, for which he won a university-wide teaching award. Previously he was a Marshall

369

Scholar at the University of Sussex in England and taught sociology at the University of Tennessee at Chattanooga. He has also taught in the College Counseling Certificate Program at the University of California, Berkeley. He is a nationally known speaker and essayist in the admissions profession and is widely cited in the media for his candid opinions and willingness to speak hard truths. He is a member of the National Association for College Admission Counseling and has served as the chair of its Committee on Current Trends and Future Issues.

Joyce Vining Morgan is a certified educational planner specializing in college admissions with an online individualized practice. She has over 17 years of experience in college admissions, including service as director of college counseling at the Putney School in Vermont and vice president of the New England Association for College Admission Counseling. Earlier in her career, she wrote and translated books and articles on Russian theater history and taught in several disciplines (Russian language and literature, French language, humanities and English) in a variety of public and private schools and colleges, including Phillips Exeter Academy, the Exeter AREA Junior and Senior High Schools, the American Embassy School of New Delhi, Vassar College, and the University of New Hampshire. She was named New Hampshire Teacher of the Year in 1994. She has coordinated and led student exchanges to Russia, France, Ukraine, and Kazakhstan and was herself an exchange student twice in the Soviet Union. She holds a doctorate in Slavic languages and literature from Yale University and a bachelor's in Russian from Manhattanville College, and is a professional member of the Independent Educational Consultants Association and the Higher Education Consultants Association and an associate member of the Overseas Association for College Admission Counseling. As a member of the National Association for College Admission Counseling, she has served on its Committee on Current Trends and Future Issues and its Ad Hoc Committee on Standardized Testing.

Index

Americans with Disabilities Act (ADA), 223–224

Amherst College, 85, 201, 286

Appeals, of financial aid offers, 255, 266–267, 302–303

Applicant pool, competitiveness of, 1–5, 50, 52–53

Applications: advantage of submitting early, 158–159; disclosing disabilities on, 228–229; to-do list, 175–178; in electronic form, 46, 162; final decisions on, 51–53; following directions for, 164; highlighting extracurricular activities, 192–194; how many to submit, 4, 118–119; making copies of everything, 323; neatness and completeness of, 163–164; reading and evaluation of, 45, 47–49; stealth applications, 112; tentative decisions on, 49–51; Universal College Application, 165, 183. *See also* Common Application; Essays; Interviews; Letters of recommendation

Applications process: arts students, 212–220; Canadian colleges, 194–195; international students, 273–274, 281–285; Irish colleges, 197–198; parents' role in, 57–58, 315–321; procrastinating on, 162–163, 318–319, 323; students with special talents, 212–220; studying abroad, 194–198; transfer students, 237–241; United Kingdom (UK) colleges, 194–197

Arizona State University, 68, 143, 144

Arts students, 208–220; applications process, 212–220; auditions, 213, 216–219; college search by, 211–212; portfolios, 213, 214–216; resources for, 359; types of colleges, 210–211; types of degrees, 209–210

Asbury College, 70

Athletes: academic eligibility, 203–204; admissions advantage, 39–40, 199–200; college search by, 201–202, 204–205; college support for, 208; female, 207; not recruited, 208; postgraduate (PG) years for, 312; recruited, 39–40, 202–207; resources for, 359; and *U.S. News* ranking data, 14

Athletics: baccalaureate colleges, 70; liberal arts colleges, 65; master's universities, 69; research universities, 67; structure of, at college level, 200–201

Attention deficit/hyperactivity disorder (ADHD). *See* Students with disabilities

Auditions, arts students, 213

Auditions, arts students, 216–219

Avery, Christopher, 151

Babson College, 71

Baccalaureate colleges, 69–70

Bard College, 34

Barnard College, 65, 73, 101, 210

Bates College, 143

Bauld, Harry, 166

Beach, Barry, 214

Beloit College, 63

Bentley College, 71

Berklee College of Music, 211

BigFuture website: career planning tools, 82; college search tool, 96–97, 103; college selectivity information, 112; expected family contribution calculator, 249; information on selectivity of colleges, 113–114; international students, 275; merit aid information, 263; net price calculators, 265

Bollinger, Lee, 11, 122

Boston College, 72, 134, 153

Boston Conservatory, 216

Boston University, 281

Data: determining *U.S. News* rankings, 10–11, 13–14; to look at when developing college lists, 115–118; for scattergrams, 116–118

Davenport, David, 18

Davidson College, 63, 72, 183

Deacon, Charles, 37

Deferral, early decision (ED), 156–157, 295–297

Degrees: for arts students, 209–210; career planning and, 83–85; dual-degree programs, 84–85, 210

Demonstrated interest: EA application as showing, 154; as factor in admissions decisions, 13, 111–112, 305; interviews as showing, 187; and *PSAT* scores notification, 141

Demonstrated need, 257; colleges meeting, 253, 254, 256, 266, 286; colleges not meeting, 254–255, 257, 286; defined, 244

Denial: competitiveness of applicant pool and, 52–53; early acceptance programs, 156, 157, 295; parental support after, 321; in review process, 50–51; to selective colleges, 53–54

DePaul University, 143

Deposits: gap years, 310, 311; wait lists, 308–309

Development admits, 38

Dickinson College, 148

Disabilities. *See* Students with disabilities

Disappointment, 299–300

Diversity: of admissions staff, 45; as hook, 40–42

Double depositing, 308–309

Dream Act, 288

Drexel University, 87

Dual-degree programs, 84–85, 210

Duke University, 42, 66, 72, 100, 134, 157

Earlham College, 148

Early acceptance programs, 147–160; applying to additional colleges, 153, 156, 294; comparison of, 153; deciding if right for you, 154–155; denial or deferral, 295–297; early notification, 158; likely letters, 157, 158; notification of admissions decision, 158, 291, 292–295; overview of, 147–148; parody of application for, 159–160. *See also* Early action (EA); Early decision (ED)

Early action (EA): acceptance of admission, 294; compared to early decision (ED), 152, 153; deciding if right for you, 154–155; defined, 147; keeping commitment with, 153; with restrictions, 147, 153

Early decision (ED): compared to early action (EA), 152, 153; deciding if right for you, 154–155; defined, 147; denial or deferral, 156–157, 295–297; financial aid and, 150–151, 267–268, 293–294; as increasing yield and reducing admissions rate, 12; keeping commitment with, 153; notification of admissions decision, 291, 292–294; PROFILE form and, 247–248; pros and cons, 148–152; recruited athletes, 206–207

Echo boomers, 2–3

Educational compacts, 262–263

Educational Talent Search, 55

EducationUSA, 275–276, 277

Elizabethtown College, 70

Elon University, 69

Emory University, 201

England. *See* United Kingdom (UK)

Erasmus Programme, 75

Erdmann, David, 29, 128

George Mason University, 144

Georgetown University, 47, 72, 100, 145, 153, 164, 295

Gettysburg College, 148

Golden, Daniel, 38

Good-bet colleges, 113, 114, 118, 121

Goucher College, 65, 73, 148, 290

Gould, David, 30

Grades (GPA): as criterion for admission, 26–27, 28; early acceptance programs and, 151; homeschooled students, 232; international students, 281–282; scattergram of data on, 116–118; senioritis and, 313–314; transfer students, 238

Graduate school, selectivity and admission to, 17–18

Graham, Martha, 214

Grants, 251–252

Guide for the College-Bound Student Athlete (NCAA), 207

Hamilton College, 85

Hampshire College, 148

Hargadon, Fred, 31, 35

Haring, Chris Hooker, 285

Harvard University, 2, 8, 9, 67, 100, 153, 286, 309–310

Harvey Mudd College, 63, 65, 73, 145

Haverford College, 65, 72, 73

Hendrix College, 65

High Point University, 70

High school counselors: college search help from, 94–96, 118; discussing wait-listing with, 307–308; essay help from, 172; gap year and, 312; letters of recommendation from, 33–34, 57, 182, 184–186; role in college admissions process, 54–55; secondary school report (SR) completed by, 28–29, 184–186

High school courses, 23–26; Advanced Placement (AP), 23, 25–26, 27, 274; International Baccalaureate (IB), 25, 143, 274, 311

High schools: academic record from, 23–29; admissions officers visiting, 45–46, 99–100; limiting number of applications, 118–119; postgraduate (PG) year at, 312; profile of, 28–29; record number of graduates from, 2–3; scattergrams prepared by, 116

Historically black colleges (HBCUs), 72–73

Homeschooled students, 231–234, 360

Honors programs, 68

Hooks, 36–43; and colleges' efforts to increase diversity, 40–42; defined, 36; development admits, 38; fairness of, 35, 43; international status, 272–273, 289; legacy status, 36–38; recruited athletes, 39–40; special talents, 42

Howard University, 72

Income, selectivity and future, 16–17

Independent counselors, 56–57, 313

Indiana University, 291

Individuals with Disabilities Education Act (IDEA), 222–223

Insider's Guide to the Colleges, 103

Institutional methodology, 247, 250–251, 255

Institutional mission, 63, 276

Institutional priorities, 36, 49–50, 117

Interest. *See* Demonstrated interest

International Baccalaureate (IB), 25, 143, 274, 311

International English Language Testing System (IELTS), 279–280